Rudman's Cigar Buying Guide

*Selecting & Savoring
the Perfect Cigar for any Occasion*

THEO RUDMAN

TRIUMPH
BOOKS
CHICAGO

Cover design by Salvatore Concialdi.
Book design by Sue Knopf.
Cover photograph by John Thoeming.

This book is available in quantity at special discounts for your group or organization. For further information, contact:

Triumph Books
644 South Clark Street
Chicago, Illinois 60605
(312) 939-3330 FAX (312) 663-3557

ISBN 1-57243-233-0

Printed in the United States of America

Contents

Introduction

It is estimated that from 1992 to the present, nearly 300 new brands of cigars have been launched on the U.S. market. This has created an enormous challenge for the cigar-loving community to keep abreast of what is available.

Therefore, the need arises for an additional means of accessing the sizes and prices of cigars and their quality. So I offer this book for those who want a concise, quick reference when making cigar purchases. (My other book, *Rudman's Complete Guide to Cigars*, is available for those wanting more comprehensive information.)

This book acts as an easy reference—providing all the available knowledge on the subject that will enable you to select a smoke to suit a particular moment or mood—from the first one of the day, when the palate is freshest and most receptive, to the one rounding off a good dinner with, perchance, a good port.

If you are interested in measuring cigars by terms of quality, the **Star Rating Index** lists each rated cigar with a corresponding star rating. Flip to the World Directory listing for a complete review on all star-rated cigars.

The **Price Rating Index** lists all the cigars for which I have been able to ascertain the retail prices at the time of going to press. Find the cigar that fits both your tastes and budget by referring to this index or check your favorite brand's price in the World Directory.

The **Cigar Size Index** provides a concise list of every cigar with its corresponding size or shape. If you have a favorite size or shape, this index will identify all the cigars under that particular size. Cigars of interest can then be referred to in the World Directory for more product information.

The **World Directory** includes all brands available in the United States. Cigars are listed in alphabetical order by country of origin, with details of tobacco types, sizes, and where possible, descriptions of the cigar-smoking qualities particular to the country of origin.

The **World Directory Index** lists each brand and identifies the country of origin in the World Directory. So, if you know the brand, but not the country of origin, this index will indicate in which country's section you will find the brand.

Good smoking!

Smoking for Pleasure

Selecting Your Cigar

A lot has been said and written about selecting the size of a cigar to suit the shape of your face or the size of your frame, but I do not subscribe to this. I believe that quality, flavor and aroma are the only criteria for choosing a cigar.

The size of a cigar is also most important.

Whenever you try a new brand it is a good idea to buy just one cigar. Most tobacconists sell cigars singly as well as by the box. Although buying by the box can, of course, often entitle one to a discount, I suggest the beginner should start by exploring the small cigars from Holland or Denmark. These include the range from Villiger, Gallaher, Henry Winterman, Ritmeester, Willem, Schimmelpenninck, Christian of Denmark and Agio. These are inexpensive and, in most cases, represent good value. These mild cigars have a pleasant aroma. An excellent transition to cigars with more body would be small cigars from Jamaica, the Philippines and the Dominican Republic.

If you are now looking for a more full-bodied or stronger smoke, it would be a good idea to progress to the small cigars from Honduras and Nicaragua (particularly Joya de Nicaragua), as these are, in my opinion, closer in body to cigars from Cuba than those from any other country.

Coronas, which are the most popular size in the world, are the middle of the road, allowing not too much smoke on each draw, while the length is such that it provides the right quantity (time) for most people.

The intermediate cigar smoker will, by this time, not only have experimented with different brands and different sizes from different countries, but will have done this at different times of the day. He will be looking to see what cigar suits him best for given times and given occasions. Generally indicated is a small cigar in the morning, a medium-bodied and medium-sized one after lunch and a bigger, full-bodied cigar to follow a heavy dinner. The occasion also affects the smoker's choice. An Arturo Fuente Masterpiece or a Fuente Fuente Opus X Double Corona from the Dominican Republic would be suitable for a special celebration, such as the birth of a child or the closing of a good business deal.

Strength of Different Tobaccos

A general guide to the strength of cigars from various countries may now be helpful for the beginner. I suggest we rate countries on a scale of one to five. One would be extremely mild and five very strong. Two and three would be the middle of the road, covering, for example, most of the cigars from the Dominican Republic.

Brazil Dark, rich and smooth. Has a natural, slightly sweet flavor: 4.

Cameroon Heavy aroma with a spicy taste: 3 to 4.

Dominican Republic Usually smooth, mild and slow-burning. Popular in the U.S.: 2 to 3. Honeyed, earthy and floral tones are common.

Ecuador Good flavor but mild: 2 to 3.

Havana Medium- to full-bodied: 4 to 5. Earthy, coffee, spicy and honeyed tones are often found. Note: Apart from local manufacture, the tobacco is often used as part of the filler blend in many European (but not American) dry cigars.

Honduras More full-bodied than those from Dominican Republic. Nearly as rich as tobacco from Cuba, but with a slightly different flavor: 3 to 4. Much spicier, with pronounced cinnamon.

Jamaica Mild and subtle: 2.

Mexico Not a particularly refined taste, and not particularly consistent, ranging from very mild up to full-bodied and coarse: 1 to 4.

Nicaragua Full-bodied and aromatic. Wrappers are slightly sweet: 3 to 4.

Sumatra Very mild but spicy: 2.

Cigar Sizes

There are over 70 possibilities. Some of the Havana ranges are confusingly extensive and cover hand-made and machine-made models.

Non-Cuban ranges are usually much smaller, with hand-mades, mostly, being limited from six to ten different sizes.

There are many minor variations in the standard sizes from brand to brand and this can sometimes cause confusion—a confusion which is increased when some brands use size names such as churchill, rothchild or corona for cigars which are not technically those sizes. The Primo del Rey Churchill (165mm/6½ ins x 16.27mm/41) from the Dominican Republic is actually a lonsdale, whose standard size is 165mm/6½ ins x 16.67mm/42.

Cigars are measured in inches in the U.S. and in millimeters in Europe and countries using metric measurement. The thickness of the cigar is measured by the "ring gauge." In the United States this is expressed in ¹⁄₆₄th of an inch. It is not used in Europe, where the thickness is measured in millimeters. Hence, if a corona-sized cigar is described as 5½ x 42 in the United States, it will translate to 142mm x 16.67mm in Europe.

Flavor and Taste

The soil in which tobacco seed is grown enormously influences the flavor of the leaf. In fact, the same seed grown in different areas, even if similar in climate and altitude, will produce tobacco with distinctly different taste characteristics. That is what happened when, after the Castro revolution in Cuba, all the cigar businesses were taken over by the state. The previous owners left, with little or no possessions except, in many cases, small quantities of best-quality Cuban tobacco seed and they started new cigar businesses in several other countries, often using the same brand names that they had before. Although, in some cases, the resulting quality was excellent, the flavor and style of tobacco were still quite different from that of Cuba.

Personal preference for most things is subjective and taste and flavor are no exception. All the tongue can taste is bitter, sweet, salt and sour. Terms commonly used to describe cigars are spicy, floral, fruity, woody, aromatic and green, which are all aroma-related, a function of the nose. Other terms often used are harsh, heavy, medium, light, dusty, mellow, strong and subtle, which are terms to describe texture. Rich, complex, fresh, character and lively are related to impression. Because of this personal subjectiveness, it is difficult to generalize on taste and aroma.

Aroma

The purpose of aging a cigar is to marry or blend the different aromas of the different leaves together with those of the cedar cigar box or the cedar-lined humidor. Fragrance and aroma are present in the oil of the leaf, particularly that of the wrapper. If the wrapper has little or no oil, there is little to be gained in aging that cigar. This also applies to a cigar that started out with a good, oily wrapper; but, due to bad storage (lack of sufficient humidity or too great a temperature) has dried out.

The aroma or bouquet of a cigar should never be confused with its strength. A cigar could be mild and rich in aroma or, on the other hand, be strong with little or no aroma. Bouquet or aroma will affect the smoker's sense of taste and smell, while the strength of the cigar will affect his throat. If the cigar is too strong for a particular smoker, he will experience harshness on the back of his throat.

Because the nose has a wider range than the palate or tongue, aroma is a most important quality in a cigar. The burning ability can also have a profound effect on enjoyment.

Many believe size affects strength. In reality, size has

little influence on strength. Strength and flavor come, largely, from the filler blend. The strength of a cigar leaf can be altered during curing, from a pale-green light leaf (light in both color and taste) to a deep chocolate-brown heavy "mudoro" leaf, which is much stronger. So, choosing a cigar that is the right strength for you can really only be achieved as a result of experimentation—and that is an almost endless journey of surprise and delight—making cigar smoking one of the more civilized pleasures in life.

And remember that your own strength criteria may well vary according to your mood, the time of day and whether the smoke is pre- or post-prandial. A good tobacconist will have a selection of open boxes of cigars to be sold singly so that you can easily keep a selection of brands and sizes to suit your needs.

Selecting the Correct Length

Length determines the quantity you wish to smoke at any one time. Often you may think a particular cigar is too strong, but it may just be that the cigar is too long, in other words, too large for the occasion, and that you have had enough before you have reached its end. Sometimes, when in the right mood or occasion, one can drink a whole bottle of wine; however, at other times, a glass or two is appropriate. The same applies to a cigar.

Shape and Thickness

All cigars fall into two categories: parejos being straight or parallel-sided and figurados covering all the irregular shapes. The main groups in the parejos category are coronas, churchills, lonsdales, robustos (also known as rothchilds), panetelas and cigarillos.

For almost a hundred years the corona size had been the most popular. Classic size for a Cuban corona is 142mm/5⁵⁄₁₆ ins x 16.67mm/42. Lonsdales are the same ring gauge as coronas (16.67mm/42, but longer, up to 165mm/6½ ins). The traditional size for a churchill is 178mm/7 ins x 18.65mm/47, and for a robusto, 124mm/4⅞ ins x 19.84mm/50.

Panetelas are much thinner. Their ring gauges vary from 11.51mm/29 to 15.48mm/39. The length can be anything from 117mm/4⁹⁄₁₆ ins (small panetela) to 178mm/7 ins (long panetela). Cigarillos are short, very thin cigars, with ring gauges from 7.9mm/20 to 11.51mm/29. Length can range from 3⅜ ins/85mm to 4³⁄₁₆ ins/106mm.

There are six major figurado shapes.

Torpedo has a pointed closed head, an open foot or tuck with a bulge in the middle; *pyramid* also has a pointed closed head and widens steadily to an open foot or tuck; *belicosos* is a pyramid shape with a round head rather than a point; *perfecto* has both ends closed, with a bulge in the middle; *diademas* is a large cigar, usually 8 ins/203.2mm or longer, with an open foot or tuck and pointed head; *culebras* comprises three thin cigars plaited together with a thread. This is undone and the cigars are smoked individually.

Each shape can be appropriate for differing occasions.

The thickness of the cigar, measured in either millimeters or, in the United States, in "ring size" or "ring gauge," contributes to the richness and coolness of the smoke. Generally, a well-rolled, thicker cigar provides a much easier draw. This gives a large, satisfying amount of smoke with less effort, so the cigar can be smoked slower and, therefore, cooler.

The coolness of the smoke is of paramount importance. If you are used to taking a big pull on the cigar to obtain a big mouthful of smoke, then you will probably be more comfortable with a cigar with a bigger ring gauge, as a big pull on a thinner cigar makes the smoke hot and harsh. A sign that this is happening is when the lighted part becomes long and pointed.

A thinner cigar may suit those who like a smaller volume of smoke per draw, but if it is fairly tightly packed, you will find it necessary to draw too hard to get a satisfying quantity of smoke, and this can result in a hot smoke. In such cases, try drawing in a little air with the smoke. Do not be afraid to experiment with cigars of different thicknesses to find the one most satisfying for you. To encourage this, a number of manufacturers are packaging their cigars in packs of five, even the prestigious Havana Cohiba range are now being offered in this new trend.

A cigar should be the correct size for the amount of time available to smoke it. Bear in mind that a long, thin cigar may smoke for the same time as a short, thick cigar. Remember, too, that you only smoke between two-thirds and three-quarters of the cigar; that is, up to the cigar band, as the build-up of tars and juices can make the remaining section rather bitter.

Wrapper Colors

The next step is consideration of the wrapper. There are about 65 different shades of these wrappers. The cigar smoker likes to see the same shade of wrapper on each cigar. This does not make the cigar smoke any better, but it is an indication of the pride each company takes in its product, with the resulting assurance of the quality of the rolling.

Within the wide spectrum of shades there are seven basic colors, namely:

Claro Claro: At one time, the majority of cigars on the American market used to come in this shade which, as a result, became known as AMS, or American Market Selection. It is also known as *Candela*. The light greenish brown color is achieved by fixing the chlorophyll with rapid high-temperature drying that also reduces the natural oils and flavor. Such wrappers can taste slightly sweet.

Claro: A pale ginger or yellowish brown color. Often found on Havana brands like H. Upmann and American brands using Connecticut Shade wrappers. This is the color of the classic mild cigar.

Colorado Claro: A light tawny brown, sometimes called "natural." It is frequently grown in the full sun as are the Cameroon wrappers commonly found on Dominican Partagas.

Colorado: Reddish brown and called EMS, or English Market Selection. Used to appeal mostly to the English market, but today has gained tremendous popularity in the United States. It has a rich flavor and a subtle aroma. Its color normally indicates well-matured cigars.

Colorado Maduro: Collage brown, medium strength and very aromatic. Has the rich flavor found in many premium Honduran cigars.

Maduro: Coffee brown and comes from the Spanish word for "ripe," which refers to the extra length of time needed to produce a rich, dark brown wrapper. Maduro is sometimes thought of as the traditional Cuban color and should be oily and silky with strong flavor and mild aroma. The full-bodied Cuban Bolivar is normally this color, as are Mexican wrappers. It is also occasionally referred to as SMS, or Spanish Market Selection.

Oscuro: Means dark and is blackish brown. It is also called negro (black) in tobacco-producing countries. It is usually left longer on the plant and is longer matured. This color can be produced artificially by "cooking" the leaves in ovens or pressure cookers. These wrappers are strong, with little aroma, and come mainly from Brazil, Mexico, Nicaragua and the sun-grown Connecticut Broadleaf.

Opening a New Box

Be careful when opening a new box. If it is a dress box (where much of the wood is covered by paper which has been heavily printed with labels and separate edging designs), the lid will be nailed down. Do not run a knife along the front split to ease up the lid as you can damage cigars on the top layer. Rather, use a flat rounded tool on each side of the single nail, after slitting the label or government seal that may also keep the box shut. Many guillotine cutters have such a device with a small slit or notch that can be inserted around the nail, enabling the lid to be pried open without going too far into the box and, thus, protecting the top layer.

The Final Choice

Before making the final choice, it is important to consider the cigar's physical appearance and condition. Take a close look at the wrapper. In a premium cigar, this should be free from discoloration and evenly rolled. Occasionally one will find spots on premium cigars. These arise from drops of rain on the tobacco leaf, before it is picked, and the sun's magnification through those drops bleach out the color. Such spots are harmless and do not affect the taste or burning qualities of the cigar. Blemishes and discolorations on the wrapper are common on many bundle cigars.

Except in the case of the dry Dutch (European) cigar, the wrapper should not be dry and dead, but rather have some texture and an oily sheen, particularly in the case of the darker wrappers. This is an indication that the tobacco has been properly cured. Preferably the veins should be visible, albeit fine. They should run as parallel as possible to the length of the cigar, as this ensures that the cigar will burn evenly. This will indicate that it has been properly rolled. If the wrapper is beginning to unravel or crack, it has been stored in conditions that are too dry.

A loosely packed cigar will indent easily when pressed, feel lighter than one that is more tightly rolled and will, probably, provide an easier draw. However, if too loose, it will burn too quickly and, therefore, be hot and harsh.

If there is no give over the entire length of the cigar, then it is probably overfilled and will be hard to draw. Hardness in just one spot can indicate that the cigar is "plugged," which, again, affects the draw. If the cigar is, indeed, "plugged" (a fault in construction), you can try kneading the hard spot in the hope of breaking up the blockage. However, there is a major probability that you will damage the wrapper and, if that happens, then either throw the cigar away or try taking it back to your tobacconist.

Rolling a cigar next to your ear to hear a crackle as an indication that the cigar is too dry serves no useful purpose. All it does is risk damaging the delicate wrapper. In any case, even if the cigar has been kept at a perfect humidity, you will still hear a faint crackle.

If you examine the foot (the end to be lighted) you will be able to see if the filler has been "booked." That is, the filler will show in straight lines, instead of appearing to flow around in curves.

The Cigar Band

The bands on non-Cuban cigars with Havana brand names tend to be similar to the Cuban originals, although they vary in small details that often include the date of origin of the brand in the space where the Cuban version has the word "Habana."

Should you leave a cigar band on or take it off? This is an often-asked question. I think the answer really lies in the circumstances or company in which the cigar is smoked. In Britain many consider it "not done" to advertise the brand you are smoking. In the rest of the world, the band is usually left on, although sometimes it is removed after the cigar has been smoked part of the way.

Care must be taken if the band is to be removed, as quite often, a drop of the glue that joins the band may have oozed out on to the delicate wrapper. This may then tear when the band is taken off. If you are going to remove the band, it is probably safer to do so after the cigar has been lit and smoked for about 20 percent of its length, as the heat of the smoke will loosen any offending drop of glue. Never slide the band off down the length of the cigar as it will, most likely, dig in and tear the wrapper.

Cutting

All hand-made cigars are sealed at the head, that is, the end to be cut and put into your mouth. The cigar has, during manufacture, been sealed with a thumb-nail-sized round piece of tobacco which has been cut from wrapper leaf thus ensuring that the color matches the wrapper itself.

There are several ways to cut the end off the cigar. Mechanical cutters range from simple and inexpensive models (around $3) to elaborate, gold-plated ones, costing anything up to $100, for those incorporated with a lighter.

Some smokers prefer to bite the end off, or pinch it off with their fingernail, which often can result in a large rough opening which may cause the wrapper to unroll and ruin the cigar, or to use a sharp knife. Whatever method you choose, it is important that the cut be clean and level, otherwise you can have difficulties with the draw. A popular method is to use a small, portable guillotine, with either a single or double blade. My favorite is a small pair of cigar scissors that can be sharpened when necessary.

You should aim to cut off only the part of the cap that actually covers the end, so that the rest of the seal remains, creating a thin ring that will stop the wrapper from unravelling. If the whole cap is removed the wrapper will, almost certainly, unravel.

Some people use a cutter that takes a v-shaped wedge out of the end. For a long time this was considered a most effective method, as it created a two-sided surface to provide an adequate draw and bitter juices and tars were kept away from the tongue. However there are two main disadvantages to this method: few clippers are capable of making a clean v-shaped cut without damaging the end, and a v-cutter cannot effectively handle sizes thicker than a 47- or 48-ring gauge.

Yet another method is to pierce the end with a cigar drill or piercer. This is not recommended as it gives a narrow opening with the edges of the filler compressed and can cause a concentration of hot oils and smoke on the tongue.

Many machine-made cigars are cut before they are packaged. This is particularly the case with the dry Dutch or European cigars. The cutting, v-wedging and piercing methods are often to be found in these "ready-to-smoke" cigars.

Lighting the Cigar

An old-fashioned practice is that of licking the whole cigar before lighting it. This stems from times before humidors were commonplace. But even then it was pointless, as it is impossible to humidify a cigar (remember, the filler and binder also need moisture) by simply licking the outside wrapper.

Gasoline lighters or cardboard matches should never be used to light a cigar. The smell of the fuel from the lighter and the chemicals and wax on the cardboard can affect the aroma. Use a butane lighter, wooden matches (preferably special long, slow-burning ones available from quality tobacco shops) or a cedar-wood taper (made from the thin sheets of cedar wood found in most boxes of premium Havanas). When using a match, make sure the sulfur has completely burnt off, otherwise this will make your first few draws unpleasant.

It is important to light the cigar properly, so take your time when doing it. The ritual of lighting a cigar adds as much to enjoyment as feeling and smelling it do at selection.

When lighting, the foot should be held just above the tip of the flame and at about 45 degrees to it. Then, rotate the cigar, slowly, gently and evenly, toasting the entire end until it is completely charred.

At this stage, hold the cigar horizontally, with the end about half an inch from the flame and begin gently to draw, gradually lighting the entire foot. It is important to have an even burn, so do not forget to rotate the cigar. To facilitate an even light, blow on the glowing end. When you first do this, you will be able to see clearly those areas that still need to be lit. Drawing quickly on the cigar will increase the temperature which, in turn, introduces a harshness that will spoil the cigar's flavor.

Smoking the Cigar

Now draw to enjoy the rich, full flavor and aroma. Do not inhale. You will get sufficient pleasure from the taste and aroma simply by swirling or holding the smoke in your mouth for a few minutes. A cigar should be smoked slowly. It should not be pulled on or puffed too frequently as this will lead to overheating and will spoil the flavor. When a cigar is well made, the wrapper, binder and filler will burn in harmony. If this does not happen you will not get the maximum enjoyment from that cigar. A clear sign that the wrapper is not burning at the same rate as the binder and filler is when a heavy, pronounced black ring appears around the cigar, just below the actual burning part.

The flavor of the cigar changes as you smoke down its length, the smoke filtering through the tobacco and intensifying the flavor as the cigar grows shorter.

Sometimes, even with a top brand, you will find that the cigar will start to burn unevenly, one side faster than the other. When this happens, you can clip the burning end straight. This treatment only helps for a short while, but it is all you can do. Assuming the cigar has been lit properly, this phenomenon can be caused by any of the following problems: incorrect humidification, poor burning-quality tobacco, a booked filler or a fault in the actual construction of the cigar. The two most common reasons are incorrect humidification and poor construction of the cigar. Although you can't do much about the other problems, you can at least ensure that your cigars are properly humidified.

To achieve maximum satisfaction, it is important for the cigar to burn at its optimum temperature and speed. So, it is necessary to develop a pace that will suit you and, at the same time, allow the cigar to burn at its slowest effective rate without going out. It is not the end of the world if the cigar does, in fact, go out. We all relight cigars. But, remember, when drawing the flame over the burnt end you suck in some of the carbonized tobacco and each time you relight the cigar, it gets a little harsher. If you allow the cigar to get cold, the oils and tars will concentrate and saturate the rest of the tobacco and, on relighting, will affect the taste.

If you are not going to finish the cigar and intend to continue smoking it later, then it is best to blow out the smoke before laying it down and then to knock off the ash after it has gone out. It would also be better to cut off a portion just behind the burnt end. This is not quite the same as a fresh smoke, but, if it's a good cigar, why waste it?

A lot has also been said and written about keeping the ash on a cigar. Long ash on a premium cigar indicates a healthy wrapper and a well-formed long-leaf filler bunch. Many believe that long ash cools the smoke, but I do not think this has ever been proven. Experiment for yourself.

Long ash on a cigar certainly looks attractive. Sometimes, if there is a soft spot in the filler, the ash will fall off unexpectedly at that point. It is not possible to get long ash on machine-made, short-filler cigars, so short ash is normally taken as an indicator of a short filler.

When you reach the last third of the cigar, the build-up of tars and juices will make this remaining section harsh, with a rather bitter aftertaste. When this happens, it is time to abandon the cigar. It is not necessary to stub it out, as is done with cigarettes. It will go out soon enough if left in the ashtray. But it is a good idea to dispose of the dead stubs as soon as possible, as their pungent, stale aroma will permeate the room. I keep a medium-sized ashtray (or a small bowl may be used) in my sitting room and another small bowl at the bottom of my wardrobe, half filled with baking soda. This absorbs, overnight, the heavy cigar aromas. The baking soda only needs to be changed every six months or so, but should be stirred around with the finger every two or three weeks.

Ideal Temperature and Humidity

Ideally, cigars should be stored at between 65 and 70 percent relative humidity (RH), with the temperature up to about 70 degrees F. In hot, dry climates, a cigar can dry out within a couple of days. Many people, particularly in the United States, believe the ideal storage conditions are a 70/70 mix (70 percent RH and 70 degrees F).

The British taste, however, is for a much drier cigar. Top British merchants store at a humidity level of between 60 and 65 percent . Years ago stock used to be kept by merchants at between 55 and 60 percent RH. One such British merchant once said: "A dry, aged cigar gives you the taste of pure tobacco, not simply water."

The ideal is for your cigar to be neither too dry nor too damp. If a cigar is far too moist, it will feel damp to the touch and, in extreme cases, there will be small bubbles on the wrapper.

The real humidity on your cigars is affected by the temperature in your humidor. The hygrometer could be reading 70 percent, but your cigars could be dry, if the temperature is below 70 degrees F.

RH is the volume of moisture (water vapor) in the air, relative to the maximum amount it could hold at that temperature. Therefore, if the temperature inside the humidor is 74 degrees F, the hygrometer should read 61 percent RH. Conversely, if the temperature drops to 66 degrees F, the RH reading should be 80 percent.

RH has little meaning without knowing the temperature. So install a thermometer together with the hygrometer.

Free humidity/temperature conversion charts, together with instructions, are available from Coast Creative Services, P.O. Box 113, Julian, California 92036, U.S. Telephone/fax: (1)(619) 765-3455.

Sometimes cigars develop a "plume," also called "bloom." This is a whitish dust on the surface of the wrapper and arises from the crystallization of oils in the cigar tobacco. Plume, which can evolve over a long period in the dark, moist confines of a humidor, is not harmful and can be brushed off with a soft brush, a dry tissue or sponge. Some smokers even believe it is beneficial to a cigar's taste.

Mold, however, has a bluish tint and will mark the wrapper. It can also be removed like plume, but is a sign that your cigars are being stored in too hot and/or humid conditions. If you allow mold to remain and do not reduce the humidity in which your cigars are stored, the cigars will begin to smell musty and seriously affect your smoking enjoyment.

Storing Cigars in Humidors

If you are a regular smoker, then it is worthwhile to invest in a good quality humidor. It should be able to hold a realistic number of cigars. They come in all sizes, storing from 25 to 200 cigars. Your humidor should approximate to your usual brand. If you wish to store up to 25 churchill-sized cigars, then a humidor that can store 25 coronas will not suffice.

It is preferable to have a humidor that has been lined with cedar wood, as its spicy aroma is ideal for intermingling with tobacco aromas. If it is a high-quality container, it will come with a hygrometer (a gauge for measuring the level of humidity) as well as a humidifier (a device for putting moisture into the air in your humidor). These devices range from those that work on sponges or chemical compounds to plain bottles containing water.

A humidor should always be measured against its ability to provide a constant performance over a long period, which means that it should not warp or crack over the years. And make sure the lid closes tightly. Remember that the humidor will only provide the correct humidity inside if it is stored in an environment not exceeding 75 degrees F and preferably around 70 degrees F.

Humidors come in a wide range of finishes and wood—from painted exteriors in different colors to lacquers in either matte or gloss finishes. A humidor should not overwhelm its surroundings. It should be both handsome and functional.

Star Rating Index

The author's subjective ratings for cigars take into account
the following: appearance; construction; quality of wrapper
and color; smoking characteristics and texture of the smoke;
flavor and aroma; and overall impression, including enjoyment of the cigar.

★★★★★ Outstanding. A classic.
★★★★ Excellent.
★★★ Good.
★★ Fair, ordinary.
★ Poor or faulty.

FIVE STARS ★★★★★

Aromas de San Andreas Gourmet	Mex
Arturo Fuente Dantes	Dom
Arturo Fuente Don Carlos Robusto	Dom
Arturo Fuente Double Chateau Fuente	Dom
Arturo Fuente Hemingway Masterpiece	Dom
Arturo Fuente Hemingway Short Story	Dom
Arturo Fuente Hemingway Signature	Dom
Arturo Fuente Spanish Lonsdale	Dom
Astral Maestro	Hon
Avo "XO" Intermezzo	Dom
Avo "XO" Preludio	Dom
Bahia Robusto	CR
Bahia IV	CR
Bances Presidents	Hon
Bauza Casa Grande	Dom
Bauza Grecos	Dom
Bauza Jaguar	Dom
Bauza Robusto	Dom
Butera Royal Vintage Dorado 652	Dom
C.A.O. Churchill	Hon
C.A.O. Corona Gorda	Hon
Calixto Lopez Palma Royale	Phi
Calle Ocho Churchill	USA
Calle Ocho Gordito Largo	USA
Canaria D'Ora Inmensos	Dom
Canaria D'Ora Supremos	Dom
Canonero No 3	Bra
Canonero No 4	Bra
Columbus Churchill	Hon
Columbus Double Corona	Hon

Columbus Short Churchill . . . . Hon
Columbus Tubos. . . . . Hon
Cuba Aliados Churchill . . . . Hon
Da Vinci Monalisa. . . . . Hon
Daniel Marshall Dominican Honduran Reserve . . . . . Hon
Daniel Marshall Dominican Reserve Churchill . . . . . . Dom
Daniel Marshall Dominican Reserve Robusto . . . . Dom
Davidoff 4000. . . . . Dom
Davidoff Double "R" . . . . Dom
Davidoff Special "T". . . . . Dom
Diamond Crown Robusto No 2 . . . . Dom
Diamond Crown Robusto No 5 . . . . Dom
Dom Tomas Corona Grandes. . . . . Hon
Dom Tomas No 500 . . . . Hon
Don Lino Churchill . . . . Hon
Don Marcos Monarch . . . . Dom
Don Tomas Epicures . . . . Dom
Don Tomas Epicures. . . . . Hon
Dunhill Altimiras . . . . Dom
Dunhill Centenas. . . . . Dom
Dunhill Pervias. . . . . Dom
El Canelo No 1 . . . . USA
El Incomparable Churchill. Hon
El Rey del Mundo Corona . . . . Hon
El Rey del Mundo Double Corona. . . . . Hon
El Rey del Mundo Flor de Llaneza. . . . . Hon
El Rey del Mundo Originale. . . . . Hon
El Rey del Mundo Robusto Suprema . . . . Hon
El Rey del Mundo Robusto. Hon
El Sublimado Churchill . . . . Dom
El Sublimado Regordete . . . . Dom
El Sublimado Torpedo. . . . . Dom
Evelio Double Corona . . . . Hon
Evelio Robusto Larga . . . . Hon
Evelio Robusto . . . . Hon
Evelio Torpedo . . . . Hon
Excalibur I . . . . Hon
Excalibur III . . . . Hon
Excalibur VII. . . . . Hon
Excelsior No 3. . . . . Mex
Flor de Florez Cabinet Selection Gigante . . . . USA
Flor de Florez Cabinet Selection Gran Panatela . . . . . USA
Fonseca 2-2. . . . . Dom

Nat Sherman No 711 . . . . Dom
Nat Sherman University. . . . . Dom
Nestor Vintage 654 . . . . Hon
Opus X Double Corona. . . . . Dom
Opus X (Fuente Fuente Opus X) Robusto . . . . Dom
Opus X Perfecxion No 5 . . . . Dom
Opus X Reserva D'Chateau . . . . Dom
Partagas Limited Reserve Regale . . . . Dom
Partagas No 1 . . . . Dom
Partagas No 2 . . . . Dom
Partagas No 3 . . . . Dom
Partagas No 10 . . . . Dom
Partagas Robusto . . . . Dom
Partagas Sabroso . . . . Dom
Peterson Presidente . . . . Dom
Petrus Tabacage 89 Double Corona . . . . Hon
Petrus Tabacage 89 Palma Fina . . . . Hon
Pleiades Plutton . . . . Dom
Punch Cafe Royal . . . . Hon
Punch De Luxe Chateau Lafitte . . . . Hon
Punch Gran Cru Superiors . . . . Hon
Punch Pitas . . . . Hon
Punch Presidents . . . . Hon
Puros Indios Nacionales . . . . Hon
Puros Indios Petit Perla . . . . Hon
Puros Indios Presidente . . . . Hon
Puros Indios Rothschild . . . . Hon
Ramon Allones Trumps . . . . Dom
Romeo Y Julieta Vintage III . . . . Dom
Santa Damiana Petit Corona . . . . Dom
Santiago Cabana Corona . . . . USA
Santiago Cabana Torpedo . . . . USA
Savinelli Extremely Limited Reserve No 6 Robusto . . . Dom
Serengeti Corona Bushbuck . . . . SA
Serengeti Corona Kudu. . . . . SA
Serengeti Churchill Buffalo. . . . . SA
Serengeti Churchill Rhino . . . . SA
Signature Collection by Santiago Cabana Churchill . . USA
Thomas Hinds Honduran Selection Churchill . . . . . . Hon
Thomas Hinds Honduran Selection Royal Corona . . . Hon
Thomas Hinds Honduran Selection Torpedo . . . . Hon
V Centennial Cetros . . . . Hon
V Centennial Numero 1 . . . . Hon

FOUR STARS ★★★★

Fonseca 10-10. . . . . Dom
Fundadores Rothchild . . . . Jam
Gilberto Oliva Churchill. Hon
Gilberto Oliva Viajante . . . . Hon
Griffin's Prestige . . . . Dom
H. Upmann Churchills . . . . Dom
H. Upmann Pequenos No 100. . . . . Dom
H. Upmann Robusto . . . . Dom
Habana Gold Corona . . . . Hon
Havana Blend Delicado . . . . USA
Havana Blend Rothschild. . . . . USA
Henry Clay Brevas . . . . Dom
Hoyo de Monterrey Churchill . . . . Hon
Hoyo de Monterrey Double Corona . . . . Hon
Hoyo de Monterrey President . . . . Hon
Hoyo de Nicaragua Maduro Deluxe Toro . . . . Nic
Hugo Cassar Diamond Selection Corona . . . . Dom
Hugo Cassar Private Collection Robusto . . . . Hon
Hugo Cassar Private Collection Robusto . . . . Mex
J. R. Ultimate Rothschild . . . . Hon
Jose Benito Churchill. . . . . Dom
Jose Llopis No 1. . . . . Pan
Jose Llopis No 4. . . . . Pan
Jose Marti Robusto. . . . . Dom
Joya de Nicaragua No 6 . . . . Nic
Joya de Nicaragua Consul . . . . Nic
Juan Clemente Churchill. Dom
Juan Clemente Club Selection No 4 . . . . Dom
Juan Clemente Demi-Corona. . . . . Dom
King No 7. . . . . Dom
Knockando No 1 . . . . Dom
La Aurora Robusto. . . . . Dom
La Flor de la Isabela Coronas Sumatra . . . . Phi
La Fontana Vintage Dante . . . . Hon
La Fontana Vintage Galileo . . . . Hon
La Gloria Cubana Coronas Extra Large. . . . . USA
La Invicta Corona. . . . . Hon
La Paz Wilde Brazil . . . . Hol
La Paz Wilde Cigarillos Havana. . . . . Hol
La Paz Wilde Havana. . . . . Hol
La Plata Maduros Magnificos . . . . USA
Las Cabrillas Magellan . . . . Hon
Lempira Churchills. . . . . Hon

Peterson Corona . . . . Dom
Petrus Tabacage 89 Palma Fina . . . . Hon
Primo del Rey Almirantes . . . . Dom
Primo del Rey Seleccion No 2 . . . . Dom
Private Stock No 8 . . . . Dom
Punch Double Corona . . . . Hon
Punch Gran Cru Britania . . . . Hon
Punch Gran Cru Monarcas. . . . . Hon
Punch Gran Cru Robustos . . . . Hon
Puro Nicaragua Rothschild . . . . Nic
Puros Indios Churchill Especial . . . . Hon
Puros Indios Piramide No 1 . . . . Hon
Ramon Allones A . . . . Dom
Ramon Allones B . . . . Dom
Ramon Allones Crystals . . . . Dom
Ramon Allones D . . . . Dom
Ritmeester Wilde Havana . . . . Hol
Romeo Y Julieta Delgados . . . . Dom
Santa Rosa Regulares . . . . Hon
Savinelli Extremely Limited Reserve No 3 Lonsdale . . Dom
Siglo 21-4 . . . . Dom
Te-Amo Figurado . . . . Mex
Te-Amo Presidente . . . . Mex
Te-Amo Robusto . . . . Mex
Temple Hall No 550 . . . . Jam
Thomas Hinds Honduran Selection Presidente. . . . . . Hon
Topper Old Fashioned . . . . USA
Troyo No 27 Corona . . . . Dom
Troyo No 81 . . . . CR
V Centennial Churchills. . . . . Hon
V Centennial Robustos. . . . . Hon
V Centennial Torpedo . . . . Hon
Valdrych 1904. . . . . Dom
Valdrych Anacaona . . . . Dom
Virtuoso Torano Presidente . . . . Hon
Vueltabajo Toros . . . . Dom
W & D Cetros No 2. . . . . Hon
Wallstreet Panetela. . . . . Aus
Willem II Petitos . . . . Hol
Zino Cigarillos . . . . Hol
Zino Connoisseur No 100. . . . . Hon

THREE STARS ★★★

Agio Biddies. . . . . Hol
Agio Elegant Rich & Light . . . . Hol
Antonio Y Cleopatra Grenadiers Mini . . . . USA
Arango Sportsman . . . . USA
Arango Statesman Barrister . . . . Hon
Avo No 4 . . . . Dom
Backwoods . . . . USA
Bauza Florete . . . . Dom
C.A.O. Corona Gordo. . . . . Hon
Camacho Churchill . . . . Hon
Camorra Imported Limited Reserve Genova . . . . Hon
Canaria D'Ora Lonsdale . . . . Dom
Canaria D'Ora Rothschild . . . . Dom
Casa Blanca Jeroboam . . . . Dom
Cervantes Senadores. . . . . Hon
Chambrair Ceremonial . . . . Dom
Chambrair Faible. . . . . Dom
Chambrair Finesse . . . . Dom
Cuba Aliados Figurin . . . . Hon
Cuba Aliados Rothchild . . . . Hon
Directors. . . . . USA
Don Diego Royal Palmas . . . . Dom
Don Lino Oro Toro . . . . Hon
Don Rene Robusto . . . . USA
Don Rex Cetros No 2 . . . . Hon
Double Happiness Bliss . . . . Phi
Dunhill Corona Grandes CI
Dutch Masters. . . . . USA
Dutch Masters Corona Deluxe . . . . PR
Dutch Masters Panetela. . . . . PR
Dutch Treats . . . . USA
El Canelo Churchill . . . . USA
El Canelo Miniatures . . . . USA
El Canelo San Marcos. . . . . USA
El Canelo St. George . . . . USA
El Producto. . . . . USA
Fighting Cock Texas Red . . . . Phi
Flor de Manila Cetro Largo . . . . Phi
Garcia Y Vega . . . . USA
Gilberto Oliva No 1 . . . . Hon
H. Upmann Coronas Brevas . . . . Dom

H. Upmann Demi Tasse........................ Dom
H. Upmann Petit Corona .... Dom
Habana Gold Double Corona .... Hon
Habana Gold Presidente .... Hon
Havana Blend Coronado .... USA
Henry Clay Brevas Fina .... Dom
Jamaica Gold Baron........................ Jam
Jose Llopis No 2........................... Pan
Jose Marti................................ Dom
Justus Van Maurik Caresse................... Hol
King Edward............................... USA
La Corona Vintage Directors.................. Dom
La Diligencia Gran Corona .... Hon
La Flor de la Isabela Brevas .... Phi
La Fontana Vintage Da Vinci .... Hon
La Fontana Vintage Verdi.................... Hon
La Gloria Inmensas.......................... USA
La Native Cetros........................... Hon
La Native Moderno.......................... Hon
La Paz Cherie.............................. Hol
La Paz Mini Wilde .... Hol
Lamb's Club Churchill....................... Dom
Lamb's Club Corona Extra .... Dom
Las Cabrillas Cortez .... Hon
Macanudo Ascots............................ Jam
Macanudo Hyde Park .... Jam
Nat Sherman Hobart .... Hon
Nording Corona............................ Hon
P & K Guardsmen No 2....................... Dom
Padron Serrie de Aniversario Superior .... Hon
Partagas 8-9-8 .... Dom
Partagas Almirante.......................... Dom
Partagas Humitube .... Dom
Partagas No 6.............................. Dom
Partagas No 10............................. Dom
Partagas Tubos............................. Dom
Particulares Royal Coronas................... Hon
Peterson Petit Corona .... Dom
Punch Gran Cru Diademas .... Hon
Punch Rothschilds .... Hon
Puros Indios Figurin......................... Hon
Ramon Allones Redondos .... Dom
Repeater Churchill.......................... Hon

TWO STARS ★★

Ritmeester Rozet . . . . Hol
Robert Burns Cigarillos . . . . USA
Rustlers . . . . USA
Super Value Pipe Tobacco Cigars . . . . USA
Supre Sweets . . . . USA
Supre Value Little Cigars . . . . USA
Swisher Sweets . . . . USA
Tijuana Smalls Cherry . . . . USA
Villiger Premium No 7 . . . . Swi
White Owl Blunts . . . . USA
White Owl Panetela Deluxe . . . . USA

ONE STAR ★

Agio Mehari's Mild & Light . . . . Hol
Canaria D'Ora Babies . . . . Dom
Clubmaster Superior Sumatra/Brazil . . . . Ger
Ritmeester PiKeur . . . . Hol
Tijuana Smalls Regular . . . . USA
Willem II Optimum . . . . Hol
William Penn Braves . . . . USA

Price Rating Index

$$$$$	$20+
$$$$	$8–20.00
$$$	$5–8.00
$$	$3–5.00
$	$1–3.00
¢	Under $1.00

$$$$$ — $20+

Davidoff Aniversario No 2 . . . . Dom
Davidoff Grand Cru No 1 . . . . Dom
Davidoff Special "C" . . . . Dom
Ornelas 250 . . . . Mex

$$$$ — $8–20.00

Arturo Fuente Hemingway Masterpiece . . . . Dom
Ashton Cabinet Selection No 1 . . . . Dom
Ashton Cabinet Selection No 2 . . . . Dom
Ashton Cabinet Selection No 3 . . . . Dom
Ashton Cabinet Selection No 7 . . . . Dom
Ashton Cabinet Selection No 8 . . . . Dom
Ashton Cabinet Selection No 10 . . . . Dom
Avo Belicoso . . . . Dom
Avo Especiales . . . . Dom
Avo No 1 . . . . Dom
Avo No 2 . . . . Dom
Avo Pyramide . . . . Dom
Butera Royal Vintage Capo Grande . . . . Dom
Calle Ocho Embajador . . . . USA
Calle Ocho Immenso . . . . USA
Calle Ocho Pyramide . . . . USA
Calle Ocho Torpedo . . . . USA
Cifuentes Churchill . . . . Jam
Cifuentes Corona Gorda . . . . Jam
Cifuentes Lonsdale . . . . Jam
Cuba Aliados Figurin . . . . Hon
Cuba Aliados General . . . . Hon
Davidoff 4000 . . . . Dom
Davidoff 5000 . . . . Dom
Davidoff Aniversario No 2 . . . . Dom
Davidoff Double "R" . . . . Dom
Davidoff Grand Cru No 2 . . . . Dom
Davidoff No 1 . . . . Dom
Davidoff No 2 . . . . Dom
Davidoff No 3 . . . . Dom

Davidoff Special "R"............................ Dom
Davidoff Special "T"............................ Dom
Davidoff Tubos................................ Dom
Diamond Crown No 1 .... Dom
Diamond Crown No 2 .... Dom
Diamond Crown No 3 .... Dom
Diamond Crown No 4 .... Dom
Don Lino Supremos............................ Hon
El Sublimado Churchill .... Dom
El Sublimado Corona........................... Dom
El Sublimado Robusto .... Dom
El Sublimado Torpedo.......................... Dom
Excelsior Individuale .... Mex
Felipe Gregorio Belicoso .... Hon
Felipe Gregorio Glorioso .... Hon
Felipe Gregorio Suntouso....................... Hon
Griffin's Don Bernado .... Dom
Griffin's Griffinos............................. Dom
Havana Classico Malelcon .... USA
Havana Classico Presidente .... USA
Havana Classico Pyramide .... USA
Havana Classico Torpedo .... USA
Hugo Cassar Mystique Churchill .... Dom
Hugo Cassar Mystique Lonsdale .... Dom
Hugo Cassar Mystique Toro..................... Dom
Hugo Cassar Private Collection Churchill........... Jam
Hugo Cassar Private Collection Corona .... Jam
Hugo Cassar Private Collection Robusto............ Jam
Hugo Cassar Private Collection Rothschild.......... Jam
Hugo Cassar Private Collection Toro .... Jam
Jose Benito Magnum .... Dom
Juan Clemente Club Selection No 1 .... Dom
Juan Clemente Club Selection No 3 .... Dom
Juan Clemente Gargantua....................... Dom
Juan Clemente Gigante .... Dom
Juan Clemente Obelisco .... Dom
La Diva Robusto .... USA
Macanudo Vintage No I......................... Jam
Macanudo Vintage No II........................ Jam
Macanudo Vintage No III....................... Jam
Macanudo Vintage No IV .... Jam
Macanudo Vintage No V........................ Jam
Macanudo Vintage No VII....................... Jam
Montecristo No 2 Torpedo .... Dom
Ornelas LTD 40 Al Cognac...................... Mex

Oscar Don Oscar . . . . Dom
Oscar Supreme . . . . Dom
Partagas Limited Reserve Epicure . . . . Dom
Partagas Limited Reserve Regale . . . . Dom
Partagas Limited Reserve Robusto . . . . Dom
Partagas Limited Reserve Royale . . . . Dom
Paul Garmirian P. G. Belicoso . . . . Dom
Paul Garmirian P. G. Celebration . . . . Dom
Paul Garmirian P. G. Churchill . . . . Dom
Paul Garmirian P. G. Corona Grande . . . . Dom
Paul Garmirian P. G. Double Corona . . . . Dom
Paul Garmirian P. G. Magnum . . . . Dom
Paul Garmirian P. G. No 1 . . . . Dom
Playboy by Don Diego Churchill . . . . Dom
Playboy by Don Diego Double Corona . . . . Dom
Playboy by Don Diego Gran Corona . . . . Dom
Playboy by Don Diego Lonsdale . . . . Dom
Playboy by Don Diego Robusto . . . . Dom
Pleiades Aldebran . . . . Dom
Pleiades Saturne . . . . Dom
Romeo Y Julieta Vintage VI . . . . Dom
Royal Jamaica Goliath . . . . Dom
Royal Jamaica Ten Downing Street . . . . Dom
Santa Damiana Seleccion No 100 . . . . Dom
Santa Damiana Seleccion No 800 . . . . Dom
Savinelli Extremely Limited Reserve No 1 Churchill . . Dom
Savinelli Extremely Limited Reserve
             No 2 Corona Extra . . . . Dom
Signature Collection by Santiago Cabana Torpedo . . . USA
Zino Pantellas Brazil . . . . Hon
Zino Pantellas Sumatra . . . . Hon

$$$ — $5–8.00

Arturo Fuente Hemingway Classic . . . . Dom
Arturo Fuente Hemingway Signature . . . . Dom
Ashton 8-9-8 . . . . Dom
Ashton Aged Maduro No 20 . . . . Dom
Ashton Aged Maduro No 30 . . . . Dom
Ashton Aged Maduro No 40 . . . . Dom
Ashton Aged Maduro No 50 . . . . Dom
Ashton Aged Maduro No 60 . . . . Dom
Ashton Cabinet Selection No 6 . . . . Dom
Ashton Churchill . . . . Dom
Ashton Magnum . . . . Dom
Ashton Prime Minister . . . . Dom

Astral Besos. . . . . Hon
Astral Favorito. . . . . Hon
Astral Lujos. . . . . Hon
Astral Maestro. . . . . Hon
Astral Perfeccion . . . . Hon
Avo No 3 . . . . Dom
Avo No 4 . . . . Dom
Avo No 5 . . . . Dom
Avo No 6 . . . . Dom
Avo No 7 . . . . Dom
Avo No 8 . . . . Dom
Avo No 9 . . . . Dom
Avo Petit Belicoso . . . . Dom
Butera Royal Vintage Bravo Corto. . . . . Dom
Butera Royal Vintage Cedro Fino . . . . Dom
Butera Royal Vintage Dorado 652 . . . . Dom
Butera Royal Vintage Fumo Dolce. . . . . Dom
Butera Royal Vintage Mira Bella . . . . Dom
C.A.O. Churchill. . . . . Hon
C.A.O. Corona . . . . Hon
C.A.O. Corona Gorda. . . . . Hon
C.A.O. Lonsdale . . . . Hon
C.A.O. Robusto. . . . . Hon
C.A.O. Triangulare . . . . Hon
Calle Ocho Churchill . . . . USA
Calle Ocho Festivale . . . . USA
Calle Ocho Gordito . . . . USA
Calle Ocho Gordito Largo . . . . USA
Calle Ocho Laquito . . . . USA
Calle Ocho Ninas . . . . USA
Calle Ocho Perfect Corona . . . . USA
Camorra Imported Limited Reserve Genova . . . . Hon
Camorra Imported Limited Reserve Napoli. . . . . Hon
Camorra Imported Limited Reserve Roma . . . . Hon
Camorra Imported Limited Reserve San Remo. . . . . . Hon
Camorra Imported Limited Reserve Venzia. . . . . Hon
Carrington VIII . . . . Dom
Cifuentes Petit Corona . . . . Jam
Colorado Lonsdale . . . . Hon
Colorado Presidente. . . . . Hon
Colorado Robusto. . . . . Hon
Colorado Torpedo . . . . Hon
Credo Dominican Arcane . . . . Dom
Credo Dominican Magnificat . . . . Dom
Credo Dominican Pythagoras . . . . Dom

Don Xavier Robusto. CI
Dunhill (Vintage) Cabreras. . . . . Dom
Dunhill (Vintage) Centenas. . . . . Dom
Dunhill (Vintage) Peravias. . . . . Dom
Evelio Double Corona . . . . Hon
Evelio Robusto Larga . . . . Hon
Evelio Torpedo . . . . Hon
Excelsior No 2. . . . . Mex
Excelsior No 3. . . . . Mex
Excelsior No 4. . . . . Mex
Excelsior No 5. . . . . Mex
Fonseca Triangular. . . . . Dom
Franco Magnum. . . . . Dom
Franco Regios . . . . Dom
Griffin's No 100 . . . . Dom
Griffin's No 200 . . . . Dom
Griffin's No 300 . . . . Dom
Griffin's No 400 . . . . Dom
Griffin's Prestige . . . . Dom
H. Upmann Cabinet Selection. . . . . Dom
H. Upmann Monarch Tubes . . . . Dom
Habanica Serie 546. . . . . Nic
Habanica Serie 550. . . . . Nic
Habanica Serie 638. . . . . Nic
Habanica Serie 646. . . . . Nic
Habanica Serie 747. . . . . Nic
Havana Classico Churchill . . . . USA
Havana Classico Corona Classic . . . . USA
Havana Classico Double Corona . . . . USA
Havana Classico Puntas . . . . USA
Havana Classico Robusto . . . . USA
Havana Classico Robusto Largo . . . . USA
Havana Classico Varadero. USA
Havana Reserve Churchills. Hon
Havana Reserve No 1 . . . . Hon
Havana Reserve Panetelas . . . . Hon
Havana Reserve Robusto . . . . Hon
Havana Reserve Rothchild . . . . Hon
Havana Reserve Toros . . . . Hon
Havana Reserve Torpedo . . . . Hon
Havana Reserve Tubes . . . . Hon
Hugo Cassar Diamond Selection Chairman. . . . . Hon
Hugo Cassar Diamond Selection Corona . . . . Dom
Hugo Cassar Diamond Selection Corona. . . . . Hon
Hugo Cassar Diamond Selection Double Corona . . . . Hon

Hugo Cassar Diamond Selection El Presidente...... Dom
Hugo Cassar Diamond Selection Grand Corona..... Dom
Hugo Cassar Diamond Selection Lonsdale .... Dom
Hugo Cassar Diamond Selection Lonsdale .... Hon
Hugo Cassar Diamond Selection Presidente .... Hon
Hugo Cassar Diamond Selection Robusto.......... Dom
Hugo Cassar Diamond Selection Robusto .... Hon
Hugo Cassar Diamond Selection Toro .... Dom
Hugo Cassar Diamond Selection Torpedo.......... Hon
Hugo Cassar Private Collection Corona .... Dom
Hugo Cassar Private Collection Emperador........ Hon
Hugo Cassar Private Collection Presidente .... Dom
Hugo Cassar Private Collection Robusto........... Dom
Hugo Cassar Private Collection Toro.............. Dom
Hugo Cassar Private Collection Torpedo.......... Dom
Indian Chief.................................. Hon
Indian TeePee................................ Hon
Joya de Nicaragua Viajante...................... Nic
Juan Clemente Churchill....................... Dom
Juan Clemente Club Selection No 2 .... Dom
Juan Clemente Club Selection No 4 .... Dom
Juan Clemente Especiale .... Dom
Juan Clemente Grand Corona.................... Dom
Juan Clemente Rothschild...................... Dom
Kingston Corona Grande .... Jam
Kingston Giant Corona .... Jam
Kingston Panetela Extra .... Jam
Kingston Rothschild .... Jam
Kingston Royal Corona .... Jam
Kingston Toro .... Jam
Kingston Viajante............................. Jam
La Diva Churchill .... USA
La Diva Corona............................... USA
La Diva Robusto .... USA
Licenciados Figurado.......................... Dom
Los Libertadores Alcade .... Dom
Los Libertadores Belicoso Reserva Especial .... Dom
Los Libertadores Churchill Reserva Especial .... Dom
Los Libertadores Diplomaticos .... Dom
Los Libertadores Exiliados...................... Dom
Los Libertadores Figurado...................... Dom
Los Libertadores Insurrectos.................... Dom
Los Libertadores Maceo........................ Dom
Los Libertadores Macheteros.................... Dom
Los Libertadores Mambises .... Dom

Los Libertadores Robusto Reserva Especial. . . . . Dom
Macabi Belicoso Fino . . . . USA
Macanudo Duke of Wellington . . . . Jam
Macanudo Prince of Wales . . . . Jam
Macanudo Prince Philip . . . . Jam
Marsh Deluxe . . . . USA
Marsh Mountaineer . . . . USA
Marsh Old Reliable. . . . . USA
Marsh Pioneer . . . . USA
Marsh Virginian . . . . USA
Matacan Bundles No 1. . . . . Jam
Matacan Bundles No 8. . . . . Jam
Matacan Bundles No 10. . . . . Jam
Match Play Olympic. . . . . Dom
Match Play Troon. . . . . Dom
Mexican Emperador . . . . Mex
Monte Canario Imperiales. CI
Monte Canario No 3 CI
Monte Canario Nuncios. CI
Monte Canario Panetelas. CI
Montecristo Churchills . . . . Dom
Montecristo No 1. . . . . Dom
Montecristo No 3. . . . . Dom
Montecristo No 4. . . . . Dom
Montecristo Robustos . . . . Dom
Montecristo Tubos . . . . Dom
Nat Sherman City Desk Selection Dispatch. . . . . Dom
Nat Sherman City Desk Selection Gazette. . . . . Dom
Nat Sherman City Desk Selection Telegraph. . . . . Dom
Nat Sherman City Desk Selection Tribune . . . . Dom
Nat Sherman Exchange Selection Butterfield No 8 . . Dom
Nat Sherman Exchange Selection Oxford No 5 . . . . . Dom
Nat Sherman Exchange Selection Trafalgar No 4. . . . Dom
Nat Sherman Gotham Selection No 500 . . . . Dom
Nat Sherman Gotham Selection No 1400 . . . . Dom
Nat Sherman Landmark Selection Algonquin . . . . . . Dom
Nat Sherman Landmark Selection Dakota . . . . Dom
Nat Sherman Landmark Selection Vanderbilt. . . . . . . Dom
Nat Sherman Metropolitan Selection Anglers. . . . . . . Dom
Nat Sherman Metropolitan Selection Explorers . . . . . Dom
Nat Sherman Metropolitan Selection Metropolitan . . Dom
Nat Sherman Metropolitan Selection Nautical . . . . . . Dom
Nat Sherman Metropolitan Selection University. . . . . Dom
Nestor Vintage 454. . . . . Hon
Nestor Vintage 654. . . . . Hon

Petrus Tabacage 89 Lord Byron . . . . Hon
Petrus Tabacage 89 No I. . . . . Hon
Petrus Tabacage 89 No II . . . . Hon
Petrus Tabacage 89 No III . . . . Hon
Petrus Tabacage 89 No IV . . . . Hon
Pleiades Antares. . . . . Dom
Pleiades Mars . . . . Dom
Pleiades Neptune. . . . . Dom
Pleiades Orion . . . . Dom
Pleiades Pluto . . . . Dom
Pleiades Sirius . . . . Dom
Pleiades Uranus . . . . Dom
Puros Indios Churchill Especial . . . . Hon
Puros Indios No 1 Especial. Hon
Puros Indios Presidente . . . . Hon
Ramon Allones Redondos . . . . Dom
Rolando Blend Numero 2 . . . . USA
Rolando Blend Perfecto. . . . . USA
Rolando Blend Pyramid . . . . USA
Romeo Y Julieta Vintage I . . . . Dom
Romeo Y Julieta Vintage II. Dom
Romeo Y Julieta Vintage III . . . . Dom
Romeo Y Julieta Vintage IV . . . . Dom
Romeo Y Julieta Vintage V. Dom
Royal Jamaica Churchill. . . . . Dom
Royal Jamaica Double Corona. . . . . Dom
Royal Jamaica Giant Corona . . . . Dom
Royal Jamaica Park Lane . . . . Dom
Royal Jamaica Tube No 1. . . . . Dom
Santa Damiana Seleccion No 200 . . . . Dom
Santa Damiana Seleccion No 300 . . . . Dom
Santa Damiana Seleccion No 400 . . . . Dom
Santa Damiana Seleccion No 500 . . . . Dom
Santa Damiana Seleccion No 600 . . . . Dom
Santa Damiana Seleccion No 700 . . . . Dom
Savinelli Extremely Limited Reserve
        No 3 Lonsdale . . . . Dom
Savinelli Extremely Limited Reserve
        No 4 Double Corona . . . . Dom
Savinelli Extremely Limited Reserve
        No 5 Extraordinaire. Dom
Savinelli Extremely Limited Reserve
        No 6 Robusto . . . . Dom
Serengeti Churchill Buffalo. SA
Serengeti Churchill Rhino . . . . SA

Signature Collection by Santiago Cabana Caribe. . . . . USA
Signature Collection by Santiago Cabana Chicas. . . . . USA
Signature Collection by Santiago Cabana Churchill . . USA
Signature Collection by Santiago Cabana Corona . . . . USA
Signature Collection by Santiago Cabana
       Double Corona. . . . . USA
Signature Collection by Santiago Cabana Lancero . . . USA
Signature Collection by Santiago Cabana Presidente. . . USA
Signature Collection by Santiago Cabana Robusto . . . USA
Sosa Family Selection No 2 . . . . Dom
Sosa Family Selection No 9 . . . . Dom
Sosa Piramides No 2 . . . . Dom
Temple Hall Belicoso. . . . . Jam
Temple Hall No 1 Trump . . . . Jam
Temple Hall No 2 Trump . . . . Jam
Temple Hall No 3 Trump . . . . Jam
Temple Hall No 4 Trump . . . . Jam
Temple Hall No 450 Maduro. . . . . Jam
Temple Hall No 500 . . . . Jam
Temple Hall No 550 . . . . Jam
Temple Hall No 625 . . . . Jam
Temple Hall No 675 . . . . Jam
Temple Hall No 685 . . . . Jam
Temple Hall No 700 . . . . Jam
Thomas Hinds Nicaraguan Selection Torpedo . . . . . . Mex
Troya No 81 Torpedo. . . . . Dom
Virtuoso Torano Presidente . . . . Hon
Zino Veritas. . . . . Hon

$$ — $3–5.00

Adante No 405 Petit Corona . . . . Dom
Adante No 504 Corona . . . . Dom
Adante No 603 Palma Fina . . . . Dom
Adante No 702 Cetro. . . . . Dom
Adante No 801 Elegante . . . . Dom
Al Capone. . . . . Hon
Arturo Fuente Chateau Fuente Royal Salute. . . . . . . Dom
Arturo Fuente Hemingway Short Story . . . . Dom
Ashton Cordial. . . . . Dom
Ashton Corona. . . . . Dom
Ashton Elegante. . . . . Dom
Ashton Panetela. . . . . Dom
Bauza Casa Grande . . . . Dom
Bauza Fabulosos. . . . . Dom
Bauza Jaguar . . . . Dom

Bauza Medalla d'Oro No 1 .... Dom
Bauza Presidente .... Dom
Bauza Robusto .... Dom
C.A.O. Petit Corona .... Hon
Caballeros Churchill .... Dom
Caballeros Corona .... Dom
Caballeros Petit Corona........................ Dom
Caballeros Rothschild .... Dom
Cabanas Exquistos .... Dom
Cabelleros Double Corona .... Dom
Cacique Caribes............................... Dom
Cacique Incas................................. Dom
Camacho Churchill .... Hon
Camacho El Cesar............................. Hon
Camacho Executives........................... Hon
Camacho No 1 .... Hon
Camorra Imported Limited Reserve Padova .... Hon
Carrington I.................................. Dom
Carrington II .... Dom
Carrington III .... Dom
Carrington IV................................ Dom
Carrington V .... Dom
Carrington VI................................ Dom
Carrington VII .... Dom
Credo Dominican Athanor .... Dom
Credo Dominican Jubilate...................... Dom
Cruz Real No 1 .... Mex
Cruz Real No 2 .... Mex
Cruz Real No 14 .... Mex
Cruz Real No 19 .... Mex
Cruz Real No 24 .... Mex
Cruz Real No 25 .... Mex
Cruz Real No 28 .... Mex
Cubita Delicias............................... Dom
Cubita No 2 .... Dom
Dannemann Espada Brazil...................... Swi
Dannemann Espada Sumatra.................... Swi
Dannemann Lights Brazil....................... Swi
Dannemann Lights Brazil Boy/Girl .... Swi
Dannemann Lights Sumatra..................... Swi
Davidoff Ambassadice .... Dom
Don Diego Corona............................ Dom
Don Diego Corona Major .... Dom
Don Diego Coronas Bravas .... Dom
Don Diego Coronas EMS/AMS.................. Dom

Don Diego Coronas Major Tubes EMS . . . . Dom
Don Diego Grandes EMS. . . . . Dom
Don Diego Grecos . . . . Dom
Don Diego Grecos EMS. . . . . Dom
Don Diego Imperial EMS . . . . Dom
Don Diego Lonsdales. . . . . Dom
Don Diego Lonsdales EMS/AMS. . . . . Dom
Don Diego Pequenos No 100 . . . . Dom
Don Diego Pequenos No 200 . . . . Dom
Don Diego Pequenos No 300 . . . . Dom
Don Diego Royal Palmas . . . . Dom
Don Juan Churchills. . . . . Nic
Don Juan Presidents. . . . . Nic
Don Leo Churchill. . . . . Dom
Don Lino Churchill . . . . Hon
Don Lino Corona . . . . Hon
Don Lino No 1 . . . . Hon
Don Lino No 3 . . . . Hon
Don Lino No 5 . . . . Hon
Don Lino Oro No 1 . . . . Hon
Don Lino Oro Panetelas. . . . . Hon
Don Lino Oro Toro . . . . Hon
Don Lino Panetelas . . . . Hon
Don Lino Peticetro. . . . . Hon
Don Lino Robustos. . . . . Hon
Don Lino Rothchild . . . . Hon
Don Lino Toros . . . . Hon
Don Marcus Cetros . . . . Dom
Don Marcus Coronas. . . . . Dom
Don Marcus Double Corona . . . . Dom
Don Marcus Naturals. . . . . Dom
Don Marcus Toros . . . . Dom
Don Melo Churchill . . . . Hon
Don Melo Corona Extra. . . . . Hon
Don Melo Corona Gorda . . . . Hon
Don Melo Numero Dos . . . . Hon
Don Rex Gigantes Maduro. . . . . Hon
Don Rex Presidentes . . . . Hon
Don Tomas Gigantes. . . . . Hon
Don Tomas Imperiales No 1. Hon
Don Tomas Presidentes . . . . Hon
Don Tomas Special Edition No 100 . . . . Hon
Don Tomas Special Edition No 200 . . . . Hon
Don Tomas Special Edition No 300 . . . . Hon
Don Tomas Special Edition No 400 . . . . Hon

Don Tomas Special Edition No 500 . . . . Hon
Dunhill (Vintage) Altiamaras . . . . Dom
Dunhill (Vintage) Condados . . . . Dom
Dunhill (Vintage) Diamantes . . . . Dom
Dunhill (Vintage) Romanas. . . . . Dom
Dunhill (Vintage) Tabaras . . . . Dom
Dunhill Canary Island Corona Grandes CI
Dunhill Canary Island Coronas Extra CI
Dunhill Canary Island Lonsdale Grandes CI
El Rey del Mundo Flor de Llaneza . . . . Hon
El Rey del Mundo Flor del Mundo. . . . . Hon
El Rico Habano Gran Habanero Deluxe . . . . USA
Elegante Especial . . . . USA
Elegante Grande. . . . . USA
Evelio Corona. . . . . Hon
Evelio No 1 . . . . Hon
Evelio Robusto . . . . Hon
Excalibur Banquets. . . . . Hon
Excelsior No 1. . . . . Mex
F. D. Grave & Son Churchill. . . . . Hon
F. D. Grave & Son Corona Grande. . . . . Hon
Felipe Gregorio Nino . . . . Hon
Felipe Gregorio Robusto . . . . Hon
Felipe Gregorio Sereno . . . . Hon
Fonseca 5-50. . . . . Dom
Fonseca 7-9-9 . . . . Dom
Fonseca 8-9-8 . . . . Dom
Fonseca 10-10. . . . . Dom
Franco Condados. . . . . Dom
Franco Eminentes . . . . Dom
Franco Gourmets . . . . Dom
Fundadores King Ferdinand . . . . Jam
Griffin's Privilege . . . . Dom
Griffin's Robusto . . . . Dom
H. Upmann Amatista. . . . . Dom
H. Upmann Cabinet Selection Corsario . . . . Dom
H. Upmann Cabinet Selection Robusto . . . . Dom
H. Upmann Churchills . . . . Dom
H. Upmann Corona Bravas . . . . Dom
H. Upmann Coronas . . . . Dom
H. Upmann Coronas Imperiales . . . . Dom
H. Upmann Coronas Major Tubes. . . . . Dom
H. Upmann Director Royale . . . . Dom
H. Upmann El Prado. . . . . Dom
H. Upmann Emperadores . . . . Dom

H. Upmann Extra Finos Gold Tube. . . . . Dom
H. Upmann Finos Gold Tube . . . . Dom
H. Upmann Lonsdales. . . . . Dom
H. Upmann Naturales Tubes. . . . . Dom
H. Upmann No 2000 SBN . . . . Dom
H. Upmann Pequenos No 100. . . . . Dom
H. Upmann Topacios SBN. . . . . Dom
H. Upmann Tubos Gold Tube . . . . Dom
Habana Gold Churchill . . . . Hon
Habana Gold Double Corona . . . . Hon
Habana Gold No 2 . . . . Hon
Habana Gold Presidente . . . . Hon
Habana Gold Torpedo . . . . Hon
Habanos Hatuey Churchills. . . . . Dom
Habanos Hatuey Lonsdales . . . . Dom
Habanos Hatuey Robustos. . . . . Dom
Harrows Esquire. . . . . Phi
Harrows No 1 . . . . Phi
Harrows Regent . . . . Phi
Henry Clay Anitas . . . . Dom
Henry Clay Brevas . . . . Dom
Henry Clay Brevas à la Conserva . . . . Dom
Henry Clay Brevas Fina . . . . Dom
Henry Clay Largas. . . . . Dom
Henry Clay Londres. . . . . Dom
Henry Clay Panetelas. . . . . Dom
Henry Clay Slim Panetela . . . . Dom
Hoyo de Nicaragua Maduro Deluxe Presidente . . . . . . Nic
Hoyo de Nicaragua Maduro Deluxe Robusto . . . . Nic
Hoyo de Nicaragua Maduro Deluxe Toro . . . . Nic
Hugo Cassar Private Collection Elegantes . . . . Hon
Hugo Cassar Private Collection Imperiale . . . . Hon
Hugo Cassar Private Collection Matador . . . . Hon
Hugo Cassar Private Collection Robusto . . . . Hon
Indian Arrow . . . . Hon
Indian Boxer. . . . . Hon
Indian Warrior . . . . Hon
J. F. Llopis Gold Churchill. . . . . Pan
J. F. Llopis Gold No 1. . . . . Pan
J. F. Llopis Gold No 2. . . . . Pan
J. F. Llopis Gold Palma Extra. . . . . Pan
J. F. Llopis Gold Rothschild . . . . Pan
J. F. Llopis Gold Viajante . . . . Pan
Jose Benito Churchill. . . . . Dom
Jose Benito Presidente. . . . . Dom

Jose Benito Rothschild.........................Dom
Jose Llopis Soberano..........................Pan
Jose Llopis Viajante..........................Pan
Jose Marti....................................Dom
Jose Marti Maceo.............................Dom
Jose Marti Palma.............................Dom
Jose Marti Robusto...........................Dom
Joya de Nicaragua Churchill..................Nic
Joya de Nicaragua Consul.....................Nic
Joya de Nicaragua No 3.......................Nic
Juan Clemente 530............................Dom
Juan Clemente Corona.........................Dom
Juan Clemente Demi Corona....................Dom
Juan Clemente Demi Tasse.....................Dom
Juan Clemente Panetela.......................Dom
La Aurora Bristol Especiales.................Dom
La Aurora Double Corona......................Dom
La Aurora Robusto............................Dom
La Aurora Sublimes...........................Dom
La Diligencia Churchill......................Hon
La Diligencia Gran Corona....................Hon
La Diligencia Presidente.....................Hon
La Diligencia Robusto........................Hon
La Diligencia Toro...........................Hon
La Flor de la Isabela 1881...................Phi
La Flor de la Isabela Brevas.................Phi
La Flor de la Isabela Coronas................Phi
La Flor de la Isabela Coronas Largas.........Phi
La Flor de la Isabela Coronas Largas Especiale.......Phi
La Flor de la Isabela Coronas Sumatra........Phi
La Flor de la Isabela Half Coronas...........Phi
La Fontana Vintage Belicoso..................Hon
La Fontana Vintage Da Vinci..................Hon
La Fontana Vintage Galileo...................Hon
La Fontana Vintage Michelangelo..............Hon
La Fontana Vintage Mona Lisa.................Hon
La Fontana Vintage Puccini...................Hon
La Gloria Cubana Crown Imperial..............USA
La Gloria Cubana Soberano....................USA
La Maximiliana Optimus.......................Hon
Las Cabrillas Maximilian.....................Hon
Lempira Churchills...........................Hon
Lempira Lanceros.............................Hon
Lempira Presidentes..........................Hon
Lempira Toro.................................Hon

Montecruz Individuales . . . . Dom
Montecruz No 200 . . . . Dom
Montecruz No 201 . . . . Dom
Montecruz No 205 . . . . Dom
Montecruz No 210 . . . . Dom
Montecruz No 220 . . . . Dom
Montecruz No 230 . . . . Dom
Montecruz No 240 . . . . Dom
Montecruz No 250 . . . . Dom
Montecruz No 255 . . . . Dom
Montecruz No 265 . . . . Dom
Montecruz No 270 . . . . Dom
Montecruz No 275 . . . . Dom
Montecruz No 276 . . . . Dom
Montecruz No 277 . . . . Dom
Montecruz No 280 . . . . Dom
Montecruz No 281 . . . . Dom
Montecruz No 282 . . . . Dom
Montecruz Robusto . . . . Dom
Montecruz Senores . . . . Dom
Montecruz Tubo. . . . . Dom
Montecruz Tubulares . . . . Dom
Montesino Gran Corona . . . . Dom
Moreno Maduro No 528 . . . . Dom
Nat Cicco's Supremos Dominicanos Deliciosos. . . . . . Dom
Nat Cicco's Supremos Dominicanos Exquisitos. . . . . . Dom
Nat Cicco's Supremos Dominicanos Grandiosos. . . . . Dom
Nat Cicco's Supremos Dominicanos Lindos . . . . Dom
Nat Cicco's Supremos Dominicanos Sabrosos. . . . . . . Dom
Nat Sherman Exchange Selection Academy No 2 . . . . Dom
Nat Sherman Exchange Selection Murray Hill No 7. . Dom
Nat Sherman Gotham Selection No 65 . . . . Dom
Nat Sherman Gotham Selection No 711 . . . . Dom
Nat Sherman Host Selection Hamilton . . . . Hon
Nat Sherman Host Selection Hampton . . . . Hon
Nat Sherman Host Selection Harrington. . . . . Hon
Nat Sherman Host Selection Hobart . . . . Hon
Nat Sherman Host Selection Hunter . . . . Hon
Nat Sherman Landmark Selection Hampshire . . . . . . Dom
Nat Sherman Landmark Selection Metropole. . . . . . . Dom
Nat Sherman Manhattan Selection Chelsea . . . . Dom
Nat Sherman Manhattan Selection Gramercy. . . . . . . Dom
Nat Sherman Manhattan Selection Sutton . . . . Dom
Nat Sherman VIP Selection Astor . . . . Dom
Nat Sherman VIP Selection Carnegie . . . . Dom

Nat Sherman VIP Selection Morgan . . . . Dom
Nat Sherman VIP Selection Zigfeld "Fancytale" . . . . . Dom
Onyx No 852 . . . . Dom
Ornelas Cafetero Chico . . . . Mex
Ornelas Cafetero Grande . . . . Mex
Ornelas Matinee Lights. . . . . Mex
Ornelas Matinee Lights Vanilla. . . . . Mex
Ornelas Matinee Vanilla . . . . Mex
Ornelas Matinee . . . . Mex
Ornelas No 1. . . . . Mex
Ornelas No 2. . . . . Mex
Ornelas No 3. . . . . Mex
Ornelas No 4. . . . . Mex
Ornelas No 5. . . . . Mex
Ornelas No 6. . . . . Mex
Ornelas Robusto . . . . Mex
Padron 2000 . . . . Hon
Padron 3000 . . . . Hon
Padron Ambassador . . . . Hon
Padron Chicos . . . . Hon
Padron Churchill . . . . Hon
Padron Delicias. . . . . Hon
Padron Executive . . . . Hon
Padron Grand Reserve . . . . Hon
Padron Londres . . . . Hon
Padron Magnum. . . . . Hon
Padron Palmas . . . . Hon
Padron Panetela . . . . Hon
Partagas Almirante. . . . . Dom
Partagas Maduro . . . . Dom
Partagas Naturales . . . . Dom
Partagas No 1. . . . . Dom
Partagas No 4. . . . . Dom
Partagas Robusto . . . . Dom
Partagas Sabroso . . . . Dom
Partagas Tubos. . . . . Dom
Particulares Executive. . . . . Hon
Particulares Presidentes . . . . Hon
Particulares Viajantes . . . . Hon
Penamil No 5. CI
Penamil No 6. CI
Penamil No 16 CI
Penamil No 17 CI
Penamil No 18 CI
Penamil No 25 CI

Penamil No 50 CI
Peter Stokkebye Santa Maria . . . . Dom
Peter Stokkebye Santa Maria No 2 . . . . Dom
Peter Stokkebye Santa Maria No 3 . . . . Dom
Petrus Tabacage 89 Chantaco . . . . Hon
Petrus Tabacage 89 Corona Sublime . . . . Hon
Petrus Tabacage 89 Duchess . . . . Hon
Petrus Tabacage 89 Gregorius . . . . Hon
Petrus Tabacage 89 No IV . . . . Hon
Petrus Tabacage 89 Palma Fina . . . . Hon
Petrus Tabacage 89 Rothschild . . . . Hon
Pleiades Perseus . . . . Dom
Primo del Rey Aguilas . . . . Dom
Primo del Rey Soberanos . . . . Dom
Punch Gran Cru Diademas . . . . Hon
Punch Gran Cru Monarcas . . . . Hon
Punch Gran Cru Prince Consorts . . . . Hon
Punch Presidents . . . . Hon
Punch Slim Panetela . . . . Hon
Puros Indios Figurin . . . . Hon
Puros Indios General . . . . Hon
Puros Indios Nacionales . . . . Hon
Puros Indios No 2 Especial . . . . Hon
Puros Indios No 4 Especial . . . . Hon
Puros Indios Palmas Real . . . . Hon
Puros Indios Piramide No 1 . . . . Hon
Puros Indios Piramide No 2 . . . . Hon
Puros Indios Rothschild . . . . Hon
Puros Indios Toro Especial . . . . Hon
Ramon Allones A . . . . Dom
Ramon Allones B . . . . Dom
Ramon Allones D . . . . Dom
Ramon Allones Ramonitos . . . . Dom
Ramon Allones Trumps . . . . Dom
Rico Havana Blend Churchill . . . . USA
Rico Havana Blend Double Corona . . . . USA
Rico Havana Blend Rough Rider . . . . USA
Rolando Blend Numero No 3 . . . . USA
Rolando Blend Numero No 4 . . . . USA
Rolando Blend Robusto . . . . USA
Roller's Choice RC Corona . . . . Dom
Roller's Choice RC Double Corona . . . . Dom
Roller's Choice RC Fino . . . . Dom
Roller's Choice RC Lonsdale . . . . Dom
Roller's Choice RC Pequeno . . . . Dom

Roller's Choice RC Robusto. . . . . Dom
Roller's Choice RC Torpedo . . . . Dom
Romeo Y Julieta Cetros . . . . Dom
Romeo Y Julieta Churchills . . . . Dom
Romeo Y Julieta Delgados . . . . Dom
Romeo Y Julieta Monarcas. Dom
Romeo Y Julieta Presidentes . . . . Dom
Romeo Y Julieta Romeo. . . . . Dom
Romeo Y Julieta Rothschild . . . . Dom
Royal Jamaica Buccaneer. . . . . Dom
Royal Jamaica Corona . . . . Dom
Royal Jamaica Corona Grande. . . . . Dom
Royal Jamaica Director 1 . . . . Dom
Royal Jamaica Doubloon . . . . Dom
Royal Jamaica Navarro. . . . . Dom
Royal Jamaica New York Plaza . . . . Dom
Royal Jamaica Petit Corona . . . . Dom
Royal Jamaica Rapier . . . . Dom
Royal Jamaica Robusto. . . . . Dom
Royal Jamaica Royal Corona . . . . Dom
Rum Runner Pirate. . . . . USA
Santa Clara "1830" No I . . . . Mex
Santa Clara "1830" Premier Tubes . . . . Mex
Santa Rosa Churchill . . . . Hon
Santa Rosa Corona . . . . Hon
Santa Rosa Elegante . . . . Hon
Santa Rosa Embajadore . . . . Hon
Santa Rosa Finas. . . . . Hon
Santa Rosa President . . . . Hon
Santa Rosa Sancho Panza. . . . . Hon
Santa Rosa Toro . . . . Hon
Santa Rosa Torpedo . . . . Hon
Serengeti Corona Bushbuck . . . . SA
Serengeti Corona Kudu. . . . . SA
Sosa Churchill . . . . Dom
Sosa Family Selection No 1 . . . . Dom
Sosa Family Selection No 3 . . . . Dom
Sosa Family Selection No 4 . . . . Dom
Sosa Family Selection No 5 . . . . Dom
Sosa Family Selection No 6 . . . . Dom
Sosa Family Selection No 7 . . . . Dom
Sosa Family Selection No 8 . . . . Dom
Sosa Governor . . . . Dom
Sosa Lonsdale. . . . . Dom
Sosa Wavell. . . . . Dom

Tabacalera Brevas a la Conserva . . . . Phi
Tabacalera Corona Larga . . . . Phi
Tabacalera Cortado . . . . Phi
Tabacalera Don Q. . . . . Phi
Tabacalera El Conde de Guell Sr . . . . Phi
Tabacalera Gigantes . . . . Phi
Tabacalera Panatella . . . . Phi
Tabacalera Panatella Larga . . . . Phi
Te-Amo C.E.O. . . . . Mex
Te-Amo Celebration . . . . Mex
Te-Amo Churchill . . . . Mex
Te-Amo Grand Piramides . . . . Mex
Te-Amo Maximo . . . . Mex
Te-Amo Piramides . . . . Mex
Te-Amo Presidente . . . . Mex
Thomas Hinds Honduran Selection Churchill . . . . . . Hon
Thomas Hinds Honduran Selection Presidente . . . . . . Hon
Thomas Hinds Honduran Selection Short Churchill . Hon
Thomas Hinds Honduran Selection Torpedo . . . . Hon
Torcedor Churchill . . . . Nic
Torcedor Vijante . . . . Nic
Troya No 18 Rothschild . . . . Dom
Troya No 27 Corona . . . . Dom
Troya No 36 Palma Fina . . . . Dom
Troya No 45 Cetro . . . . Dom
Troya No 54 Elegante . . . . Dom
Troya No 63 Churchill . . . . Dom
Troya No 72 Executive . . . . Dom
V Centennial Churchills . . . . Hon
V Centennial Numero 1 . . . . Hon
V Centennial Numero 2 . . . . Hon
V Centennial Presidente . . . . Hon
V Centennial Torpedo . . . . Hon
Virtuoso Torano Cetros . . . . Hon
Virtuoso Torano Double Corona . . . . Hon
Virtuoso Torano Lonsdale . . . . Hon
Virtuoso Torano Robusto . . . . Hon
Vueltabajo Churchill . . . . Dom
Vueltabajo Gigante . . . . Dom
Vueltabajo Lonsdale . . . . Dom
Zino Classic Brazil . . . . Hon
Zino Classic Sumatra . . . . Hon
Zino Diamond . . . . Hon
Zino Elegance . . . . Hon
Zino Junior . . . . Hon

Zino Mouton Cadet No 1 . . . . Hon
Zino Mouton Cadet No 2 . . . . Hon
Zino Mouton Cadet No 3 . . . . Hon
Zino Mouton Cadet No 4 . . . . Hon
Zino Mouton Cadet No 5 . . . . Hon
Zino Mouton Cadet No 6 . . . . Hon
Zino Princesse. . . . . Hon
Zino Relax Sumatra . . . . Hon
Zino Tradition . . . . Hon
Zino Tubos No 1. . . . . Hon

$ — $1-3.00

Alhambra Corona Grande . . . . Phi
Alhambra Corona. . . . . Phi
Alhambra Double Grande . . . . Phi
Alhambra Duque . . . . Phi
Alhambra Especiale . . . . Phi
Arango Sportsman No 300 . . . . USA
Arango Sportsman No 350 . . . . USA
Arango Sportsman No 400 . . . . USA
Arango Statesman Barrister . . . . Hon
Arango Statesman Counselor . . . . Hon
Arango Statesman Executor . . . . Hon
Arturo Fuente Canones . . . . Dom
Arturo Fuente Chateau Fuente . . . . Dom
Arturo Fuente Churchill . . . . Dom
Arturo Fuente Corona Imperial. . . . . Dom
Arturo Fuente Cuban Corona . . . . Dom
Arturo Fuente Dantes . . . . Dom
Arturo Fuente Don Carlos Robusto. . . . . Dom
Arturo Fuente Double Chateau Fuente. . . . . Dom
Arturo Fuente Flor Fina 8-5-8 . . . . Dom
Arturo Fuente Fumas. . . . . Dom
Arturo Fuente Panetela Fina . . . . Dom
Arturo Fuente Petit Corona. Dom
Arturo Fuente Rothschild . . . . Dom
Arturo Fuente Seleccion Privada No 1 . . . . Dom
Arturo Fuente Spanish Lonsdale . . . . Dom
Baccarat Havana Selection Bonita . . . . Hon
Baccarat Havana Selection Churchill. . . . . Hon
Baccarat Havana Selection Luchadore. . . . . Hon
Baccarat Havana Selection No 1. . . . . Hon
Baccarat Havana Selection Panetela. . . . . Hon
Baccarat Havana Selection Petit Corona . . . . Hon
Baccarat Havana Selection Platinum . . . . Hon

Baccarat Havana Selection Polo . . . . Hon
Baccarat Havana Selection Rothschild . . . . Hon
Bauza Florete . . . . Dom
Bauza Grecos . . . . Dom
Bauza Petit Corona . . . . Dom
Belinda Belinda . . . . Hon
Belinda Breva Conserva . . . . Hon
Belinda Corona Grande . . . . Hon
Belinda Medagla D'Oro . . . . Hon
Belinda Ramon . . . . Hon
Bering Barons . . . . Hon
Bering Casinos-Glass Tubes . . . . Hon
Bering Cazadores . . . . Hon
Bering Corona Royale . . . . Hon
Bering Coronados . . . . Hon
Bering Gold No 1 . . . . Hon
Bering Grande . . . . Hon
Bering Hispanos . . . . Hon
Bering Imperials . . . . Hon
Bering Imperials Boy/Girl . . . . Hon
Bering Inmensas . . . . Hon
Bering Plazas . . . . Hon
Bering Robusto . . . . Hon
Bering Torpedo . . . . Hon
Bermejo Cazadores . . . . Hon
Bermejo Fumas . . . . Hon
Blue Label Bulvon . . . . Hon
Blue Label Churchill . . . . Hon
Blue Label Finos . . . . Hon
Blue Label Imperial . . . . Hon
Blue Label No 1 . . . . Hon
Blue Label No 2 . . . . Hon
Blue Label Palma . . . . Hon
Blue Label Presidente . . . . Hon
Blue Label Rothschild . . . . Hon
Blue Label Toro . . . . Hon
Blue Ribbon No 500 . . . . Nic
Cabanas Corona . . . . Dom
Cabanas Corona Grande . . . . Dom
Cabanas Lonsdale . . . . Dom
Cabanas Premier . . . . Dom
Cabanas Royale . . . . Dom
Cacique Apache . . . . Dom
Cacique Azteca . . . . Dom
Cacique Jaraqua . . . . Dom

Cacique Siboneyes . . . . Dom
Cacique Tainos. . . . . Dom
Calixto Lopez/Carlos V Corona Exquisito. . . . . Phi
Calixto Lopez/Carlos V Corona Numero 1 . . . . Phi
Calixto Lopez/Carlos V Czars . . . . Phi
Calixto Lopez/Carlos V Gigantes. . . . . Phi
Calixto Lopez/Carlos V Lonsdale Suprema. . . . . Phi
Calixto Lopez/Carlos V Nobles Extrafinos . . . . Phi
Calixto Lopez/Carlos V Palma Royale . . . . Phi
Camacho Cazadores . . . . Hon
Camacho Cetros . . . . Hon
Camacho Conchitas . . . . Hon
Camacho Elegante . . . . Hon
Camacho Monarca . . . . Hon
Camacho Nacionales . . . . Hon
Camacho No 1 . . . . Hon
Camacho Palmas. . . . . Hon
Camacho Pan Especial . . . . Hon
Camorra Imported Limited Reserve Capri . . . . Hon
Canaria D'Ora Corona. . . . . Dom
Canaria D'Ora Fino . . . . Dom
Canaria D'Ora Immensos . . . . Dom
Canaria D'Ora Lonsdale . . . . Dom
Canaria D'Ora Rothschild . . . . Dom
Canaria D'Ora Supremos. . . . . Dom
Caramba Twin-Pack No 1 . . . . Hon
Caramba Twin-Pack No 2 . . . . Hon
Caramba Twin-Pack No 3 . . . . Hon
Caramba Twin-Pack No 4 . . . . Hon
Caramba Twin-Pack No 5 . . . . Hon
Caramba Twin-Pack No 6 . . . . Hon
Caramba Twin-Pack No 7 . . . . Hon
Caramba Twin-Pack No 8 . . . . Hon
Casa Blanca Bonita . . . . Dom
Casa Blanca Corona. . . . . Dom
Casa Blanca De Luxe . . . . Dom
Casa Blanca Half Jeroboam . . . . Dom
Casa Blanca Jeroboam . . . . Dom
Casa Blanca Lonsdale . . . . Dom
Casa Blanca Magnum. . . . . Dom
Casa Blanca Panetela . . . . Dom
Casa Blanca Presidente . . . . Dom
Casa Martin Churchills . . . . Dom
Casa Martin Majestad. . . . . Dom
Casa Martin Matador . . . . Dom

Casa Martin Numero Uno Plus . . . . Dom
Casa Martin Petit Coronas . . . . Dom
Casa Martin Regulares . . . . Dom
Casa Martin Seleccion Especial . . . . Dom
Caz-Bar Cazadores . . . . Hon
Caz-Bar Churchills . . . . Hon
Caz-Bar Corona Lonsdale . . . . Hon
Caz-Bar Fumas . . . . Hon
Caz-Bar Petit Cazadore . . . . Hon
Cervantes Churchill . . . . Hon
Cervantes Corona . . . . Hon
Cervantes Senadores . . . . Hon
Chevere Antonio . . . . Jam
Chevere Kingston . . . . Jam
Chevere Montego . . . . Jam
Chevere Ocho Rios . . . . Jam
Chevere Spanish Town . . . . Jam
Clementine Inmensas . . . . Hon
Clementine Torpedo . . . . Hon
Clementine Viajante . . . . Hon
Cruz Real No 3 . . . . Mex
Cuba Aliados Cazadore . . . . Hon
Cuba Aliados Churchill . . . . Hon
Cuba Aliados Corona Deluxe . . . . Hon
Cuba Aliados Fuma . . . . Hon
Cuba Aliados Lonsdale . . . . Hon
Cuba Aliados Number 4 . . . . Hon
Cuba Aliados Palma . . . . Hon
Cuba Aliados Petite Cetro . . . . Hon
Cuba Aliados Remedios . . . . Hon
Cuba Aliados Rothschild . . . . Hon
Cuba Aliados Toro . . . . Hon
Cuba Aliados Valentino . . . . Hon
Cuesta-Rey Cabinet Selection Cabinet No 2 . . . . Dom
Cuesta-Rey Cabinet Selection Cabinet No 95 . . . . Dom
Cuesta-Rey Cabinet Selection Cabinet No 898 . . . . . . Dom
Cuesta-Rey Cabinet Selection Cabinet No 1884 . . . . . Dom
Cuesta-Rey Caravelle . . . . USA
Cuesta-Rey No 120 . . . . USA
Cuesta-Rey No 240 . . . . USA
Cuesta-Rey Palma Supreme . . . . USA
Cyrilla Kings . . . . USA
Cyrilla Nationals . . . . USA
Cyrilla Senators . . . . USA
Cyrilla Slims . . . . USA

Don Melo Petit Corona .... Hon
Don Rex Blunts .... Hon
Don Rex Cetros No 2 .... Hon
Don Rex Coronas............................. Hon
Don Rex Panetela Largas .... Hon
Don Tomas Cetros No 2 .... Hon
Don Tomas Corona Grandes .... Hon
Don Tomas Coronas........................... Hon
Don Tomas Epicures........................... Hon
Don Tomas International Series No 1 .... Hon
Don Tomas International Series No 2 .... Hon
Don Tomas International Series No 3 .... Hon
Don Tomas International Series No 4 .... Hon
Don Tomas It's a Boy/Girl .... Hon
Don Tomas Matadors .... Hon
Don Tomas Panetela Largas..................... Hon
Don Tomas Panetelas.......................... Hon
Don Tomas Rothschild......................... Hon
Don Tomas Supremos .... Hon
Don Tomas Toros .... Hon
Dunhill (Vintage) Samanas .... Dom
Dunhill (Vintage) Valverdes .... Dom
Dunhill Canary Island Corona.................. CI
Dunhill Canary Island Panetelas CI
Dunhill Corona CI
Dunhill Panetela CI
El Rey del Mundo Cafe au Lait .... Hon
El Rey del Mundo Cedar .... Hon
El Rey del Mundo Choix Supreme............... Hon
El Rey del Mundo Corona .... Hon
El Rey del Mundo Coronation .... Hon
El Rey del Mundo Double Corona............... Hon
El Rey del Mundo Petit Lonsdale............... Hon
El Rey del Mundo Rectangulare................. Hon
El Rey del Mundo Robusto Suprema .... Hon
El Rey del Mundo Robusto Zavalia............... Hon
El Rey del Mundo Rothschilde.................. Hon
El Rey del Mundo Tino .... Hon
El Rico Habano Club .... USA
El Rico Habano Coronas .... USA
El Rico Habano Double Coronas................. USA
El Rico Habano Gran Coronas.................. USA
El Rico Habano Lonsdale Extra................. USA
El Rico Habano No 1 .... USA
El Rico Habano Petit Habanos................. USA

Hoja de Mexicali Lonsdale Natural . . . . Mex
Hoja de Mexicali Royal Corona Natural. . . . . Mex
Hoja de Mexicali Soberano Natural . . . . Mex
Hoja de Mexicali Toro Natural/Maduro . . . . Mex
Hoja de Mexicali Viajante Natural/Maduro. . . . . Mex
Hoja de Oro . . . . Mex
Hoja de Oro 100. . . . . Mex
Hoja de Oro 101. . . . . Mex
Hoja de Oro 103. . . . . Mex
Hoja de Oro 104. . . . . Mex
Hoja de Oro 105. . . . . Mex
Hoja de Oro 106. . . . . Mex
Hoja de Oro 107. . . . . Mex
Honduran Import Maduro Bandidos. . . . . Hon
Honduran Import Maduro Delicosos. . . . . Hon
Honduran Import Maduro Granadas. . . . . Hon
Honduran Import Maduro Majestics . . . . Hon
Honduran Import Maduro Petzels. . . . . Hon
Honduran Import Maduro Superbos. . . . . Hon
Hoyo de Monterrey Ambassador . . . . Hon
Hoyo de Monterrey Cafe Royale . . . . Hon
Hoyo de Monterrey Churchill . . . . Hon
Hoyo de Monterrey Corona . . . . Hon
Hoyo de Monterrey Cuban Largos. . . . . Hon
Hoyo de Monterrey Culebras . . . . Hon
Hoyo de Monterrey Delights . . . . Hon
Hoyo de Monterrey Demitasse . . . . Hon
Hoyo de Monterrey Double Corona . . . . Hon
Hoyo de Monterrey Governor . . . . Hon
Hoyo de Monterrey Largo Elegantes . . . . Hon
Hoyo de Monterrey Margaritas . . . . Hon
Hoyo de Monterrey No 1 . . . . Hon
Hoyo de Monterrey No 55 . . . . Hon
Hoyo de Monterrey President . . . . Hon
Hoyo de Monterrey Sabrosos . . . . Hon
Hoyo de Monterrey Sultan . . . . Hon
Hoyo de Monterrey Super Hoyos. . . . . Hon
Hugo Cassar Durango . . . . Jam
Hugo Cassar Monterey . . . . Jam
Hugo Cassar No 1. . . . . Hon
Hugo Cassar No 2. . . . . Hon
Hugo Cassar No 3. . . . . Hon
Hugo Cassar No 4. . . . . Hon
Hugo Cassar No 5. . . . . Hon
Hugo Cassar No 6. . . . . Hon

Jamaica Gold Baron. . . . . Jam
Jamaica Gold Count. . . . . Jam
Jamaica Gold Duke . . . . Jam
Jamaica Gold Earl . . . . Jam
Jamaica Gold Prince . . . . Jam
Jamaica Gold Queen . . . . Jam
Jose Benito Chico. . . . . Dom
Jose Benito Corona . . . . Dom
Jose Benito Havanitos . . . . Dom
Jose Benito Palma . . . . Dom
Jose Benito Panetela . . . . Dom
Jose Benito Petite. . . . . Dom
Jose Llopis Churchill . . . . Pan
Jose Llopis No 1. . . . . Pan
Jose Llopis No 2. . . . . Pan
Jose Llopis No 4. . . . . Pan
Jose Llopis Palma Extra. . . . . Pan
Jose Llopis Rothschild . . . . Pan
Jose Marti Corona . . . . Dom
Jose Marti Creme . . . . Dom
Jose Melendi Rothschild Maduro . . . . USA
Jose Melendi Vega I . . . . USA
Jose Melendi Vega II. . . . . USA
Jose Melendi Vega III . . . . USA
Jose Melendi Vega IV . . . . USA
Jose Melendi Vega V. . . . . USA
Jose Melendi Vega VII . . . . USA
Jose Melendi Wild Maduro. USA
Joya de Nicaragua Corona . . . . Nic
Joya de Nicaragua No 1 . . . . Nic
Joya de Nicaragua No 2 . . . . Nic
Joya de Nicaragua No 5 . . . . Nic
Joya de Nicaragua No 6 . . . . Nic
Joya de Nicaragua Petit . . . . Nic
Juan Lopez No 300. . . . . Hon
Juan Lopez No 301. . . . . Hon
Juan Lopez No 302. . . . . Hon
Juan Lopez No 303. . . . . Hon
Juan Lopez No 304. . . . . Hon
King No 1. . . . . Dom
King No 2. . . . . Dom
King No 3. . . . . Dom
King No 5. . . . . Dom
King No 6. . . . . Dom
King No 7. . . . . Dom

King No 8. . . . . Dom
King No 9. . . . . Dom
King No 10. . . . . Dom
King No 13. . . . . Dom
Kiskeya Cetros . . . . Dom
Kiskeya Churchills . . . . Dom
Kiskeya Numero Dos . . . . Dom
Kiskeya Numero Uno. . . . . Dom
Kiskeya Palma Fina. . . . . Dom
Kiskeya Presidentes . . . . Dom
Kiskeya Rothschild. . . . . Dom
Kiskeya Toros . . . . Dom
Kiskeya Viajantes . . . . Dom
La Aurora Cetro. . . . . Dom
La Aurora Corona . . . . Dom
La Aurora No 4 . . . . Dom
La Aurora Palmas Extra. Dom
La Aurora Petite Corona . . . . Dom
La Flor de la Isabela Brevas . . . . Phi
La Flor de la Isabela Caprichos . . . . Phi
La Flor de la Isabela Cigarillos. . . . . Phi
La Flor de la Isabela Conchas . . . . Phi
La Flor de la Isabela Damas . . . . Phi
La Flor de la Isabela Half Coronas. . . . . Phi
La Flor de la Isabela Ideales. . . . . Phi
La Flor de la Isabela Isabela. . . . . Phi
La Flor de la Isabela Panetelas. . . . . Phi
La Flor de la Isabela Panetelas Largas . . . . Phi
La Flor de la Isabela Tips. Phi
La Fontana Vintage Dante . . . . Hon
La Fontana Vintage Rossini . . . . Hon
La Fontana Vintage Verdi. . . . . Hon
La Maximiliana Dulcis . . . . Hon
La Maximiliana Fumas . . . . Hon
La Maximiliana Luxus . . . . Hon
La Primodora Emperor . . . . Hon
La Primodora Excellentes . . . . Hon
La Primodora Falcon . . . . Hon
La Primodora Petite Cetros . . . . Hon
La Primodora Solitaire. . . . . Hon
La Primodora Starbite . . . . Hon
La Unica No 100 . . . . Dom
La Unica No 200 . . . . Dom
La Unica No 300 . . . . Dom
La Unica No 400 . . . . Dom

La Unica No 500 . . . . Dom
Las Cabrillas Balboa . . . . Hon
Las Cabrillas De Soto . . . . Hon
Las Cabrillas Magellan . . . . Hon
Las Cabrillas Ponce de Leon . . . . Hon
Legacy Corona Grande . . . . Hon
Legacy Elegante . . . . Hon
Legacy Monarch . . . . Hon
Legacy Napoleon . . . . Hon
Legacy Rothchild . . . . Hon
Legacy Super Cetro . . . . Hon
Lempira Lonsdale . . . . Hon
Lempira Robusto . . . . Hon
Leon Jimenes No 5 . . . . Dom
Licenciados Expresso . . . . Dom
Licenciados No 4 . . . . Dom
Licenciados Panetela Linda . . . . Dom
Macabi Media Corona . . . . USA
Macabi No 1 . . . . USA
Macanudo Caviar . . . . Jam
Macanudo Quill . . . . Jam
Maria Mancini Corona Classico . . . . Hon
Maria Mancini Coronas Largas . . . . Hon
Maria Mancini De Gaulle . . . . Hon
Maria Mancini Grandes . . . . Hon
Maria Mancini Palma Delgado . . . . Hon
Maya Coronas . . . . Hon
Maya Matador . . . . Hon
Maya Robustos . . . . Hon
Mocha Supreme Allegro . . . . Hon
Mocha Supreme Baron de Rothschild . . . . Hon
Mocha Supreme Lords . . . . Hon
Mocha Supreme Patron . . . . Hon
Mocha Supreme Petites . . . . Hon
Mocha Supreme Rembrandt . . . . Hon
Mocha Supreme Renaissance . . . . Hon
Mocha Supreme Sovereign . . . . Hon
Montecassino Cazadores . . . . Hon
Montecassino Imperial . . . . Hon
Montecruz Chicos . . . . Dom
Montecruz Junior . . . . Dom
Montesino Diplomatico . . . . Dom
Montesino Napoleon Grande . . . . Dom
Montesino No 1 . . . . Dom
Montesino No 2 . . . . Dom

Primo del Rey Chavon . . . . Dom
Primo del Rey Churchill . . . . Dom
Primo del Rey Club Selection Aristocrats . . . . Dom
Primo del Rey Club Selection Barons . . . . Dom
Primo del Rey Club Selection Nobles . . . . Dom
Primo del Rey Club Selection Regals. . . . . Dom
Primo del Rey Panetela Extras. . . . . Dom
Primo del Rey Panetelas . . . . Dom
Primo del Rey Presidentes . . . . Dom
Primo del Rey Reales . . . . Dom
Primo del Rey Seleccion No 1 . . . . Dom
Primo del Rey Seleccion No 2 . . . . Dom
Primo del Rey Seleccion No 3 . . . . Dom
Primo del Rey Seleccion No 4 . . . . Dom
Primo del Rey Seleccion No 5 . . . . Dom
Private Stock No 1 . . . . Dom
Private Stock No 2 . . . . Dom
Private Stock No 3 . . . . Dom
Private Stock No 4 . . . . Dom
Private Stock No 5 . . . . Dom
Private Stock No 6 . . . . Dom
Private Stock No 7 . . . . Dom
Private Stock No 8 . . . . Dom
Private Stock No 9 . . . . Dom
Private Stock No 10 . . . . Dom
Private Stock No 11 . . . . Dom
Punch After Dinner . . . . Hon
Punch Amatistas . . . . Hon
Punch Cafe Royal . . . . Hon
Punch Card Royal. . . . . Hon
Punch Casa Grandes. . . . . Hon
Punch De Luxe Chateau Lafitte. . . . . Hon
Punch De Luxe Chateau Margaux . . . . Hon
Punch De Luxe Coronas . . . . Hon
Punch De Luxe Royal Coronations . . . . Hon
Punch Double Corona . . . . Hon
Punch Elites . . . . Hon
Punch Gran Cru Britania . . . . Hon
Punch Gran Cru Robustos . . . . Hon
Punch Gran Cru Superiors. Hon
Punch Largo Elegantes. . . . . Hon
Punch London Club. . . . . Hon
Punch Lonsdale . . . . Hon
Punch No 1. . . . . Hon
Punch No 75. . . . . Hon

Romeo Y Julieta Palmas . . . . Dom
Romeo Y Julieta Panetelas . . . . Dom
Royal Jamaica Gaucho . . . . Dom
Royal Jamaica Pirate . . . . Dom
Royal Manna Churchill . . . . Hon
Royal Manna Laro Extra Fino Rothschild . . . . Hon
Royal Manna Manchego . . . . Hon
Royal Manna No 1 . . . . Hon
Royal Manna No 4 . . . . Hon
Royal Manna Toro . . . . Hon
Rum Runner Bucaneer . . . . USA
Rum Runner Wench . . . . USA
Sabroso Numero Cinco . . . . Nic
Sabroso Numero Dos . . . . Nic
Sabroso Numero Quatro . . . . Nic
Sabroso Numero Tres . . . . Nic
Sabroso Numero Uno . . . . Nic
Santa Clara "1830" No II . . . . Mex
Santa Clara "1830" No III . . . . Mex
Santa Clara "1830" No IV . . . . Mex
Santa Clara "1830" No V . . . . Mex
Santa Clara "1830" No VI . . . . Mex
Santa Clara "1830" No VII . . . . Mex
Santa Clara "1830" No VIII . . . . Mex
Santa Clara "1830" Robusto . . . . Mex
Santa Rosa Cetros . . . . Hon
Santa Rosa Largos . . . . Hon
Santa Rosa Numero Quatro . . . . Hon
Santa Rosa Regulares . . . . Hon
Santiago No 1 . . . . Dom
Santiago No 2 . . . . Dom
Santiago No 3 . . . . Dom
Santiago No 4 . . . . Dom
Santiago No 5 . . . . Dom
Segovia Crown Royal . . . . Nic
Segovia Primo Gorda . . . . Nic
Segovia Robusto . . . . Nic
Segovia Toro . . . . Nic
Segovia X-O . . . . Nic
Sosa Brevas . . . . Dom
Sosa Family Selection Intermezzo . . . . Dom
Sosa Santa Fe . . . . Dom
Suerdieck Brasilia . . . . Bra
Suerdieck Caballero . . . . Bra
Suerdieck Corona Brasil Luxo . . . . Bra

Topstone Supremes . . . . USA
Torcedor No 1 . . . . Nic
Torcedor Rothchild . . . . Nic
Torcedor Toro . . . . Nic
Tresado No 100 . . . . Dom
Tresado No 200 . . . . Dom
Tresado No 300 . . . . Dom
Tresado No 400 . . . . Dom
Tresado No 500 . . . . Dom
V Centennial Cetros . . . . Hon
V Centennial Coronas . . . . Hon
V Centennial Robustos . . . . Hon
Villazon Deluxe Chairman . . . . USA
Voyager Atlantis . . . . Hon
Voyager Columbia . . . . Hon
Voyager Enterprise . . . . Hon
Vueltabajo Corona . . . . Dom
Vueltabajo Robusto . . . . Dom
Vueltabajo Toros . . . . Dom
William Ascot Palma . . . . USA
Zino Demi Tasse . . . . Hon

¢ — UNDER $1.00

Antonio Y Cleopatra Classics Corona . . . . USA
Antonio Y Cleopatra Grenadiers . . . . USA
Antonio Y Cleopatra Grenadiers Boy/Girl . . . . USA
Antonio Y Cleopatra Grenadiers Mini . . . . USA
Antonio Y Cleopatra Grenadiers Mini Dark . . . . USA
Antonio Y Cleopatra Grenadiers Mini Light . . . . USA
Antonio Y Cleopatra Grenadiers/Presidentes . . . . . . USA
Antonio Y Cleopatra Grenadiers Tubos . . . . USA
Antonio Y Cleopatra Grenadiers Whiffs . . . . USA
Antonio Y Cleopatra Panetelas Deluxe . . . . USA
Antonio Y Cleopatra Tribunes . . . . USA
Arango Sportsman No 100 . . . . USA
Arango Sportsman No 200 (Boy & Girl) . . . . USA
Arturo Fuente Brevas Royale . . . . Dom
Arturo Fuente Curly Head . . . . Dom
Arturo Fuente Curly Head Deluxe . . . . Dom
Arturo Fuente Don Carlos No 3 . . . . Dom
As You Like It No 18 . . . . USA
As You Like It No 22 . . . . USA
As You Like It No 32 . . . . USA
As You Like It No 35 . . . . USA
B-H Blunt . . . . USA

Clementine Rothchild . . . . Hon
Clementine Toro . . . . Hon
Corps Diplomatique After Dinner 10s . . . . Bel
Corps Diplomatique Panetela. Bel
Danlys Churchill. . . . . Hon
Danlys Luchadore. . . . . Hon
Danlys No 1 . . . . Hon
Danlys No 4 . . . . Hon
Danlys Panetela. . . . . Hon
Danlys Toro. . . . . Hon
Dannemann Imperial . . . . Ger
Dannemann Lonja. . . . . Ger
Dannemann Menor . . . . Ger
Dannemann Moods . . . . Ger
Dannemann Originale Sweet Brazil . . . . Swi
Dannemann Pierrot. . . . . Ger
Dannemann Speciale. . . . . Ger
Davidoff Long Cigarillos . . . . Den
Davidoff Mini Cigarillos . . . . Den
Davidoff Mini Light. . . . . Den
Denobili Kings . . . . USA
Denobili Popular Amm. . . . . USA
Denobili Toscani. . . . . USA
Denobili Toscani Longs . . . . USA
Denobili Twin Pack. . . . . USA
Don Diego Babies SMS . . . . Dom
Don Diego Preludes. . . . . Dom
Don Diego Preludes EMS . . . . Dom
Don Mateo No 1. . . . . Hon
Don Mateo No 2. . . . . Hon
Don Mateo No 3. . . . . Hon
Don Mateo No 4. . . . . Hon
Don Mateo No 5. . . . . Hon
Don Mateo No 6. . . . . Hon
Don Mateo No 7. . . . . Hon
Don Mateo No 8. . . . . Hon
Don Mateo No 9. . . . . Hon
Don Mateo No 10. . . . . Hon
Dutch Masters Belvedere . . . . USA
Dutch Masters Cadet . . . . USA
Dutch Masters Cadet Tip . . . . USA
Dutch Masters Carona Deluxe . . . . USA
Dutch Masters Elites. . . . . USA
Dutch Masters Palma . . . . USA
Dutch Masters Panetela Deluxe . . . . USA

Garcia Y Vega Presidente .... USA
Garcia Y Vega Romeros......................... USA
Garcia Y Vega Senators........................ USA
Garcia Y Vega Tips .... USA
Garcia Y Vega Whiffs.......................... USA
H. Upmann Aperitif............................ Dom
H. Upmann Demi Tasse......................... Dom
Harvester Perfecto .... USA
Harvester Record Breaker .... USA
Hav-A-Tampa Classic.......................... USA
Hav-A-Tampa Jewel .... USA
Hav-A-Tampa Jewel Sweet...................... USA
Hecho-A-Mano-Caz-Bar Cazadores................ Hon
Hecho-A-Mano-Caz-Bar Churchills............... Hon
Hecho-A-Mano-Caz-Bar Corona Lonsdale .... Hon
Hecho-A-Mano-Caz-Bar Fumas................... Hon
Henry Winterman Cigars Cello .... Hol
Henry Winterman Cigars Corona de Luxe .... Hol
Henry Winterman Cigars Excellentes .... Hol
Henry Winterman Cigars Golden Panetella .... Hol
Henry Winterman Cigars Half Corona .... Hol
Henry Winterman Cigars Kentucky Kings........... Hol
Henry Winterman Cigars Long Panatella .... Hol
Henry Winterman Cigars Royales .... Hol
Henry Winterman Cigars Scooters .... Hol
Henry Winterman Cigars Slim Panatella........... Hol
Jamaica Gold Duchess .... Jam
Jamaica Heritage No 100........................ Jam
Jamaica Heritage No 200........................ Jam
Jamaica Heritage No 600........................ Jam
Jamaica Heritage No 1000....................... Jam
Jamaica Heritage No 1002....................... Jam
King Edward Cigarillo Deluxe .... USA
King Edward Imperial........................... USA
King Edward Invincible Deluxe .... USA
King Edward Panetela Deluxe .... USA
King Edward Specials .... USA
King Edward Tip Cigarillo .... USA
King Edward Wood Tip Cigarillo .... USA
La Corona Vintage Aristocrats .... USA
La Corona Vintage Corona Chicas .... USA
La Corona Vintage Coronas...................... USA
La Corona Vintage Directors .... USA
La Corona Whiffs .... USA
Las Cabrillas Columbus .... Hon

Panter Domino Cameroun . . . . Hol
Panter Domino Wild & Light . . . . Hol
Panter Lights . . . . Hol
Panter Mignon . . . . Hol
Panter Small . . . . Hol
Panter Sprint . . . . Hol
Panter Tango . . . . Hol
Pedroni Classico . . . . Swi
Primo del Rey Cortos . . . . Dom
Republica Dominica No 2 . . . . Dom
Republica Dominica No 3 . . . . Dom
Republica Dominica No 4 . . . . Dom
Republica Dominica No 5 . . . . Dom
Republica Dominica No 6 . . . . Dom
Republica Dominica No 7 . . . . Dom
Republica Dominica No 8 . . . . Dom
Rigoletto Black Arrow . . . . Dom
Rigoletto Black Magic . . . . Dom
Rigoletto Dominican Lights . . . . Dom
Robert Burns Black Watch . . . . USA
Robert Burns Cigarillos . . . . USA
Santa Clara "1830" Quino . . . . Mex
Santa Fe Biltmore . . . . USA
Santa Fe Fairmont . . . . USA
Santa Fe Panetela . . . . USA
Santa Fe Patties . . . . USA
Schimelpennick Florina . . . . Hol
Schimelpennick Half Corona . . . . Hol
Schimelpennick Media . . . . Hol
Schimelpennick Mono . . . . Hol
Schimelpennick Montego Milds . . . . Hol
Schimelpennick Nostra . . . . Hol
Schimelpennick Vada . . . . Hol
Swisher Sweets Cigarillo . . . . USA
Swisher Sweets Coronella . . . . USA
Swisher Sweets Kings . . . . USA
Swisher Sweets Perfecto Slims . . . . USA
Swisher Sweets Tip Cigarillo . . . . USA
Swisher Sweets Wood Tip Cigarillo . . . . USA
Tampa Sweet Cheroot . . . . USA
Tampa Sweet Perfecto . . . . USA
Tampa Sweet Tip Cigarillo . . . . USA
Te-Amo Elegante . . . . Mex
Te-Amo Intermezzo . . . . Mex
Te-Amo Pauser . . . . Mex

Willem II Whiff & Miniature Sigretto . . . . Hol
Willem Long Panetella . . . . Hol
William Ascot Panetela . . . . USA
William Penn Braves . . . . USA
William Penn Panetela . . . . USA
William Penn Perfecto . . . . USA
William Penn Willow Tips . . . . USA
Winchester 100's Little Cigars . . . . USA
Winchester Little Cigars . . . . USA
Winchester Menthol Little Cigars. . . . . USA
Winchester Sweet 100's Little Cigars . . . . USA
Wolf Brothers Crooks Sweet Vanilla . . . . USA
Wolf Brothers Nippers . . . . USA
Wolf Brothers Rum Crooks. . . . . USA
Zino Cigarrillos Brazil. . . . . Hon
Zino Cigarrillos Sumatra . . . . Hon

Cigar Size Index

There are many variations in standard cigar sizes from brand to brand and this can sometimes cause confusion—a confusion which is increased when some brands use size names such as churchill, rothchild/robusto or corona for cigars which are technically not those sizes.

For the purposes of this index, all of the cigars in this book have been grouped into 16 broad categories according to the table below. The first column indicates the classical size for the respective shape.

CLASSICAL DIMENSIONS	LENGTH RANGE	GAUGE RANGE
Gigante/Gran Corona/Giant		
235mm/9½ ins x 47	219mm/8⅝ ins+	47+
Double Corona		
194mm/7⅝ ins x 49	170mm/6¾ ins–216mm/8½ ins	48–54
Churchill		
178mm/7 ins x 47	170mm/6¾ ins–191mm/7½ ins	45–49
Corona Extra/Corona Gorda		
143mm/5⅝ ins x 46	132mm/5$\frac{3}{16}$ ins–165mm/6½ ins	44–47
Robusto/Rothchild		
124mm/4⅞ ins x 50	114mm/4½ ins–140mm/5½ ins	48–54
Lonsdale		
165mm/6½ ins x 42	159mm/6¼ ins–178mm/7 ins	40–44
Corona		
142mm/5$\frac{9}{16}$ ins x 42	140mm/5½ ins–156mm/6⅛ ins	40–44
Petit/Half Corona		
129mm/5$\frac{1}{16}$ ins x 42	102mm/4 ins–132mm/5$\frac{3}{16}$ ins	40–43
Long Panetela		
192mm/7$\frac{9}{16}$ ins x 38	180mm/7$\frac{1}{16}$ ins–197mm/7¾ ins	35–39
Panetela		
152mm/6 ins x 38	140mm/5½ ins–178mm/7 ins	35–39
Slim Panetela		
152mm/6 ins x 32	127mm/5 ins–178mm/7 ins	28–34
Short Panetela		
127mm/5 ins x 37	114mm/4½ ins–127mm/5 ins	35–39
Small Panetela		
117mm/4$\frac{9}{16}$ ins x 34	89mm/3½ ins–114mm/4½ ins	30–34
Cigarillo		
106mm/4$\frac{3}{16}$ ins x 29	89mm/3$\frac{1}{2}$ ins–114mm/4$\frac{1}{2}$ ins	26–29
Figurado		
Any irregular shape of any size	102mm/4 ins–254mm/10 ins	42–60
Odd Size	Cigar sizes other than the above.	

GIGANTES/GRAN CORONAS/GIANTS

Andujar Azuo............................... Dom
Arturo Fuente Hemingway Masterpiece .... Dom
Ashton Cabinet Selection No 1 .... Dom
Avo Especiales .... Dom
Calle Ocho Embajador....................... USA
Carbonell Gigante .... Dom
Casa Blanca Jeroboam....................... Dom
Cibao Magnum .... Dom
Columbus Eleven Fifty .... Hon
Connisseur Gold Label Goliath .... Hon
Cuba Aliados Figurin .... Hon
Cuba Aliados General........................ Hon
Davidoff Aniversario No 1 .... Dom
Diamond Crown No 1 .... Dom
Dominican Original Fat Tub .... Dom
Don Oscar .... Dom
Griffin's Don Bernado....................... Dom
Griffin's Prestige .... Dom
Havana Classico Malelcon .... USA
Jose Benito Magnum .... Dom
Juan Clemente Gargantua..................... Dom
Juan Clemente Gigante .... Dom
King No 9................................. Dom
La Coradoba Viajantes....................... Nic
La Gloria Cubana Crown Imperial............... USA
La Venga No 80 .... Hon
Mexican Emperador......................... Mex
Nat Cicco's Grandiosos .... Dom
Ornelas 250............................... Mex
Ortiz Mexican Emperadors .... Mex
P. G. Celebration .... Dom
Padron Magnum............................ Hon
Premium Dominican Selection Giant .... Dom
Puros Indios Figurin........................ Hon
Puros Indios General .... Hon
Rico Havana Blend Rough Rider............... USA
Royal Jamaica Goliath .... Dom
Special Jamaican Rey del Rey .... Dom
Tabacalera Gigantes......................... Phi
Tabantillas A .... Dom
Valdrych Quisqueya Real..................... Dom

DOUBLE CORONAS

Aguila Brevas 49............................ Dom
Aguila Brevas 50............................ Dom

Don Julio Fabulosos. . . . . Dom
Don Lino Churchill . . . . Hon
Don Lino Oro Churchill . . . . Hon
Don Lino Supremos. . . . . Hon
Don Manolo Churchill . . . . Dom
Don Mateo No 10. . . . . Hon
Don Mateo No 9. . . . . Hon
Don Melo Presidente . . . . Hon
Don Miguel Double Coronas. . . . . Dom
Don Miguel Ejecutivos. . . . . Dom
Don Miguel Presidents . . . . Dom
Don Pepe Double Corona . . . . Bra
Don Pishu Macintosh. CI
Don Pishu Tenerife CI
Don Rene Churchill. . . . . USA
Don Rene Presidente . . . . USA
Don Rex Gigantes. . . . . Hon
Don Rex Presidentes . . . . Hon
Don Rubio Monarchs. . . . . Hon
Don Rubio President . . . . Hon
Don Rubio Soberanos . . . . Hon
Don Tomas Gigantes . . . . Hon
Don Tomas International Series No 1 . . . . Hon
Don Tomas Panetela Largas. . . . . Hon
Don Tomas Presidentes . . . . Hon
Don Tomas Special Edition No 100 . . . . Hon
Don Vito Troncas. . . . . Dom
El Beso Churchill . . . . Mex
El Canelo Churchill . . . . USA
El Canelo Soberanos . . . . USA
El Incomparable Churchill. Hon
El Paraiso Grande. . . . . Hon
El Paraiso Presidente . . . . Hon
El Rey del Mundo Corona Inmensa. . . . . Hon
El Rey del Mundo Coronation. . . . . Hon
El Rey del Mundo Double Corona. . . . . Hon
El Rey del Mundo Flor del Mundo . . . . Hon
El Rey del Mundo Imperiale . . . . Hon
El Rey del Mundo Robusto Suprema. . . . . Hon
El Sublimado Churchill. . . . . Dom
El Triunfo No 1 Mayans . . . . Mex
Elegante Especial . . . . USA
Elegante Grande. . . . . USA
Elysee No 7-50 . . . . Bra
Encanto Viajantes. . . . . Hon
Espada Executive . . . . Hon

Habana Gold Presidente . . . . Hon
Habanos Hatuey Churchills. Dom
Harrows Londonderry . . . . Phi
Havana Classico Churchill . . . . USA
Havana Classico Presidente . . . . USA
Havana Reserve Churchills. . . . . Hon
Havana Sunrise Churchill . . . . USA
Havana Sunrise Presidente. . . . . USA
Hecho-A-Mano-Caz-Bar Churchills. . . . . Hon
Hidalgo Double Corona . . . . Pan
Hidalgo Monarch . . . . Pan
Hoja de Mexicali Soberano Natural. . . . . Mex
Hoja de Mexicali Viajante Natural/Maduro. . . . . Mex
Hoja de Oro 100. . . . . Mex
Hoja de Oro 101. . . . . Mex
Hoja del Regal Soberano . . . . Hon
Honduran Gold General . . . . Hon
Honduran Gold Presidente . . . . Hon
Honduran Import Maduro Majestics . . . . Hon
Honduras Cuban Tobaccos Gigantes. . . . . Hon
Honduras Cuban Tobaccos Monarch. . . . . Hon
Honduras Cuban Tobaccos Presidente . . . . Hon
Honduras Cuban Tobaccos Soberano . . . . Hon
Honduras Viajantes . . . . Hon
Hoyo de Monterrey Double Corona . . . . Hon
Hoyo de Monterrey President . . . . Hon
Hoyo de Monterrey Sultan. . . . . Hon
Hoyo de Nicaragua Presidente . . . . Nic
Hugo Cassar Diamond Chairman . . . . Hon
Hugo Cassar Diamond Selection El Presidente. . . . . . Dom
Hugo Cassar Mystique Churchill. . . . . Dom
Hugo Cassar No 5. . . . . Hon
Hugo Cassar No 6. . . . . Hon
Hugo Cassar No 7. . . . . Hon
Hugo Cassar Private Collection Churchill . . . . Mex
Hugo Cassar Sierra Madre . . . . Mex
Hugo Cassar Signature Series Giant . . . . Nic
Hugo Cassar Veracruz. . . . . Mex
Hugo Cassar Yucatan . . . . Mex
Indian Chief. . . . . Hon
Indian Head Emperador . . . . Hon
Indian Head Gigantes . . . . Hon
Indian Head Monarch . . . . Hon
Indian Head Soberanos . . . . Hon
Indian Head Viajante. . . . . Hon
Indian Tabac Chief. . . . . Hon

La Llorona No 4 . . . . Hon
La Llorona No 6 . . . . Hon
La Native Gigantes . . . . Hon
La Palma de Oro Double Corona CI
La Palma de Oro Piramedes*** CI
La Palma de Oro Superior CI
La Plata Enterprise Classic . . . . USA
La Plata Maduros Royal Wilshire . . . . USA
La Primadora Emperor . . . . Hon
La Primera Churchill. . . . . Dom
La Primera Presidente. . . . . Dom
La Real Imperials . . . . Hon
La Regenta Emperador CI
La Unica No 100 . . . . Dom
La Unica No 200 . . . . Dom
La Venga No 59 . . . . Hon
Lambs Club Churchill . . . . Dom
Las Cabrillas Balboa . . . . Hon
Las Cabrillas Columbus . . . . Hon
Las Cabrillas De Soto . . . . Hon
Legacy Monarch. . . . . Hon
Legacy Napoleon . . . . Hon
Lempira Churchills . . . . Hon
Lempira Presidentes. . . . . Hon
Licenciados Churchill . . . . Dom
Licenciados No 500 . . . . Dom
Licenciados Presidentes. . . . . Dom
Licenciados Soberanos . . . . Dom
Lord Clinton President . . . . USA
Macabi Super Corona. . . . . USA
Macanudo Vintage No I . . . . Jam
Matacan Bundles No 1 . . . . Mex
Matacan Bundles No 8 . . . . Mex
Match Play Olympic. . . . . Dom
Match Play Troon. . . . . Dom
Maya Executive. . . . . Hon
Medal of Honor No 500. . . . . Hon
Medal of Honor No 700. . . . . Hon
Micubano No 852. . . . . Nic
Mocambo Churchill . . . . Mex
Mocha Supreme Patron . . . . Hon
Mocha Supreme Rembrandt . . . . Hon
Montecassino Imperial. . . . . Hon
Montecassino Super Diamentes. . . . . Hon
Montecruz Individuales. . . . . Dom
Montelimar Presidente. . . . . Hon

Montero Presidente . . . . Dom
Montesino Gran Corona . . . . Dom
Moreno Maduro No 507 . . . . Dom
Morro Castle Churchill. . . . . USA
Nat Cicco's Exquisitos . . . . Dom
Nat Sherman City Desk Tribune . . . . Dom
Nat Sherman Gotham No 500. . . . . Dom
Nat Sherman Host Selection Hampton . . . . Hon
National Brand Churchill. . . . . Hon
National Brand Imperial . . . . Hon
Nestor Vintage 747. . . . . Hon
Nicaragua Especial Presidente. . . . . Nic
Nicaragua Especial Viajante. Nic
Nording Presidente . . . . Hon
Nude Dominican 42 . . . . Dom
Nude Dominican 44 . . . . Dom
Nude Mexican 912 . . . . Mex
Nude Mexican 914 . . . . Mex
Ocho Rios President . . . . Jam
Ocho Rios Vijantes . . . . Jam
Olar Cacique . . . . Dom
Olar Colossus. . . . . Dom
Old Harbour No 400. . . . . Jam
Onyx No 750 . . . . Dom
Onyx No 852 . . . . Dom
Opus X Fuente Double Corona. . . . . Dom
Oro Blend •24 . . . . USA
Ortiz Churchill . . . . Mex
Oscar No 700. . . . . Dom
Oscar Supreme . . . . Dom
P. G. Double Corona . . . . Dom
P. G. Magnum . . . . Dom
P & K Guardsman No 1. . . . . Dom
P & K Guardsman No 2. . . . . Dom
Padron Executive . . . . Hon
Padron Serrie de Aniversario Diplomatico . . . . Hon
Padron Serrie de Aniversario Pyramide*** . . . . Hon
Panorea Churchill . . . . Dom
Particulares Executive . . . . Hon
Particulares Presidentes . . . . Hon
Particulares Viajantes . . . . Hon
Penamil No 57. CI
Peter Stokkebye Santa Maria. . . . . Dom
Peterson Presidente . . . . Dom
Petrus Tabacage 89 Churchill. . . . . Hon
Petrus Tabacage 89 Double Corona. . . . . Hon

Plasencia Gigante . . . . Hon
Plasencia Viajante . . . . Hon
Playboy Churchill. . . . . Dom
Pleiades Aldebran . . . . Dom
Por Larranaga Fabulosos . . . . Dom
Premium Dominican Selection Super Soberanos . . . . Dom
Premium Dominican Selections Presidente . . . . Dom
Pride of Copan No 1 . . . . Hon
Pride of Jamaica Monarch. . . . . Jam
Primo del Cristo Generals . . . . Hon
Primo del Cristo Inmensos. . . . . Hon
Primo Del Rey Aguilas . . . . Dom
Primo Del Rey Barons . . . . Dom
Primo Del Rey Regals . . . . Dom
Primo Del Rey Soberanos . . . . Dom
Private Stock No 1 . . . . Dom
Profesor Sila Majestad CI
Pueblo Dominicano Baruhona . . . . Dom
Punch De Luxe Chateau Lafitte. . . . . Hon
Punch Gran Cru Diademas . . . . Hon
Punch Gran Cru Prince Consorts . . . . Hon
Punch Presidents . . . . Hon
Purios Indios Churchill Especial . . . . Hon
Puro Nicaragua Gigantes . . . . Nic
Puro Nicaragua Soberano . . . . Nic
Puro Nicaragua Viajantes. . . . . Nic
Quorum Chairman . . . . Dom
RC Double Corona . . . . Dom
Red Label Emperadore . . . . Hon
Red Label Magnifico . . . . Hon
Republica Dominica No 2 . . . . Dom
Republica Dominica No 1 . . . . Dom
Riata No 900. . . . . Hon
Rico Havana Blend Churchill. . . . . USA
Rico Havana Blend Double Corona. . . . . USA
Ricos Dominicanos Churchill . . . . Dom
Romanticos Marc Anthony . . . . Dom
Romanticos Valentino . . . . Dom
Romeo Y Julieta Churchills . . . . Dom
Romeo Y Julieta Gigante . . . . Hon
Romeo Y Julieta Monarcas. Dom
Romeo Y Julieta Vintage V. . . . . Dom
Royal Court Presidente. . . . . Hon
Royal Court Viajante . . . . Hon
Royal Dominicana Churchill . . . . Dom
Royal Honduras Czar . . . . Hon

Thomas Hinds Honduran Presidente	Hon
Topper Centennial Churchill	Dom
Torcedor Churchill	Nic
Torcedor Vijante	Nic
Torquino	USA
Torquino Delicioso	USA
Traditionales Cuban Round Larga	USA
Traditionales Presidente	USA
Tresado No 100	Dom
Troya No 72 Executive	Dom
Tulas No 4	Hon
Tulas No 6	Hon
V Centennial Presidente	Hon
Valdrych Monumento	Dom
Vargas Churchill	CI
Vegas Gran Reserva Churchill	Nic
Veracruz Magnum, Owner's Reserve	Mex
Vintage Honduran President	Hon
Vintage Honduran Sultans	Hon
Virtuoso Torano Presidente	Hon
Vueltabajo Gigante	Dom
W & D Gigantes	Hon
W & D Presidentes	Hon
Yago Churchill	Hon
Zino Connoisseur No 100	Hon
Zino Veritas	Hon

CHURCHILLS

8-9-8 Collection Churchill	Jam
8-9-8 Collection Monarch	Jam
Aguila Brevas 44	Dom
American Eagle Statesman	USA
Antelo Churchill	USA
Antelo Super Cazadore	USA
Arango Sportsman No 300	USA
Arango Sportsman No 400	USA
Arango Statesman Barrister	Hon
Armenter Reserva No 6	CI
Arturo Fuente Churchill	Dom
Ashton Aged Maduro No 50	Dom
Ashton Cabinet Selection No 2	Dom
Ashton Churchill	Dom
Ashton Prime Minister	Dom
Astral Favorito	Hon
Astral Perfeccion	Hon
Avo Belicoso***	Dom

Avo No 5 . . . . Dom
Bahia Churchill. . . . . CR
Balboa Churchill . . . . Pan
Ballena Suprema Danli Collection Alma . . . . Hon
Ballena Suprema San Andres Collection Concordia . . Mex
Bances Corona Immensas . . . . Hon
Bauza Casa Grande . . . . Dom
Belinda Ramon. . . . . Hon
Bering Inmensas. . . . . Hon
Beverly Hills VIP No 749 . . . . Hon
Blue Label Churchill . . . . Hon
Bohio Churchill. . . . . Dom
Butera Royale Vintage Capo Grande. . . . . Dom
Caballeros Double Corona . . . . Dom
Cacique Caribes. . . . . Dom
Camacho Churchill . . . . Hon
Camorra San Remo . . . . Hon
Canaria D'Ora Supremos . . . . Dom
Canonero No 4 . . . . Bra
Carbonell Churchill. . . . . Dom
Carbonell Presidente. . . . . Dom
Caribbean Family Rounds . . . . USA
Carlin Churchill . . . . Nic
Carlos Torano Carlos VI . . . . Dom
Carrington V . . . . Dom
Casa de Nicaragua Churchill . . . . Nic
Casa Martin Churchills . . . . Dom
Casa Martin Grandes . . . . Dom
Casanova Churchill CI
CCI Gold Silk No 2. . . . . Hon
CCI Royal Satin No 2 . . . . Hon
Cervantes Churchill . . . . Hon
Chairman's Reserve Churchill. . . . . Dom
Charles Fairmorn Churchill . . . . Hon
Chavelo Churchill. . . . . USA
Chevere Kingston . . . . Jam
Cibao Churchills . . . . Dom
Cibao Churchills. . . . . USA
Cienfugo Detroit 1805 . . . . Hon
Cimero Lonsdale . . . . Dom
Clementine Churchills . . . . Hon
Cohiba Esplendido . . . . Dom
Columbus Churchill. . . . . Hon
Connisseur Gold Label Churchill . . . . Hon
Connisseur Gold Label Churchill . . . . USA
Connisseur Silver Label Churchills . . . . USA

Conquistador No 700 . . . . USA
Credo Dominican Magnificent . . . . Dom
Cuba Aliados Cazadore . . . . Hon
Cuba Aliados Valentino . . . . Hon
Cuban Twist No 600 . . . . Hon
Cuesta-Rey Centennial Aristocrat . . . . Dom
Cuesta-Rey Centennial Dominican No 2 . . . . Dom
Cusano Hermanos Churchill . . . . Dom
Cyrilla Kings . . . . USA
Cyrilla Senators . . . . USA
Da Vinci Ginerva de Benci . . . . Hon
Daniel Marshall Dominican Reserve Churchill . . . . . . Dom
Diana Silvius 2000 . . . . Dom
Diana Silvius Churchill . . . . Dom
Dominican Original Churchill . . . . Dom
Dominicana Superba No 2 . . . . Dom
Dominico No 702 . . . . Dom
Don Alberto Grand Cruz Corona . . . . Dom
Don Barco Marinero . . . . Dom
Don Diego Imperial EMS . . . . Dom
Don Diego Imperiale . . . . Dom
Don Diego Monarchs Tubes EMS . . . . Dom
Don Estaban Churchill . . . . Dom
Don Fife Churchill . . . . Dom
Don Juan Churchills . . . . Nic
Don Leo Churchill . . . . Dom
Don Marcos Monarch . . . . Dom
Don Mateo No 6 . . . . Hon
Don Melo Churchill . . . . Hon
Don Ramos Gigantes . . . . Hon
Don Rubio Churchill . . . . Hon
Don Tonioli Churchill . . . . Hon
Don Xavier Churchill CI
Double Happiness Ectasy . . . . Phi
Dunhill (Vintage) Cabreras . . . . Dom
Dunhill (Vintage) Peravias . . . . Dom
El Canelo Cazadores . . . . USA
El Imperio Cubano Churchill . . . . USA
El Paraiso Double Corona . . . . Hon
El Rey del Mundo Principale . . . . Hon
El Rico Habano Double Coronas . . . . USA
Elegante Blend Especial . . . . Hon
Elysee No 7-46 . . . . Bra
Encanto Churchill . . . . Hon
Espanola Excellente . . . . Dom
Espanola Reserve Churchill . . . . Dom

Jamaica Bay No 300 . . . . Jam
Jamaica Gem Double Corona . . . . Jam
Jamaica Gem Giant Corona. . . . . Jam
Jamaica Heritage No 1000. . . . . Jam
Jamaican Pride Double Corona. . . . . Jam
John Aylesbury Santa Dominga Churchill. . . . . Dom
John T's Magnum Amaretto . . . . Dom
John T's Magnum Brown Gold . . . . Dom
John T's Magnum Cappuccino . . . . Dom
John T's Magnum Cherry Cream . . . . Dom
John T's Magnum Expresso. . . . . Dom
Jose Llopis Churchill . . . . Pan
Jose Marti. . . . . Dom
Joya de Nicaragua Churchill . . . . Nic
Joya Del Rey Numero 49 . . . . USA
Juan Clemente Churchill. . . . . Dom
King No 10. . . . . Dom
Kiskeya Churchills . . . . Dom
Knockando No 1 . . . . Dom
La Aurora Bristol Especiales . . . . Dom
La Balla. . . . . Hon
La Cordoba Churchill . . . . Nic
La Diligencia Churchill . . . . Hon
La Flor Dominicana Churchill Reserva Especial. . . . . Dom
La Fontana Da Vinci. . . . . USA
La Fontana Vintage Da Vinci . . . . Hon
La Gianna Churchill. . . . . Hon
La Gloria Cubana Glorias Inmensas. . . . . USA
La Habanera Churchill . . . . Dom
La Hoja Selecta Cosiac . . . . USA
La Invicta Churchill . . . . Hon
La Llorona No 3. . . . . Hon
La Native Churchill . . . . Hon
La Native Corona Grande . . . . Hon
La Palma de Oro Don Ricardo CI
La Regenta Gran Corona. CI
La Venga No 63 . . . . Hon
La Venga No 70 . . . . Hon
Legacy Corona Grande . . . . Hon
Leon Jimenes No 1 . . . . Dom
Leon Jimenes No 2 . . . . Dom
Lord Beaconsfield Directors. USA
Lord Beaconsfield Rounds. . . . . USA
Lord Clinton Churchill . . . . USA
Los Libertadores Churchill Reserva Especial . . . . Dom
Los Libertadores Mambises . . . . Dom

Puros Indios No 1 Especial. . . . . Hon
Puros Indios Presidente . . . . Hon
Quorum President. . . . . Dom
Ramon Allones A. . . . . Dom
Ramon Allones Redondos . . . . Dom
Red Label Lonsdale . . . . Hon
Red Label Presidente . . . . Hon
Repeater Churchill. . . . . Hon
Republica Dominica No 5 . . . . Dom
Rey del Mar Churchill . . . . USA
Riata No 600. . . . . Hon
Rigoletto Black Magic . . . . Dom
Rolando Blend Numero No 2 . . . . USA
Romeo Y Julieta Vintage IV. . . . . Dom
Royal Honduras Sovereign. Hon
Royal Jamaica Double Corona. . . . . Dom
Royal Jamaica Giant Corona . . . . Dom
Royal Jamaica Ten Downing Street . . . . Dom
Royal Nicaraguan Numero 8 . . . . Nic
Rum Runner Pirate . . . . USA
Sabroso Numero Quatro . . . . Nic
Santa Cruz Bristol . . . . Jam
Santa Cruz Monarch . . . . Jam
Santa Damiana Churchill . . . . Dom
Santa Rosa Churchill . . . . Hon
Santiago Cabana Double Corona. . . . . USA
Savinelli No 1 Churchill. . . . . Dom
Sebastian Reserva No 5 . . . . Nic
Serengeti Churchill Buffalo . . . . SA
Serengeti Churchill Rhino . . . . SA
Siglo 21-4 . . . . Dom
Solo Aroma Churchill . . . . Hon
Solo Aroma Corona Gorda . . . . Hon
Sosa Churchill . . . . Dom
Sosa Family No 8 . . . . Dom
Special Caribbean Churchill . . . . Dom
Super Special Churchill . . . . Hon
Tabaquero No 746. . . . . Dom
Temple Hall No 4 Trump . . . . Jam
Temple Hall No 675 . . . . Jam
Temple Hall No 700 . . . . Jam
Thomas Hinds Honduran Churchill . . . . Hon
Thomas Hinds Nicaraguan Churchill . . . . Nic
Topstone Directors. . . . . USA
Topstone—Natural Darks Executives. . . . . USA
Tresado No 200 . . . . Dom

Troya No 63 Churchill . . . . Dom
Tulas No 3 . . . . Hon
V Centennial Churchills . . . . Hon
Valdrych 1904 . . . . Dom
Vargas Presidentes CI
Villa de Cuba Corona Grande . . . . USA
Voyager Atlantis . . . . Hon
Vueltabajo Churchill . . . . Dom
West Indies Vanilla Carmella . . . . USA
Yumuri Churchill . . . . Dom
Zino Connoisseur No 200 . . . . Hon

CORONA EXTRAS/CORONA GORDAS

Aguila Brevas 46 . . . . Dom
Arango Statesman Counsetor . . . . Hon
Arturo Fuente Corona Imperial . . . . Dom
Arturo Fuente Cuban Corona . . . . Dom
Arturo Fuente Flor Fina 8-5-8 . . . . Dom
Arturo Fuente Hemingway Signature . . . . Dom
Ashton Aged Maduro No 20 . . . . Dom
Ashton Cabinet Selection No 3 . . . . Dom
Ashton Corona . . . . Dom
Avo No 7 . . . . Dom
Avo XO Notturno . . . . Dom
B-H Blunt . . . . USA
B-H Blunt Boy & Girl . . . . USA
Bahia No 3 . . . . CR
Bances No 3 . . . . Hon
Bances No 3 . . . . USA
Belinda Breva Conserva . . . . Hon
Belinda Cabinet . . . . Hon
Ben Bey Crystals . . . . USA
Bering Cazadores . . . . Hon
Bering Coronadoes . . . . Hon
Bermejo Cazadores . . . . Hon
Bermejo Fumas . . . . Hon
Beverly Hills VIP No 644 . . . . Hon
Blackhawk Chief . . . . USA
Blue Ribbon No 503 . . . . Nic
Bohio Corona . . . . Dom
Bouquet Special . . . . USA
Butera Royale Vintage Fumo Dolce . . . . Dom
Cabanas Corona Grande . . . . Dom
Cabanas Royale . . . . Dom
Cabanas Royales . . . . USA
Calixto Lopez/Carlos V Corona Numero 1 . . . . Phi

Calle Ocho Festivale . . . . USA
Camacho Nacionales . . . . Hon
Camorra Genova . . . . Hon
Camorra Venzia . . . . Hon
Canonabo Guanines . . . . Dom
Caramba No 6 . . . . Hon
Caribbean Family Casinos . . . . USA
Carlos Torano Carlos V . . . . Dom
Casa Martin Cazadores . . . . Dom
Casa Martin Cetros . . . . Dom
Casa Martin Numero Cuatro . . . . Dom
CCI Royal Satin No 4 . . . . Hon
Cervantes Coronas . . . . Hon
Chevere Montego . . . . Jam
Cimero Cetros . . . . Dom
Clementine No 4 . . . . Hon
Columbus Columbus . . . . Hon
Connisseur Gold Label Corona . . . . Hon
Connisseur Gold Label Corona . . . . USA
Conquistador No 300 . . . . USA
Cuba Aliados Corona Deluxe . . . . Hon
Cuba Aliados Fuma . . . . Hon
Cuba Aliados Number 4 . . . . Hon
Cusano Hermanos Corona . . . . Dom
Daniel Marshall Honduran Reserve Corona . . . . Hon
Davidoff 5000 . . . . Dom
Domingold President . . . . Dom
Dominican Original Cetros . . . . Dom
Don Abreu Churchill . . . . Dom
Don Alberto Comandante Double Corona . . . . Dom
Don Alberto Oro de Habana Double Corona . . . . Dom
Don Alberto Santiago Double Corona . . . . Dom
Don Diego Monarch . . . . Dom
Don Lino Oro Toro . . . . Hon
Don Lino Toros . . . . Hon
Don Manolo Corona . . . . Dom
Don Mateo No 4 . . . . Hon
Don Melo Corona . . . . Hon
Don Melo Corona Gorda . . . . Hon
Don Miguel Churchill . . . . Dom
Don Pishu Canary Island CI
Don Pishu Fuerte Ventura CI
Don Pishu Lanzarote CI
Don Pishu Rare CI
Don Rene Toro . . . . USA
Don Rubio Corona . . . . Hon

Pride of Copan No 2 . . . . Hon
Pride of Jamaica Petit Churchill . . . . Jam
Primera Bundles No 2. . . . . Ecu
Primo Del Rey Cazadores . . . . Dom
Primo Del Rey Presidentes . . . . Dom
Private Stock No 2 . . . . Dom
Private Stock No 6 . . . . Dom
Profesor Sila Excelencia. CI
Profesor Sila Presidente. CI
Pueblo Dominicano La Romana . . . . Dom
Punch Cafe Royal. . . . . Hon
Punch Card Royal. . . . . Hon
Punch De Luxe Chateau Margaux. . . . . Hon
Punch De Luxe Coronas . . . . Hon
Punch De Luxe Royal Coronations . . . . Hon
Punch Elites . . . . Hon
Punch No 75. . . . . Hon
Puro Nicaragua Corona Gorda . . . . Nic
Puros Indios No 2 Especial. Hon
Puros Indios No 4 Especial. Hon
Puros Indios Piramide No 2 . . . . Hon
Red Label Amatista . . . . Hon
Riata No 400. . . . . Hon
Ricos Dominicanos Breva . . . . Dom
Rigoletto Cigars Black Jack. . . . . USA
Rigoletto Dominican Lights. . . . . Dom
Romeo Y Julieta Romeo. . . . . Dom
Romeo Y Julieta Vintage II . . . . Dom
Royal Dominicana Corona. Dom
Royal Jamaica Corona . . . . Dom
Royal Jamaica Director 1 . . . . Dom
Royal Jamaica Park Lane . . . . Dom
Royal Jamaica Royal Corona . . . . Dom
Rum Runner Bucaneer . . . . USA
Sabana No 3 . . . . Ven
Sabroso Numero Dos. . . . . Nic
San Fernando Corona . . . . Hon
Santa Clara "1830" No V. . . . . Mex
Santa Damiana Seleccion No 300 . . . . Dom
Santa Rosa Regulares . . . . Hon
Santiago Cabana Caribe . . . . USA
Santiago No 3 . . . . Dom
Santiago No 4 . . . . Dom
Savinelli No 5 Ordinaire . . . . Dom
Sebastian Reserva No 8 . . . . Nic
Segovia X-O . . . . Nic

ROBUSTOS/ROTHCHILDS

Andujar Vega . . . . Dom
Arango Sportsman No 350 . . . . USA
Aromas de San Andreas Robusto . . . . Mex
Arturo Fuente Chateau Fuente . . . . Dom
Arturo Fuente Don Carlos Robusto . . . . Dom
Arturo Fuente Rothschild . . . . Dom
Ashton Magnum . . . . Dom
Astral Besos . . . . Hon
Avo No 9 . . . . Dom
Avo XO Intermezzo . . . . Dom
Bahia Robusto . . . . CR
Ballena Suprema Danli Collection Consuelo . . . . Hon
Bances Crown . . . . USA
Bances Crowns Maduro . . . . Hon
Bauza Robusto . . . . Dom
Belinda Medagla D'Oro . . . . Hon
Bering Robusto . . . . Hon
Beverly Hills VIP No 550 . . . . Hon
Black Label Robusto . . . . Mex
Blue Label Rothschild . . . . Hon
Blue Ribbon No 502 . . . . Nic
Bohio Robusto . . . . Dom
Butera Royal Vintage Bravo Corto . . . . Dom
C.A.O. Robusto . . . . Hon
Caballeros Rothschild . . . . Dom
Cacique Azteca . . . . Dom
Calle Ocho Gordito . . . . USA
Camacho Monarca . . . . Hon
Camorra Roma . . . . Hon
Canaria D'Ora Immensos . . . . Dom
Canaria D'Ora Rothschild . . . . Dom
Canonabo Petit Premier . . . . Dom
Canonero No 2 . . . . Bra
Canonero No 3 . . . . Bra
Carbonell Toro . . . . Dom
Carlin Robusto . . . . Nic
Carlos Torano Carlos VII . . . . Dom
Carrington VI . . . . Dom
Casa Blanca Half Jeroboam . . . . Dom
Casa de Nicaragua Petit Corona . . . . Nic
Casa de Nicaragua Rothschild . . . . Nic
Casa Martin Rothschild . . . . Dom
Casa Mayan Robusto . . . . Hon
Casa Mayan Rothschild . . . . Hon
Casanova Consul CI
Caz-Bar Corona Lonsdale . . . . Hon

Don Lino Corona. . . . . Hon
Don Lino Robustos. . . . . Hon
Don Lino Rothchild. . . . . Hon
Don Manolo Robusto . . . . Dom
Don Mateo No 7. . . . . Hon
Don Melo Nom Plus. . . . . Hon
Don Miguel Big Toros . . . . Dom
Don Miguel Petit . . . . Dom
Don Miguel Toros . . . . Dom
Don Pepe Robusto. . . . . Bra
Don Pishu Tu y Yo CI
Don Ramos Gordas**. . . . . Hon
Don Rene Robusto. . . . . USA
Don Rex Coronas. . . . . Hon
Don Rubio Nom Plus. . . . . Hon
Don Tomas Coronas. . . . . Hon
Don Tomas International Series No 2 . . . . Hon
Don Tomas Rothschild. . . . . Hon
Don Tomas Special Edition No 300 . . . . Hon
Don Tonioli Robusto . . . . Hon
Don Vito Robusto . . . . Dom
Don Xavier Robusto. CI
Double Happiness Bliss . . . . Phi
Double Happiness Rapture . . . . Phi
Dunhill (Vintage) Altimiras (tubed) . . . . Dom
Dunhill (Vintage) Romanas (Rothschild) . . . . Dom
Dunhill Canary Islands Coronas CI
El Imperio Cubano Robusto . . . . USA
El Incomparable Robusto. . . . . Hon
El Producto Escepcionales . . . . USA
El Producto Favoritas . . . . USA
El Rey del Mundo Robusto . . . . Hon
El Rey del Mundo Robusto Zavalia . . . . Hon
El Rey del Mundo Rothschilde. . . . . Hon
El Rico Habano Club . . . . USA
El Sublimado Regordete . . . . Dom
Elegante Blend Queen. . . . . Hon
Elegante Queen . . . . USA
Encanto Rothschild . . . . Hon
Espada Rothschild . . . . Hon
Espanola Reserve Robusto. . . . . Dom
Espanola Robusto . . . . Dom
Evelio Robusto . . . . Hon
Executor Rothschild. . . . . Hon
Fat Cat Robusto . . . . Dom
Felipe Gregorio Robusto . . . . Hon

LONSDALES

Antonio Y Cleopatra Grenadiers Tubos . . . . USA
Arango Sportsman No 200 (Boy & Girl) . . . . USA
Armenter Reserva No 5 CI
Aromas de San Andreas Gourmet . . . . Mex
Arturo Fuente Curley Head. . . . . Dom
Arturo Fuente Curley Head Deluxe . . . . Dom
Arturo Fuente Fumas. . . . . Dom
Arturo Fuente Seleccion Privada No 1 . . . . Dom
Arturo Fuente Spanish Lonsdale. . . . . Dom
Ashton 8-9-8. . . . . Dom
Ashton Aged Maduro No 30 . . . . Dom
Astral Lujos. . . . . Hon
Avo No 1 . . . . Dom
B-H Corona . . . . USA
B-H Golden Corona Boy & GIrl. . . . . USA
B-H Kings . . . . USA
B-H Special No 76 . . . . USA
Baccarat Havana No 1 . . . . Hon
Balboa No 1. . . . . Pan
Balboa No 2. . . . . Pan
Ballena Suprema Danli Collection Ventaja . . . . Hon
Ballena Suprema San Andres Collection Cortes . . . . . Mex
Bances Cazadores. . . . . Hon
Bauza Jaguar . . . . Dom
Bauza Medalla d'Oro No 1 . . . . Dom
Belinda Corona Grande. . . . . Hon
Bering Barons. . . . . Hon
Bering Casinos . . . . Hon
Blue Label No 1 . . . . Hon
Butera Royal Vintage Cedro Fino . . . . Dom
C.A.O. Lonsdale. . . . . Hon
Cabanas Lonsdale . . . . Dom
Cabanas Premier . . . . Dom
Cacique Siboneyes. . . . . Dom
Calixto Lopez/Carlos V Lonsdale Suprema. . . . . Phi
Calle Ocho Perfect Corona . . . . USA
Camacho Cazadores. . . . . Hon
Camacho Cetros. . . . . Hon
Camacho No 1 . . . . Hon
Camorra Venzia . . . . Hon
Canaria D'Ora Lonsdale . . . . Dom
Canonero No 10. . . . . Bra
Capote No 3. CI
Cara Mia Lonsdale. CI
Caramba No 4 . . . . Hon
Carbonell Corona . . . . Dom

Cuesta-Rey Centennial Dominican No 4 . . . . Dom
Danlys No 1 . . . . Hon
Davidoff Grand Cru No 2 . . . . Dom
Diana Silvius Corona . . . . Dom
Domingold Lonsdale . . . . Dom
Dominican Estates Lonsdale . . . . Dom
Dominican Original No 1 . . . . Dom
Dominicana Superba No 3 . . . . Dom
Dominico No 704 . . . . Dom
Domino Park Corona . . . . USA
Don Abreu Big Toros . . . . Dom
Don Abreu Coronas . . . . Dom
Don Abreu Coronitas . . . . Dom
Don Alberto Oro de Habana Corona . . . . Dom
Don Alberto Santiago Corona . . . . Dom
Don Asa Cetros . . . . Hon
Don Diego Lonsdales . . . . Dom
Don Diego Lonsdales EMS/AMS . . . . Dom
Don Diego Privada 1 . . . . Dom
Don Estaban Elegante . . . . Dom
Don Fife Double Corona . . . . Hon
Don Fife Numero 1 . . . . Hon
Don Juan Numero Uno . . . . Nic
Don Leo Cetro . . . . Dom
Don Lino No 1 . . . . Hon
Don Lino No 5 . . . . Hon
Don Lino Oro No 1 . . . . Hon
Don Marcus Cetros . . . . Dom
Don Mateo No 5 . . . . Hon
Don Miguel Coronas . . . . Dom
Don Miguel Coronitas . . . . Dom
Don Miguel Lonsdale (No 1) . . . . Dom
Don Pishu Gomera CI
Don Ramos Magnum** . . . . Hon
Don Rene Corona . . . . USA
Don Rex Cetros No 2 . . . . Hon
Don Rubio Cazadore . . . . Hon
Don Rubio Corona Gorda . . . . Hon
Don Rubio No 1 . . . . Hon
Don Tomas Cetros No 2 . . . . Hon
Don Tomas Corona Grandes . . . . Hon
Don Tomas It's a Boy/Girl . . . . Hon
Don Tomas Special Edition No 200 . . . . Hon
Don Tomas Supremos . . . . Hon
Don Vito Lonsdale . . . . Dom
Don Xavier Lonsdale CI

Dunhill (Vintage) Diamantes (Lonsdale) . . . . Dom
Dunhill (Vintage) Diamantes (Lonsdale) . . . . Dom
Dunhill Canary Hill Islands Lonsdale Grandes CI
Dunhill Corona Grande. CI
Dunhill Lonsdale Grande CI
El Beso No 1 . . . . Mex
El Canelo Cetros No 2 . . . . USA
El Canelo Fumas. . . . . USA
El Canelo No 1 . . . . USA
El Imperio Cubano Lonsdale . . . . USA
El Rey del Mundo Cedar . . . . Hon
El Triunfo No 6 Mitlas . . . . Mex
Elegante Blend Centimo . . . . Hon
Elegante Centimo. . . . . USA
Encanto Corona Larga. . . . . Hon
Encanto Elegantes . . . . Hon
Encanto Luchadores . . . . Hon
Espada Corona Gorda . . . . Hon
Espanola Excellent . . . . Dom
Evelio No 1. . . . . Hon
Executor No 1 . . . . Hon
F. D. Grave & Son Lonsdale . . . . Hon
Figaro . . . . USA
Five Star Seconds No 100 . . . . Dom
Flor de Consuegra Lonsdale . . . . Hon
Flor de Florez Cetros . . . . USA
Flor de Manila Corona Largo . . . . Phi
Flor de Mexico No 1. . . . . Mex
Flor de Nicaragua No 1 . . . . Nic
Flor de Orlando Corona . . . . Dom
Flor de Orlando No 1 . . . . Dom
Flor del Caribe No 1. . . . . Hon
Franco Condados. . . . . Dom
Free Cuba Corona . . . . USA
Fundadores Rothchild. . . . . Jam
Gilberto Oliva No 1 . . . . Hon
Gloria Palmera Lonsdale CI
Goya Cetro. CI
Griffin's No 200 . . . . Dom
Griffin's No 300 . . . . Dom
Guaranteed Jamaica No 100 . . . . Jam
H. A. Ladrillo Lancero . . . . Hon
H. Upmann Director Royale . . . . Dom
H. Upmann Lonsdales. . . . . Dom
H. Upmann No 2000 SBN . . . . Dom
Habanos Hatuey Lonsdale. . . . . Dom

Harrows Camelot . . . . Phi
Harrows No 1 . . . . Phi
Havana Blend Doubloon . . . . USA
Havana Classico Corona Classic . . . . USA
Havana Reserve No 1 . . . . Hon
Havana Reserve Tubes . . . . Hon
Hecho-A-Mano-Caz-Bar Cazadores . . . . Hon
Hecho-A-Mano-Caz-Bar Fumas . . . . Hon
Henry Clay J. A. Leather . . . . Dom
Henry Winterman Excellentes . . . . Hol
Hidalgo Cazadore . . . . Pan
Hidalgo Fuma . . . . Pan
Hoja de Mexicali Lonsdale Natural . . . . Mex
Hoja del Regal Corona Gorda . . . . Hon
Honduran Gold Senator . . . . Hon
Honduran Import Maduro Delicosos . . . . Hon
Honduras Elegantes . . . . Hon
Hoyo de Monterrey Ambassador . . . . Hon
Hoyo de Monterrey Cetros . . . . Hon
Hoyo de Monterrey No 1 . . . . Hon
Hugo Cassar Diamond Selection Lonsdale . . . . Dom
Hugo Cassar Mystique Lonsdale . . . . Dom
Hugo Cassar No 3 . . . . Hon
Hugo Cassar Signature Series Lonsdale . . . . Nic
Indian Head Cazadores . . . . Hon
Indian Head Coronas Gorda . . . . Hon
Indian Head Fumas . . . . Hon
Indian Head Numero Dos . . . . Hon
Indian Head Numero Uno . . . . Hon
Iracema Macumba . . . . Ger
J. F. Gold No 2 . . . . Pan
J. F. Llopis Gold No 1 . . . . Pan
J. R. Ultimate Cetro . . . . Hon
Jamaica Bay No 400 . . . . Jam
Jamaica Gem Corona Grande . . . . Jam
Jamaica Gold Baron . . . . Jam
Jamaica Gold Queen . . . . Jam
Jamaica Heritage No 100 . . . . Jam
Jamaican Kings Buccaneers . . . . Jam
Jamaican Kings Double Coronas . . . . Jam
Jamaican Pride Corona Deluxe . . . . Jam
John Aylesbury Santa Dominga Lonsdale . . . . Dom
Jose Benito Corona . . . . Dom
Jose Llopis No 1 . . . . Pan
Jose Llopis No 2 . . . . Pan
Jose Marti Maceo . . . . Dom

Medal of Honor No 300 . . . . Hon
Micubano No 644 . . . . Nic
Mina de Veracruz, Reserva Especial . . . . Mex
Mocambo Premier . . . . Mex
Mocha Supreme Lords . . . . Hon
Monte Canario Imperiales CI
Monte Canario Nuncios CI
Montecassino Cazadores . . . . Hon
Montecristo No 1 . . . . Dom
Montecruz No 205 . . . . Dom
Montecruz No 210 . . . . Dom
Montelimar Luchadore Mad . . . . Hon
Montelimar Luchadore Nat . . . . Hon
Montelimar No 1 . . . . Hon
Montesino Fumas . . . . Dom
Montesino No 1 . . . . Dom
Montesino No 2 . . . . Dom
Moreno Maduro No 426 . . . . Dom
Morro Castle Corona . . . . USA
Nat Cicco's Deliciosos . . . . Dom
Nat Sherman Exchange Butterfield No 8 . . . . Dom
Nat Sherman Gotham No 1440 . . . . Dom
Nat Sherman Host Selection Harrington . . . . Hon
Nat Sherman Landmark Alonquin . . . . Dom
Nat Sherman Manhattan Gramercy . . . . Dom
Nat Sherman VIP Morgan . . . . Dom
National Brand Lonsdale . . . . Hon
Nestor Vintage No 1 . . . . Hon
New York, New York Park Avenue . . . . Mex
Nording Lonsdale . . . . Hon
Nude Dominican 32 . . . . Dom
Nude Dominican 50 . . . . Dom
Nude Dominican 54 . . . . Dom
Nude Mexican 910 . . . . Mex
Ocho Rios No 1 . . . . Jam
Oh Que Bueno No 1 CI
Olar Lonsdale . . . . Dom
Old Harbour No 200 . . . . Jam
Ornelas LTD 40 AL Cognac . . . . Mex
Ornelas No 1 . . . . Mex
Ornelas No 1 Vanilla . . . . Mex
Oro Blend •22 . . . . USA
Oro de Cuba El Aquila . . . . Dom
Oro de Cuba El Pantero . . . . Dom
Ortiz Double Corona . . . . Mex
Oscar No 200 . . . . Dom

Romeo Y Julieta Cetros . . . . Dom
Romeo Y Julieta Delgados . . . . Dom
Romeo Y Julieta Presidentes . . . . Dom
Royal Dominicana No 1. . . . . Dom
Royal Honduras Prince . . . . Hon
Royal Jamaica Corona Grande. . . . . Dom
Royal Jamaica Tube No 1. . . . . Dom
Royal Nicaraguan Numero 10 . . . . Nic
Royales No 5 . . . . Dom
San Luis Corona. . . . . Hon
San Luis Corona. . . . . USA
San Vicente Blend Supremo . . . . USA
Santa Clara "1830" No III. . . . . Mex
Santa Damiana Seleccion No 700 . . . . Dom
Santa Rosa Corona. . . . . Hon
Santa Rosa Elegante. . . . . Hon
Santiago Cabana Corona . . . . USA
Savinelli No 3 Lonsdale. . . . . Dom
Sebastian Reserva No 6 . . . . Nic
Serendipity Coronita . . . . Dom
Serengeti Corona Bushbuck . . . . SA
Serengeti Corona Kudu . . . . SA
Siglo 21-2 . . . . Dom
Solo Aroma Cazadores . . . . Hon
Solo Aroma Fumas. . . . . Hon
Sosa Family No 1 . . . . Dom
Sosa Lonsdale . . . . Dom
Special Caribbean No 2. . . . . Dom
Special Caribbean No 898 . . . . Dom
Special Jamaica A. . . . . Dom
Special Jamaica Fancytale Shape . . . . Dom
Super Special No 1. . . . . Hon
Tabacalera Corona Larga. . . . . Phi
Tabacalera Don Q . . . . Phi
Tabacalera El Conde De Guell Sr . . . . Phi
Te-Amo Caballero. . . . . Mex
Te-Amo Celebration . . . . Mex
Te-Amo Contemplation . . . . Mex
Te-Amo Relaxation . . . . Mex
Te-Amo Segundo Relaxation . . . . Mex
Temple Hall No 1 Trump . . . . Jam
Temple Hall No 625 . . . . Jam
Tena y Vega No 1 . . . . Hon
Tesoros de Copan Cetros . . . . Hon
Thomas Hinds Honduran Supremo . . . . Hon
Thomas Hinds Nicaraguan Lonsdale. . . . . Nic

CORONAS

Bances Palmas . . . . USA
Bances Palmas (Girl or Boy) . . . . USA
Bauza Grecos . . . . Dom
Bering Corona Royale . . . . Hon
Bering Plazas . . . . Hon
Black Label Acapulco . . . . Mex
Blue Label No 2 . . . . Hon
Blue Ribbon No 504 . . . . Nic
Bohio Petit Corona . . . . Dom
C.A.O. Corona . . . . Hon
Caballeros Corona . . . . Dom
Caballeros Petit Corona . . . . Dom
Cabanas Corona . . . . Dom
Cabanas Coronas . . . . USA
Cabanas Premiers . . . . USA
Cacique Tainos . . . . Dom
Calixto Lopez/Carlos V Corona Exquisto . . . . Phi
Camacho Palmas . . . . Hon
Canaria D'Ora Corona . . . . Dom
Canonabo Nabories . . . . Dom
Canonero No 20 . . . . Bra
Cara Mia Corona CI
Carbonell Palma Short . . . . Dom
Cariges No 1 . . . . Spa
Carlin Corona . . . . Nic
Carlos Torano Carlos IV . . . . Dom
Carrington II . . . . Dom
Carrington IV . . . . Dom
Casa Blanca Corona . . . . Dom
Casa de Nicaragua Corona . . . . Nic
Casa Martin Numero Dos . . . . Dom
Casa Martin Regulares . . . . Dom
Cervantes Senadores . . . . Hon
Chambrair Faible . . . . Dom
Charles Denby Invincible . . . . USA
Chevere Antonio . . . . Jam
Cibao Corona Deluxe . . . . Dom
Cibao Corona Deluxe . . . . USA
Cienfugo Richmond 1865 . . . . Hon
Cimero Corona . . . . Dom
Columbus Tubos . . . . Hon
Competere No 200 . . . . Hon
Condal No 3 CI
Connisseur Gold Label No 4 . . . . Hon
Connoisseur Gold Label No 4 . . . . USA
Connoisseur Silver Label Corona . . . . USA

Dunhill Corona CI
Dutch Masters Corona Deluxe . . . . PR
Dutch Masters Palmas Maduro . . . . PR
Dutch Masters President . . . . PR
Dutch Masters President . . . . USA
El Beso Cetros . . . . Mex
El Canelo No 4 . . . . USA
El Imperio Cubano Corona . . . . USA
El Paraiso Corona . . . . Hon
El Producto Blunts . . . . USA
El Producto Coronas . . . . USA
El Producto Queens . . . . USA
El Rey del Mundo Habana Club . . . . Hon
El Rico Habanos Coronas . . . . USA
El Trelles Bankers . . . . USA
El Trelles Club House . . . . USA
El Trelles Kings . . . . USA
El Triunfo No 7 Pueblas . . . . Mex
Elegante Blend Petit Cetro . . . . Hon
Elegante Petit Cetro . . . . USA
Elysee No 5-42 . . . . Bra
Elysee No 6-42 . . . . Bra
Encanto Cetros . . . . Hon
Encanto Petit Corona . . . . Hon
Espanola Corona . . . . Dom
Evelio Corona . . . . Hon
Evermore Palma . . . . USA
Executor No 4 . . . . Hon
Felipe Gregorio Sereno . . . . Hon
Flamenco Brevas . . . . Dom
Flamenco Brevas SMS . . . . USA
Flor de Consuegra Corona . . . . Hon
Flor de Consuegra Corona Extra . . . . Hon
Flor de Mexico No 2 . . . . Mex
Flor de Nicaragua No 6 . . . . Nic
Flor de Nicaragua Seleccion B . . . . Nic
Flor de Orlando No 4 . . . . Dom
Flor de Palicio No 2 . . . . Hon
Flor del Caribe Duques . . . . Hon
Fonseca 8-9-8 . . . . Dom
Franco Eminentes . . . . Dom
Garcia Y Vega Crystals No 200 . . . . USA
Garcia Y Vega English Coronas . . . . USA
Garcia Y Vega English Coronas Boy/Girl . . . . USA
Garcia Y Vega Gran Coronas . . . . USA
Garcia Y Vega Gran Premios . . . . USA

Private Stock No 5 . . . . Dom
Puro Nicaragua Numero 4 . . . . Nic
Quorum Corona . . . . Dom
RC Corona . . . . Dom
Red Label Cetro . . . . Hon
Red Label Chico . . . . Hon
Repeater 100 . . . . Hon
Repeater 200 . . . . Hon
Republica Dominica No 7 . . . . Dom
Rey del Mar Corona . . . . USA
Riata It's A Boy/Girl . . . . Hon
Riata No 300 . . . . Hon
Rico Havana Blend Corona . . . . USA
Rigoletto Cigars Natural Coronas . . . . USA
Rigoletto Cigars Palma Grande . . . . USA
Roi-Tan Blunts . . . . PR
Rolando Blend Numero No 4 . . . . USA
Romanticos Cleopatra . . . . Dom
Romeo Y Julieta Coronas . . . . Dom
Romeo Y Julieta Palmas . . . . Dom
Romeo Y Julieta Vintage I . . . . Dom
Royal Court Cetro . . . . Hon
Royal Dominicana Nacional . . . . Dom
Royal Honduras Joker . . . . Hon
Royal Nicaraguan Numero 16 . . . . Nic
Royal Nicaraguan Numero 18 . . . . Nic
Royales No 1 . . . . Dom
Royales No 6 . . . . Dom
Sabana No 2 . . . . Ven
San Vicente Blend Matador . . . . USA
Santa Clara "1830" No IV . . . . Mex
Santa Cruz Corona . . . . Jam
Santa Cruz Corona Grande . . . . Jam
Santa Damiana Carona . . . . Dom
Santa Damiana Seleccion No 200 . . . . Dom
Santa Fe Biltmore . . . . USA
Santa Fe Fairmont . . . . USA
Santa Fe Patties . . . . USA
Santa Rosa Cetros . . . . Hon
Sebastian Reserva No 7 . . . . Nic
Segovia Primo Gorda . . . . Nic
Solo Aroma Numero Cuatro . . . . Hon
Solo Aroma Numero Dos . . . . Hon
Sosa Brevas . . . . Dom
Special Caribbean Corona . . . . Dom
Super Special Cetros . . . . Hon

Swisher Sweets Kings . . . . USA
Te-Amo Meditation . . . . Mex
Te-Amo Segundo Meditation . . . . Mex
Temple Hall No 3 Trump . . . . Jam
Tena Y Vega Cetros . . . . Hon
Thomas Hinds Honduran Corona . . . . Hon
Thomas Hinds Honduran Royal Corona . . . . Hon
Thomas Hinds Nicaraguan Corona . . . . Nic
Tiburon Great White . . . . Hon
Tiburon Mako . . . . Hon
Topper Corona . . . . Hon
Topstone Supremes . . . . USA
Torquino Breva Corona . . . . USA
Traditionales Corona . . . . USA
Tresado No 500 . . . . Dom
Troya Clasico Executive . . . . Dom
Troya No 27 Corona . . . . Dom
V Centennial Coronas . . . . Hon
Valdrych Anacaona . . . . Dom
Vegas Gran Reserva Corona . . . . Nic
Veracruz Poemas de Veracruz . . . . Mex
Villazon Deluxe Aromatics Commodores . . . . USA
Vintage Honduran Matador . . . . Hon
Virtuoso Torano Cetros . . . . Hon
Voyager Enterprise . . . . Hon
VSOP Corona . . . . Hon
Vueltabajo Corona . . . . Dom
White Owl Invincible (Boy/Girl) . . . . USA
White Owl New Yorker . . . . USA
Yumuri Corona . . . . Dom
Zino Diamond . . . . Hon
Zino Drie . . . . Hol

PETIT/HALF CORONAS

Adante No 405 Petit Corona . . . . Dom
Alhambra Corona . . . . Phi
Antelo No 5 . . . . USA
Arango Statesman Executor . . . . Hon
As You Like It No 22 . . . . USA
Avo No 8 . . . . Dom
Balmoral Corona de Luxe . . . . Hol
Bering Imperials . . . . Hon
Bering Imperials Boy/Girl . . . . Hon
C.A.O. Petit Corona . . . . Hon
Camorra Padova . . . . Hon
Caramba No 7 . . . . Hon

Caribes No 2 .... Spa
Casa Martin Petite Coronas.................... Dom
Casa Mayan No 4 .... Hon
Celestino Vega Petit Corona .... Ind
Cohiba Robusto................................ Dom
Condal No 4................................... CI
Connisseur Silver Label Corona .... Dom
Cubita $500 .... Dom
Cuesta-Rey Centennial Dominican No 5.......... Dom
Danlys No 4 .... Hon
Davidoff 2000................................. Dom
Davidoff Grand Cru No 3 .... Dom
Davidoff Grand Cru No 4 .... Dom
Davidoff Grand Cru No 5 .... Dom
Dexter Londres .... USA
Dominicana Superba No 5 .... Dom
Don Asa Blunts................................ Hon
Don Diego Corona Major .... Dom
Don Diego Coronas Major Tubes EMS .... Dom
Don Diego Pequenos No 300 .... Dom
Don Diego Petit Corona .... Dom
Don Diego Petit Coronas EMS/AMS............... Dom
Don Lino No 4................................. Hon
Don Melo Cremos .... Hon
Don Miguel Petit Corona (No 4) .... Dom
Don Ramos Petit Corona .... Hon
Don Ramos Tres Petit Corona .... Hon
Don Rex Blunts .... Hon
Dutch Masters Belvedere .... PR
El Producto Bouquets .... USA
El Producto Finos............................. USA
El Producto Panetelas .... USA
El Rey del Mundo Petit Lonsdale............... Hon
El Rico Petit Habanos......................... USA
Emerson Diplomat.............................. USA
Espanola Petit Corona......................... Dom
Excalibur VII .... Hon
Farios Centenario .... Spa
Farios Superiores............................. Spa
Felipe Gregorio Nino.......................... Hon
Flor de Florez Blunt.......................... USA
Flor de Florez Coronitas...................... USA
Flor de Mexico No 4........................... Mex
Flor de Nicaragua No 2 .... Nic
Fonseca 2-2 .... Dom
Garcia Y Vega Blunts .... USA

Odin Viking	USA
Oh Que Bueno Corona	CI
Optimo Coronas	USA
Optimo Sports	USA
Opus X Fuente Perfecxion No 5	Dom
Ornelas No 4	Mex
Oro de Cuba El Falcon	Dom
Oro de Cuba El Pasofina Tube	Dom
P. G. No 5	Dom
P. G. Petit Corona	Dom
Partagas No 3	Dom
Peter Stokkebye Santa Maria No 3	Dom
Peterson Petit Corona	Dom
Petrus Tabacage 89 Gregorius	Hon
Phillies Blunts	USA
Phillies Junior	USA
Pleiades Antares	Dom
Primera Bundles Toro	Ecu
Primo del Cristo Reyes	Hon
Private Stock No 10	Dom
Private Stock No 7	Dom
Pueblo Dominicano Samana	Dom
Pueblo Dominicano Santiago	Dom
Punch London Club	Hon
Quorum Trumph	Dom
Ramon Allones D	Dom
RC Fine	Dom
RC Pequeno	Dom
Rico Havana Habanero	USA
Ritmeester Corona	Hol
Ritmeester Corona Delecta	Hol
Roi-Tan Bankers	PR
Royal Jamaica Petit Corona	Dom
Santa Damiana Petit Corona	Dom
Santa Damiana Seleccion No 400	Dom
Santa Rosa Numero Cuatro	Hon
Santiago No 5	Dom
Sosa Family No 4	Dom
Suerdieck Mata Fina Esp	Bra
Tabacalera Brevas a la Conserva	Phi
Tabacalera Corona	Phi
Tabantillas No 4	Dom
Tabaquero No 542	Dom
Tampa Nugget Blunt Blunt	USA
Tampa Nugget Sublime Perfecto	USA
Te-Amo No 4	Mex

LONG PANETELAS

Petrus Tabacage 89 Lord Byron . . . . Hon
Primo del Cristo Palmas . . . . Hon
Primo del Cristo Palmas Reales . . . . Hon
Royal Manna Laro Fino Rothschild . . . . Hon
Royal Nicaraguan Numero 12 . . . . Nic
Santiago No 2 . . . . Dom
Tabacalera Banderilla . . . . Phi
Troya No 36 Palma Fina . . . . Dom
Valdrych Cabellero . . . . Dom
Vintage Honduran Panetela Large . . . . Hon
W & D Panetela Largas . . . . Hon

PANETELAS

Andujar Samana . . . . Dom
Arturo Fuente Panetela Fina . . . . Dom
Avo No 6 . . . . Dom
Baccarat Havana Panetela . . . . Hon
Bances El Prados . . . . Hon
Bances Uniques . . . . Hon
Belinda . . . . Hon
Bering Hispanos . . . . Hon
Black Label Guadalajara . . . . Mex
Blue Label Palma . . . . Hon
Butera Royal Vintage Mira Belle . . . . Dom
Cacique Jaragua . . . . Dom
Calle Ocho Laquito . . . . USA
Camacho Elegante . . . . Hon
Camorra Napoli . . . . Hon
Canonabo Caciques . . . . Dom
Capote No 4 CI
Caramba No 8 . . . . Hon
Carbonell Panetela . . . . Dom
Carbonell Panetela Grande . . . . Dom
Carlos Torano Carlos VIII . . . . Dom
Casa Blanca Panetela . . . . Dom
Casa Martin Palma Fina . . . . Dom
Casa Martin Seleccion Especial . . . . Dom
Chambrair Plaisir . . . . Dom
Charles Fairmorn Elegante . . . . Hon
Chavelo Panatela . . . . USA
Cibao Diamantes . . . . USA
Cibao Diamantes . . . . Dom
Cojimar Cortaditos . . . . USA
Cojimar Laguito . . . . USA
Connisseur Gold Label No 3 Nat . . . . USA
Connisseur Silver Label Diamantes . . . . USA

Flor de Palicio No 1 . . . . Hon
Flor del Caribe Petit Cetro . . . . Hon
Franco Gourmets . . . . Dom
Griffin's No 100 . . . . Dom
Griffin's No 400 . . . . Dom
Guaranteed Jamaica No 300 . . . . Jam
H. Upmann Finos Gold Tube . . . . Dom
H. Upmann Naturales Tubes . . . . Dom
Habanica Serie 638 . . . . Nic
Hauptmann's Panetela . . . . USA
Havana Sunrise Lancero . . . . USA
Henry Clay Largas . . . . Dom
Hoja del Regal Slim Panetela . . . . Hon
Honduras Lindas . . . . Hon
Hoyo de Monterrey Delights . . . . Hon
Indian Head Lindas . . . . Hon
Indian Head Panetelas . . . . Hon
J. Cortes Long Filler No 1 . . . . Bel
J. R. Ultimate Palma . . . . Hon
J. R. Ultimate Petit Cetro . . . . Hon
J. R. Ultimate Slims . . . . Hon
Jamaica Bay No 500 . . . . Jam
Jamaica Gold Count . . . . Jam
Jamaica Gold Earl . . . . Jam
John Aylesbury Santa Dominga Elegante . . . . Dom
John T's Amaretto . . . . Dom
John T's Brown Gold . . . . Dom
John T's Cafe Ole . . . . Dom
John T's Capuccino . . . . Dom
John T's Cherry Cream . . . . Dom
Jon Piedro Acapulco Slims . . . . USA
Jose Benito Panetela . . . . Dom
Jose Benito Petite . . . . Dom
Joya de Nicaragua No 5 . . . . Nic
Joya de Nicaragua Petit . . . . Nic
King No 3 . . . . Dom
King No 5 . . . . Dom
La Aurora Palmas . . . . Dom
La Corona Vintage Aristocrats . . . . USA
La Fontana Dante . . . . USA
La Fontana Vintage Dante . . . . Hon
La Habanera Selectos . . . . Dom
La Hoja Selecta Bel Aires . . . . USA
La Paz Especiales CK 164 . . . . Hol
La Regenta Olimpicas CI
Lambs Club Palma . . . . Dom

Petrus Tabacage 89 No IV . . . . Hon
Petrus Tabacage 89 Palma Fina . . . . Hon
Plasencia No 3 . . . . Hon
Por Larranaga Delicados . . . . Dom
Premium Dominican Selection No 3. . . . . Dom
Premium Dominican Selection No 4. . . . . Dom
Premium Dominican Selection Super Fino. . . . . Dom
Pride of Copan No 4 . . . . Hon
Pride of Jamaica President . . . . Jam
Primo Del Rey Reales . . . . Dom
Primo Del Rey Seleccion No 3. . . . . Dom
Primo Del Rey Seleccion No 5. . . . . Dom
Private Stock No 4 . . . . Dom
Profesor Sila Principe CI
Puro Nicaragua Lindas. . . . . Nic
Puro Nicaragua Panetela Especial . . . . Nic
Puros Indios Palmas Real . . . . Hon
Quorum Whillo . . . . Dom
Red Label Elegante . . . . Hon
Republica Dominica No 8 . . . . Dom
Rey del Mar Petit Corona. . . . . USA
Riata No 200. . . . . Hon
Roi-Tan Panetelas . . . . PR
Romeo Y Julieta Brevas . . . . Dom
Royal Court Petit Corona. . . . . Hon
Royal Dominicana Super Fino. . . . . Dom
Royal Manna Manchego. . . . . Hon
Royales No 7 . . . . Dom
Sabana No 1 . . . . Ven
San Luis Panetelas . . . . Hon
San Luis Panetelas . . . . USA
San Luis Panetelas Boy/Girl. USA
Santa Clara "1830" Premier Tubes . . . . Mex
Santa Cruz Majestic. . . . . Jam
Santa Rosa Largos . . . . Hon
Santiago Cabana Lancero. . . . . USA
Sosa Family No 6 . . . . Dom
Sosa Santa Fe . . . . Dom
Tabacalera Conde De Guell . . . . Phi
Tabantillas Havana 1866 No 1 . . . . Dom
Tabantillas Havana Club . . . . Dom
Tabaquero No 638. . . . . Dom
Tampa Nugget Panetela Panetela. . . . . USA
Te-Amo Segundo Torero . . . . Mex
Te-Amo Torero . . . . Mex
Topstone—Natural Darks Panetela . . . . USA

SLIM PANETELAS

Davidoff 3000.	Dom
Davidoff No 3.	Dom
Don Diego Babies SMS	Dom
Don Mateo No 1.	Hon
Don Pepe Slim Panetela	Bra
Don Rene Senoritas	USA
Don Rubio Panatella	Hon
Don Vito Alfonsitos	Dom
Dunhill (Vintage) Fantinos (Panetela)	Dom
Dunhill Canary Hill Islands Panetelas	CI
Dunhill Panetela	CI
Dutch Masters Cadet Tip	USA
Dutch Masters Elites	PR
Dutch Masters Elites	USA
El Canelo St George	USA
El Paraiso Pequenos	Hon
El Rey del Mundo Elegante	Hon
El Rey del Mundo Plantation	Hon
El Verso Mellow	USA
Entrefinos Java Largos	Spa
Executor Panetela	Hon
Five Star Seconds No 600	Dom
Five Star Seconds No 900	Dom
Flor de Nicaragua No 7	Nic
Flor de Nicaragua Senoritas	Nic
Flor de Orlando Panetela	Dom
Garcia Y Vega Bravura	USA
Garcia Y Vega Crystals No 100	USA
Garcia Y Vega Delgado Panetela	USA
Garcia Y Vega Elegantes	USA
Garcia Y Vega Gallantes	USA
Garcia Y Vega Granadas	USA
Garcia Y Vega Panatella Deluxe	USA
Garcia Y Vega Romeros	USA
Garcia Y Vega Tips	USA
Gold & Mild Pipe Tobacco Cigars	USA
Griffin's Privilege	Dom
Harrows Esquire	Phi
Havana Blend Palma Fina	USA
Havana Sunrise Panetela—Cache	USA
Henry Clay Panetelas	Dom
Henry Clay Slim Panetela	Dom
Henry Winterman Long Panatella	Hol
Honduras Clasico	Hon
Honduras Pincel	Hon
House of Windsor Magnate	USA

Montecruz No 277 . . . . Dom
Montecruz No 280 . . . . Dom
Montecruz No 281 . . . . Dom
Montelimar Elegante . . . . Hon
Moreno Maduro No 326 . . . . Dom
Muniemaker Panetela 100's Oscura . . . . USA
Muriel Air Tips Menthol . . . . PR
Muriel Air Tips Pipe Aroma . . . . PR
Muriel Air Tips Regular . . . . PR
Muriel Air Tips Sweet . . . . PR
Nat Sherman Exchange Academy No 2 . . . . Dom
Nat Sherman Gotham No 65 . . . . Dom
Nat Sherman Landmark Hampshire . . . . Dom
Nat Sherman Landmark Metropole . . . . Dom
Nat Sherman Manhattan Beekman . . . . Dom
Nat Sherman Manhattan Tribeca . . . . Dom
Nat Sherman VIP Zigfeld "Fancytale" . . . . Dom
Nobel Grand Panetela Sumatra . . . . Den
Nude Dominican 58 . . . . Dom
Nude Dominican 60 . . . . Dom
Optimo Diplomat . . . . USA
Optimo Panetela . . . . USA
Ornelas Matinee . . . . Mex
Ornelas Matinee Vanilla . . . . Mex
Oro de Cuba El Flamingo . . . . Dom
Oscar Prince . . . . Dom
Partagas No 5 . . . . Dom
Partagas No 6 . . . . Dom
Partagas Tubos . . . . Dom
Particulares Petit . . . . Hon
Phillies Cheroot . . . . USA
Phillies King Cheroot . . . . USA
Phillies Panatella . . . . USA
Plasencia No 5 . . . . Hon
Pleiades Mars . . . . Dom
Pleiades Perseus . . . . Dom
Pleiades Uranus . . . . Dom
Pollack Crown Drum . . . . USA
Pride of Copan No 5 . . . . Hon
Primo del Rey Panetelas . . . . Dom
Prince Albert Cool Mint . . . . USA
Prince Albert Soft & Sweet Vanilla . . . . USA
Prince Albert Traditional . . . . USA
Private Stock No 3 . . . . Dom
Punch Largo Elegantes . . . . Hon
Red Dot Panetela . . . . USA

Zino Relax Brazil . . . . Hon
Zino Relax Sumatra . . . . Hon
Zino Santos . . . . Bra
Zino Tubos No 1. . . . . Hon

SHORT PANETELAS

Arturo Fuente Petit Corona. . . . . Dom
Ashton Panetela. . . . . Dom
Avo XO Allegro . . . . Dom
Bauza Petit Corona . . . . Dom
Beverly Hills VIP No 535 . . . . Hon
Calle Ocho Ninas . . . . USA
Canonabo Nitainos . . . . Dom
Caribbean Family Petite . . . . USA
Casa Blanca Bonita . . . . Dom
Clubmaster Half Corona Sumatra/Brazil . . . . Ger
Connisseur Silver Label Diamantes . . . . Dom
Cuba Aliados Petite Cetro . . . . Hon
Cuban Twist No 200 . . . . Hon
Don Pepe Half Corona . . . . Bra
El Rey del Mundo Cafe Au Lait . . . . Hon
El Rey del Mundo Reynita . . . . Hon
Espanola Reserve Demi Tasse . . . . Dom
Flor de Consuegra Panetela . . . . Hon
Flor de Manila Panetela. . . . . Phi
Free Cuba Miniature . . . . USA
Havana Blend Petit Corona . . . . USA
Havana Classico Puntas . . . . USA
Hoyo de Monterrey Demitasse. . . . . Hon
Island Amaretto Bellissima. . . . . USA
J. Cortes High Class . . . . Bel
J. Cortes Long Filler No 2 . . . . Bel
Justus Van Maurik After Dinner . . . . Hol
King Edward Panetela Deluxe . . . . USA
La Aurora Corona . . . . Dom
La Aurora Petite Corona . . . . Dom
La Aurora Sublimes. . . . . Dom
La Flor de la Isabela Panetelas. . . . . Phi
Leon Jimenes No 5 . . . . Dom
Licenciados Expresso. . . . . Dom
Macanudo Petit Corona . . . . Jam
Matasa Palmita. . . . . Dom
Montecruz No 270. . . . . Dom
Morro Castle Miniature . . . . USA
Ornelas No 6 . . . . Mex
Ornelas No 6 Vanilla. . . . . Mex

P. G. Petit Bouquet . . . . Dom
Partagas No 4 . . . . Dom
Peterson Tres Petit Corona . . . . Dom
Petrus Tabacage 89 Chantaco . . . . Hon
Por Larranga Petit Cetro . . . . Dom
Pride of Copan No 3 . . . . Hon
Private Stock No 8 . . . . Dom
Purios Indios Petit Perla . . . . Hon
Romeo Y Julieta Panetelas . . . . Dom
Rum Runner Wench . . . . USA
Santa Damiana Panetela . . . . Dom
Santa Damiana Seleccion No 600 . . . . Dom
Santiago Cabana Chicas . . . . USA
Suerdieck Mandarim Pai . . . . Bra
Suerdieck Panatella Fina . . . . Bra
Te-Amo Pauser . . . . Mex

SMALL PANETELAS

Ashton Europe Coronita . . . . Dom
Ashton Europe Dutch Corona . . . . Dom
Ashton Europe Senorita . . . . Dom
Avo XO Serenata . . . . Dom
Baccarat Havana Bonita . . . . Hon
Baccarat Havana Platinum . . . . Hon
Balmoral Cardinal*** . . . . Hol
Balmoral Highlands . . . . Hol
Balmoral Midlands . . . . Hol
Bances Demitasse . . . . Hon
Bances Demitasse . . . . USA
Canaria D'Ora Babies . . . . Dom
Celestino Vega Senorita . . . . Ind
Charles Fairmorn Super Finos . . . . Hon
Christian of Denmark Mini Cigarillos . . . . Den
Columbus Tinas . . . . Hon
Cuesta-Rey Centennial Cameo . . . . Dom
Davidoff 1000 . . . . Dom
Dominican Original Miniatures . . . . Dom
Don Lino Epicures . . . . Hon
Don Tomas Epicures . . . . Hon
El Canelo Miniatures . . . . USA
El Producto Little Coronas . . . . USA
Encanto Princesse . . . . Hon
Entrefinos Java Superiors . . . . Spa
Farios Chico . . . . Spa
Flor de Nicaragua Piccolino . . . . Nic
Flor de Veracruz Carinas . . . . Mex

H. Upmann Demi Tasse. . . . . Dom
Henry Winterman Half Corona . . . . Hol
Honduras Super Fino. . . . . Hon
Hoyo de Monterrey Petit . . . . Hon
Indian Head Princesse . . . . Hon
J. Cortes Club . . . . Bel
J. Cortes Milord . . . . Bel
J. Cortes Mini . . . . Bel
Jamaica Gold Dutchess . . . . Jam
Jose Benito Chico . . . . Dom
Juan Clemente Demi Tasse . . . . Dom
Justus Van Maurik Classique . . . . Hol
Justus Van Maurik Sumatra Tuitnak***. . . . . Hol
La Favorita Buds. . . . . USA
La Native Super Fino . . . . Hon
La Paz Wilde Corona. . . . . Hol
Muriel Coronella. . . . . PR
Muriel Coronella Pipe Aroma. . . . . PR
Muriel Coronella Sweet. . . . . PR
Muriel Sweet Minis . . . . PR
Nat Sherman Host Selection Hudson . . . . Hon
Nobel Petit Corona. . . . . Den
Ornelas Matinee Lights . . . . Mex
Ornelas Matinee Lights Vanilla . . . . Mex
Partagas Puritos. . . . . Dom
Pedroni Classico. . . . . Swi
Petrus Tabacage 89 Duchess. . . . . Hon
Phillies Mexicali Slim . . . . USA
Pride of Copan No 6 . . . . Hon
Ramon Allones Ramonitos . . . . Dom
Ritmeester Quick. . . . . Hol
Royal Jamaica Pirate . . . . Dom
Suerdieck Cigarillos Palomitas. . . . . Bra
Tampa Nugget Juniors Miniature. . . . . USA
Tampa Nugget Juniors Panetela. . . . . USA
Tarantos . . . . Spa
White Owl Demi-Tip. . . . . USA
Willem II Senoritas . . . . Hol
Zino Jong Cigarillos. . . . . Hol
Zino Par Favor . . . . Bra

CIGARILLOS

Agio Biddies. . . . . Hol
Agio Biddies Light. . . . . Hol
Agio Elegant Rich & Light . . . . Hol
Agio Filter Tip . . . . Hol

Montecristo Mini . . . . Spa
Montecruz Chicos . . . . Dom
Nobel Medium Panetela Sumatra. . . . . Den
Nobel Petit Lights. . . . . Den
Nobel Petit Sumatra . . . . Den
Oscar Oscarito . . . . Dom
Petrus Tabacage 89 Petrushkas. . . . . Hon
Phillies Tip Sweet . . . . USA
Phillies Tips . . . . USA
Plasencia Imperial I . . . . Hon
Pride of Copan No 7 . . . . Hon
Primo Del Rey Cortos . . . . Dom
Private Stock No 9 . . . . Dom
Punch Slim Panetela . . . . Hon
Ritmeester Half Corona. . . . . Hol
Ritmeester Junior . . . . Hol
Ritmeester Livarde. . . . . Hol
Ritmeester Livarde Light. . . . . Hol
Ritmeester Livarde Mini Light . . . . Hol
Ritmeester Pikeur . . . . Hol
Ritmeester Pikeur Mini Light . . . . Hol
Ritmeester Riant . . . . Hol
Ritmeester Royal Dutch Cigarillo . . . . Hol
Ritmeester Royal Dutch Fresh and Mild . . . . Hol
Ritmeester Royal Dutch Half Corona . . . . Hol
Ritmeester Royal Dutch Panatella. . . . . Hol
Ritmeester Senior. . . . . Hol
Ritmeester Tip. . . . . Hol
Ritmeester Whiff . . . . Hol
Rustlers Black 'n' Cherry . . . . USA
Rustlers Menthol . . . . USA
Rustlers Sweets . . . . USA
Santa Clara "1830" VII . . . . Mex
Suerdieck Cigarillos Arpoador. . . . . Bra
Suerdieck Cigarillos Brasillia Petit. . . . . Bra
Suerdieck Cigarillos Copacabana Sumatra . . . . Bra
Suerdieck Cigarillos Nino . . . . Bra
Supre Sweets Cigarillo . . . . USA
Supre Sweets Little Cigars . . . . USA
Supre Sweets Tip Cigarillo . . . . USA
Supre Value Little Cigars Cherry . . . . USA
Supre Value Little Cigars Menthol. . . . . USA
Supre Value Little Cigars Sweet . . . . USA
Supre Value Little Cigars Ultra Mild . . . . USA
Swisher Sweets. . . . . Hol
Swisher Sweets Cigarillo . . . . USA

Swisher Sweets Outlaws . . . . Hon
Swisher Sweets Tip Cigarillo. . . . . USA
Swisher Sweets Wood Tip Cigarillo . . . . USA
Tijuana Smalls Aromantic . . . . USA
Tijuana Smalls Cherry . . . . USA
Tijuana Smalls Regular. . . . . USA
Tiparillo Aromatic . . . . USA
Tiparillo Menthol. . . . . USA
Tiparillo Mild Blend. . . . . USA
Tiparillo Sweet Blend . . . . USA
VSOP Churchill . . . . Hon
Vegafina Delicias . . . . Spa
Vegafina Mini. . . . . Spa
Wallstreet Cigararillo. . . . . Aus
White Owl Coronetta . . . . USA
White Owl Miniatures. . . . . USA
Willem II Half Corona. . . . . Hol
Willem II Indioz . . . . Hol
Willem II Indioz Mini . . . . Hol
Willem II Java . . . . Hol
Willem II Java Mini . . . . Hol
Willem II No 30. . . . . Hol
Willem II Petitos . . . . Hol
Willem II Primo. . . . . Hol
Willem II Sigretto . . . . Hol
Willem II Wee Willem Extra Mild . . . . Hol
Willem II Wee Willem Mild. Hol
Willem II Wings No 105 . . . . Hol
Willem II Wings No 75 . . . . Hol
William Penn Braves. . . . . USA
William Penn Willow Tips . . . . USA
Zino Cigarillos. . . . . Hol
Zino Princesse . . . . Hon

FIGURADOS

Avo Petit Belicoso . . . . Dom
Ballena Suprema San Andres Collection Cordura. . . . Mex
Ballena Suprema San Andres Collection Patron . . . . . Mex
Balmoral Regentes. . . . . Hol
Bering Torpedo . . . . Hon
Bohio Piramides . . . . Dom
Budd Sweet Perfecto . . . . USA
Calle Ocho Pyramide . . . . USA
Calle Ocho Torpedo CI
Cara Mia Pyramide CI
Carbonell Piramide . . . . Dom

Havana Classico Pyramide .... USA
Havana Classico Torpedo .... USA
Havana Reserve Torpedo .... Hon
Havana Sunrise Pyramid .... USA
Havana Sunrise Torpedo .... USA
Honduras Cuban Tobaccos Torpedo .... Hon
Hoyo de Monterrey Culebras .... Hon
Hugo Cassar Diamond Selection Torpedo .... Hon
Hugo Cassar Private Collection Torpedo .... Dom
Indian Head Torpedos .... Hon
Indian Tabac TeePee .... USA
Indian TeePee .... Hon
Jamaica Gold Torpedo .... Jam
Juan Clements Obelisco .... Dom
La Flor Dominicana Belicoso Reserva Especial ...... Dom
La Flor Dominicana Figurado .... Dom
La Gianna Torpedo .... Hon
La Gloria Cubana Piramides .... USA
La Gloria Cubana Torpedo No 1 .... USA
Los Libertadores Belicoso Reserva Especial .... Dom
Los Libertadores Figurado .... Dom
Macabi Belicoso Fino .... USA
Montecristo No 2 Torpedo .... Dom
Montero Torpedo .... Dom
Morro Castle Perfecto .... USA
Morro Castle Torpedo .... USA
Muniemaker Perfecto 100's .... USA
Old Hermitage Golden Perfecto .... USA
Opus X Fuente Perfecxion No 2 .... Dom
P. G. Belicoso .... Dom
P. G. Belicoso Fino .... Dom
Panorea Belicoso .... Dom
Petrus Tabacage 89 Antonius .... Hon
Phillies Perfecto .... USA
Puros Indios Piramide No 1 .... Hon
Red Dot Perfecto .... USA
Roi-Tan Perfectos .... PR
Rolando Blend Pyramid .... USA
Royal Honduras Kings .... Hon
Royal Honduras Princess .... Hon
Santiago Cabana Torpedo .... USA
Siglo 21-3 .... Dom
Sosa Piramides No 2 .... Dom
Special Coronas Pyramides .... Dom
Special Coronas Victoria Obesquio .... Dom
Special Jamaican Nobles (flared) .... Dom

ODD SIZES

Flor de Jalapa Toro . . . . Nic
Flor de Mexico Toro. . . . . Mex
Flor de Nicaragua Duke. . . . . Nic
Flor de Orlando Governor . . . . Dom
Fonseca "Vintage Vitolas" Corona Gorda . . . . Dom
Free Cuba Robusto Largo . . . . USA
Fundadores Ultra . . . . Jam
Gilberto Oliva Viajante. . . . . Hon
Gloria Palmera Toro CI
Goya Reales CI
Grand Nica Lonsdale. . . . . Nic
Grand Nica Toro . . . . Nic
Guaranteed Jamaica No 600 . . . . Jam
H. Upmann Coronas Bravas . . . . Dom
H. Upmann Emperadores . . . . Dom
Havana Classico Robusto Largo. . . . . USA
Havana Sunrise Double Corona. . . . . USA
Havana Sunrise Emperador . . . . USA
Henry Clay Milla Fleurs. Dom
Hoja de Mexicali Toro Natural/Maduro . . . . Mex
Hoja del Regal El Toro. . . . . Hon
Hoja del Regal Viajante . . . . Hon
Honduran Gold Governor . . . . Hon
Honduran Import Maduro Granadas . . . . Hon
Honduras Cuban Matador. . . . . Hon
Honduras Cuban Palma de Mayorca . . . . Hon
House of Windsor Crook . . . . USA
House of Windsor Imperiales. . . . . USA
Hoyo de Monterrey Governor . . . . Hon
Hoyo de Nicaragua Toro . . . . Nic
Hugo Cassar Diamond Selection Double Corona . . . . Hon
Hugo Cassar Diamond Selection Lonsdale . . . . Hon
Hugo Cassar Diamond Selection Toro . . . . Dom
Hugo Cassar Mystique Toro. . . . . Dom
Hugo Cassar Private Collection Toro . . . . Dom
Hugo Cassar Private Collection Toro . . . . Mex
Hugo Cassar Signature Series Toro . . . . Nic
Indian Head Toros. . . . . Hon
Indian Tabac Buffalo . . . . USA
Iracema Mata Fina. . . . . Ger
J. R. Ultimate Corona Tubos . . . . Hon
J. R. Ultimate Padrons . . . . Hon
J. R. Ultimate Super Cetro . . . . Hon
J. R. Ultimate Toro. . . . . Hon
Jamaica Bay No 200. . . . . Jam
Jamaica Gold King. . . . . Jam

Montelimar Toro . . . . Hon
Montero Toro . . . . Dom
Montesino No 3 . . . . Dom
Moreno Maduro No 486 . . . . Dom
Morro Castle Robusto Largo . . . . USA
Nat Cicco's Sabrosos . . . . Dom
Nat Sherman City Desk Telegraph . . . . Dom
Nat Sherman Gotham No 711 . . . . Dom
Nat Sherman Metropolitan University . . . . Dom
National Brand Super Rothschild . . . . Hon
Nestor Vintage 654 . . . . Hon
New York, New York Wall Street . . . . Mex
Nicaragua Especial Matador . . . . Nic
Nording Corona Grande . . . . Hon
Nude Mexican 906 . . . . Mex
Ocho Rios Toros . . . . Jam
Olar Paco . . . . Dom
Onyx No 646 . . . . Dom
Onyx No 650 . . . . Dom
Oro de Cuba El Tigre . . . . Dom
Ortiz Club House . . . . Mex
P. G. Connoisseur . . . . Dom
P & K Guardsman No 3 . . . . Dom
Padron Grand Reserve . . . . Hon
Partagas Aristocrat . . . . Dom
Particulares Matador . . . . Hon
Pedro Iglesias Crowns . . . . Hon
Penamil No 50 CI
Peterson Toro . . . . Dom
Petrus Tabacage 89 No III . . . . Hon
Plasencia Elegante . . . . Hon
Plasencia Toro . . . . Hon
Playboy Double Corona . . . . Dom
Pleiades Neptune . . . . Dom
Pleiades Saturne . . . . Dom
Premium Dominican Selection El Cid . . . . Dom
Premium Dominican Selection Regulares . . . . Dom
Pride of Jamaica Magnum . . . . Jam
Primo del Cristo Churchills . . . . Hon
Primo del Cristo Toros . . . . Hon
Primo del Rey Almirantes . . . . Dom
Pueblo Dominicano Santo Domingo . . . . Dom
Punch Gran Cru Britania . . . . Hon
Punch Pitas . . . . Hon
Puro Nicaragua Toro . . . . Nic
Puros Indios Toro Especial . . . . Hon

Tena Y Vega Double Corona .... Hon
Tesoros de Copan Toros........................ Hon
Thomas Hinds Honduran Short Churchill .... Hon
Thomas Hinds Nicaraguan Short Churchill .... Nic
Topper Centennial Toro .... Dom
Topper Churchill .... Hon
Topper Toro.................................. Hon
Torcedor Toro .... Nic
Torquino Toro .... USA
V Centennial Numero 2........................ Hon
Valdrych Taino............................... Dom
Villazon Deluxe Chairman...................... USA
Vintage Honduran Governor.................... Hon
Vintage Honduran Imperial..................... Hon
Virtuoso Torano Double Corona .... Hon
Vueltabajo Toros .... Dom
Yumuri Toro................................. Dom
Zino Classic Brazil .... Hon
Zino Classic Sumatra .... Hon

*mm means machine-made.
**only available in the U.K.
***cigar should be considered a figurado.

The following figurado shapes inadvertently appear in some
of the previous size indexes:
Avo Belicoso .... Dom
Avo Pyramide .... Dom
Balmoral Cambridge .... Hol
Balmoral Cardinal .... Hol
Balmoral Oxford .... Hol
Balmoral Valentine .... Hol
C.A.O. Triangulare .... Hon
Justus Van Maurik Sumatra Tuitnak .... Hol
La Palma de Oro Piramedes CI
Nat Sherman Metropolitan Explorers .... Dom
Nat Sherman Metropolitan Nautical .... Dom
Padron Serrie de Anniversario Pyramide .... Hon
Ritmeester Gracia .... Hol
Special Jamaican Pyramid .... Dom

World Directory

Star Rating

The author's subjective ratings for cigars take into account the following: appearance; construction; quality of wrapper and color; smoking characteristics and texture of the smoke; flavor and aroma; and over-all impression, including enjoyment of the cigar.

★★★★★	Outstanding. A classic.
★★★★	Excellent.
★★★	Good.
★★	Fair, ordinary.
★	Poor or faulty.
No Star	Not evaluated.

Price Rating

$$$$$	$20+
$$$$	$8–20.00
$$$	$5–8.00
$$	$3–5.00
$	$1–3.00
¢	Under $1.00

Austria

Austria Tabak

This state-owned monopoly makes all cigars and cig-arettes in Austria. It owns or has license agreements with more than 200 brands and produces about 29 million cigars a year. Established in 1784, it is one of Europe's oldest cigar manufacturers, mainly using tobacco imported from Sumatra, Java, and Brazil, with a small quantity from Cuba for cigarillos.

In 1996, plans were put in motion to privatize the group which was estimated to be worth $1.2 billion to $1.5 billion.

Generally, cigarillos are of a particularly good quality.

Most cigars produced by Austria Tabak are machine-made with short filler.

WALLSTREET

Machine-made. Quality, superior. Wrapper from Sumatra. Filler is a blend of tobacco from Cuba, Java and Brazil. Medium- to full-bodied. Launched 1995. Available through most of Europe.

Classic Corona . . . . ★★★★★
150mm/5¹⁵⁄₁₆ ins x 18mm/47. Medium strength, but full flavor. Dusty finish. Good daytime smoke.
Panetela . . . . ★★★★
145mm/5¹¹⁄₁₆ ins x 11.1mm/28. Easy draw. Slow burning. Shows some character.
Cigararillo . . . . ★★★★★
90mm/3½ ins x 9mm/23. Rich, spicy floral aroma. Medium- to full-bodied. Smooth. Good quick smoke.

Belgium

Cigarillos account for about 90 percent of local cigar sales.

CORPS DIPLOMATIQUE

Machine-made.

¢ **Deauville**
¢ **Panetela**
   Wapped in tissue. Sumatra wrapper. Java and Brazilian filler.
¢ **After Dinner 10s**

J. CORTES

Machine-made. All tobacco.

Long Filler No 1 . . . . 140mm/5½ ins x 15.1mm/38
Long Filler No 2 . . . . . . 127mm/5 ins x 15.1mm/38
Club . . . . 114mm/4½ ins x 11.9mm/30
Grand Luxe . . . . 101mm/4 ins x 9.9mm/25
High Class . . . . 127mm/5 ins x 15.1mm/38
Milord . . . . 108mm/4¼ ins x 11.9mm/30
Royal Class . . . . 133mm/5¼ ins x 11.9mm/30
Mini . . . . 89mm/3½ ins x 7.5mm/19

Brazil

Large producer of tobacco used predominantly in

German cigar industry. Most famous is Bahia, north of Brazil. Commercial tobacco industry started by Portuguese who shipped the best quality to Lisbon and used lower grades for exchange of slaves imported from Africa. In 1962, total production peaked at over 400,000 bales, with Germany, Switzerland, Holland, Denmark, France, the United Kingdom and Belgium consuming around 230,000 bales. Present production is about 80,000 bales.

Despite adverse weather conditions in some growing regions, the 1995–1996 crop showed an increase in both quantity and price.

CANONERO

Hand-made. Quality, superior. Launched early 1996. Connecticut Shade wrapper. Brazilian binder and filler. Distributed by Diamente Intl., Kentucky, USA.

> **No 1** . . . . 190mm/7½ ins x 19.84mm/50
> **No 2** . . . . ★★★★
> 140mm/5½ ins x 19.84mm/58. Medium-bodied. Good flavor with hint of spice. Well balanced. Elegant. A daytime smoke.
> **No 3** . . . . ★★★★★
> 127mm/5 ins x 20.6mm/52. Medium-bodied, rich, good balance. Much more character than one expects from a Brazilian cigar. A classy daytime smoke.
> **No 4** . . . . ★★★★★
> 178mm/7 ins x 18.3mm/46. Medium strength and integrated flavors. Elegant. For the connoisseur.
> **No 10** . . . . ★★★★
> 165mm/6½ ins x 16.67mm/42. A bit milder than the thicker ring gauges. Good finish. Elegant, well made. Daytime smoke.
> **No 20** . . . . ★★★★
> 140mm/5½ ins x 16.67mm/42. Well-made. Slow, even burning. Medium-bodied, complex with hint of sweetness. Smooth. An elegant daytime smoke for discerning smoker.
> **Potra** . . . . 108mm/4¼ ins x 15.08mm/38

DON PEPE

Hand-made. All Brazilian tobacco. Made by Suerdieck.

Double Corona . . . . ★★★★
191mm/7½ ins x 19.84mm/50. Unusual silky,
Colorado wrapper for Brazilian cigar. Good draw. Slow
even burning. Mild to medium-bodied. Well-made.
Churchill . . . . 111mm/4⅜ ins x 18.7mm/47
Robusto . . . . 127mm/5 ins x 19.84mm/50
Petit Lonsdale . . . . 153mm/6 ins x 15.9mm/4
Half Corona. . . . . 114mm/4½ ins x 14.3mm/36
Slim Panetela . . . . 133mm/5¼ ins x 11.9mm/30

ELYSEE

Hand-made. Feature is luxury leather-bound boxes of 25.

Elysee No 7-50 . . . . . 190mm/7½ ins x 19.84mm/50
Elysee No 7-46 . . . . . . 178mm/7 ins x 18.26mm/46
Elysee No 6-50 . . . . . . 153mm/6 ins x 19.84mm/50
Elysee No 6-42 . . . . . 153mm/6¾ ins x 16.67mm/42
Elysee No 5-42 . . . . . 146mm/5¾ ins x 16.67mm/42

FIDELIO BUNDLES

Fidelio Bundle No 11
Fidelio Bundle No 22
Finlandia Little Cigars

IRACEMA

$ **Autentico-Fuma** . . . . . 133mm/5¼ ins x 17.5mm/44
$ **Macumba** . . . . 165mm/6½ ins x 16.67mm/42
$ **Matafina Especiale** . . 133mm/5¼ ins x 17.5 mm/44

SUERDIECK

Hand-made. Dark—Brazilian wrapper. Light—Sumatran
wrapper. Not for the connoisseur.

Fiesta. . . . . 152mm/6 ins x 12mm/30
Valencia. . . . . 152mm/6 ins x 12mm/30
Caballero. . . . . 152mm/6 ins x 12mm/30
Mandarim Pai*. . . . . . 127mm/5 ins x 15.08mm/38
Brasilia . . . . 133mm/5¼ ins x 12mm/30
Nips . . . . 152mm/6 ins x 12.7mm/32
Finos . . . . 147mm/5¾ ins x 18.26mm/46
Fiesta. . . . . 160mm/6¼ ins x 12mm/30
Corona Brasil Luxo . 140mm/5½ ins x 17.86mm/45

Corona
Imperial Luxo . . . . . 140mm/5½ ins x 17.86mm/45
Mata Fino Especiale. 133mm/5¼ ins x 16.67mm/42
Panatella Fina . . . . . 136mm/5⅜ ins x 14.29mm/36
Sumatran leaf (light wrapper)

SUERDIECK CIGARILLOS

Machine-made. See also German section. Dark—Brazilian wrapper. Has 10 percent of Brazilian cigar and cigarillo market.

Arpoador . . . . 113mm/4½ ins x 9.3mm/23
Nina . . . . 165mm/6 ins x 8.73mm/22
Palomitas . . . . 89mm/3½ ins x 12.7mm/32
Copacabana Sumatra . 140mm/5 ins x 11.51mm/29
Brasillia Petit . . . . 79mm/3⅛ ins x 8.73mm/22

SUERDIECK PREMIUM CIGARS

Hand-made.

Corona Brasil
Luxo. . . . . 140mm/5½ ins x 17.86mm/45
Corona Imperial
Luxo. . . . . 140mm/5½ ins x 17.86mm/45
Mata Fina Esp. . . . . . . 133mm/5¼ ins x 16.67mm/42
Panatella Fina . . . . . 147mm/5⅜ ins x 14.29mm/36

ZINO

Hand-made.

Zino Santos . . . . 152mm/6½ ins x 13.49mm/34
Zino Par Favor . . . . 102mm/4 ins x 12mm/30

Canary Islands

Main producer is CITA, subsidiary of giant Spanish monopoly, Tabacalera.

ARMENTAR RESERVA

Hand-made. Quality, good. All Canary Islands tobacco. Distributed by Armenter Cigar Holding, New York, USA.

No 7 . . . . 191mm/7½ ins x 19.8mm/50
No 6 . . . . 178mm/7 ins x 18.3mm/46
No 5 . . . . 168mm/6⅝ ins x 16.67mm/42
No 4 . . . . 143mm/5⅝ ins x 16.67mm/42
No 3 . . . . 191mm/7½ ins x 19.8mm/50

CAPOTE

Hand-made. Distribution in USA by Mike's Cigars, Bay Harbour, Florida, USA.

$$$	No 1	178mm/7 ins x 19.8mm/50
$$$	No 2	152mm/6 ins x 19.8mm/50
$$$	No 3	165mm/6½ ins x 17.1mm/43
$$$	No 4	140mm/5½ ins x 15.5mm/39

CARA MIA

Hand-made. Quality, good. Connecticut Shade wrapper. All Canary Island tobacco. Distributed by Metaco, New York, USA.

Pyramide	179mm/7 ins x 20.6mm/52
Churchill	179mm/7 ins x 19.8mm/50
Toro	152mm/6 ins x 19.8mm/50
Lonsdale	165mm/6½ ins x 16.67mm/42
Corona	140mm/5½ ins x 16.67mm/42

CASANOVA

Hand-made. Connecticut wrapper. Brazilian binder. Filler, blend of tobacco from Caribbean. International distribution by Distabacasa, Distribuidora de Tabaccos Canarios, Las Palmas, Canary Islands.

Churchill	178mm/7 ins x 19.1mm/48
Sublime	165mm/6½ ins x 17.5mm/44
Superfino	165mm/6½ ins x 16.67mm/42
Consul	140mm/5½ ins x 19.1mm/48

CONDAL

Hand-made.

No 1	168mm/6⅝ ins x 16.67mm/42
No 3	143mm/5⅝ ins x 16.67mm/42
No 4	132mm/5¼ ins x 16.67mm/42
No 6	160mm/6¼ ins x 13.89mm/35
Inmenso	184mm/7¼ ins x 16.67mm/42

DON PISHU

Hand-made. Connecticut wrapper.

Macintosch	178mm/7 ins x 19.84mm/50
Tenerife	171mm/6¾ ins x 19.1mm/48
Hierro	165mm/6½ ins x 19.84mm/50
Rare	152mm/6 ins x 19.1mm/48
Canary Island	146mm/5¾ ins x 19.1mm/48
Lanzarote	165mm/6½ ins x 18.3mm/46

	Tu y Yo	127mm/5 ins x 19.84mm/50
	Gomera	165mm/6½ ins x 16.67mm/42
	Fuerte Ventura	140mm/5½ ins x 18.3mm/46

DON XAVIER

Hand-made. Imported into USA by Marcas Miguel Tobacco, Dallas, Texas.

$$$	**Panetela**	191mm/7½ ins x 15.5mm/39
$$$	**Petit Panetela**	143mm/5⅝ ins x 15.5mm/39
$$$	**Lonsdale**	168mm/6⅝ ins x 16.67mm/42
$$$	**Petit Lonsdale**	143mm/5⅝ ins x 16.67mm/42
$$$	**Corona**	178mm/7 ins x 18.3mm/46
$$$	**Gran Corona**	168mm/5⅝ ins x 18.3mm/46
$$$	**Churchill**	191mm/7½ ins x 19.84mm/50
$$$	**Robusto**	118mm/4⅝ ins x 19.84mm/50
$$$	**Pyramid**	178mm/7 ins x 20.6mm/52

DUNHILL

Hand-made. Long filler. Connecticut wrapper. Black and white band.

	Lonsdale Grande	190mm/7½ ins x 16.67mm/42
	Corona Grande	165mm/6½ ins x 16.67mm/42
	Corona Extra	145mm/5¹¹⁄₁₆ ins x 19.84mm/50
$	**Panetela**	155mm/8⅛ ins x 12mm/30
$	**Corona**	140mm/5½ ins x 16.67mm/40

DUNHILL CANARY ISLANDS CIGARS

Hand-made. Cameroon wrapper. Canary Islands filler and binder. Distributed in USA by Lane Ltd.

$	**Coronas**	140mm/5½ ins x 17.07mm/43
$$	**Coronas Extra**	140mm/5½ ins x 19.84mm/50
$$	**Coronas Grandes**	★★★ 165mm/6½ ins x 17.07mm/43. Good draw. Well made. Slow, even burning. Light- to medium-bodied. One dimensional. Ideal for beginner or early morning smoke for experienced smoker.
$$	**Lonsdale Grandes**	190mm/7½ ins x 16.67mm/42
$	**Panetelas**	152mm/6 ins x 12mm/30

GLORIA PALMERA

Hand-made. Quality, superior. Connecticut Shade wrapper. Filler is a blend of tobacco from Brazil, Canary Islands and Dominican Republic. Distributed by Compania de Tabacos Del Mediterranea, Madrid, Spain.

$$$$	**Double Corona**	. . . . . 191mm/7½ ins x 19.8mm/50
$$$$	**Toro**	. . . . 152mm/6 ins x 19.8mm/50
$$$	**Robusto**	. . . . 127mm/5 ins x 19.8mm/50
$$$	**Lonsdale**	. . . . 165mm/6½ ins x 17.1mm/43

GOYA

Hand-made. Quality, good. Made by CITA, Tobacos de Canarias. Distributed in USA by Mike's Cigars, Bay Harbour, Florida, USA.

$$$	**Gran Corona**	. . . . 184mm/7¼ ins x 19.8mm/50
$$$	**Reales**	. . . . 152mm/6 ins x 19.8mm/50
$$$	**Cetro**	. . . . 168mm/6⅝ ins 17.1mm/43
$$$	**Corona**	. . . . 140mm/5½ ins x 17.1mm/43

LA FAMA

Hand-made. Quality, superior. Made by CITA, Tabacos de Canarias.

Fama Platas	. . . . 165mm/6½ ins x 16.3mm/41
Gran Fama	. . . . 165mm/6½ ins x 16.3mm/41
Fama Coronas	. . . . . . 130mm/5⅛ ins x 15.9mm/40

LA FAVORITA

Hand-made. Quality, superior. Connecticut Shade wrapper. Filler is a blend of tobacco from Brazil, Canary Islands and Dominican Republic. Distributed in USA by Arango Cigar.

$$$$	**Double Corona**	. . . . . 191mm/7½ ins x 19.8mm/50
$$$$	**Toro**	. . . . 152mm/6 ins x 19.8mm/50
$$$	**Robusto**	. . . . 121mm/4¾ ins x 19.8mm/50
$$$	**Lonsdale**	. . . . 165mm/6½ ins x 17.1mm/43

LA PALMA DE ORO

Hand-made. Distributed in USA by Cuban Cigar Factory, San Diego, California.

Double Corona	. . . . . 171mm/6¾ ins x 19.8mm/50
Robusto	. . . . 127mm/5 ins x 19.8mm/50
Don Ricardo	. . . . 171mm/6¾ ins x 18.3mm/46
Cafe	. . . . 140mm/5½ ins x 17.5mm/44
Don Jorge	. . . . 159mm/6¼ ins x 19.8mm/50
Superior	. . . . 191mm/7½ ins x 21.4mm/54
Piramedes	. . . . 171mm/6¾ ins x 20.6mm/52

¢ – Under $1.00 $ – $1–3.00 $$ – $3–4.00
$$$ – $5–8.00 $$$$ – $8–20.00 $$$$$ – $20+

LA REGENTA

Hand-made. Long filler. Connecticut Shade wrappers.

       Emperador. . . . . . . 190mm/7½ ins x 20.64mm/52
       Gran Corona . . . . . . 184mm/7¼ ins x 18.26mm/46
       Findos. . . . . 178mm/7 ins x 14.29mm/36
       Premier . . . . 178mm/7 ins x 16.67mm/42
       No 1. . . . . 165mm/6½ ins x 16.67mm/42
       No 2. . . . . 165mm/6½ ins x 18.26mm/46
       No 3. . . . . 140mm/5½ ins x 16.67mm/42
       No 4. . . . . 130mm/5⅛ ins x 16.67mm/42
       Olimpicas. . . . . 155mm/6⅛ ins x 14.29mm/36
       Elegantes . . . . 152mm/6 ins x 11.51mm/29
       Rothschild . . . . 113mm/4½ ins x 19.84mm/50

MONTE CANARIO

Hand-made. Imported into USA by Marcas Miguel Tobacco, Dallas, Texas.

$$$ **Nuncios** . . . . 171mm/6¾ ins x 17.5mm/44
$$$ **Imperiales** . . . . 165mm/6½ ins x 16.67mm/42
$$$ **No 3** . . . . 146mm/5¾ ins x 16.67mm/42
$$$ **Panetelas** . . . . 152mm/6 ins x 15.1mm/38

OH QUE BUENO

Hand-made. Connecticut wrapper. Indonesian binder. Filler, blend of tobacco from Dominican Republic and Brazil.

       No 1 . . . . 178mm/7 ins x 16.3mm/41
       Corona. . . . . 133mm/5¼ ins x 16.3mm/41

PENAMIL

Hand-made. Cameroon wrapper. Dominican binder. Filler blend from Dominican Republic, Mexico and Brazil. Distributed in USA by Swisher Intl.

$$ **No 5**. . . . . 143mm/5⅛ ins x 16.27mm/41
$$ **No 6**. . . . . 149mm/5⅞ ins x 16.27mm/41
$$ **No 16** . . . . 181mm/7⅛ ins x 152mm/38
$$ **No 17**. . . . . 169mm/6⅔ ins x 16.27mm/41
$$ **No 18**. . . . . 181mm/7⅛ ins x 17.46mm/44
$$ **No 25**. . . . . 190mm/7½ ins x 17.86mm/45
$$$ **No 30**. . . . . 195mm/7⅔ ins x 17.86mm/45
$$ **No 50**. . . . . 153mm/6 ins x 19.84mm/50
$$$ **No 57**. . . . . 190mm/7½ ins x 19.84mm/50

PROFESOR SILA

Hand-made. Quality, superior. Cuban seed, Canary Island filler and binder. Connecticut Shade wrapper. Generally, mild and aromatic. Distributed by Las Palmas Tobacco Co., Fairfax, Virginia, USA.

$$$	**Majestad**	203mm/8 ins x 19.8mm/50
$$$	**Excelencia**	165mm/6½ ins x 17.9mm/45
$$$	**Presidente**	137mm/5⅜ ins x 17.9mm/45
$$$	**Robusto**	118mm/4⅝ ins x 19.8mm/50
$$$	**Principe**	185mm/7⁹⁄₁₆ ins x 15.1mm/38

VARGAS

Hand-made. Quality, good. All Canary Island tobacco. Distributed by Marcos Miguel Tobacco Corp., Dallas, Texas, USA.

Churchill	191mm/7½ ins x 19.8mm/50
Presidentes	171mm/6¾ ins x 18.3mm/46
Senadores	140mm/5½ ins x 18.3mm/46
Capitolios	130mm/5⅛ ins x 17.5mm/44
Robustos	121mm/4¾ ins x 19.8mm/50
Diplomaticos	140mm/5½ ins x 14.3mm/36

Costa Rica

BAHIA

Hand-made. Quality, superior. Ecuadorian wrapper. Nicaraguan binder and filler, aged for five years. Cigars also aged for several months after rolling. 1989 vintage rolled in June 1996, released in February 1997. Production 490,000. Distributed in USA by Tony Borhani Cigars, La Jolla, California, who specialize in setting up humidors in wine trade.

$$$$	**Double Corona**	203mm/8 ins x 19.8mm/50
$$$	**Churchill**	175mm/6⅞ ins x 19.1mm/48
$$$	**Esplendido**	152mm/6 ins x 19.8mm/50
$$$	**Robusto**	★★★★

127mm/5 ins x 19.8mm/50. Mild to medium-bodied. Good flavors with a hint of sweetness. Good balance and finish. To follow meal. For discerning smoker.

$$	**No III**	152mm/6 ins x 18.3mm/46

$$ **No IV** . . . . ★★★★★
140mm/5½ ins x 16.67mm/42. Firm draw. Flavor
develops. Spicy with creamy finish. Smooth.
Daytime smoke. For connoisseur.

FLORENTINO

Hand-made. Distributed in USA by Arango Cigar.

Viajante	. . . .	209mm/8¼ ins x 19.84mm/50
Churchill	. . . .	178mm/7 ins x 19.05mm/48
No 1	. . . .	178mm/7 ins x 17.46mm/44
No 2	. . . .	152mm/6 ins x 17.46mm/44
Toro	. . . .	152mm/6 ins x 19.84mm/50
Presidente	. . . .	190mm/7½ ins x 19.84mm/50

PINTOR

Viajante
Churchill
No 1
No 2
No 4
No 5
No 6

Denmark

Denmark is the largest consumer of cigars per capita
in the world.

CHRISTIAN OF DENMARK

Machine-made. Dry cigars. Dominican, Java and Brazil filler.
Java binder and Sumatran wrapper.

¢ **Mini Cigarillos** . . . . ★★★★
89mm/3½ ins. Smooth. Plenty of flavor. Well-made
cigarillo.
¢ **Long Cigarillos** . . . . 102mm/4 ins
¢ **Midi** . . . . 95mm/3¾ ins

DAVIDOFF CIGARILLOS

Machine-made. Superior quality. All tobacco.

¢ **Davidoff Mini Cigarillos** . . . . ★★★★
88mm/3½ ins. Rich, smooth, elegant.
¢ **Davidoff Mini Light** . . . . ★★★★
88mm/3½ ins. Mild, good flavor, smooth, elegant.
¢ **Davidoff Long Cigarillos** . . . . 114mm/4½ ins

NOBEL CIGARS

Largest cigar maker in Europe. Launched in 1898. Sold 400 million cigars (all brands) in 1990–91. Machine-made. (Dry cigars.)

- ¢ **Petit Sumatra** . . . . ★★★★
  89mm/3½ ins. Rich, full flavored, smooth. Elegant.
- ¢ **Medium Panetela Sumatra**
  89mm/3½ ins x 8.73mm/22
- ¢ **Grand Panetela Sumatra**
  140mm/5½ ins x 11.11mm/28
- ¢ **Petit Corona** . . . . 95mm/3¾ ins x 12.7mm/32
- ¢ **Petit Lights** . . . . 89mm/3½ ins

Dominican Republic

The Dominican Republic has become the largest seller of premium cigars to the United States, exporting in 1996 around 138.6 million cigars. The figure for the first six months of 1997 was 113 million.

After Fidel Castro came to power in Cuba in 1959, later expropriating businesses, many previous owners fled, with little or no possessions except Cuban seed tobacco, to various countries which they thought had similar soil and climatic conditions to those of Cuba. Such countries included Honduras, Nicaragua, Dominican Republic, Jamaica and even the Canary Islands.

In the 1960s and 1970s, there was little development in the Dominican cigar industry, until in 1976, the American company General Cigar established a leaf processing facility for all types of leaves, particularly wrappers. The Dominican Republic previously exported about 5 million cigars to the United States. When General Cigar became a fully fledged cigar manufacturing operation in 1979, these exports rose to 11 million.

Between 1979 and 1981, the other American giant, Consolidated Cigar, moved its activities from the Canary Islands to La Romana on the Dominican Republic's southeast coast, and sales to the United States then exploded to 33 million cigars.

During this period the country changed from a tobacco processor to a producer of premium, hand-rolled cigars and started to gain a reputation as important supplier of quality hand-made products.

In 1995, the Dominican Republic exported almost 83 million cigars to the United States, this accounting for an estimated 43 percent of imports into the U.S. of premium cigars. The main tobacco growing area is Cibao River Valley, close to the capital of Santiago. Another important tobacco growing area is Real Valley. The island's tropical climate, predominantly hot days and high humidity, as well as its fertile soil, is ideal for growing tobacco.

Despite the Dominican Republic's importance as a producer of filler and binder tobacco leaf, the country continues to import such leaf from Cameroon and Nicaragua while leaf for wrappers is bought from Cameroon, Connecticut in the United States, Ecuador and Mexico. In the 1980s, unsuccessful attempts were made to grow wrappers from Connecticut wrapper seed. However, in 1992, Carlos Fuente Jr., son of legendary Carlos Fuente Sr., started growing good quality shade wrapper from Cuban seed.

In Cuba, the *torcedor*, or cigar roller, combines the different leaves to form the filler, before rolling it in a binder and then applying the delicate wrapper.

In the Dominican Republic, workers, called bunchers, roll the binder around the filler to create the bunch for the *torcedor* to apply the wrapper and thereby finish the cigar. In some factories, a team consists of three rollers to two bunchers. At Consolidated Cigar, factory teams comprise six rollers and four bunchers.

Strict quality control is employed in most Dominican factories. Many smokers do not believe any non-Cuban cigar can compete with Havanas. There is certainly a difference in taste, with Dominicans being, generally, milder than Havanas. However, the local industry is striving to improve the tobacco it uses by experimenting with different combinations of imported leaf to provide the best flavor.

As mentioned under "Strength of Different Tobacco" in the chapter on "Smoking for Pleasure," tobacco from the Dominican Republic could be described as smooth, honeyed, earthy, floral and spicy flavored, mild and slow burning. It is popular in the U.S. and probably rates in strength, on a scale from one to five, as a two or three.

Main producers are: Tabacalera Arturo Fuente, making about 28 million cigars annually (Arturo Fuente, Ashton, Cuesta Rey, Don Carlos, Hemingway, Opus, La Unica); Consolidated Cigars, about 35 million (Don Diego, Flamenco, Henry Clay, H. Upmann, La Corona, Nat Sherman, Primo Del Rey, Santa Damiana); General Cigar, about 16 million (Canaria D'Oro, Macanudo Partagas, Temple Hall, Ramon Allones; MATASA, about 6.5 million (Jose Benito, JR, Romeo & Julieta); Tabacos Dominicanos, about nine million (Avo, Davidoff, Griffin's, PG, Troya). The brands shown are those owned by the respective producers as well as private labels and is not exhaustive.

ABREU ANILLO DE ORO

Hand-made. Quality, superior. Connecticut Shade wrapper. Dominican filler and binder. Distributed by Mike's Cigars, Bay Harbour, Florida.

$$	**Presidente**	203mm/8 ins x 19.8mm/50
$$	**Churchill**	165mm/6½ ins x 18.3mm/46
$$	**Torito**	127mm/5 ins x 19.8mm/50
$$	**Corona**	178mm/7 ins x 17.5mm/44
$	**Especiales**	127mm/5 ins x 10.3mm/26
$$	**Panetela**	191mm/7½ x 15.1mm/38

ADANTE

Hand-made. Short filler. Mexican wrapper. Binder and filler from Dominican Republic. Mild. Distributed in USA by Lignun-2 Inc.

$$	**No 405 Petit Corona**	113mm/4½ ins x 16.67mm/42
$$	**No 504 Corona**	140mm/5½ ins x 16.67mm/42
$$	**No 603 Palma Fina**	160mm/6¼ ins x 13.49mm/34
$$	**No 702 Cetro**	152mm/6 ins x 16.67mm/42
$$	**No 801 Elegante**	168mm/6⅜ ins x 17.07mm/43

AGUILA

Hand-made. Connecticut Shade wrapper. Dominican binder and filler. Distributed in USA by F&K Cigar.

Coronita. . . . . 140mm/5½ ins x 15.87mm/40
Brevas 44 . . . . 190mm/7½ ins x 17.46mm/44
Brevas 46 . . . . ★★★★
165mm/6½ ins x 18.26mm/46. Good, consistent construction. Cool. Slow, even burning. Light-bodied. Touch of sweetness. Value for money.
Brevas 49 . . . . 178mm/7 ins x 19.84mm/50
Brevas 50 . . . . 190mm/7½ ins x 19.84mm/50
Petit Gordo . . . . ★★★★
120mm/4¾ ins x 19.84mm/50. Well-made. Good draw, slow, even burning. Flavorful. Not for the beginner.

ANDUJAR

Hand-made. Connecticut Shade wrapper. Dominican binder and filler.

Samana. . . . . 152mm/6 ins x 15.08mm/38
Vega . . . . 127mm/5 ins x 19.84mm/50
Azuo . . . . 228mm/9 ins x 18.26mm/46
Macorix . . . . 165mm/6½ ins x 17.46mm/44
Romana . . . . 127mm/5 ins x 9.92mm/25
Santiago . . . . 190mm/7½ ins x 19.84mm/50

ARTURO FUENTE

Hand-made. Cameroon wrapper. Quality, superior. Binder and filler from Dominican Republic, Brazil, Mexico and Nicaragua. There is also a range of machine cigars made in Tampa, Florida. Medium- to full-flavored. Good value. Old established tobacco family which, since 1900, has owned factories in Tampa, Honduras and Nicaragua and now for the past 15 years in the Dominican Republic.

While I was in the United States, the industry was full of news of destruction by fire of one of family's tobacco warehouses, the sixth fire in their history. Third factory planned to open in 1995. In 1995 had 85 acres under cultivation, with option to buy another 25-acre farm. In 1994 sold over 10 million cigars across Arturo Fuente range. Same year family exported over 24 million cigars spread over seven brands.

Sold about 10 million Arturo Fuente cigars in 1994. Price range $1-95 to $3+. Late 1995, early 1996 plan to introduce series with Conecticut shade wrapper. Distributed in U.S. by

FANCO, a joint venture between Fuente family and Newman family's M&N, whose main brand is Cuesta Rey.

One of few manufacturers who use as many as four different types of tobacco in their filler blends. Each cigar model has a different blend.

$$$$ **Hemingway Masterpiece** . . . . ★★★★★
228mm/9 ins x 20.64mm/52. Figurado shape. Dark oily wrapper. Full-bodied. Spicy with coffee undertones. Rich. Cigar for special occasion.

$$$ **Hemingway Classic** . . . . ★★★★
178mm/7 ins x 19.05mm/48. Figurado shape. Medium-bodied. Good balance between strength and flavor. Good daytime smoke. For connoisseur and novice alike.

$$$ **Hemingway Signature** . . . . ★★★★★
152mm/6 ins x 18.65mm/47. Figurado shape. Dark oily wrapper. Smooth. Spicy with leathery undertones. Wonderful smoke.

$$ **Hemingway Short Story** . . . . ★★★★★
102mm/4 ins x 17.86mm/45. Figurado shape. Medium- to full-bodied. Rich. Spicy, coffee flavors. Well-made. Hedonistic delight.

$$ **Chateau Fuente Royal Salute**
193mm/7 ⅝ ins x 21.43mm/54

$ **Canones** . . . . 216mm/8½ ins x 20.64mm/52

$ **Double Chateau Fuente** . . . . ★★★★★
172mm/6¾ ins x 19.84mm/50. Medium- to full-bodied. Spicy. Cool. Good balance cigar for connoisseur. Well-made. After dinner smoke.

$ **Dantes** . . . . ★★★★★
178mm/7 ins x 19.84mm/50. Dark oily wrapper. Packs plenty of punch and flavor. Long finish. Ideal after-dinner cigar.

$ **Churchill** . . . . ★★★★
184mm/7¼ ins x 19.05mm/48. Rich, full flavor. Medium-bodied. Spicy with touch of coffee. Good after-lunch cigar.

$ **Corona Imperial** . . . . ★★★★
165mm/6½ ins x 19.05mm/46. Slightly hard draw. Good burning qualities. Medium strength. Integrated herbaceous aromas. Well-made.

$ **Flor Fina 8-5-8** . . . . ★★★★
152mm/6 ins x 18.65mm/47. Subtle aroma. Spicy. Touch of sweetness. Mild. Dry finish. Good burning. Well-made.

$ **Chateau Fuente** . . . . ★★★★
113mm/4½ ins x 19.84mm/50. Woody. Spicy.
Elegant. Good daytime smoke.

$ **Cuban Corona** . . . . . 133mm/5¼ ins x 17.86mm/45

$ **Seleccion Privada No 1**
172mm/6¾ ins x 17.46mm/44

Don Carlos Robusto . . . . ★★★★★
127mm/5 ins x 19.84mm/50. Dark oily wrapper.
Full-bodied. Rich, spicy. Well-made. Delight to
smoke after dinner.

$ **Rothschild** . . . . 113mm/4½ ins x 19.84mm/50

$ **Panetela Fina** . . . . ★★★★
178mm/7 ins x 15.08mm/38. Medium-bodied.
Good balance and finish. Daytime smoke.

$ **Spanish Lonsdale** . . . . ★★★★★
165mm/6½ ins x 16.67mm/42. Dark oily wrapper.
Rich. Smooth. Firm draw. Herbaceous, spicy flavors.
Well-made.

$ **Petit Corona** . . . . ★★★★
127mm/5 ins x 15.08mm/38. Firm draw. Good
burning. Smooth. Hint of sweetness. Well-made.
Daytime smoke.

$ **Fumas** . . . . ★★★★
178mm/7 ins x 17.46mm/44. Medium strength.
Full flavors. Slightly spicy. Extra girth improves
draw.

¢ **Curley Head Deluxe** 165mm/6½ ins x 17.07mm/43

¢ **Curley Head** . . . . . . 165mm/6½ ins x 17.07mm/43

Don Carlos No 3 . . . . ★★★★
140mm/5 1/2 ins x 17.46mm/44. Dark oily wrap-
per. Medium- to full-bodied. Smooth. Good daytime smoke.

¢ **Brevas Royale** . . . . ★★★★
140mm/5½ ins x 16.67mm/42. Well-made. Smooth.
Spicy. Good daytime smoke.

ASHTON

Hand-made. Quality, superior. Connecticut Shade wrapper.
Cuban seed, Dominican binder and fillers. Mild and aromatic.
Launched in 1985. Owned by Ashton Products.

$$$ **Churchill** . . . . 190mm/7½ ins x 20.64mm/52

$$$ **Prime Minister** . . . . . 175mm/6⅞ ins x 19.05mm/48

| $$$ | 8-9-8 | .... ★★★★ |

165mm/6½ ins x 17.46mm/44. Well-made. Good draw. Slow, even burning. Medium to strong, with rich flavor and touch of sweetness. Smooth, good finish. A daytime smoke for beginners and experienced smokers alike. Good value.

$$	**Panetela**	. . . . 127mm/6 ins x 14.29mm/36
$$	**Corona**	. . . . 140mm/5½ ins x 17.46mm/44
$$	**Cordial**	. . . . 127mm/5 ins x 12mm/30
$$$	**Magnum**	. . . . 127mm/5 ins x 19.84mm/50
$$	**Elegante**	. . . . 165mm/6½ ins x 35

ASHTON AGED MADURO

Hand-made.

$$$	**No 60**	. . . . 190mm/7½ ins x 20.64mm/52
$$$	**No 50**	. . . . 178mm/7 ins x 19.05mm/48
$$$	**No 40**	. . . . 152mm/6 ins x 19.84mm/50
$$$	**No 30**	. . . . 172mm/6¾ ins x 17.46mm/44
$$$	**No 20**	. . . . 140mm/5½ ins x 17.46mm/44

ASHTON CABINET SELECTION
(VINTAGE LIMITED EDITION)

Hand-made. Selected Connecticut Shade wrapper. Aged for one year. All are shaped cigars featuring a rounded head and Perfecto-style foot. Among best of vintage cigars. Introduced in 1988.

Cabinet

$$$$	**No 1**	. . . . 228mm/9 ins x 20.64mm/52
$$$$	**No 2**	. . . . 178mm/7 ins x 18.26mm/46
$$$$	**No 3**	. . . . 152mm/6 ins x 18.26mm/46
$$$	**No 6**	. . . . 140mm/5½ ins x 18.26mm/46
$$$$	**No 7**	. . . . 159mm/6¼ ins x 20.64 mm/52
$$$$	**No 8**	. . . . 198mm/7 ins x 19.5mm/49
$$$$	**No 10**	. . . . 190mm/7½ ins x 20.64mm/52

ASHTON EUROPE CIGARS

	Petit	. . . . 79mm/3⅛ ins cigarillo
	Coronita	. . . . 82mm/3¼ ins x 12mm/30
	Senorita	. . . . 89mm/3½ ins x 12mm/30
	Dutch Corona	. . . . . 111mm/4⅜ ins x 13.89mm/35
	Royal	. . . . 147mm/5¾ ins x 16.67mm/42

AVO

Hand-made. Quality, superior. Connecticut Shade wrapper. Cuban seed binder. Filler is blend of four tobaccos. Elegant pale pink, gold, black and white band. Made by Tabacos Dominicanos.

These cigars were created by a renowned musician Avo Uvezian. While a young man, was official pianist to the late Shah of Iran. Imported and distributed exclusively internationally by Davidoff of Geneva. Sold over 1.4 million cigars in 1995.

$$$$ **Avo No 1** . . . . ★★★★
172mm/6¾ ins x 16.67mm/42. A good example of lonsdale shape. Ideal to follow a meal.

$$$$ **Avo No 2** . . . . ★★★★
152mm/6 ins x 19.84mm/50. Well-made. Good flavor. Long finish. Daytime smoke.

$$$ **Avo No 3** . . . . ★★★★
190mm/7½ ins x 20.64mm/52. Good wrapper. Spicy with dusty finish.

$$$ **Avo No 4**. . . . . ★★★
198mm/7 ins x 15.08mm/38. Hard draw, difficult burning qualities. Harsh finish.

$$$ **Avo No 5** . . . . 172mm/6¾ ins x 18.26mm/46

$$$ **Avo No 6** . . . . 165mm/6½ ins x 14.29mm/36

$$$ **Avo No 7** . . . . 152mm/6 ins x 17.46mm/44

$$$ **Avo No 8** . . . . 133mm/5½ ins x 15.87mm/40

$$$ **Avo No 9** . . . . 120mm/4¾ ins x 19.05mm/48

$$$$ **Especiales**. . . . . 223mm/8 ins x 19.05mm/48

$$$$ **Pyramide** . . . . ★★★★
178mm/7 ins x 21.43mm/54. Well-made. Spicy, leathery flavors. Medium-bodied. Satisfying. A cigar for special occasion.

$$$$ **Belicoso** . . . . 152mm/6 ins x 19.84mm/50

$$$$ **Petit Belicoso**. . . . . . 120mm/4¾ ins x 19.84mm/50

AVO "XO"

Hand-made. Quality, superior. Connecticut Shade wrapper. Cuban seed binder. Filler is blend of four tobaccos. Elegant peach, gold, black and white band. Imported and distributed exclusively internationally by Davidoff of Geneva.

        Maestoso . . . . ★★★★
178mm/7 ins x 19.05mm/48. Medium-bodied. Smooth. Spicy, leathery. Daytime smoke or to follow light lunch.

Fantasia . . . . ★★★★
152mm/6 ins x 20.64mm/52. Full-bodied. Spicy
earthy flavors. Well-made. Cigar for special occasion.
Preludio . . . . ★★★★★
152mm/6 ins x 15.87mm/40. Full-bodied. Good
balance between strength and flavor. Integrated.
Spicy, herbaceous aroma. Good daytime cigar or to
follow meal. Cigar for the connoisseur.
Notturno . . . . 152mm/6 ins x 17.46mm/44
Intermezzo . . . . ★★★★★
140mm/5½ ins x 19.84mm/50. Beautifully made with
oily wrapper. Smooth. Medium-bodied with attractive
integrated flavors. A cigar to be appreciated.
Allegro . . . . 127mm/5 ins x 15.08mm/38
Serenata. . . . . 114mm/4½ ins x 13.5mm/34

BAUZA

Hand-made. Quality, superior. Made by Tabacalera A Fuente.
Owned by Mike's Cigars, Miami, Florida, USA. Named after
Cuban-born owner, Oscar Boruchin. Cameroon wrappers.
Mexican binder. Medium-bodied. Premium-priced.

\$\$ **Fabulosos**. . . . . 190mm/7½ ins x 19.84mm/50
\$ **Grecos**. . . . . ★★★★★
           140mm/5½ ins x 16.67mm/42. Dark brown, oily
           wrapper. Good flavor. Smooth. Cigar for connois-
           seur.
\$\$ **Jaguar** . . . . ★★★★★
           165mm/6½ ins x 16.67mm/42. Medium- to
           full-bodied. Rich, spicy.
\$\$ **Casa Grande** . . . . ★★★★★
           172mm/6½ ins x 19.05mm/48. Full flavors. Hint of
           coffee. Good finish.
\$ **Florete** . . . . ★★★
           175mm/6⅞ ins x 13.89mm/35. Hard to draw.
           Touch of spice on palate. Slightly harsh burn.
\$ **Petit Corona**. . . . . . . 127mm/5 ins x 15.08mm/38
\$\$ **Robusto**. . . . . ★★★★★
           140mm/5½ ins x 19.84mm/50. Beautiful natural
           maduro. Oily, smooth wrapper. Lots of flavor.
           Touch of cinnamon. More flavor than normally
           associated with Dominican Republic. New style.
\$\$ **Presidente** . . . . 190mm/7½ ins x 19.84mm/50
\$\$ **Medalla d'Oro No 1**. . 175mm/6⅞ ins x 17.46mm/44

BOHIO

Hand-made. Quality, superior. Connecticut Shade wrapper. Dominican binder and filler. Distributed by T&R Tobacco Sales Co., St. Albans, New York, USA.

Presidente . . . . 191mm/7½ ins x 19.8mm/50
Churchill . . . . 178mm/7 ins x 18.3mm/46
Corona . . . . 152mm/6 ins x 17.5mm/44
Petit Corona. . . . . . 140mm/5½ ins x 16.67mm/42
Robusto . . . . 127mm/5 ins x 19.8mm/50
Piramides . . . . 152mm/6 ins x 20.6mm/52

BUTERA ROYAL VINTAGE

Hand-made. Connecticut Shade wrapper. Dominican binder and filler. Owned by Butera Pipe Co.

$$$ **Bravo Corto** . . . . 114mm/4½ ins x 19.8mm/50
$$$ **Cedro Fino** . . . . ★★★★
165mm/6½ ins x 17.46mm/44. The finely made cap adds to an already excellently made cigar. The flavor does not match the construction. Short finish. Good morning cigar to start the day.
$$$ **Dorado 652** . . . . ★★★★★
152mm/6 ins x 20.64mm/52. Good, consistent construction. Good draw. Even burn. Smooth. Complex, full flavored. Long finish. For the connoisseur.
$$$$ **Capo Grande** . . . . 190mm/7½ ins x 19.1mm/48
$$$ **Fumo Dolce** . . . . 140mm/5½ ins x 17.5mm/44
$$$ **Mira Bella** . . . . 171mm/6¾ ins x 15.1mm/38

CABALLEROS

Hand-made. Quality, superior. Connecticut Shade wrapper. Dominican filler and binder. Distributed by Metaco, New York, USA.

$$ **Churchill** . . . . ★★★★
178mm/7 ins x 19.8mm/50. Spicy. Creamy finish. Good draw. Medium- to full-bodied. For discerning smoker.
$$ **Double Corona** . . . . . 171mm/6¾ ins x 19.1mm/48
$$ **Rothchild** . . . . ★★★★
127mm/5 ins x 19.8mm/50. Well-made. Medium-bodied. Spicy.
$$ **Corona** . . . . ★★★★
146mm/5¾ ins x 17.1mm/43. Good draw. Well-made. Mild to medium-bodied. Daytime smoke. Ideal for beginners.
$$ **Petit Corona**. . . . . . 140mm/5½ ins x 16.67mm/42

CABANAS

Hand-made by Consolidated Cigar. Connecticut Shade wrapper. Binder and filler from Domincan Republic. Good value.

$$	**Exquisitos**	165mm/6½ ins x 19.05mm/48
$	**Corona Grande**	152mm/6 ins x 19.05mm/48
$	**Premier**	168mm/6⅜ ins x 16.67mm/42
$	**Lonsdale**	168mm/6⅜ ins x 16.67mm/42
$	**Corona**	140mm/5½ ins x 16.67mm/42
$	**Royale**	★★★★

143mm/5⅝ ins x 18.26mm/46. Medium-bodied. Earthy. Lacks subtlety.

CACIQUE

Hand-made. Available with Connecticut and Cameroon wrappers. Owned by Tropical Tobacco. Good value.

$	**Jaraqua**	172mm/6¾ ins x 14.29mm/36
$	**Tainos**	152mm/6 ins x 16.67mm/42
$	**Siboneyes**	172mm/6¾ ins x 17.07mm/43
$$	**Caribes**	175mm/6⅞ ins x 18.26mm/46
$$	**Incas**	178mm/7½ ins x 20.64mm/50
$	**Azteca**	120mm/4¾ ins x 20.64mm/50

Available in maduro wrapper only.

$	**Apache**	152mm/6 ins x 20.64mm/50

Available in maduro and Connecticut wrapper.

CANARIA D'ORA

Hand-made. Quality, superior. Cameroon wrapper. Dominican, Jamaican and Mexican filler and binder. Light, sweet tasting. Owned by General Cigar. Good value.

$	**Supremos**	★★★★★

178mm/7 ins x 17.86mm/45. Slow, even burning. Spicy with honeyed undertones. Medium- to full-bodied. Ideal to follow meal that is not too spicy.

$	**Lonsdale**	★★★

165mm/6½ ins x 16.67mm/42. One dimensional. Slightly harsh and becomes bitter towards the end. Medium-bodied, vegetal finish on palate.

$	**Fino**	★★

152mm/6 ins x 12.3mm/31. Medium- to full-bodied. Not size for inexperienced smoker. Becomes tiring to smoke.

$ **Immensos** . . . . ★★★★★
140mm/5½ ins x 19.45mm/49. Smooth, silky claro
wrapper. Multi-layered flavors with honeyed undertones. Smooth. Ideal to follow meal.

$ **Corona**. . . . . ★★★★
140mm/5½ ins x 16.67mm/42. Smooth, oily claro
wrapper. Mild. Flavor somewhat one dimensional.

$ **Rothschild** . . . . ★★★
108mm/4½ ins x 19.84mm/50. Maduro, almost
oscuro wrapper. Slow, even burn. Honeyed
overtones on palate. Surprisingly dull finish for
this size.

¢   **Babies** . . . . ★
108mm/4½ ins x 12.7mm/32. Hard draw.
Little flavor.

         Vista. . . . . 160mm/6¼ ins x 12.7mm/32

CANONABO

Hand-made. Quality, superior. All Dominican filler and
binder. Connecticut Shade wrapper. Named after heroic
Cibao Indian chief, who died in 1495 as a prisoner of the
Spanish. Owned by Palm Business Services, Miami, Florida,
USA.

$$$	**Grand Premier**.	191mm/7½ ins x 19.89mm/50
$$$	**Guanines**	152mm/6 ins x 17.5mm/44
$$$	**Nabories**	140mm/5½ ins x 16.67mm/42
$$$	**Caciques**	191mm/7½ ins x 15.1mm/38
$$$	**Nitainos**.	127mm/5 ins x 143mm/36
$$$	**Petit Premier**	114mm/4½ ins x 19.8mm/50
$$	**Helennas**	127mm/5 ins x 11.9mm/30

CARBONELL

Hand-made. Packed in boxes of 10 and 20. Distributed by
Howard House Tobacco, Celine, Ohio, USA.

$$$	**Piramide Gigante**	203mm/8 ins x 27mm/68
$$$	**Piramide**	191mm/7½ ins x 16.67mm/42
$$	**Piramide Breva**	140mm/5½ ins x 22.2mm/56
$$$	**Gigante**.	254mm/10 ins x 22.2mm/56
$$$	**Soberano**	216mm/8½ ins x 20.6mm/52
$$	**Toro**.	140mm/5½ ins x 19.8mm/50
$$$	**Presidente**	191mm/7½ ins x 19.5mm/49
$$	**Churchill**	191mm/7½ ins x 18.3mm/46
$$	**Corona**.	165mm/6½ ins x 17.5mm/44
$$	**Palma Extra**	178mm/7 ins x 16.67mm/42
$$	**Palma**.	165mm/6½ ins x 16.67mm/42
$$	**Palma Short**	140mm/5½ ins x 16.67mm/42

$$	**Panetela Grande** . . . . ins x 15.1mm/38	
$$	**Panetela** . . . . 152mm/6 ins x 14.3mm/36	
$$	**Panetela Thins** . . . . 178mm/7 ins x 12.7mm/32	
$	**Demi Tasse** . . . . 127mm/5 ins x 11.9mm/30	
$	**Palmaritos** . . . . 101mm/4 ins x 11.1mm/28	

CARLOS TORANO

Hand-made. Quality, superior. Connecticut Shade wrapper. Mexican binder. Dominican and Nicaraguan filler. Also available in Europe. A Cuban, Carlos Torano is credited with introducing Pilolo Cuban seed from Cuba in the Dominican Republic in the mid-1960s. Distributed by Torano Cigars, Miami, Florid, USA.

$$$	**Carlos I** . . . . 152mm/6 ins x 19.8mm/50	
$$$	**Carlos II** . . . . 171mm/6¾ ins x 17.1mm/43	
$$$	**Carlos III** . . . . 191mm/7½ ins x 20.6mm/52	
$$	**Carlos IV** . . . . 146mm/5¾ ins x 17.1mm/43	
$$	**Carlos V** . . . . 152mm/6 ins x 18.3mm/46	
$$$	**Carlos VI** . . . . 178mm/7 ins x 19.1mm/48	
$$	**Carlos VII** . . . . 121mm/4¾ ins x 20.6mm/52	
$$	**Carlos VIII** . . . . 165mm/6½ ins x 14.3mm/36	

CARRINGTON

Hand-made. Quality, superior. Connecticut Shade warpper. Dominican binder and filler. Made by Tobacos Dominicas for House of Oxford.

$$	**I** . . . . 190mm/7½ ins x 19.8mm/50	
$$	**II** . . . . ★★★★	
	152mm/6 ins x 16.67mm/42. Medium-bodied. Spicy. Smooth and creamy.	
$$	**III** . . . . ★★★★	
	178mm/7 ins x 14.3mm/36. Slow, even burning. Smooth. Medium strength. Discreet flavors. Well-made for this size. Good daytime smoke. Ideal for beginners.	
$$	**IV** . . . . 140mm/5½ ins x 15.9mm/40	
$$	**V** . . . . ★★★★	
	175mm/6 ins x 18.3mm/46. Good draw. Burns evenly. Ash tends to fall off easily. Touch of cinnamon. Ideal for beginners.	

★★★★★ Outstanding. A classic.   ★★★★ Excellent.
★★★ Good.   ★★ Fair, ordinary.   ★ Poor or faulty.
No Star Not evaluated.

$$ **VI** . . . . ★★★★
114mm/4½ ins x 19.8mm/50. Good texture.
Subtle. Mild to medium-bodied. Well-made.
Daytime smoke.

$$ **VII** . . . . 152mm/6 ins x 19.8mm/50

$$$ **VIII** (pyramid) . . . . 175mm/6 ins x 23.8mm/60
Note the gigantic ring gauge.

CASA BLANCA

Hand-made. Quality, superior. Connecticut Shade and maduro
wrappers. Filler both from Dominican Republic and Brazil.
Binder is Mexican. Originally created for use in U.S. White
House and was the cigar offered at the inauguration dinner
of Ronald Reagan. Jeroboam and Half Jeroboam have massive
66 ring gauges. Exclusive to Santa Clara, N.A. Good value.

$ **Jeroboam*** . . . . ★★★
254mm/10 ins x 26.19mm/66. Because of size most
smokers would find this too tiring to finish. Smooth.

$ **Half Jeroboam*** . . . . . 127mm/5 ins x 26.19mm/66

$ **Magnum*** . . . . 178mm/7 ins x 23.81mm/60

$ **Presidente*** . . . . 190mm/7½ ins x 19.84mm/50

$ **De Luxe*** . . . . 152mm/6 ins x 19.84mm/50

$ **Lonsdale*** . . . . ★★★★
165mm/6½ ins x 16.67mm/42. Easy draw. Even
burn. Mild to medium-bodied.

$ **Corona** . . . . ★★★★
140mm/5½ ins x 16.67mm/42. Good oily wrapper.
Herbaceous. Smooth. Good cigar for beginner.

$ **Panetela** . . . . 152mm/6 ins x 14.29mm/36

$ **Bonita** . . . . 102mm/4 ins x 14.29mm/36
Also available in maduro wrapper.

CASA MARTIN

Hand-made bundles. Available with Cameroon and
Connecticut wrapper. Owned by Tropical Tobacco. Named
after owner, Pedro Martin.

$ **Petit Coronas** . . . . . . 133mm/5¼ ins x 16.67mm/42

$ **Seleccion Especial** . . 172mm/6¾ ins x 14.29mm/36

$ **Regulares** . . . . 152mm/6 ins x 17.07mm/43

$ **Numero Uno Plus** . . 172mm/6¾ ins x 17.46mm/44

$ **Matador** . . . . 152mm/6 ins x 19.84mm/50

$ **Majestad** . . . . 190mm/7½ ins x 19.84mm/50

$ **Churchill** . . . . 175mm/6⅞ ins x 18.26mm/46

CHAIRMAN'S RESERVE BY H. UPMANN

Hand-made. Quality, superior. Launched towards end 1996.
Made by Consolidated Cigar. Super-premium line.

> **Torpedo**
> **Robusto** . . . . 121mm/4¾ ins x 19.84mm/50
> **Churchill** . . . . 171mm/6¾ ins x 19.1mm/48
> **Double Corona**. . . . . . 178mm/7 ins x 19.84mm/50

CHAMBRAIR

Hand-made. Quality, superior. Made specially for restaurants
in Germany.

> **Ceremonial**. . . . . ★★★
> 190.5mm/7½ ins x 19.7mm/50. Mild and aromatic.
> Palate slightly sweet.
> **Elite** . . . . ★★★★
> 184.0mm/7¼ ins x 18.9mm/48. Rich and full-bod-
> ied flavor.
> **Moreau** . . . . ★★★★
> Dark wrappers. Full-bodied and herbaceous flavors.
> **Elegance** . . . . ★★★★
> 171.5mm/6¾ ins x 17.3mm/43. Tightly rolled. For
> the experienced smoker.
> **Plaisir**. . . . . ★★★★
> 171.5mm/6¾ ins x 13.8mm/35. Has character and
> powerful flavors. For the experienced smoker.
> **Faible** . . . . ★★★
> 139.7mm/5½ ins x 16.9mm/43. Mild and elegant.
> Ideal for beginners.
> **Finesse** . . . . ★★★
> 127.0mm/5 ins x 11.8mm/28. Very light with
> finesse. Cigar for ladies and beginners.
> **Mademoiselles**. . . . . ★★★★
> 124.0mm/4¹³⁄₁₆ ins x 8mm/20. Blend of four differ-
> ent tobaccos. Mild with herbaceous flavor. The
> name suggests it is made for ladies.

CIBAO

Hand-made. Distributed in USA by Indian Head Sales.

> **Magnum** . . . . 254mm/10 ins x 19.84mm/50
> **Especiales**. . . . . 203mm/8 ins x 19.84mm/50
> **Piramid** . . . . 178mm/7 ins x 21.4mm/54
> **Elegantes** . . . . 178mm/7 ins x 17.46mm/44
> **Diamantes** . . . . 165mm/6½ ins x 13.89mm/35
> **Churchill** . . . . 172mm/6¾ ins x 18.26mm/46

Brevas . . . . 133mm/5¼ ins x 19.84mm/50
Corona Deluxe. . . . . 140mm/5½ ins x 17.07mm/43

CIMERO

Hand-made. Quality, superior. All Dominican tobacco. Distributed by Jonathan Drew Inc., New York, USA.

Churchill . . . . 178mm/7 ins x 19.8mm/50
Toro . . . . 152mm/6 ins x 19.8mm/50
Robusto . . . . 127mm/5 ins x 19.8mm/50
Lonsdale . . . . 175mm/6⅞ ins x 18.3mm/46
Corona. . . . . 140mm/5½ ins x 16.67mm/42
Cetros. . . . . 152mm/6 ins x 17.5mm/44
Demi Tasse. . . . . 127mm/5 ins x 13.5mm/34

COHIBA

Hand-made by General Cigars. Not yet widely available. Same name as flagship brand made in Cuba. Dominican version unbanded.

Robusto . . . . 140mm/5½ ins x 19.84mm/50
Corona Especiale. . . 165mm/6½ ins x 16.67mm/42
Esplendido . . . . 178mm/7 ins x 19.45mm/49

CONNISSEUR SILVER LABEL

Hand-made. Bundles. Honduran wrapper. Distributed in USA by Indian Head Sales.

Corona. . . . . 133mm/5¼ ins x 17.07mm/43
Brevas. . . . . 152mm/6 ins x 19.84mm/50
Elegantes . . . . 178mm/7 ins x 17.46mm/44
Especiales. . . . . 203mm/8 ins x 19.84mm/50
Diamantes . . . . 228mm/7 ins x 13.89mm/35
Churchills. . . . . 190mm/7½ ins x 19.84mm/50

CREDO DOMINICAN

Hand-made. Connecticut Shade wrapper. Binder is aged Dominican leaf. Filler is blend of Dominican Olor and Piloto Cuban leaf for medium strength. Owned by Credo and distributed exclusively in USA by Hollco Rohr.

$$$ **Pythagoras** . . . . 178mm/7 ins x 21.43mm/50
$$$ **Magnificat** . . . . 175mm/6⅞ ins x 18.26mm/46

★★★★★ Outstanding. A classic.   ★★★★ Excellent.
★★★ Good.   ★★ Fair, ordinary.   ★ Poor or faulty.
No Star Not evaluated.

$$$ **Arcane** . . . . 127mm/5 ins x 19.84mm/50
$$ **Athanor** . . . . ★★★★
147mm/5¾ ins x 16.67mm/42. Easy draw. Even
burn. Medium-bodied. Good early morning smoke
or ideal for casual smoker.
$$ **Jubilate** . . . . 127mm/5 ins x 13.49mm/34

CUBITA

Created for European market, where smokers prefer full body
and rich aroma. Connecticut wraper. Binder and filler from
Dominican Republic. Made by MATASA. Distributed in USA
by S.A.G. Imports.

$$$ **No 2000** . . . . 178mm/7 ins x 19.84mm/50
$$$ **No 8-9-8** . . . . 172mm/6¾ ins x 17.07/43
No 500 . . . . 133mm/5½ ins x 17.07mm/43
$$ **No 2** . . . . 160mm/6¼ ins x 15.1mm/38
$$$ **No 7** . . . . 152mm/6 ins x 18.84mm/50
$$ **Delicias** . . . . 130mm/5⅛ ins x 11.9mm/30

CUESTA-REY CABINET SELECTION

Hand-made. Quality, superior. Mild. Founded in 1884 by
Angel LaMadrid Cuesta, Spanish cigar maker who did appren-
ticeship in Cuba. Partner was Peregrino Rey. Owners' sur-
names provided name of company. In 1985, bought by
Newman family's M&N company in USA. In 1995, celebrated
100th anniversary; marked by launch of new brand, Diamond
Crown. M&N first U.S. company to wrap cigars in cellophane.
Made by Tabacalera Arturo Fuente. Available in both light-
natural and maduro wrapper.

$ **Cabinet No 1884** . . . 172mm/6¾ ins x 17.46mm/44
$ **Cabinet No 95** . . . . ★★★★
160mm/6¼ ins x 16.67mm/42. Mild. Well-
balanced. Elegant. Good daytime.
$ **Cabinet No 898** . . . . . 178mm/7 ins x 19.84mm/50
$ **Cabinet No 2** . . . . 178mm/7 ins x 14.29mm/36

CUESTA-REY CENTENNIAL COLLECTION

Hand-made. Quality, superior. Owned by Newman family's
M&N company in USA. Made by Tabacalera Arturo Fuente.

$$$ **Dominican No 1** . . . . 216mm/8½ ins x 20.64mm/52
$$$ **Dominican No 2** . . . . ★★★★
184mm/7¼ ins x 19.05mm/48. Easy draw. Even
burn. Medium-bodied. Smooth. Elegant, although
finishes rather flat. Daytime smoke. Ideal for occasional smoker.

$$$	**Dominican No 3** . . . . . 178mm/7 ins x 14.29mm/36	
$$$	**Dominican No 4** . . . . ★★★★	

165mm/6½ ins x 16.67mm/42. Easy draw. Medium-bodied. Spicy with touch of coffee. Good balance between strength and flavor.

$$$	**Dominican No 5** . . . . 133mm/5½ ins x 17.07mm/43
$$$	**Dominican No 7** . . . 114.3mm/4½ ins x 19.8mm/50
$$$	**Dominican No 60** . . . 152.4mm/6 ins x 19.8mm/50
$$$	**Captiva** (aluminum tube) 157mm/6¾₆ ins x 16.67mm/42
$$$	**Aristocrat** (glass tubes) 184mm/7¼ ins x 19.05mm/48
$$$	**Rivera** . . . . 177.8mm/7 ins x 14.3mm/36
$$$	**Individual** . . . . 216mm/8½ ins x 20.64mm/52
$$$	**Cameo** . . . . 107.9mm/4¼ ins x 12.7mm/32

CUSANO HERMANOS

Hand-made. Quality, superior. Connecticut Shade wrapper. Dominican binder and filler. Distributed by Dom Rey Cigar, Boston.

Churchill . . . . 175mm/6⅞ ins x 18.3mm/46
Corona . . . . 152mm/6 ins x 17.5mm/44
Robusto . . . . 127mm/5 ins x 19.8mm/50
Bullet . . . . 102mm/4 ins x 19.8mm/50

CUSANO ROMANI

Hand-made. Quality, superior. Available with Connecticut, maduro and Indonesian wrappers. Dominican binder and filler. Distributed by Dom Rey Cigar, Boston, Massachusetts, USA.

Pyramid . . . . 165mm/6½ ins x 21.4mm/54

DANIEL MARSHALL DOMINICAN RESERVE

Hand-made. Quality, superior. Connecticut wrapper. Mexican binder. Dominican filler. Top humidor manufacturer, has now added a small but select range of Dominican and Honduran cigars to complement impressive range of humidors. Natural pairing—a class cigar with a class humidor. Black and silver band indicates Dominican range. Made by MATASA. Distributed by D. Marshall Inc., Tustin, California, USA.

$$$$ **Churchill** . . . . ★★★★★
178mm/7 ins x 19.1mm/48. Good, consistent construction. Slow, even burning. Cool, smooth. Good flavor. Spicy. For connoisseur.

$$$ **Robusto**. . . . . ★★★★★
       127mm/5 ins x 19.8mm/50. Good, consistent con-
       struction. Cool, smooth, with loads of flavor. Light
       to medium strength. Spicy. For discerning smoker.
$$$ **Corona**. . . . . 152mm/6 ins x 17.1mm/43

DAVIDOFF

Hand-made. Quality, superior.

Range owned by Max Oettinger Company of Basel, Switzerland and made in Dominican Republic.

New milder Davidoffs, made in the Dominican Republic by Tabacos Dominicanos (Tabadom Factory) in Santiago, must be judged in their own right. Have Connecticut Shade wrappers and Dominican filler leaves and are extremely well made. Range includes four different blends. Cigars aged at factory for three weeks before shipment. Have strict color grade standards. Sell about 6 million cigars a year worldwide.

Davidoff, highly respected marque named, in 1969, after Zino Davidoff, doyen of cigar industry in Europe, and son of Henri Davidoff, cigarette maker and merchant who, in 1911, immigrated to Switzerland from Russia. Made in Cuba until 1992.

Young Zino grew up working in his father's tobacco store in Lausanne before going to tobacco plantations in Bahia, Brazil and Cuba, to gain practical experience in all aspects of cigar-making.

On return, developed business, later opening shop on corner of Rue de Rive and Rue de La Fontaine in fashionable Geneva, which is the mecca of Europe's rich and famous.

In 1970, Zino Davidoff, then 65, sold to large import–export Max Oettinger Company based in Basel, Switzerland. This company was founded in 1875 and is one of the earliest importers of cigars from Havana, Brazil and Jamaica into France, Germany and Switzerland.

Davidoff remained in business to assist Ernst Schneider, present head of company. Internationalized business by opening additional shops. Now has chain of 45 stores (some corporate-owned, some franchised).

Davidoff range of cigars, bearing famous white and gold band, synonymous with top quality, vying with Montecristo and later Cohiba. Some sizes were produced at prestigious El Laguito factory in Havana, but majority made at Hoyo De Monterrey factory.

During 80s, conflict developed between state-owned Cubatabaco and Davidoff over quality. This coincided with 1982 launch of Cohiba, first post-revolutionary truly Cuban quality cigar. Observers believe Cubans gave Cohiba brand priority to detriment of Davidoff range.

In 1990, Davidoff announced no further production in Cuba, switching to Santiago in Dominican Republic.

Cubatabaco maintained it had right to use Davidoff name, but in 1991, court determined Cuban Davidoffs could only be sold until stocks exhausted and, in any event, no later than end of 1992.

This Cuban range has scarcity value and certain sizes can still be obtained most expensively from specialist cigar merchants in Europe.

In 1983, Davidoff's Zino range, made in Honduras, launched in United States. (Listed in the Honduras section.)

Davidoff Aniversario No 1 . . . . ★★★★
220mm/8⅔ ins x 19.05mm/48. Good draw with even burn. Mild. Smooth. Creamy. Early morning smoke.

$$$$$ **Davidoff Aniversario No 2**
178mm/7 ins x 19.05mm/48

$$$$ **Davidoff No 1** . . . . . 192mm/7½ ins x 15.08mm/38

$$$$ **Davidoff No 2** . . . . . . 152mm/6 ins x 15.08mm/38

$$$$ **Davidoff Tubos** . . . . . 152mm/6 ins x 15.08mm/38

$$$ **Davidoff No 3**. . . . . . . 126mm/5⅛ ins x 12mm/30

$$ **Davidoff Ambassadrice**
117mm/4⅝ ins x 10.32mm/26

$$$$$ **Davidoff Grand Cru No 1**. . . . . ★★★★
155mm/6³⁄₃₂ ins x 16.67mm/42. Elegant. Mild to medium-bodied. Spicy. Well-made. Daytime smoke.

$$$$ **Davidoff Grand Cru No 2**
168mm/5⅝ ins x 16.67mm/42

$$$ **Davidoff Grand Cru No 3**. . . . . ★★★★
127mm/5 ins x 16.67mm/42. Carries punch. Spicy with honeyed undertones on palate. After-lunch cigar.

$$$ **Davidoff Grand Cru No 4**
117mm/4⅝ ins x 15.87mm/40

$$$ **Davidoff Grand Cru No 5**
102mm/4 ins x 15.87mm/40

$$$ **Davidoff 1000** . . . . . 117mm/4⅝ ins x 13.49mm/34

$$$ **Davidoff 2000** . . . . . . 127mm/5 ins x 16.67mm/42

$$$ **Davidoff 3000** . . . . 178mm/7 ins x 13.1mm/33

$$$$ **Davidoff 4000** . . . . ★★★★★
155mm/6³⁄₃₂ ins x 16.67mm/42. Beautiful oily wrap-
per. Slow burning. Spicy with touch of honey. Well-
made.

$$$$$ **Davidoff Special "C"** . . 165 mm/6½ ins x 13.1mm/33

$$$$ **Davidoff 5000** . . . . . 143mm/5⅝ ins x 18.26mm/46

$$$$ **Davidoff Special "R"** (Royal)
124mm/4⅞ ins x 19.84mm/50

$$$$ **Davidoff Special "T"** (torpedo) . . . . ★★★★★
15.2mm/8 ins x 19.84mm/50. Slow burning
smooth smoke. Benefits from thick girth.
Wonderful integrated aroma and flavors. Well-made
cigar for connoisseur.

$$$$ **Davidoff Double "R"** . . . . ★★★★★
19mm/7½ ins x 19.84mm/50. Beautiful Colorado
claro wrapper. Slow burning. Spicy herbaceous
aroma with honeyed undertones on palate.
Complex and smooth. Great cigar to end wonderful meal or celebrate special occasion.

DIAMOND CROWN

Hand-made. Quality, superior. Five-year-old Connecticut
Shade wrapper. Dominican filler and binder. Up to seven leaves
used in the filler. This blend took three years to perfect in creating full-flavored cigars that are not too overpowering.
Finished cigars are cedar-aged for 12 months. Relaunch of an
old brand to commemorate M & N's 100th anniversary in 1995.
One of most expensive non-Cuban ranges on market. Made
by Tobacatera Arturo Fuente. Owned by M & N.

$$$ **4 No 1** . . . . 216mm/8½ ins x 21.4mm/54

$$$ **4 No 2** . . . . ★★★★★
191mm/7½ ins x 21.4mm/54. Attractive wrapper.
Good, consistent construction. Good draw. Slow,
even burning. Smooth. A wonderful cigar. For the
connoisseur.

$$$$ **No 3** . . . . 165mm/6½ ins x 21.4 mm/54

$$$$ **No 4** . . . . 140mm/5½ ins x 21.4mm/54

$$$ **No 5** . . . . ★★★★★
114mm/4½ ins x 21.4mm/54. Attractive wrapper.
Wonderful draw. Mild with full flavors. Hint of
spice and caramel. Smooth. A delight to smoke.

DIANA SILVIUS

Hand-made. Quality, superior. Connecticut Shade wrapper. Dominican filler and binder. Mady by Tobacalera Fuente for Diana Silvius, charismatic owner of Up Down Tobacco Shop in Chicago, Illinois, USA.

$$$ **Diana Churchill** . . . . ★★★★
179mm/7 ins x 19.8mm/50. Medium- to full-bodied. Flavor improves. Well-balanced. To follow meal.

$$$ **Diana 2000** . . . . 171mm/6¾ ins x 18.3mm/46

$$$ **Diana Corona** . . . . . . 165mm/6½ ins x 16.67mm/42

$$$ **Diana Robusto** . . . . ★★★★
124mm/4⅞ ins x 20.6mm/52. Needs ½ ins (1cm) to get benefit of its full flavor. An elegant cigar for the connoisseur. Daytime smoke or to follow lunch.

DOMINGOLD

Hand-made bundles. Cameroon wrapper. Connecticut binder and filler from Dominican Republic. Packed 20 per bundle. Exclusive to Arango Cigar Co. in Chicago, Illinois, USA.

Toro	152mm/6 ins x 19.84mm/50
Lonsdale	160mm/6¼ ins x 17.07mm/43
Rothschild	
Corona	140mm/5½ ins x 17.07mm/43
President	152mm/6 ins x 18.26mm/46
Churchill	178mm/7 ins x 19.84mm/50

DOMINICAN ESTATES

Hand-made. Connecticut wrapper. Dominican filler. Mexican binder.

Double Corona	178mm/7 ins x 19.84mm/50
Corona Gorda	152mm/6 ins x 19.84mm/50
Lonsdale	165mm/6½ ins x 17.1mm/43
Corona	140mm/5½ ins x 17.1mm/43

DOMINICAN ORIGINAL

Hand-made. Bundles. Connecticut Shade wrapper. Dominican binder and filler. Exclusive to Mike's Cigars, Miami, Florida, USA. Good value.

$ **Minatures** . . . . 108mm/4¼ ins x 12.7mm/32

$ **Cetros** . . . . 152mm/6 ins x 17.5mm/44

$ **Churchill** . . . . 175mm/6⅞ ins x 18.3mm/46

$ **Fat Tub** . . . . ★★★★
    254mm/10 ins x 26.2mm/66. Not just for laughs. It is
    worth smoking. Easy draw, Cool, slow burning. Mild.
$ **Gorilla** . . . . 127mm/5 ins x 26.2mm/66
$ **King Kong** . . . . 216mm/8½ ins x 20.6mm/52
$ **Monster** . . . . 178mm/7 ins x 23.8mm/60
$ **No 1** . . . . 165mm/6½ ins x 16.67mm/42
$ **No 2** . . . . 140mm/5½ ins x 16.67mm/42
$ **Palma Fina** . . . . 178mm/7 ins x 14.7mm/37
$ **Piramides** . . . . 152mm/6 ins x 22.2mm/56
$ **Presidents** . . . . 191mm/7½ ins x 19.84mm/50
$ **Robusto** . . . . 114mm/4½ ins x 19.84mm/50
$ **Toro** . . . . 152m/6 ins x 19.84mm/50
$ **Torpedo** . . . . 178mm/7 ins x 19.84mm/50

DOMINICAN PRIVATE STOCK

Hand-made. Exclusive to Brick-Hanauer Co.

Viajante . . . . 216mm/8½ ins x 20.64mm/52
President . . . . 178mm/7 ins x 19.84mm/50
Toro . . . . 152mm/6 ins x 19.84mm/50
Elegante . . . . 178mm/7 ins x 17.07mm/43
Numero Uno . . . . . . 172mm/6¾ ins x 17.07mm/43
Cetros . . . . 152mm/6 ins x 17.07mm/43
Numero Cuatro . . . . 133mm/5¼ ins x 17.07mm/43
Palma Elite . . . . 178mm/7 ins x 15.08mm/38
Dominican Guarantee Seal

This brand is also provided with a private label, if required.

DOMINICANA SUPERBA

Hand-made bundles. Tobacco all from Dominican Republic.
Exclusive to H. J. Bailey Co.

No 1 . . . . 216mm/8½ ins x 20.64mm/52
No 2 . . . . 178mm/7 ins x 19.45mm/49
No 3 . . . . 172mm/6¾ ins x 17.46mm/44
No 4 . . . . 113mm/4½ ins x 19.84mm/50
No 5 . . . . 127mm/5½ ins x 17.07mm/43
No 6 . . . . 190mm/7½ ins x 19.84mm/50

DOMINICO

Hand-made bundles. Connecticut Shade wrapper. Dominican
binder and filler. Exclusive to Hollco-Rohr.

No 700 . . . . 191mm/7½ ins x 23.8mm/60
No 701 . . . . 216mm/8½ ins x 20.6mm/52
No 702 . . . . 178mm/7 ins x 19.1mm/48

No 703 . . . . 152mm/6 ins x 19.84mm/50
No 704 . . . . 178mm/7 ins x 17.1mm/43
No 705 . . . . 140mm/5½ ins x 17.1mm/43
No 706 . . . . 121mm/4¾ ins x 20.6mm/52

DON ABREU

Hand-made. Quality, superior. Connecticut Shade wrapper. Dominican binder and filler. Distributed by Andre Suarez Ltd., Miami Beach, Florida, USA.

Presidente . . . . 203mm/8 ins x 19.8mm/50
Ejectivos. . . . . 191mm/7½ ins x 19.8mm/50
Double Coronas. . . . . 191mm/7½ ins x 19.5mm/49
Torpedos . . . . 165mm/6½ ins x 21mm/53
Big Toros . . . . 165mm/6½ ins x 19.8mm/50
Coronas . . . . 178mm/7 ins x 17.5mm/44
Churchill . . . . 165mm/6½ ins x 18.3mm/46
Coronitas . . . . 165mm/6½ ins x 17.5mm/44
General . . . . 140mm/5½ ins x 16.67mm/42
Toros . . . . 127mm/5 ins x 19.8mm/50
Petit . . . . 127mm/5 ins x 18.3mm/46

DON ALBERTO COMANDANTE

Hand-made. Quality, superior. Indonesian wrapper. Dominican binder and filler. Distributed by Don Alberto Cigar Co., Miami, Florida, USA.

Churchill . . . . 203mm/8 ins x 19.1mm/48
Double Corona . . . . . 165mm/6½ ins x 18.3mm/46
Robusto . . . . 127mm/5 ins x 19.8mm/50

DON ALBERTO GRAN CRUZ

Hand-made. Quality, superior. Indonesia maduro wrapper. Dominican binder and filler. Owned by Don Alberto Cigar Co., Miami, Florida, USA.

Presidente . . . . 203mm/8 ins x 19.8mm/50
Corona . . . . 178mm/7 ins x 17.5mm/44
Piramid . . . . 165mm/6½ ins x 21mm/53
Robusto . . . . 127mm/5 ins x 19.8mm/50

DON ALBERTO ORO DE HABANA

Hand-made. Quality, superior. Connecticut Shade wrapper. Dominican binder and filler. Owned by Don Alberto Cigar Co., Miami, Florida, USA.

Churchill . . . . 203mm/8 ins x 19.1mm/48
Corona . . . . 178mm/7 ins x 17.5mm/44

Double Corona ..... 165mm/6½ ins x 18.3mm/46
Piramid............ 165mm/6½ ins x 21mm/53
Robusto .... 127mm/5 ins x 19.8mm/50

DON ALBERTO SANTIAGO

Hand-made. Quality, superior. Connecticut Shade wrapper. Dominican binder and filler. Owned by Don Alberto Cigar Co., Miami, Florida, USA.

Presidente .... 203mm/8 ins x 19.8mm/50
Corona............. 178mm/7 ins x 17.5mm/44
Double Corona ..... 165mm/6½ ins x 18.3mm/46
Robusto .... 127mm/5 ins x 19.8mm/50

DON BARCO

Hand-made. Quality, superior. Indonesian wrapper. Dominican binder and filler. Distributed by Tampa Rico Cigar Co., Tampa, Florida, USA.

$$$ **Galeon**............ 191mm/7½ ins x 19.8mm/50
$$$ **Captian**............ 127mm/5 ins x 19.8mm/50
$$$ **Admiral** .... 152mm/6 ins x 19.8mm/50
$$ **Marinero** .... 171mm/6¾ ins x 18.3mm/46

DON DIEGO

Hand-made. Connecticut Shade wrappers on larger sizes. Cameroon wrappers on smaller sizes. Some sizes available in choice of double claro (AMS) or colorlab (EMS). Privados series more fully matured. Made by Consolidated Cigar. Cigars sold in Europe not same blends sold in USA.

Privada 1 .... 172mm/6¾ ins x 17.07mm/43
Privada 2 .... 168mm/6⅝ ins x 19.84mm/50
Privada 3 .... 168mm/6⅝ ins x 15.08mm/38
Privada 4 .... 147mm/5¾ ins x 16.67mm/42
Imperiale .... 168mm/6⅝ ins x 18.26mm/46
Grandes .... 152mm/6 ins x 19.84mm/50
Monarch............................★★★★
178mm/7¼ ins x 18.26mm/46. Smooth, oily dark wrapper. Medium-bodied. Hint of coffee on palate. After-dinner cigar for occasional smoker.
Amatista.......... 149mm/5⅞ ins x 15.87mm/40
$$ **Corona**........... 143mm/5⅝ ins x 16.67mm/42
$$ **Lonsdales**......... 168mm/6⅝ ins x 16.67mm/42
$$ **Grecos** .... 165mm/6½ ins x 15.08mm/38

$$ **Royal Palmas** . . . . ★★★
155mm/6⅛ ins x 14.29mm/36. Burns slightly hot causing some harshness. Good draw. Hint of coffee on palate.

$ **Petit Corona**. . . . . . 130mm/5⅛ ins x 16.67mm/42

$$ **Corona Major** . . . . . 129mm/5⅟₁₆ ins x 16.67mm/42

$$ **Pequenos No 100**. . . 113mm/4½ ins x 19.84mm/50

$$ **Pequenos No 200**. . . 113mm/4½ ins x 18.26mm/46

$$ **Pequenos No 300**. . . 113mm/4½ ins x 16.67mm/42

¢   **Preludes** . . . . 102mm/4 ins x 11.11mm/28
Good value.

$ **Amigos EMS**. . . . . . . 165mm/6½ ins x 14.29mm/36

¢   **Babies SMS** . . . . 129mm/5⅟₁₆ ins x 13.1mm/33

$$ **Coronas Bravas** . . . . 165mm/6½ ins x 19.05mm/48

$$ **Coronas Major Tubes EMS**
129mm/5⅟₁₆ ins x 16.67mm/42

$$ **Coronas EMS/AMS**
143mm/5⅝ ins x 16.67mm/42

$$ **Coronas EMS**. . . . . . 143mm/5⅝ ins x 16.67mm/42

$$ **Grandes EMS** . . . . 152mm/6 ins x 19.84mm/50

$$ **Grecos EMS** . . . . 165mm/6½ ins x 15.08mm/38

$$ **Imperial EMS** . . . . . 186mm/7⅟₁₆ ins x 18.26mm/46

$$ **Lonsdales EMS/AMS**
168mm/6⅝ ins x 16.67mm/42

$$$ **Monarchs Tubes EMS**
184mm/7¼ ins x 18.26mm/46

¢   **Preludes EMS**. . . . . . . 102mm/4 ins x 11.11mm/28

$ **Royal Palmas Tubes EMS**
155mm/6⅛ ins x 14.29mm/36

DON ESTABAN

Hand-made bundles. In natural and maduro wrappers. Cameroon wrapper. Micon binder and filler blend of tobacco from Mexico and Dominican Republic. Exclusive to H. J. Bailey Co.

       Churchill . . . . 175mm/6⅞ ins x 19.05mm/48
       Puritano . . . . 147mm/5¾ ins x 16.67mm/42
       Selector . . . . 178mm/7 ins x 15.08mm/38
       Elegante . . . . 172mm/6¾ ins x 16.67mm/42
       Emperador . . . . 152mm/6 ins x 19.84mm/50
       President . . . . 190mm/7½ ins x 19.84mm/50

★★★★★ Outstanding. A classic.   ★★★★ Excellent.
★★★ Good.   ★★ Fair, ordinary.   ★ Poor or faulty.
No Star Not evaluated.

DON JULIO

Hand-made bundles. Connecticut wrapper. Binder and filler from Dominican Republic. Owned by Swisher Intl.

$	**Corona Deluxe**	147mm/5¾ ins x 17.07mm/43
$	**Fabulosos**	178mm/7 ins x 19.84mm/50
$	**Miramar**	147mm/5¾ ins x 17.07mm/43
$	**Private Stock No 1** . .	160mm/6¼ ins x 17.07mm/43
$	**Supremos**	172mm/6¾ ins x 15.1mm/38

DON LEO

Hand-made. Quality, superior. All Dominican tobacco. Launched 1996. Made by a family of tobacco farmers, Puros de Villa Gonzalez, newest cigar factory in Santiago. Distributed by House of Oxford.

$	**Cetro**	165mm/6½ ins x 17.5mm/44
$$	**Churchill**	191mm/7½ ins x 19.84mm/50
$	**Corona**	140mm/5½ ins x 16.67mm/42
$	**Robusto**	114mm/4½ ins x 19.84mm/50
$	**Toro**	152mm/6 ins x 19.84mm/50
$$$	**Torpedo**	171mm/6¾ ins x 20.6mm/52

DON MANOLO

Hand-made. Quality, good. Sumatran wrapper. Dominican binder and filler. Also available with maduro wrappers. Distributed by Capone Cigar.

$$$	**Churchill**	178mm/7 ins x 19.8mm/50
$$	**Pyramid**	152mm/6 ins x 21.4mm/54
$$$	**Robusto**	140mm/5½ ins x 19.8mm/50
$$$	**Corona**	152mm/6 ins x 17.5mm/44

DON MARCUS

Hand-made. Connecticut wrapper. Dominican binder and filler. Old brand relaunched in 1995. Distributed by Phillips & King.

$$	**Coronas** . . . . ★★★★
	140mm/5½ ins x 16.67mm/42. Medium-bodied.
	Rich flavor with hint of coffee. Well-made.
$$	**Cetros**	165mm/6½ ins x 16.67mm/42
$$	**Naturals** (tubed)	156mm/6⅛ ins x 14.3mm/36
$$	**Double Corona**	165mm/6½ ins x 19.1mm/48
$$	**Toros**	152mm/6 ins x 19.84mm/50
$$$	**Torpedo**	152mm/6 ins x 19.84mm/50

\$\$\$ **Monarch** . . . . ★★★★★
178mm/7 ins x 18.3mm/46. Well-made. Cool, even
burning. Medium- to full-bodied strength with
loads of flavor. A cigar that can be appreciated.

DON MIGUEL

Hand-made. Sold only in Europe, although sales are not
restricted. Made by Consolidated Cigars.

Lonsdale (No 1). . . . 164mm/6½ ins x 16.67mm/42
Tubos (aluminum tube)
156mm/6⅛ ins x 16.67mm/42
Corona (No 3) . . . . . 140mm/5½ ins x 16.67mm/42
Petit Corona (No 4)
131mm/5⅙ ins x 16.67mm/42
Grecos . . . . 165mm/6½ ins x 15.1mm/38

DON MIGUEL

Hand-made. Quality, superior. All Dominican tobacco.
Available with maduro wrappers. Distributed by Andre Suarez
Ltd., Miami Beach, Florida, USA.

Presidents. . . . . 203mm/8 ins x 19.8mm/50
Ejecutivos. . . . . 191mm/7½ ins x 19.8mm/50
Double Coronas. . . . . 191mm/7½ ins x 19.5mm/49
Torpedos . . . . 165mm/6½ ins x 21mm/53
Big Toros . . . . 165mm/6½ ins x 19.8mm/50
Coronas . . . . 178mm/7 ins x 17.5mm/44
Churchills. . . . . 165mm/6½ ins x 18.3mm/46
Coronitas . . . . 165mm/6½ ins x 17.5mm/44
Generals. . . . . 140mm/5½ ins x 16.67mm/42
Toros . . . . 127mm/5 ins x 19.8mm/50
Petits . . . . 127mm/5 ins x 18.3mm/46

DON VITO

Hand-made. All Dominican tobacco. Distributed by Marcos
Miquel Tobacco, Dallas, Texas, USA.

Troncas. . . . . 203mm/8 ins x 19.84mm/50
Robusto . . . . 127mm/5 ins x 19.84mm/50
Virginianos. . . . . 152mm/6 ins x 17.5mm/44
Lonsdale . . . . 171mm/6¾ ins x 16.67mm/42
Caobas . . . . 140mm/5½ ins x 16.67mm/42
Padrinos. . . . . 191mm/7½ ins x 15.1mm/38
Alfonsitos. . . . . 127mm/5 ins x 11.9mm/30

DUNHILL (VINTAGE)

Hand-made. Quality, superior. Long filler, Connecticut Shade wrappers. Aged for at least three months before distribution. Well-made, slow burning. Dominican Dunhills have a blue and white band.

All the tobacco comes from one year's harvest. Only good years are chosen. First vintage from 1986 crop went on sale in 1989. 1987 vintage sold from 1991. The 1989 vintage on sale from 1993. The current 1994 one in 1996. Limited stock still available for all vintages, except 1986.

Dunhill also makes a hand-made range, with black bands and Connecticut wrappers, in the Canary Islands.

Brand made by Consolidated Cigar, distributed by Lane Ltd.

$$$	**Cabreras** (tubed) . . . . 178mm/7 ins x 19.05mm/48	
$$$	**Peravias** (Churchill) . . . . ★★★★★	
	178mm/7 ins x 19.84mm/50. (1987 vintage) Medium-bodied. Smooth. An elegant cigar for the connoisseur.	
$$	**Tabaras** . . . . 140mm/5½ ins x 16.67mm/42	
$$	**Condados**. . . . . ★★★★	
	152mm/6 ins x 19.05mm/48. Medium-bodied. Spicy. Smooth. Well-made. Daytime smoke.	
$$	**Diamantes** (lonsdale) 168mm/6⅜ ins x 16.67mm/42	
$	**Samanas** (especial) 165mm/6½ ins x 15.08mm/38	
$	**Valverdes** (corona) 140mm/5½ ins x 16.67mm/42	
$$	**Altiamaras** (tubed) . . . . ★★★★★	
	127mm/5 ins x 19.05mm/48. (1989 vintage) Oily wrapper. Elegant, smooth. Earthy flavors. For discerning smoker.	
$$	**Romanas** (rothschild) 113mm/4½ ins x 19.84mm/50	
	Fantinos (panetela) 178mm/7 ins x 11.11mm/28	
$$$	**Centenas** . . . . ★★★★★	
	152mm/6 ins x 19.84mm/50. (1994 vintage). Tapered with curly head. Good draw. Fine balance between strength and flavor. Well-made. Definitely for connoisseur.	

ESPANOLA

Hand-made. Quality, superior. Connecticut Shade wrapper. Dominican binder and filler. Exclusive to JM Tobacco, Los Angeles, California, USA.

$$$	**Presidente**	178mm/7 ins x 19.8mm/50
$$$	**Churchill**	171mm/6¾ ins x 19.8mm/50
$$$	**Sassoun**	152mm/6 ins x 19.8mm/50
$$$	**Robusto**	127mm/5 ins x 19.8mm/50
$$$	**Excellente**	175mm/6⅞ ins x 18.3mm/46
$$	**Corona**	140mm/5½ ins x 16.67mm/42
$$	**Torito**	152mm/6 ins x 14.3mm/36

ESPANOLA RESERVE

Hand-made. Quality, superior. Connecticut Shade wrapper. Dominican binder and filler. Exclusive to JM Tobacco, Los Angeles, California, USA.

Fabuloso	203mm/8 ins x 20.6mm/52
Belicoso	140mm/5½ ins x 20.6mm/52
Double Corona	191mm/7½ ins x 19.8mm/50
Toro	152mm/6 ins x 19.8mm/50
Robusto	127mm/5 ins x 19.8mm/50
Churchill	178mm/7 ins x 19.1mm/48
Corona Grande	152mm/6 ins x 17.5mm/44
Excellente	165mm/6½ ins x 16.67mm/42
Petit Corona	127mm/5 ins x 16.67mm/42
Demi Tasse	114mm/4½ ins x 74.3mm/36

FAT CAT

Hand-made. Quality, good. Dominican-grown Cuban seed filler and binder. Sumatra wrapper. In spite of the name, is a serious cigar. Owned by Fat Cat Cigars Ltd., Sunrise, Florida, USA.

$$$	**Torpedo**	165mm/6½ ins x 20.6mm/52
$$	**Churchill**	179mm/7 ins x 19.8mm/50
$$	**Robusto**	127mm/5 ins x 20.6mm/52

FIVE STAR SECONDS

Hand-made. Connecticut Shade wrappers. Mild. Good value. Exclusive to Santa Clara, N.A.

No 100	165mm/6½ ins x 17.46mm/44
No 200	152mm/6 ins x 17.46mm/44
No 300	140mm/5½ ins x 17.46mm/44
No 400	178mm/7 ins x 19.84mm/50
No 500	152mm/6 ins x 19.84mm/50
No 600	152mm/6 ins x 13.49mm/34
No 700	127mm/5 ins x 19.84mm/50

No 800 . . . . 216mm/8½ ins x 20.64mm/52
No 900 . . . . 172mm/6¾ ins x 13.49mm/34

FLAMENCO

Hand-made. Quality, superior. Not active brand but in process of being revived. Production limited by manufacturing capacity. Made by Consolidated Cigars.

Brevas . . . . 141mm/5⁵⁄₁₆ ins x 16.67mm/42

FLOR DE ORLANDO

Hand-made bundles. Connecticut Shade wrapper. Dominican filler and binder.

Emperador . . . . 197mm/7¾ ins x 19.84mm/50
Churchill . . . . 178mm/7 ins x 19.1mm/48
Governor . . . . 152mm/6 ins x 19.84mm/50
No 1 . . . . 178mm/7 ins x 17.1mm/43
No 4 . . . . 140mm/5½ ins x 16.67mm/42
Corona . . . . 165mm/6½ ins x17.5mm/44
Panetela Extra . . . . 178mm/7 ins x 14.3mm/36
Panetela . . . . 140mm/5½ ins x 13.5mm/34

FONSECA

Hand-made. Quality, superior. Cabinet selection cigars. Uses Connecticut Shade wrapper. Dominican filler. Mexican binders. Owned by Manufactura de Tabacos SA (MATASA). Same name as brand made in Cuba, also famous Port House.

$$ **8-9-8**. . . . . ★★★★★
152mm/6 ins x 17.07mm/43. Firm, but good draw. Slow, even burning. Mild, but flavors build up as cigar is smoked. Long finish. For discerning smoker.

$$ **7-9-9*** . . . . ★★★★
165mm/6½ ins x 18.26mm/46. Well-made, consistent construction. Smooth. Even burning. A light cigar. Smoke for beginner.

$$ **10-10*** . . . . ★★★★
178mm/7 ins x 19.84mm/50. Medium-bodied. Smooth. Even burn, but fairly hard draw. Daytime smoke.

$$ **5-50*** . . . . ★★★★★
127mm/5 ins x 19.84mm/50. Medium-bodied.
Smooth. Coffee and honeyed flavors. Well-made.
Top cigar.

$ **2-2*** . . . . ★★★★★
108mm/4¼ ins x 15.87mm/40. Extremely well-
made. Slow, even burning. Mild, with creamy
flavors. A pleasant, quick, daytime smoke. For
discerning smoker.

$$$ **Triangular** . . . . ★★★★★
133mm/5½ ins x 22.23mm/56. Figurado. Difficult
shape to make. Concentrated flavors. Elegant.
Cigar for discerning smoker.
*Also available in maduro Connecticut Shade wrapper.

FONSECA "VINTAGE VITOLAS"

Hand-made. Quality, superior. Small quantities of selected
tobacco is further aged. Made by MATASA. Distributed by
SAG Imports.

$$$$ **Corona Doble** . . . . . 190mm/7½ ins x 20.64mm/52
$$$$ **Corona Gorda** . . . . . . 152mm/6 ins x 19.84mm/50
$$$$ **Cetro Extra** . . . . 172mm/6¾ ins x 19.05mm/48

FRANCO

Hand-made. Connecticut Shade wrapper. Dominican binder
and filler. Owned by House of Oxford.

$$ **Condados** . . . . 165mm/6½ ins x 17.46mm/44
$$ **Eminentes** . . . . 140mm/5½ ins x 16.67mm/42
$$ **Gourmets** . . . . 178mm/7 ins x 15.1mm/38
$$$ **Magnum** . . . . 190mm/7½ ins x 19.84mm/50
$$$ **Regios** . . . . 140mm/5½ ins x 19.84mm/50

GRIFFIN'S

Hand-made. Quality, superior. Connecticut Shade wrappers.
Made by Tobacos Dominicas in Santiago. Exclusively dis-
tributed by Davidoff.

$$$$ **Griffin's Don Bernado** . . 228mm/9 ins x 18.26mm/46
$$$ **Griffin's Prestige** . . . . ★★★★
152mm/8 ins x 19.05mm/48. Mild and elegant
with good flavors, but loses interest towards end.
Good daytime smoke.

$$$ **Griffin's No. 100** . . . . 178mm/7 ins x 15.08mm/38
$$$ **Griffin's No. 200** . . . . 178mm/7 ins x 17.46mm/44
$$$ **Griffin's No. 300** . . . 160mm/6¼ ins x 17.46mm/44

$$$	**Griffin's No. 400** . . . . 152mm/6 ins x 15.08mm/38
$$	**Griffin's Robusto** . . . . ★★★★★
	127mm/5 ins x 19.84mm/50. Smooth, integrated flavors. Medium-bodied. Well-made. A top cigar.
$$	**Griffin's Privilege** . . . . ★★★★★
	127mm/5 ins x 12mm/30. Mild and elegant but good flavors. Well-made. Good daytime smoke.
$$$$	**Griffin's Griffinos** . . . . 95mm/3¾ ins x 7.14mm/18

HABONOS HATUEY

Hand-made. Connecticut Shade wrapper. Dominican filler and binder. Owned by Los Libertadores Cigars. Coral Gables, Florida, USA. Distributed by Mike's Cigars, Miami, Florida, USA.

$$	**Churchills**. . . . . 175mm/6⅞ ins x 19.1mm/48
$	**Coronas** . . . . 140mm/5½ ins x 16.67mm/42
$$	**Lonsdales**. . . . . 165mm/6½ ins x 17.5mm/44
$$	**Robustos** . . . . 127mm/5 ins x 19.1mm/48

HENRY CLAY

Hand-made. All with maduro wrappers. This was one of the most famous old Havana brands, created in the 19th century and named after a famous American senator. The cigars sold in Europe are not the same blends as those sold in the United States. Made by Consolidated Cigars.

$	**J. A. Leather**. . . . . 178mm/7 ins x 16.7mm/42
$	**Milla Fleurs**. . . . . 165mm/6½ ins x 19mm/48
$$	**Brevas Fina**. . . . . ★★★
	152mm/6½ ins x 19.05mm/48. Oily, but rough dark wrapper. Smooth, but short on flavor. Good for beginner.
$$	**Londres** . . . . 152mm/6 ins x 18.2mm/46
$$	**Brevas a la Conserva** 143mm/5⅝ ins x 18.26mm/46
$$	**Anitas** . . . . 141mm/5⁵⁄₁₆ ins x 16.7mm/42
$$	**Brevas** . . . . ★★★★
	140mm/5½ ins x 16.67mm/42. Even burning. Medium-bodied. Smooth. Daytime smoke.
$$	**Largas**. . . . . 171mm/6¾ ins x 15mm/38
$$	**Panetelas** . . . . 152mm/6 ins x 12.7mm/32
$$	**Slim Panetelas**. . . . . . . 127mm/5 ins x 13mm/33

★★★★★ Outstanding. A classic.   ★★★★ Excellent.
★★★ Good.   ★★ Fair, ordinary.   ★ Poor or faulty.
No Star Not evaluated.

HUGO CASSAR DIAMOND SELECTION

Hand-made. Connecticut Shade wrappers. Binder and filler from Dominican Republic Brand owned by Hugo Cassar Cigars, California, USA.

$$$ **Corona**................................ ★★★★
140mm/5½ ins x 16.67mm/42. Slow, even burning. Peppery. Full-bodied. To follow a meal.

$$$ **Robusto** .... 121mm/4¾ ins x 19.84mm/50

$$$ **Grand Corona** .... 152mm/6 ins x 18.3mm/46

$$$ **Toro**............. 165mm/6½ ins x 20.6mm/52

$$$ **Lonsdale**........... 178mm/7 ins x 17.5mm/44

$$$ **El Presidente** .... 203mm/8 ins x 19.84mm/50

HUGO CASSAR MYSTIQUE

Hand-made. All Dominican tobacco

$$$$ **Lonsdale**........... 178mm/7 ins x 17.5mm/44

$$$$ **Toro**............. 159mm/6¼ ins x 19.84mm/50

$$$$ **Churchill** .... 203mm/8 ins x 19.84mm/50

HUGO CASSAR PRIVATE COLLECTION

Hand-made. All Dominican tobacco.

$$$ **Corona** .... 152mm/6 ins x 16.67mm/42

$$$ **Robusto** .... 127mm/5 ins x 19.8mm/50

$$$ **Torpedo** .... 152mm/6 ins x 19.1mm/48

$$$ **Toro**............. 165mm/6½ ins x 20.6mm/52

$$$ **Presidente** .... 191mm/7½ ins x 19.5mm/49

H. UPMANN

Hand-made. Quality, superior. Cameroon wrappers. Central American filler. Well made, mild to medium smoke. Band reads "H. Upmann 1844." On Cuban version date replaced with "Habana." Made by Consolidated Cigar.

$$ **Amatista** .... 149mm/5⅞ ins x 15.87mm/40

¢ **Aperitif** .... 102mm/4 ins x 11.11mm/28

$$ **Churchills** .... ★★★★
143mm/5⅝ ins x 18.26mm/46. Spicy and herbaceous flavors. Good daytime smoke or to follow light meal.

$$ **Coronas Imperiales** .. 178mm/7 ins x 18.26mm/46

$$ **Lonsdales** .... 168mm/6⅝ ins x 16.67mm/42

$$ **Coronas Major Tubes**
128mm/5¹⁄₁₆ ins x 16.67mm/42

$$ **Coronas**.......... 141mm/5⁹⁄₁₆ ins x 16.67mm/42

$$ **Coronas Bravas**. . . . . ★★★
165mm/6½ ins x 19.05mm/48. Well-made. Good
draw and burning qualities. Bland.

¢   **Demi Tasse**. . . . . ★★★
113mm/4½ ins x 13.1mm/33. Good draw. Slow,
even burning. Medium-bodied with robust flavors.
Daytime smoke.

$$ **Director Royale** . . . . 165mm/6½ ins x 16.67mm/42

$$ **El Prado** . . . . 178mm/7 ins x 14.29mm/36

$$ **Emperadores** . . . . . . 197mm/7¾ ins x 18.26mm/46

$$ **Extra Finos Gold Tube**
172mm/6¾ ins x 15.08mm/38

$$ **Finos Gold Tube** . . . 155mm/6⅛ ins x 14.29mm/36

$$$ **Monarch Tubes**. . . . . ★★★★★
178mm/7 ins x 17.86mm/45. Good draw. Slow,
even burning. Smooth. Rich, creamy flavors. Good
balance between strength and flavor. Good consis-
tent construction.

$$ **Naturales Tubes**. . . . 156mm/6⅛ ins x 14.29mm/36

$$ **No. 2000 SBN** . . . . . . 178mm/7 ins x 16.67mm/42

$$ **Pequenos No. 100** . . . . ★★★★
113mm/4½ ins x 19.84mm/50. Dark oily wrapper.
Spicy with coffee undertones on palate. Medium-
bodied. Satisfying.

$ **Pequenos No. 200** . . 113mm/4½ ins x 18.26mm/46

$ **Pequenos No. 300** . . 113mm/4½ ins x 16.67mm/42

$ **Petit Corona**. . . . . ★★★
128mm/5¹⁄₁₆ ins x 16.67mm/42. Easy draw. Flavors
increase as cigar smoked. Consistent construction.
Value for money.

$$ **Topacios SBN** . . . . . 133mm/5¼ ins x 17.07mm/43

$$ **Tubos Gold Tube** . . 128mm/5¹⁄₁₆ ins x 16.67mm/42

H. UPMANN CABINET SELECTION

Hand-made. Quality, superior. Cameroon wrappers. Central
American filler.

$$$ **Columbo** . . . . 203mm/8 ins x 19.84mm/50

$$ **Corsario**. . . . . 140mm/5½ ins x 19.84mm/50

$$ **Robusto** . . . . ★★★★
120mm/4¾ ins x 19.84mm/50. Medium-bodied.
Good flavors. To follow meal.

JOHN AYLESBURY EL FUMO

Hand-made. Superior quality. Does not have the elegant "JA" band. See entry under Germany and Honduras.

Brevas
Palomas
Exquisitos

JOHN AYLESBURY FLOR DE ORLANDO

Hand-made. Superior quality. Has a red, white and gold "Flor de Orlando" band and not the "JA" band. One model only. See entry under Germany and Honduras.

JOHN AYLESBURY SANTA DOMINGA

Hand-made. Mild and subtle. See entry under Germany and Honduras. Produced for John Aylesbury chain of cigar shops in Germany. Also exported to USA where distributed by F & K Cigar.

Churchill	178mm/7 ins x 18.3mm/46
Lonsdale	168mm/6⅝ ins x 16.67mm/42
Rothschild	114mm/4½ ins x 19.84mm/50
Corona	140mm/5½ ins x 16.67mm/42
Panetela	152mm/6 ins x 12.27mm/32
Elegante	171mm/6¾ ins x 15.08mm/38

JOHN T'S

Hand-made. Tubed in bundles of 20. Untubed in boxes. Connecticut wrapper. Dominican binder. Pipe tobacco filler. Distributed by Indian Head Sales.

Brown Gold	140mm/5½ ins x 15.1mm/38
Cherry Cream	140mm/5½ ins x 15.1mm/38
Capuccino	140mm/5½ ins x 15.1mm/38
Cafe Ole	140mm/5½ ins x 15.1mm/38
Amaretto	140mm/5½ ins x 15.1mm/38
Magnum Amaretto . . .	171mm/6¾ ins x 18.3mm/46
Magnum Brown Gold .	171mm/6¾ ins x 18.3mm/46
Magnum Cherry Cream	
171mm/6¾ ins x 18.3mm/46	
Magnum Capuccino . .	171mm/6¾ ins x 18.3mm/46
Magnum Expresso . . .	171mm/6¾ ins x 18.3mm/46

★★★★★ Outstanding. A classic.   ★★★★ Excellent.
★★★ Good.   ★★ Fair, ordinary.   ★ Poor or faulty.
No Star Not evaluated.

JOSE BENITO

Hand-made. Quality, good. Indonesian (TBN) wrapper. Cuban seed Dominican filler. Central American Cuban seed binder. Medium strength. The large Magnum is one of biggest on market. Made by MATASA, small producer employing fewer than 70 bunchers and rollers. Owned by Manuel Quesada, whose family has been in tobacco business since 1877.

$$$$	**Magnum**	229mm/9 ins x 25mm/64	
$$	**Presidente**	197mm/7¾ ins x 19.84mm/50	
$$	**Churchill**	★★★★

178mm/7 ins x 19.84mm/50. Medium-bodied. Touch of honey. Good balance. After-dinner cigar.

$	**Corona**	172mm/6¾ ins x 17.07mm/43	
$	**Panetela**	ins x 15.08mm/38	
$	**Palma**	★★★★★

152mm/6 ins x 16.67mm/43. Medium-bodied. Smooth. Well-made. Appreciated by experienced smoker and novice alike.

$	**Petite**	140mm/5½ ins x 15.08mm/38
$$	**Rothschild**	120mm/4¾ ins x 19.84mm/50
$	**Chico**	108mm/4¼ ins x 12.27mm/32
$	**Havanitos**	127mm/5 ins x 9.92mm/25

JOSE MARTI

Hand-made. Connecticut wrapper. Mild and sweet. Brand named after leader of Cuban revolution against USA in 1895, also known as Apostle of Cuba. Made by Ramón Carbonell. Distributed by Cigars by Santa Clara, N.A.

$$	**José Marti**	★★★

190mm/7½ ins x 19.05mm/48 . Well-made. Rich, spicy flavors. Becomes slightly bitter.

$$	**Maceo**	175mm/6⅞ ins x 17.46mm/44
$$	**Palma**	178mm/7 ins x 16.67mm/42
$$	**Robusto**	★★★★

140mm/5½ ins x 19.84mm/50 . Well-made. Good draw. Slow, even burning. Mild. Good balance. Daytime smoke.

$	**Corona**	140mm/5½ ins x 15.87mm/40
$	**Créme**	★★★★

152mm/6 ins x 13.49mm/34. Medium-bodied. Tones of wet hay. Even burn.

JUAN CLEMENTE

Hand-made. Quality, superior. Connecticut Shade wrapper. Ages well. Launched in Europe in 1982 and in USA in 1985. Produces about 1 million cigars per year. Feature is packing of 24 cigars per box and band at tuck-end (foot) of each cigar to prevent cracking.

$$$$ **Juan Clemente Gargantua**
343mm/13½ ins x 19.84mm/50

$$$$ **Juan Clemente Gigante**
228mm/9 ins x 19.84mm/50

$$$ **Churchill** . . . . ★★★★★
175mm/6⅞ ins x 18.26mm/46. Medium-bodied. Good balance between strength and flavor. Well-made. For experienced smoker and novice alike.

$$ **Corona** . . . . ★★★★★
127mm/5 ins x 16.67mm/42. Extremely well-made and consistent. Wonderful draw. Slow, even burning. Cool. Good balance. Lovely flavors. Daytime smoke for discerning smoker.

$$$ **Grand Corona** . . . . . . 152mm/6 ins x 16.67mm/42

$$ **Panetela** . . . . 165mm/6½ ins x 13.49mm/34

$$$ **Juan Clemente Especiale**
190mm/7½ ins x 13.49mm/34

$$ **530** . . . . 127mm/5 ins x 12mm/30

$$ **Demi Corona** . . . . ★★★★
102mm/4 ins x 15.87mm/40. Well-made with good draw. Slow, even burning. Has rich flavors, unusual for this size.

$$$ **Rothschild** . . . . 124mm/4⅞ ins x 19.84mm/50

$$ **Demi Tasse** . . . . 92mm/3⅝ ins x 13.49mm/34

$$$$ **Club Selection No 1** . . 152mm/6 ins x 19.84mm/50

$$$ **Club Selection No 2**
113mm/4½ ins x 18.26mm/46

$$$$ **Club Selection No 3** . . 178mm/7 ins x 17.46mm/44

$$$ **Club Selection No 4** . . . . ★★★★★
146mm/5¾ ins x 16.67mm/42. Smooth with creamy flavors. Medium-bodied. Well-made. Daytime smoke.

$$$$ **Obelisco** . . . . 152mm/6 ins x 21.4mm/54

KING

Hand-made bundles. Natural or maduro wrapper. Made by Juan Clemente. Imported into USA by Club Imports.

$ **No 1** . . . . 165mm/6½ ins x 16.67mm/42

$ **No 2** . . . . 140mm/5½ ins x 16.67mm/42

$	**No 3**	172mm/6¾ ins x 15.08mm/38
$	**No 5**	140mm/5½ ins x 15.08mm/38
$	**No 6**	120mm/4¾ ins x 15.87mm/40
$	**No 7** . . . . ★★★★

216mm/8½ ins x 20.64mm/52. Rich, full flavored.
Smooth. Good value.

$	**No 8**	178mm/7 ins x 23.81mm/60
$	**No 9**	254mm/10 ins x 26.19mm/66
$	**No 10**	190mm/7½ ins x 19.45mm/49
$	**No 13**	127mm/5 ins x 26.19mm/66

KISKEYA

Hand-made bundles. Connecticut Shade wrapper. Made by Tabacos Dominicanos. Distributed in USA by Tropical Tobacco.

$	**Palma Fina**	178mm/7 ins x 14.29mm/36
$	**Numero Dos**	145mm/5¾ ins x 16.67mm/42
$	**Rothschild***	120mm/4¾ ins x 19.84mm/50
$	**Cetros**	152mm/6 ins x 17.46mm/44
$	**Numero Uno**	172mm/6¾ ins x 17.07mm/43
$	**Toros***	152mm/6 ins x 19.84mm/50
$	**Churchills**	175mm/6⅞ ins x 18.26mm/46
$	**Presidentes**	190mm/7½ ins x 19.84mm/50
$	**Viajantes**	216mm/8½ ins x 20.64mm/52

Also available with maduro wrapper.

KNOCKANDO

Hand-made. Connecticut Shade wrapper. Dominican binder and filler. Introduced by distillers Justerini and Brooks to go with their whiskies, particularly the well-known Knockando single malt. They are mild to medium, well-matured cigars that have been well made. Made by Tabacos Dominicanos.

    No 1 . . . . ★★★★
    175mm/6⅞ ins x 17.86mm/45. Good draw and
    burning qualities. Appreciated by connoisseurs and
    novices alike.

No 2	165mm/6½ ins x 13.89mm/35
No 3	168mm/5⅝ ins x 15.87mm/40
No 4	190mm/7½ ins x 19.05mm/48
St. James	127mm/5 ins x 16.67mm/42

LA AURORA

Hand-made. Quality, superior. Established 1903. One of oldest brands made in Dominican Republic. Cameroon wrapper. Dominican binder and filler. Distributed by Miami Cigar.

$	**Petite Corona**.	114mm/4½ ins x 14.7mm/37
$	**Palmas Extra**	171mm/6¾ ins x 13.9mm/35
$	**Corona**	127mm/5 ins x 15.1mm/38
$	**Aurora No 4**	133mm/5¼ ins x 17.1mm/43
$	**Cetros**	165mm/6½ ins x 13.5mm/34
$$	**Double Corona**	190mm/7½ ins X 19.84mm/50
$$	**Bristol Especiales**. . . .	165mm/6½ ins x 19.1mm/48
$$	**Sublimes**.	127mm/5 ins x 15.1mm/38
$$	**Robusto** . . . . ★★★★

127mm/5 ins x 19.84mm/50. Easy draw. Cool burn. Medium-bodied. Good flavor with caramel finish.

LA CORONA VINTAGE SELECTION

Hand-made. Quality, superior. This brand used to be made in the United States and is now produced by Consolidated Cigar Corporation in the Dominican Republic. They are well-made, mild to medium and use Connecticut Shade wrappers. Cigars sold in Europe not same blends as sold in USA. La Corona Whiffs machine-made in USA.

Directors. . . . . ★★★
165mm/6½ ins x 18.26mm/46. Smooth wrapper. Good draw. Creamy and smooth. Daytime smoke.
Aristocrats . . . . 155mm/6⅛ ins x 14.29mm/36
Coronas. . . . . 154mm/6¹/₁₆ ins x 17.07mm/43
Corona Chicas . . . . . 140mm/5½ ins x 16.67mm/42

LA DIVA

Hand-made. Quality, superior. Launched August 1996. Connecticut wrapper. Dominican binder and filler. Thirty-year-old cognac-scented cigar. Brand owned by Emmanuelle Marty, who brings feminine flair to masculine world and was formerly in charge of distribution of the El Sublimado brand, now made in Honduras.

$$$	**Churchill** . . . . ★★★★★

203mm/8 ins x 19.05mm/50. Smooth. Lots of distinctive flavor, but not dominated by cognac. Cigar for discerning smoker not governed by convention.
$$$$ **Torpedo** . . . . 178mm/7 ins x 21.4mm/54
$$$ **Robusto**. . . . . ★★★★★
114mm/4½ ins x 19.05mm/50. Medium-bodied. Lots of flavor with caramel undertones. Well-made. Good draw. Slow, even burning. Smooth. After dinner cigar for discerning smoker.
$$$ **Corona** . . . . 152mm/6 ins x 17.05mm/44

LA FLOR DOMINICANA

Hand-made. Quality, superior. Connecticut wrapper. Dominican binder and filler. Exclusive to Premium Imports, Coral Gables, Florida.

$$$	**Presidente**	203mm/8 ins x 19.8mm/50
$$$	**Mambises**	175mm/6⅞ ins x 19.1mm/48
$$$	**Alcalde**	165mm/6½ ins x 17.5mm/44
$$	**Insurrectos**	140mm/5½ ins x 16.67mm/42
$$$	**Maceo**	127mm/5 ins x 19.1mm/48
$$	**Macheteros**	102mm/4 ins x 15.9mm/40
$$$	**Churchill Reserva Especial** 175mm/6⅞ ins x 19.5mm/49	
$$$	**Figurado**	165mm/6½ ins x 20.6mm/52
$$$	**Robusto Reserva Especial** 127mm/5 ins x 19.1mm/48	
$$$	**Belicoso Reserva Especial** 140mm/5½ ins x 20.6mm/52	
$	**Diplomatico**	127mm/5 ins x 11.9mm/30

LA HABANERA

Hand-made. Quality, superior. Connecticut Shade wrapper. Dominican binder and filler. Distributed by Don Alberto Cigar Co., Miami, Florida, USA.

Churchill	175mm/6⅞ ins x 18.3mm/46
Diplomaticos	152mm/6 ins x 17.5mm/44
Elegante	175mm/6⅞ ins x 16.67mm/42
Emperadores	140mm/5½ ins x 19.8mm/50
Especiale	127mm/5 ins x 12.3mm/30
Presidente	191mm/7½ ins x 19.8mm/50
Puritanos	146mm/5¾ ins x 16.67mm/42
Selectos	178mm/7 ins x 14.3mm/36

LA PRIMERA

Hand-made. Quality, superior. Ecuadorian wrapper. Dominican binder. Blend of Nicaraguan and Dominican filler. Launched October 1996. Made by Manufactura de Tabacos SA (MATASA), owned by renowned Manuel Quesada. Distributed in USA by SAG Imports, Miami, Florida, USA.

$$	**Presidente**	216mm/8½ ins x 20.6mm/52
$$	**Churchill**	178mm/7 ins x 19.8mm/50
$$	**Toro**	152mm/6 ins x 19.8mm/50
$$	**Cetro Grande**	171mm/6¾ ins x 17.5mm/44

$ **Rothschild**. . . . . ★★★★★
      127mm/5 ins x 19.8mm/50. Well-made. Medium
      body, rich flavors. Good balance and finish. For dis-
      cerning smoker.
$ **Petit Corona** . . . . 146mm/4¾ ins x 17.1mm/43

LA UNICA

Premium bundles, hand-made. Available in both light-natural
and maduro wrappers. Owned by Newman family's M&N company in USA. Made by Arturo Fuente. Range also available
with maduro wrappers. Good value.

$ **No 100** . . . . ★★★★★
      216mm/8½ ins x 20.64mm/52. Well-made.
      Good draw. Medium-bodied. Spicy. An undis-
      covered cigar.
$ **No 200** . . . . ★★★★★
      178mm/7 ins x 19.84mm/50. Good balance
      between strength and flavor. Proof that bundle
      cigars need not always be lower quality. Daytime
      or after-dinner cigar.
$ **No 300** . . . . 172mm/6¾ ins x 17.64mm/44
$ **No 400** . . . . 113mm/4½ ins x 19.84mm/50
$ **No 500** . . . . 133mm/5½ ins x 17.07mm/43

LAMB'S CLUB

Hand-made. Ecuadorian wrapper. Honduran binder. Filler,
blend of tobacco from Dominican Republic and Brazil.
Distributed by Finck Cigar.

       Churchill. . . . . ★★★
       178mm/7 ins x 19.84mm/50. Full-bodied. Spicy
       and earthy.
       Corona Extra . . . . ★★★
       159mm/6¼ ins x 17.1mm/43. Good draw. Even
       burn. Full-bodied, spicy.
       Palma Extra . . . . 178mm/7 ins x 15.1mm/38
       Rothschild . . . . 121mm/4¾ ins x 19.84mm/50
       Toro . . . . 152mm/6 ins x 19.84mm/50
       Chico . . . . 114mm/4½ ins x 15.9mm/40

★★★★★ Outstanding. A classic.   ★★★★ Excellent.
★★★ Good.   ★★ Fair, ordinary.   ★ Poor or faulty.
No Star Not evaluated.

LEON JIMENES

Hand-made. Connecticut Shade wrapper. Made by La
Aurora since 1903. Distributed by Miami Cigar.

$$ **No 1**..................................★★★★
        190mm/7½ ins x 19.84mm/50. Good draw. Mild,
        but rich flavors that improve.

$$ **No 2**..................................★★★★
        178mm/7 ins x 18.65mm/47. Good draw. Smooth.
        Full-bodied with complex flavors.

$$ **No 3**............. 165mm/6½ ins x 16.67mm/42

$$ **No 4**..................................★★★★
        143mm/5⅝ ins x 16.67mm/42. Medium-bodied.
        Good balance. Well-made. Elegant.

$ **No 5**.............. 127mm/5 ins x 15.08mm/38

$$ **Robusto** .... 140mm/5½ ins x 19.84mm/50

$$ **Cristal**.......... 142mm/5¹⁹⁄₃₂ ins x 16.67mm/42

$$ **Torpedo** .... 165mm/6½ ins x 23mm/58

LICENCIADOS

Hand-made. Quality, superior. Connecticut wrapper. Hon-
duran binder. Filler from Dominican Republic. Logo simi-
lar to Cuban Diplomaticas brand. Made by MATASA. Brand
owned and distributed by Mike's Cigars, Miami, Florida, USA.

$$ **Churchill** .... 178mm/7 ins x 19.84mm/50

$$ **Excellentes**.........................★★★★
        171mm/6¾ ins x 17.1mm/43Smooth. Slow, even-
        burning. Full-Flavored. Daytime smoke for discern-
        ing smoker.

$ **Expresso** ....★★★★★
        114mm/4½ ins x 13.9mm/35. Full-flavored.
        Smooth. Well-made cigar for experienced smoker.
        Good, quick smoke to follow meal.

$ **No 4**............... 146mm/5¾ ins x 17.1mm/43

$ **Panetela Linda**....... 178mm/7 ins x 15.1mm/38

$$ **Presidentes**......... 203mm/8 ins x 19.84mm/50

$$ **Soberanos** .... 216mm/8½ ins x 20.6mm/54

$$ **No 200**............ 146mm/5¾ ins x 17.1mm/43

$$ **No 300**............ 171mm/6¾ ins x 17.1mm/43

$$ **No 400** .... 152mm/6 ins x 19.84mm/50

$$ **No 500** .... 203mm/8 ins x 19.84mm/50

$$ **Toro** . . . . ★★★★
152mm/6 ins x 19.84mm/50. Medium-bodied.
Smooth. Refined flavor improves. Daytime smoke
or to follow meal.

     Wavell . . . . ★★★★
127mm/5 ins x 19.84mm. Good draw. Mild to
medium-bodied with pleasant flavors. Daytime
smoke.

$$$ **Figurado** . . . . 152mm/6 ins x 22.2mm/56

LOS LIBERTADORES

Hand-made. Connecticut wrapper. Dominican filler and
binder. Owned by Los Libertadores Cigars, Coral Gables,
Florida, USA.

$$$ **Mambises** . . . . 175mm/6⅞ ins x 19.1mm/48

$$$ **Insurrectos** . . . . ★★★★
133mm/5½ ins x 16.67mm/42. Good, consistent
construction. Spicy, with touch of sweeness. Mild,
but flavorful. Daytime smoke.

$$$ **Exiliados** . . . . 191mm/7½ ins x 15.1mm/38

$$$ **Macheteros** . . . . 102mm/4 ins x 15.9mm/40

$$$ **Alcade** . . . . 165mm/6½ ins x 17.5mm/44

$$$ **Maceo** . . . . 127mm/5 ins x 19.1mm/48

$$$ **Figurado** . . . . 165mm/6½ ins x 20.6mm/52

$$$ **Diplomaticos** . . . . 127mm/5 ins x 11.9mm/30

$$$ **Belicoso Reserva Especial**
140mm/5½ ins x 20.6mm/52

$$$ **Robusto Reserva Especial**
127mm/5 ins x 19.1mm/48

$$$ **Churchill Reserva Especial**
175mm/6⅞ ins x 19.1mm/48

MATASA SECONDS

Hand-made. Quality, superior. Connecticut wrappers. Mild.
Overruns of some famous brands. Made by MATASA.
Exclusive to Santa Clara, N.A.

     Corona . . . . 152mm/6 ins x 17.07mm/43

     No 2 . . . . 165mm/6½ ins x 17.07mm/43

     No 4 . . . . 140mm/5½ ins x 16.67mm/42

     Palma Fina . . . . 178mm/7½ ins x 14.29mm/38

     Palmita . . . . 127mm/5 ins x 14.29mm/38

     Super Fino . . . . 152mm/6 ins x 14.29mm/36

MATCH PLAY

Hand-made. Quality, superior. Connecticut Shade wrapper. Binder and filler from Ecuador. Distributed by Dormie Imports, Portland, Oregon, USA.

$$ **Cypress** . . . . ★★★★
12.06mm/4¾ ins x 19.4mm/50. Firm draw. Cool. Medium-bodied. Touch of sweetness.

$$ **St. Andrews** . . . . 159mm/6¼ ins x 17.1mm/43

$$ **Turnberry** . . . . ★★★★★
152mm/6 ins x 19.84mm/50. Well-made. Attractive, oily wrapper. Good draw. For discerning smoker.

$$ **Prestwick** . . . . ★★★★★
175mm/6⅞ ins x 18.3mm/46. Fine, dark, oily wrapper. Good, consistent construction. Smooth. Fruity with hint of sweetness. For connoisseur.

$$$ **Olympic** . . . . 191mm/7½ ins x 19.84mm/50

$$$ **Troon** . . . . ★★★★
178mm/7 ins x 21.4mm/54 . A well-made pyramid. Burns cool and evenly. Good balance and finish. Mild, pleasant, daytime smoke.

MONTECRISTO

Hand-made by Consolidated Cigar. Quality, superior. Full-bodied, rich flavors not normally associated with cigars made in Dominican Republic. Good alternative for lovers of Havanas. Only available in selected stores. Not sold outside USA. Be advised that there is a brand, Monte Cristi, in the Dominican Republic which has no connection to the authorized, registered brand.

$$$ **Churchills** . . . . ★★★★★
178mm/7 ins x 19.05mm/48. Oily dark wrapper. Packed full of flavors. Has punch, but also finesse. Well-made. They don't get much better than this.

$$$ **No 1** . . . . 165mm/6½ ins x 17.46mm/44

$$$ **Tubos** . . . . 155mm/6⅛ ins x 16.67mm/42

$$$$ **No 2 Torpedo** . . . . ★★★★
152mm/6 ins x 19.84mm/50. Honeyed and woody undertones on finish. Good burning qualities. Becomes richer and stronger, but still remains mild. Would prefer slightly easier draw. Good daytime smoke. Much milder than Cuban version.

$$$ **No 3** . . . . 140mm/5½ ins x 17.46mm/44

$$$ **Robustos** . . . . ★★★★★
       120mm/4¾ ins x 19.84mm/50. Beautiful, smooth,
       oily reddish wrapper. Spicy, leathery aroma.
       Elegant, well-made cigar for connoisseur.
$$$ **No 4** . . . . 127mm/5 ins x 16.67mm/42

MONTECRUZ

Hand-made. Filler, blend of tobacco from Brazil and
Dominican Republic. Cameroon wrapper. Dominican binders.
Cuban seed tobacco and Brazilian filler.

When the Menendez family, former owners of
Montecristo brand, left Cuba they started a factory in the
Canary Islands making Montecruz, with labels similar to
Montecristo. In the mid-1970s the operation was taken over
by Consolidated Cigar Corporation and moved to the
Dominican Republic. Well-made. Matured medium- to full-
flavored. First cigar imported in USA with a Cameroon
wrapper.

$$ **Individuales** . . . . 203mm/8 ins x 19.84mm/50
$$ **Colossus** . . . . 165mm/6½ ins x 19.84mm/50
$$ **Senores** . . . . 146mm/5¾ ins x 13.9mm/35
$$ **Robusto** . . . . 114mm/4½ ins x 19.8mm/50
$$ **Tubo** (A/tube) . . . . . . 152mm/6 ins x 16.67mm/42
$$ **Tubulares** (A/tube) . 155mm/6⅛ ins x 14.29mm/36
$ **Junior** . . . . 124mm/4⅞ ins x 13.1mm/33
$ **Chicos** . . . . 99mm/3⅞ ins x 11.11mm/28
$$ **No 200** . . . . 184mm/7¼ ins x 18.26mm/46
$$ **No 201** . . . . 155mm/6⅛ ins x 15.08mm/38
$$ **No 205** . . . . 178mm/7 ins x 16.67mm/42
$$ **No 210** . . . . 165mm/6½ ins x 16.67mm/42
$$ **No 220** . . . . 140mm/5½ ins x 16.67mm/42
$$ **No 230** . . . . 127mm/5 ins x 16.67mm/42
$$ **No 240** . . . . 120mm/4¾ ins x 17.46mm/44
$$ **No 250** . . . . 165mm/6½ ins x 15.08mm/38
$$ **No 255** . . . . 178mm/7 ins x 14.29mm/36
$$ **No 265** . . . . 140mm/5½ ins x 15.08mm/38
$$ **No 270** . . . . 120mm/4¾ ins x 13.89mm/35
$$ **No 275** . . . . 178mm/7 ins x 12.7mm/32
$$ **No 276** . . . . 152mm/6 ins x 12.7mm/32
$$ **No 277** . . . . 127mm/5 ins x 12.7mm/32
$$ **No 280** . . . . 178mm/7 ins x 13.1mm/33
$$ **No 281** . . . . 152mm/6 ins x 13.1mm/33
$$ **No 282** . . . . 127mm/5 ins x 16.67mm/42

MONTERO

Hand-made. Quality, superior. Connecticut seed wrapper. Dominican binder and filler. Made by Tabacos Dominicos. Distributed by Tropical Tobacco, Miami, Florida, USA.

Presidente . . . . 191mm/7½ ins x 19.8mm/50
Torpedo . . . . 178mm/7 ins x 21.4mm/54
Churchill . . . . 175mm/6⅞ ins x 18.3mm/46
Toro . . . . ★★★★★
152mm/6 ins x 19.8mm/50. Well-made. Slow, even burning. Smooth. Medium body. Good balance and finish. For discerning smoker.
Cetro . . . . 152mm/6 ins x 17.5mm/44
Robusto . . . . 127mm/5 ins x 19.8mm/50

MONTERO

Hand-made. Connecticut wrapper. Dominican filler and binder. Boxes of 20. Owned by Tropical Tobacco. Named after vice-president of company, Ralph Montero.

Torpedo . . . . 178mm/7 ins x 21.4mm/54
Presidente . . . . ★★★★
191mm/7½ ins x 19.84mm/50. Good, consistent construction. Excellent draw. Smooth. Slow, even burning. Mild, but with loads of flavor. Good finish. Ideal for beginner or casual smoker.
Churchill . . . . 175mm/6⅞ ins x 18.3mm/46
Toro . . . . 152mm/6 ins x 19.84mm/50
Cetro . . . . 152mm/6 ins x 17.5mm/44
Robusto . . . . 127mm/5 ins x 19.84mm/50

MONTESINO

Hand-made. Quality, superior. Connecticut Shade wrapper. Dominican and Brazilian filler. Nicaraguan binders. Milder than Arturo Fuente range. Wrapper colors often not evenly matched in box. Good value. Made by Arturo Fuente. Distributed by FANCO.

$$ **Gran Corona** . . . . . . 172mm/6¾ ins x 19.05mm/48
$ **No. 1** . . . . 175mm/6⅞ ins x 17.07mm/43
$ **No. 2** . . . . ★★★★
160mm/6¼ ins x 17.46mm/44. Medium-bodied. Smooth. Spicy. Good balance and finish. Daytime smoke.
$ **No. 3** . . . . 172mm/6¾ ins x 14.29mm/36

$ **Diplomatico** . . . . ★★★★★
140mm/5½ ins x 16.67mm/42. Good draw. Slow,
even burning. Smooth. Spicy and earthy. Well-
made. For discerning smoker.

$ **Napoleon Grande** . . . . ★★★★★
178mm/7 ins x 18.26mm/46. Medium-bodied.
Smooth. Well-balanced. Connoisseur's cigar. Also
wonderful introduction for beginner.

¢   **Fumas** . . . . 172mm/6¾ ins x 17.46mm/44

MORENO MADURO

Hand-made. Mexican maduro wrappers. Binder from
Dominican Republic. Fill blend of tobacco from Brazil and
Dominican Republic. Made by Consolidated Cigar. Exclusive
to Phillips & King.

$ **No 445** . . . . 140mm/5½ ins x 17.46mm/44
$ **No 326** . . . . 152mm/6 ins x 14.29mm/36
$ **No 426** . . . . 165mm/6½ ins x 16.67mm/42
$ **No 486** . . . . 152mm/6 ins x 19.05mm/48
$ **No 507** . . . . ★★★★
178mm/7 ins x 19.84mm/50. Rich, spicy and hon-
eyed flavors. Good draw. Well-made.

$$ **No 528** . . . . 216mm/8½ ins x 20.6mm/52

NAT CICCO'S SUPREMOS DOMINICANOS

Hand-made bundles. Quality, good. All Dominican Republic
tobacco. Distributed in USA by Phillips & King.

$$ **Grandiosos** . . . . 228mm/9 ins x 23.81mm/60
$$ **Exquisitos** . . . . 184mm/7¼ ins x 19.84mm/50
$$ **Sabrosos** . . . . 152mm/6 ins x 19.05mm/48
$$ **Lindos** . . . . 113mm/4½ ins x 19.84mm/50
$$ **Deliciosos** . . . . 165mm/6½ ins x 17.07mm/43

NAT SHERMAN CITY DESK SELECTION

Hand-made. Quality, superior. Mexican maduro wrapper.
Dominican binder and blend of Dominican and Mexican
filler. Medium- to full-bodied. Orange, red and gold band.

   Named after famous newspapers in days when tough
cigar-smoking editors, wearing green visors, with shirt-
sleeves held up by garters, brought news to the masses in
classic style.

$$$ **Gazette** . . . . 152mm/6 ins x 16.67/42
$$$ **Dispatch** . . . . 165mm/6½ ins x 18.26mm/46

$$$ **Telegraph**. . . . . ★★★★
        152mm/6 ins x 19.84mm/50. Mild, and mellow.
        Touch of sweetness on palate. Gets rounder as you
        smoke. Daytime smoke or to follow light meal.
$$$ **Tribune** . . . . 190mm/7½ ins x 19.84mm/50

NAT SHERMAN EXCHANGE SELECTION

Hand-made. Quality, superior. Connecticut Shade wrapper.
Binders from Mexico and fillers from Dominican Republic.
Mild. Dark green, red and gold band.

Second generation, Joel Sherman, is proud of family's
deep New York roots and, accordingly, all brands named
after famous New York landmarks. Each one has different
color band for identification.

Named after celebrated New York telephone exchanges
of the past.

$$ **Academy No 2** . . . . ★★★★
        127mm/5 ins x 12.3mm/31 . Good, consistent con-
        struction. Good draw. Slow, even burning.
        Cool, light-bodied. Daytime smoke.
$$ **Murray Hill No 7** . . . . 152mm/6 ins x 15.08mm/38
$$$ **Butterfield No 8** . . . 165mm/6½ ins x 16.67mm/42
$$$ **Trafalgar No 4** . . . . . . 152mm/6 ins x 18.65mm/47
$$$ **Oxford No 5** . . . . ★★★★
        178mm/7 ins x 19.45mm/49. Mild. Delicate flavors
        with nutty aroma. An elegant cigar.

NAT SHERMAN GOTHAM SELECTION

Hand-made. Quality, superior. Connecticut Shade wrapper.
Dominican Olor binder and blend of Dominican and Cuban
seed filler. Mild. Grey, red and gold band.

Named after addresses synonymous with Sherman her-
itage. Each box covered in leather.

$$ **No 65** (Where Joel was born)
        152/6 ins x 12.7mm/32
$$$ **No 1400** (First store). . 160mm/6¼ ins x 17.46mm/44
$$ **No 711** (First Fifth Ave. store) . . . . ★★★★★
        152mm/6 ins x 19.84mm/50. Good balance
        between flavor and strength. Mild, integrated
        flavors, mellow and smooth. Thicker girth probably
        helps this blend. Great cigar.
$$$ **No 500** (Present Fifth Ave. store)
        178mm/7 ins x 19.84mm/50

NAT SHERMAN LANDMARK SELECTION

Hand-made. Quality, superior. Cameroon wrapper. Mexican binder and Dominican filler. Black, red and gold band.

Named after places that needed no address to true New Yorkers. Just name of hotel, jazz club, special building would identify address not normally found in tourist guides.

$$	**Metropole**.	152mm/6 ins x 13.49mm/34
$$	**Hampshire** . . . . ★★★★★

140mm/5½ ins x 16.67mm/42 . Attractive, dark, oily wrapper. Well-made. Good draw. Slow, even burning. Smooth. Good balance between strength and flavor. Unusually powerful cigar for this size. An after-dinner cigar for discerning smoker.

$$$	**Algonquin**	172mm/6¾ ins x 17.07mm/43
$$$	**Vanderbilt** . . . . ★★★★

127mm/5 ins x 18.65mm/47. Elegant, well-made, mild cigar. Smooth with herbaceous aroma. Excellent cigar for someone looking for lightness.

$$$	**Dakota**	190mm/7½ ins x 19.45mm/49

NAT SHERMAN MANHATTAN SELECTION

Hand-made. Quality, superior. Mexican wrapper and binder. Dominican filler. Medium-bodied with lots of flavor. Chocolate, red and gold band.

Named after small communities in Manhattan.

$	**Beekman**	133mm/5¼ ins x 11.11mm/28
$	**Tribeca**	152mm/6 ins x 12.3mm/31
$$	**Chelsea**	165mm/6½ ins x 15.08mm/38
$$	**Gramercy**	172mm/6¾ ins x 17.07mm/43
$$	**Sutton** . . . . ★★★★

140mm/5½ ins x 19.45mm/49. Lovely aromatic, leathery aromas. Tangy finish. More flavor than Landmark Vanderbilt. Good daytime smoke.

NAT SHERMAN METROPOLITAN SELECTION

Hand-made. Quality, superior. Connecticut Shade wrapper. Dominican binder and filler. Medium-bodied. Royal blue, red and gold band. Named after great New York private clubs leaving legacy of buildings reflecting permanence and discreet good taste.

$$$	**Anglers**.	140mm/5½ ins x 17.1mm/43
$$$	**Nautical** (pyramid) . . .	178mm/7 ins x 19.1mm/48

$$$ **University** . . . . ★★★★★
152mm/6 ins x 19.84mm/50. Good draw and even
burning. Good balance. Flavor develops after half
an inch (one cm). Medium-bodied. Elegant day-
time smoke for connoisseur.

$$$ **Explorers** (pyramid) . . . . ★★★★
140mm/5½ ins x 19.84mm/50. Mild. Good subtle
flavors. Burns evenly. Elegant. Daytime smoke.

$$$ **Metropolitan** (torpedo) . . . mm/7 ins x 23.8mm/60

NAT SHERMAN VIP SELECTION

Hand-made. Quality, superior. Connecticut Shade wrapper.
Dominican binder and blend of Dominican and Brazilian
filler. Medium- to full-bodied. Purple, red and gold band.
    Named after famous New York personalities.

$$ **Zigfeld "Fancytale"** . . 172mm/6¾ ins x 12.7mm/32
$$ **Morgan** . . . . 178mm/7 ins x 16.67mm/42
$$ **Astor** . . . . ★★★★
113mm/4½ ins x 19.84mm/50. Herbaceous, spicy
aromas. Strength is little ahead of flavor. Not as elegant as Landmark Vanderbilt and Gotham No 711.

$$ **Carnegie** . . . . 152mm/6 ins x 19.05mm/48

NUDE DOMINICAN

Hand-made bundles. Distributed in USA by Indian
Head Sales.

60 . . . . 127mm/5 ins x 12mm/30
38 . . . . 133mm/5¼ ins x 17.07mm/43
40 . . . . 133mm/5¼ ins x 19.84mm/50
56 . . . . 152mm/6 ins x 17.07mm/43
54 . . . . 160mm/6¼ ins x 17.46mm/44
50 . . . . 172mm/6¾ ins x 17.07mm/43
48 . . . . 175mm/6⅞ ins x 18.26mm/46
58 . . . . 178mm/7 ins x 12mm/30
52 . . . . 178mm/7 ins x 14.29mm/36
32 . . . . 178mm/7 ins x 17.46mm/44
44 . . . . 190mm/7½ ins x 19.84mm/50
42 . . . . 203mm/8 ins x 19.84mm/50

★★★★★ Outstanding. A classic.   ★★★★ Excellent.
★★★ Good.   ★★ Fair, ordinary.   ★ Poor or faulty.
No Star Not evaluated.

OLOR

Hand-made. Connecticut wrapper. Filler and binder from Dominican Republic.

Cacique . . . . 194mm/7⅝ ins x 21.4mm/54
Colossus . . . . 184mm/7¼ ins x 19.1mm/48
Lonsdale . . . . 162mm/6½ ins x 16.67mm/42
Paco . . . . 152mm/6 ins x 19.84mm/50
Rothschild . . . . . . 114mm/4½ ins x 19.84mm/50
Momento . . . . 140mm/5½ ins x 17.1mm/43

ONYX

Hand-made. Quality, good. Mexican maduro wrapper. Java binder. Dominican and Mexican filler. Launched in 1992. Made by Consolidated Cigar. Good value.

$ **No 642** . . . . 152mm/6 ins x 16.67mm/42
$ **No 646** . . . . 168mm/6⅝ ins x 18.26mm/46
$ **No 650** . . . . ★★★★
152mm/6 ins x 19.84mm/50. Good flavor with chocolate undertones. Good balance.
$ **No 750** . . . . ★★★★
190mm/7½ ins x 19.84mm/50. Medium-bodied. Rich and smooth. Touch of sweetness.
$$ **No 852** . . . . 203mm/8 ins x 20.64mm/52

OPUS X (FUENTE FUENTE OPUS X)

Hand-made. Quality, superior. Unique Dominican shade wrapper. Pioneered by Carlos Fuente Jr. Dominican filler and binder. Super-premium range. Pride of Fuente family. Among most expensive non-Havana cigars on market. Plans were to sell only 500,000 cigars in 1996. Made by Arturo Fuente. Distributed in USA by FANCO (joint venture between Fuente and M&N).

Petit Lancero . . . . ★★★★
159mm/6¼ ins x 15.5mm/39. Well-made. Medium-bodied. Full, spicy flavor. Short finish.
Perfecxion No 5 . . . . ★★★★★
124mm/4⅞ ins x 15.9mm/40. Medium-strength. Full flavors. Hint of coffee and nutmeg. Smooth. Wonderfully balanced. Do not be misled by its size, quick, satisfying smoke for connoisseur.
Fuente Fuente . . . . . . 143mm/5⅝ ins x 18.3mm/46

Reserva D'Chateau . . . . ★★★★★
178mm/7 ins x 19.1mm/48. Beautiful, oily
wrapper. Medium-bodied. Good flavor. Spicy
with touch of sweetness. To follow a meal. This
cigar is an occasion!

Double Corona . . . . ★★★★★
194mm/7⅝ ins x 18.3mm/46. Dark, oily wrapper.
Packed with flavor. Good balance. Hell of a cigar!
They do not get much better than this.

Robusto . . . . ★★★★★
133mm/5¼ ins x 19.84mm/50. Dark, oily wrapper.
Extremely well-made. Good draw. Slow, even burning. Smooth. Full-bodied, creamy. Probably the best
Dominican robusto. For a special occasion for the
connoisseur.

Perfecxion No 2 . . . . ★★★★
162mm/6⅜ ins x 20.6mm/52. Beautiful colorado
wrapper. Medium-bodied. Good flavor, but doesn't
have punch of parejos (parallel-sided) cigars. Tends
to fade towards the end. Extremely well-made.

ORO DE CUBA

Cameroon or maduro wrappers. Distributed in USA by Brick-
Hanauer Co.

El Falcon	133mm/5½ ins x 17.07mm/43
El Flamingo	172mm/6¾ ins x 13.89mm/35
El Pantero	165mm/6½ ins x 17.46mm/44
El Aquila	178mm/7 ins x 17.07mm/43
El Pasofina Tube . . .	133mm/5½ ins x 16.67mm/42
El Tigre	152mm/6 ins x 19.84mm/50
El Leon	178mm/7 ins x 19.45mm/49

OSCAR

Hand-made. Quality, superior. Connecticut Shade wrapper.
Dominican filler and binder. Brand owned by Dominican
Cigar Imports and named after owner, Oscar Rodriguez.

$$$$	**Don Oscar**	229mm/9 ins x 18.3mm/44
$$$$	**Supreme** . . . . ★★★★	

203mm/8 ins x 19.1mm/48. Full-bodied. Spicy with
good finish.

$$$	**Prince**	127mm/5 ins x 11.9mm/30
$$$	**No 100**	178mm/7 ins x 15.1mm/38
$$$	**No 200**	178mm/7 ins x 18.3mm/44
$$$	**No 300**	159mm/6¼ ins x 18.3mm/44
$$$	**No 400**	152mm/6 ins x 15.1mm/38

$$$	**No 500** . . . . 140mm/5½ ins x 19.84mm/50
$$$	**No 600** . . . . 114mm/4½ ins x 19.84mm/50
$$$	**No 700** . . . . 178mm/7 ins x 21.4mm/54
$$$	**Oscarito** . . . . 102mm/4 ins x 7.91mm/20

P & K GUARDSMAN

Hand-made. Java wrapper. Dominican binder. Filler, blend of tobacco from Mexico, Brazil and Dominican Republic Brand owned by Phillips & King.

$ **P & K Guardsmen No 1**
203mm/8 ins x 20.64mm/52

$ **P & K Guardsmen No 2** . . . . ★★★
190mm/7½ ins x 19.84mm/50. Inconsistent construction. Lots of flavor with honeyed undertones. Light- to medium-bodied. Value for money.

$ **P & K Guardsmen No 3**
152mm/6 ins x 19.84mm/50

$ **P & K Guardsmen No 4**
120mm/43/4 ins x 19.84mm/50

$ **P & K Guardsmen No 5** . . . . ★★★★
178mm/7 ins x 19.05mm/48. Medium- to full-bodied. Good value.

$ **P & K Guardsmen No 6**
133mm/5½ ins x 17.46mm/44

$ **P & K Guardsmen No 7**
152mm/6 ins x 16.67mm/42

$ **P & K Guardsmen No 8**
152mm/6 ins x 14.29mm/36

PANOREA

Hand-made. Quality, superior. Connecticut Shade wrapper. Dominican binder and filler. Distributed by CEI Group, Northfield, Illinois, USA.

| **Churchill** . . . . 178mm/7 ins x 19.8mm/50 |
| **Belicoso** . . . . 159mm/6¼ ins x 20.6mm/52 |
| **Lonsdale** . . . . 165mm/6½ ins x 17.1mm/43 |
| **Robusto** . . . . 127mm/5 ins x 19.8mm/50 |
| **Corona** . . . . 140mm/5½ ins x 17.1mm/43 |

★★★★★ Outstanding. A classic.   ★★★★ Excellent.
★★★ Good.   ★★ Fair, ordinary.   ★ Poor or faulty.
No Star Not evaluated.

PARTAGAS

Hand-made. Quality, superior. Fillers are mixture of Jamaican, Dominican and Mexican tobacco. They are well made, medium- to full-bodied, with a touch of sweetness. Relatively expensive. Second biggest brand made by giant General Cigar. Band reads "Partagas 1845." On Cuban version date replaced with "Habana." Most names different from Cuban range.

$$ **No 1** .... ★★★★★
172mm/6¾ ins x 17.07mm/43. Spicy, vegetal aroma and flavors. Well balanced between strength and flavor. Elegant. Good finish. Well-made.
No 2 .... ★★★★★
147mm/5¾ ins x 17.07mm/43. Well-made elegant cigar. Slightly salty finish. For the connoisseur.
No 3 .... ★★★★★
133mm/5¼ ins x 17.07mm/43. Medium-bodied. Good balance between integrated flavors and strength. Earthy undertones. Elegant.

$$ **No 4**............................... ★★★★
127mm/5 ins x 15.08mm/38. Smooth silky wrapper. Medium- to full-bodied. This cigar gets better as you smoke. Finishes on high note.
No 5 .... ★★
133mm/5¼ ins x 11.11mm/28. Hard draw, difficult burning. Not easy to smoke.
No 6 .... ★★★
152mm/6 ins x 13.49mm/34. Medium-bodied. Mildly aromatic.

$$$ **No 10** .... ★★★★★
190mm/7¾ ins x 19.45mm/49. New brand. Well-made. Good draw. Slow, even burning. Complex, full flavors. Ideal after-dinner cigar.

$$$ **Aniversario** .... 190mm/7 ins x 20.6 mm/52

$$$ **8-9-8** (cabinet) .... ★★★
175mm/7½ ins x 17.07mm/43, Good, dark, almost maduro wrapper. Mild. Slightly sweet. Lacks punch.

$$$ **Aristocrat**............................. ★★
152mm/6 ins x 19.84mm/50. Not very aristocratic. One dimensional and boring.

$$ **Naturales** .... ★★★★
140mm/5½ ins x 19.45mm/49. Smooth colorado maduro wrapper. Well-made. Flavor builds up after halfway. Elegant.

$$ **Maduro**........... 160mm/6¼ins x 18.65mm/47

$$ **Tubos** (aluminum tubes) . . . . ★★★
190mm/7 ins x 13.49mm/34. Elegant-looking cigar. Could do with more complexity.

$$$ **Humitube** (glass tubes) . . . . ★★★
147mm/6¾ ins x 17.07mm/43. Mild, spicy, floral aromas. Dull wrapper. Lacks punch.

$$ **Sabroso** (aluminum tubes) . . . . ★★★★★
149mm/5⅞ ins x 17.46mm/44. Full-bodied. Lots of spicy, earthy flavors. Has character. Ideal to follow spicy meal.

$$ **Almirante** . . . . ★★★
160mm/6¼ ins x 18.65mm/47. Very mild. Licorice, coffee and honeyed flavors. Lacks punch.

$$ **Robusto** . . . . ★★★★★
113mm/4½ ins x 19.45mm/49. Burns easily and evenly. Subtle, spicy aroma and flavors. Medium-bodied. Smooth. Daytime smoke or to follow light meal.

$ **Puritos** (tins) . . . . ★★★★
107mm/4³⁄₁₆ ins x 12.7mm/32. Machine-made. Short filler. Medium-bodied, floral aroma. Burns well.

$$$$ **Limited Reserve Royale** . . . . ★★★★★
147mm/6¾ ins x 17.07mm/43. Green and gold band. Lovely wrapper. Elegant, well-made cigar with integrated spicy and floral aroma and flavors with coffee undertones. Good finish. For connoisseur.

$$$$ **Limited Reserve Regale** . . . . ★★★★★
160mm/6¼ ins x 18.65mm/47. Green and gold band. Good colorado claro wrapper. Burns slowly and evenly. Thick girth allows lots of integrated flavors. For connoisseur.

$$$$ **Limited Reserve Epicure**
127mm/5 ins x 15.08mm/38

$$$$ **Limited Reserve Robusto**
140mm/5½ ins x 19.5mm/49

PARTAGAS 150 SIGNATURE SERIES

Hand-made. Quality, superior. Unique 18-year-old Cameroon wrapper leaf. This limited once-in-a-lifetime edition was created to commemorate 150th anniversary of Partagas brand, by Ramon Cifuentes who, pre-Castro, ran the Partagas factory in Cuba. Cigars packed in cedar boxes of 25, 50 and 100, bearing Cifuentes' signature and special Partagas 150 logo. Total production under 1 million. Released November 1995. For further details see 1996 edition.

PAUL GARMIRIAN—P.G.

Hand-made by Tabacos Dominicanos for P.G. Top price range.

$$$$	**P.G. Celebration**	228mm/9 ins x 19.84mm/50
$$$$	**P.G. Double Corona**	193mm/7⅝ ins x 19.84mm/50
$$$$	**P.G. Magnum**	178mm/7 ins x 19.84mm/50
$$$$	**P.G. Belicoso**	165mm/6½ ins x 20.64mm/52
$$$$	**P.G. Churchill**	178mm/7 ins x 19.05mm/48
$$$$	**P.G. No 1**	190mm/7½ ins x 15.08mm/38
$$$$	**P.G. Corona Grande**	165mm/6½ ins x 18.26mm/46
$$$	**P.G. Belicoso Fino**	140mm/5½ ins x 20.64mm/52
$$$	**P.G. Lonsdale**	165mm/6½ ins x 16.67mm/42
$$$	**P.G. Connoisseur**	152mm/6 ins x 19.84mm/50
$$$	**P.G. Epicure**	140mm/5½ ins x 19.84mm/50
$$$	**P.G. Robusto**	127mm/5 ins x 19.84mm/50
$$$	**P.G. No 2**	120mm/4½ ins x 19.05mm/48
$$$	**P.G. Petit Corona**	127mm/5 ins x 17.07mm/43
$$$	**P.G. Petit Bouquet**	113mm/4½ ins x 15.08mm/38
$$$	**P.G. No 5**	102mm/4 ins x 15.87mm/40

PETER STOKKEBYE

Hand-made. Connecticut Shade wrapper. Dominican binder. Brazilian and Cuban seed tobacco filler. Very mild. Distributed in USA by Arango Cigar.

$$	**Santa Maria**	178mm/7 ins x 19.84mm/50
$$	**Santa Maria No. 2**	172mm/6¾ ins x 15.08mm/38
$$	**Santa Maria No. 3**	133mm/5½ ins x 17.07mm/43

PETERSON

Hand-made. Quality, superior. Connecticut Shade wrapper. Dominican filler and binder from Ecuador. Owned by famous piper makers, Peterson of Dublin. Made by Cuervo Y Hermano. Distributed in USA by Hollco Rohr.

Presidente . . . . ★★★★★
190mm/7½ ins x 19.8mm/50. Medium-bodied. Touch of spice. Smooth. Good balance. Well-made cigar with finesse.

$$$	**Churchill**	178mm/7 ins x 19.1mm/48
$$$	**Toro**	152mm/6 ins x 19.8mm/50

$$$ **Corona**. . . . . ★★★★
146mm/5¾ ins x 17.1mm/43. Good draw. Mild strength, but lot of complex flavors. Ideal for beginner.

$$$ **Petit Corona**. . . . . ★★★
127mm/5 ins x 17.1mm/43. Well-made with attractive wrapper. Slow, even burning with subtle flavors. Morning smoke.

$$$ **Robusto** . . . . 120mm/4¾ ins x 19.8mm/50
Tres Petit Corona . . . 114mm/4½ ins x 15.1mm/38

PLAYBOY BY DON DIEGO

Hand-made. Quality, superior. Licensed to carry Playboy Rabbit logo. Made by Consolidated Cigar. Super premium line. Launched towards end of 1996.

$$$$ **Double Corona**. . . . . . . 152mm/6 ins x 20.6mm/52
$$$$ **Robusto** . . . . 127mm/5 ins x 19.84mm/50
$$$$ **Churchill** . . . . 146mm/5¾ ins x 19.84mm/50
$$$$ **Gran Corona** . . . . 171mm/6¾ ins x 19.1mm/48
$$$$ **Lonsdale** . . . . 165mm/6½ ins x 16.67mm/42

PLEIADES

Hand-made. Connecticut Shade wrapper. Dominican binder and filler. Brand owned by Swisher Intl.

$$$$ **Aldebran** . . . . 216mm/8½ ins x 19.84mm/50
$$$$ **Saturne**. . . . . 203mm/8 ins x 18.26mm/46
$$$ **Neptune**. . . . . 190mm/7½ ins x 16.67mm/42
$$$ **Sirius** . . . . 175mm/6⅞ ins x 18.26mm/46
$$$ **Orion** . . . . 147mm/5¾ ins x 16.67mm/42
$$$ **Uranus** . . . . 175mm/6⅞ ins x 13.49mm/34
$$$ **Antares**. . . . . 133mm/5½ ins x 15.87mm/40
$$$ **Pluton** . . . . ★★★★★
127mm/5 ins x 19.84mm/50. Good, consistent construction. Good draw. Cool. Floral aromas. Good after-dinner cigar.

$$ **Perseus**. . . . . 127mm/5 ins x 13.49mm/34
$$$ **Mars** . . . . 127mm/5 ins x 11.11mm/28

★★★★★ Outstanding. A classic.   ★★★★ Excellent.
★★★ Good.   ★★ Fair, ordinary.   ★ Poor or faulty.
No Star Not evaluated.

POR LARRANAGA

Hand-made. Connecticut Shade wrappers. Dominican binders and fillers blend of Dominican and Brazilian leaf. Brand owned in USA by Consolidated Cigar. Band carries words "La Romana," while Cuban version has word "Habana."

Fabulosos	. . . .	178mm/7 ins x 19.84mm/50
Cetros	. . . .	175mm/6⅞ ins x 16.67mm/42
Nacionales	. . . .	140mm/5½ ins x 16.67mm/42
Delicados	. . . .	165mm/6½ ins x 14.29mm/36
Robusto	. . . .	127mm/5 ins x 19.84mm/50
Petit Cetro	. . . .	127mm/5 ins x 15.1mm/38

PREMIUM DOMINICAN SELECTION

Hand-made. Quality, good. Available with Connecticut, Cameroon and maduro wrappers. (Note ring gauge of Giant and El Cid.) Distributed by Antillian Cigar Corp., Miami, Florida, USA.

$$$$	**Giant**	229mm/9 ins x 24.6mm/62
$$	**Super Soberanos**	216mm/8½ ins x 20.6mm/52
$	**Presidente**	203mm/8 ins x 19.8mm/50
$$	**El Cid**	178mm/7 ins x 23.8mm/60
$	**Churchill**	178mm/7 ins x 19.5mm/49
$	**Regulares**	152mm/6 ins x 19.8mm/50
$	**No 1**	171mm/6¾ ins x 17.1mm/43
$	**No 3**	171mm/6¾ ins x 15.1mm/38
$	**No 4**	140mm/5¼ ins x 15.1mm/38
$	**Rothschilds**	121mm/4¾ ins x 19.5mm/49
$	**Super Fino**	152mm/6 ins x 13.9mm/35

PRIMO DEL REY

Machine-bunched and hand-finished. Brazilian wrapper. Label similar to Montecruz. Made by Consolidated Cigar.

	No 100*	113mm/4½ ins x 19.84mm/50
$$	**Aguilas***	203mm/8 ins x 20.64mm/52
$	**Almirantes*** . . . . ★★★★

152mm/6 ins x 19.84mm/50. Dark, oily wrapper. Spicy with coffee undertones. Good finish. After-dinner smoke.

$	**Cazadores****	154mm/6¹⁄₁₆ ins x 17.46mm/44
$	**Chavon**	165mm/6½ ins x 16.27mm/41
$	**Churchill***	165mm/6½ ins x 19.05mm/48
¢	**Cortos**	102mm/4 ins x 11.11mm/28
$	**Panetelas Extras*** . .	151mm/5¹³⁄₁₆ ins x 13.49mm/34
$	**Panetelas***	136mm/5⅜ ins x 13.49mm/34
$	**Presidentes***	157mm/6¹³⁄₁₆ ins x 17.46mm/44

$ **Reales** . . . . 155mm/6⅛ ins x 14.29mm/36
$ **Seleccion No 1** . . . . 157mm/6¹³⁄₁₆ ins x 16.67mm/42
$ **Seleccion No 2**** . . . . ★★★★
160mm/6¼ ins x 16.67mm/42. Firm draw. Good
burning qualities. Mild to medium-bodied. Good
balance and finish. Daytime smoke.
$ **Seleccion No 3*** . . . 157mm/6¹³⁄₁₆ ins x 14.29mm/36
$ **Seleccion No 4**** . . . 140mm/5½ ins x 16.67mm/42
$ **Seleccion No 5** . . . . . 147mm/5¾ ins x 15.48mm/39
$$ **Soberanos*** . . . . 190mm/7½ ins x 19.84mm/50
*Maduro wrappers.
**Maduro and colorado wrappers.

PRIMO DEL REY CLUB SELECTION

Hand-made. Quality, superior. Connecticut Shade wrapper,
different to standard range.

$ **Nobles** . . . . 160mm/6¼ ins x 17.46mm/44
$ **Aristocrats** . . . . 172mm/6¾ ins x 19.45mm/48
$ **Regals** . . . . ★★★★
178mm/7 ins x 19.84mm/50. Attractive wrapper.
Good balance between strength and flavor. Well-
made. Mild, smooth. Good daytime smoke or after
light meal.
$ **Barons** . . . . 203mm/8½ ins x 20.64mm/52

PRIVATE STOCK

Hand-made. "Seconds" from Tobacos Dominicanos SA fac-
tory. Brand owned by Davidoff. More affordable price range.

$ **No 1** . . . . 197mm/7¾ ins x 19.05mm/48
$ **No 2** . . . . 152mm/6 ins x 19.05mm/48
$ **No 3** . . . . 165mm/6½ ins x 13.1mm/33
$ **No 4** . . . . 147mm/5¾ ins x 15.08mm/38
$ **No 5** . . . . 147mm/5¾ ins x 17.07mm/43
$ **No 6** . . . . 133mm/5¼ ins x 18.26mm/46
$ **No 7** . . . . 120mm/4¾ ins x 17.07mm/43
$ **No 8** . . . . ★★★★
117mm/4⅝ ins x 13.89mm/35. Acceptable draw.
Slow, even burning. Full-bodied. Good flavor with
touch of spice. For the connoisseur.
$ **No 9** . . . . 117mm/4⅝ ins x 10.32mm/26
$ **No 10** . . . . 102mm/4 ins x 15.87mm/40
$ **No 11** . . . . 117mm/4⅝ ins x 19.84mm/50

PUEBLO DOMINICANO

Hand-made. Quality, good. All Dominican tobacco. Each cigar is named after a pueblo in the Dominican Republic, except the Siglo V, which commemorates the 500 years of Dominican history. Brand established 1996. Owned by Pueblo Dominicano Imports, Austin, Texas, USA.

$$$$	**Baruhona**	203mm/8 ins x 19.8mm/50
$$$	**San Pedro**	114mm/4½ ins x 20.6mm/52
$$$	**Santo Domingo**	152mm/6 ins x 19.8mm/50
$$$	**La Romana**.	140mm/5½ ins x 18.3mm/46
$$	**Siglo V**	171mm/6¾ ins x 18.3mm/46
$$	**Santiago**	133mm/5¼ ins x 16.67mm/42
$$	**Samana**.	102mm/4 ins x 16.67mm/42

QUORUM

Hand-made. Connecticut Shade wrappers. Dominican binders. Originally made in Canary Islands.

Chairman	190mm/7½ ins x 19.84mm/50
President	184mm/7¼ ins x 18.26mm/46
No 1	168mm/6⅝ ins x 16.67mm/42
Corona	143mm/5⅝ ins x 16.67mm/42
Rothschild	113mm/4½ ins x 19.84mm/50
Whillo	178mm/7 ins x 14.29mm/36
Trumph	108mm/4¼ ins x 16.67mm/42

RAMON ALLONES

Hand-made by General Cigar. Quality, superior. Cameroon wrappers. Made by General Cigar. Binders from Mexico and fillers from Mexico, Jamaica and Dominican Republic. Mild. Names different to Cuban range. Bands do not include the word "Habana." Made by General Cigar.

$$ Ramonitos . . . . 113mm/5⅛ ins x 12.7mm/32

$$$ Redondos . . . . ★★★
178mm/7 ins x 19.45mm/49. Fairly hard draw. Mild to medium-bodied. Little flavor. Lacks character.

$$ A . . . . ★★★★
178mm/7 ins x 17.86mm/45. Smooth. Mild but rich flavors. Hint of coffee. A sophisticated smoke for the connoisseur.

$$ B . . . . ★★★★
165mm/6½ ins x 16.67mm/42. Rich, earthy flavors. Touch of coffee. Smooth. Slow burning. Well-made.

$$ **D** .... ★★★★
127mm/5 ins x 16.67mm/42. Beautiful colorado maduro wrapper. Spicy, floral aroma. Hint of coffee on palate. Elegant, sophisticated smoke.

$$ **Crystals** (glass tubes).................. ★★★★
165mm/6¾ ins x 16.67mm/43. Beautiful dark brown wrapper. Elegant. Good finish. Ideal to follow a meal.

$$ **Trumps** (cabinet) .... ★★★★★
172mm/6¾ ins x 17.07mm/43. Beautiful dark oily wrapper. Integrated flavors. Mild. Smooth. Well-made.

REPUBLICA DOMINICA

Hand-made. Bundles. Indonesian wrapper. Mexican binder. Dominican filler. Made by Consolidated Cigar.

$	**No 1**	204mm/8 ins x 20.6mm/52
¢	**No 2**	191mm/7½ ins x 19.84mm/50
¢	**No 3**	152mm/6 ins x 19.84mm/50
¢	**No 4**	127mm/5 ins x 19.84mm/50
¢	**No 5**	178mm/7 ins x 19.1mm/48
¢	**No 6**	168mm/6⅝ ins x 17.5mm/44
¢	**No 7**	152mm/6 ins x 16.67mm/42
¢	**No 8**	175mm/6⅞ ins x 15.1mm/38

RICOS DOMINICANOS

Hand-made. Quality, superior. Connecticut Shade wrapper. Dominican filler and binder. Also available with maduro wrappers. Made by MATASA. Distributed by SAG Imports, Miami, Florida, USA.

Churchill	178mm/7 ins x 19.8mm/50
Toro	152mm/6 ins x 19.8mm/50
Breva	140mm/5½ ins x 17.5mm/44
Cetro Largo	171mm/6¾ ins x 17.5mm/44

RIGOLETTO

Hand-made. Connecticut Shade wrapper. Filler and binder from Dominican Republic. Made by Arturo Fuente Ltd. Distributed in USA by M&N.

¢	**Black Magic**	190mm/7½ ins x 18.26mm/46
¢	**Black Arrow**	160mm/6¼ ins x 17.46mm/44
¢	**Dominican Lights**	160mm/6¼ ins x 19.05mm/48

¢ – Under $1.00 $ – $1–3.00 $$ – $3–4.00
$$$ – $5–8.00 $$$$ – $8–20.00 $$$$$ – $20+

ROLANDO BLEND

Hand-made. Connecticut Shade wrapper. Dominican filler and binder. Packed in boxes of 20. Owned by Tampa Rico Cigar Co, Tampa, Florida, USA.

> **Numero No 2** . . . . ★★★
> 190mm/7½ ins x 19.1mm/48. Drawing quality not consistent. Mild. Complex flavors.
> **Numero No 3** . . . . 152mm/6 ins x 20.2mm/50
> **Numero No 4** . . . . 152mm/6 ins x 17.1mm/43
> **Robusto** . . . . ★★★
> 121mm/4¾ ins x 20.6mm/52. Firm, acceptable, draw. Full-bodied, robust. Lacks refinement.
> **Pyramid** . . . . 165mm/6½ ins x 13.5mm/34
> **Perfecto** . . . . 178mm/7 ins x 17.5mm/44

ROLLER'S CHOICE

Hand-made in distinctive presentation. Connecticut wrapper. Mexican binder. Dominican filler. Made by MATASA. Distributed by SAG Imports.

$$	**RC Double Corona** . .	178mm/7 ins x 19.84mm/50
$$	**RC Lonsdale**	165mm/6½ ins x 18.26mm/46
$$	**RC Corona**	152mm/6 ins x 17.07mm/43
$$	**RC Fino**	133mm/5½ ins x 16.27mm/41
$$	**RC Robusto**	127mm/5 ins x 19.84mm/50
$$	**RC Pequeno**	108mm/4¼ ins x 15.87mm/40
$$	**RC Torpedo**	140mm/5½ ins x 21.8mm/56
$	**RC Cetro**	140 mm/5½ ins x 17.1mm/43
$	**RC Toro**	152 mm/6 ins x 19.84 mm/50

ROMANTICOS

Hand-made. Quality, superior. Dominican filler and binder. Connecticut Shade wrapper. Distributed by S & T Cigars, Coral Gables, Florida, USA.

> **Marc Anthony** . . . . 203mm/8 ins x 20.6mm/52
> **Valentino** . . . . 178mm/7 ins x 19.8mm/50
> **Cyrano** . . . . 152mm/6 ins x 20.6mm/52
> **Cleopatra** . . . . 146mm/5¾ ins x 17.1mm/43
> **Eros** . . . . 127mm/5 ins x 19.8mm/50
> **Venus** . . . . 127mm/5 ins x 14.3mm/36

★★★★★ Outstanding. A classic.　　★★★★ Excellent.
★★★ Good.　　★★ Fair, ordinary.　　★ Poor or faulty.
No Star Not evaluated.

ROMEO Y JULIETA

Hand-made. Quality, superior. Cameroon wrappers. Dominican and Cuban seed filler. Well-made. Medium-bodied. Until recently was also made in Honduras and Cuba. No longer made in Honduras. Made in MATASA factory in Santiago free-trade zone. The range made in Cuba also include a Churchill and a Romeo. The bands do not include the word "Habana." Owned in USA by Hollco Rohr.

$$	**Monarcas**	203mm/8 ins x 20.64mm/52
$$	**Churchills***	178mm/7 ins x 19.84mm/50
$$	**Presidentes**	178mm/7 ins x 17.07mm/43
$$	**Rothschild***	127mm/5 ins x 19.84mm/50
$	**Palmas**	152mm/6 ins x 16.67mm/43
$$	**Cetros***	165mm/6½ ins x 17.46mm/44
	Coronas	140mm/5½ ins x 17.46mm/44
$$	**Delgados** . . . . ★★★★

178mm/7 ins x 17.1mm/43. Earthy aroma. Gentle cigar with finese. Well-made. Ideal for novice.

$	**Brevas**	143mm/5⅝ ins x 15.1mm/38
$	**Panetelas**	133mm/5¼ ins x 13.89mm/35
$	**Chiquitas**	108mm/4¼ ins x 19.84mm/50
$$	**Romeo*** (torpedo) . . .	152mm/6 ins x 18.26mm/46

Available with maduro wrapper.

ROMEO Y JULIETA VINTAGE I

Hand-made. Quality, superior. Connecticut Shade wrapper. Filler blend of Cuban seed and Dominican binder is aged Mexican leaf. Packed in Spanish cedar box, fitted with French Credo humidifier.

$$$	**Vintage I**	152mm/6 ins x 17.07mm/43
$$$	**Vintage II**	152mm/6 ins x 18.26mm/46
$$$	**Vintage III** . . . . ★★★★★

113mm/4½ ins x 19.84mm/50. Excellent, consistent construction. Good draw. Slow, even burning. Complex, full flavors with cedar undertones. Ideal to smoke with an espresso. For the discerning smoker.

$$$	**Vintage IV**	178mm/7 ins x 19.05mm/48
$$$	**Vintage V**	190mm/7½ ins x 19.84mm/50
$$$$	**Vintage VI**	178mm/7 ins x 23.8mm/60

ROYAL DOMINICANA

Hand-made. Quality, superior. Connecticut wrapper. Mild to medium. Exclusive to Santa Clara, N.A..

Churchill	190mm/7½ ins x 19.84mm/50
Corona	152mm/6 ins x 18.26mm/46
Nacional	140mm/5½ ins x 17.07mm/43
No 1	172mm/6¾ ins x 17.07mm/43
Super Fino	152mm/6½ ins x 13.89mm/35

ROYAL JAMAICA

Hand-made. Quality, good. Cameroon wrapper. Java binder. Maduro wrappers from Brazil. Formerly made in Jamaica. Mild.

$$$$	**Ten Downing Street**	178mm/7 ins x 17.86mm/45
$$$	**Giant Corona***	190mm/7½ ins x 19.45mm/49
$$$$	**Goliath**	228mm/9 ins x 17.86mm/45
$$$	**Double Corona**	178mm/7 ins x 17.86mm/45
$$$	**Churchill***	203mm/8 ins x 20.24mm/51
$$	**Corona Grande***	165mm/6½ ins x 16.67mm/42
$$	**Royal Corona**	152mm/6 ins x 15.87mm/50
$$	**Director 1**	152mm/6 ins x 17.86mm/45
$$	**New York Plaza**	152mm/6 ins x 15.87mm/50
$$$	**Tube No 1**	165mm/6½ ins x 16.67mm/42
$$	**Doubloon**	178mm/7 ins x 12mm/30
$$	**Navarro**	160mm/6¼ ins x 13.49mm/34
$$	**Buccaneer***	140mm/5½ ins x 12mm/30
$$$	**Park Lane**	152mm/6 ins x 18.65mm/47
$$	**Corona***	140mm/5½ ins x 15.87mm/47
$$	**Petit Corona**	★★★

127mm/5 ins x 15.87mm/40. Medium-bodied with earthy flavors. Ideal for the beginner and value for money. Daytime smoke.

$$	**Robusto**	113mm/4½ ins x 19.45mm/49
$	**Pirate**	113mm/4½ ins x 12mm/30
$	**Gaucho**	133mm/5¼ ins x 13.1mm/33
$$	**Rapier**	165mm/6½ ins x 11.1mm/28

Maduro wrapper.

ROYALES

Hand-made.

No 1	203mm/8 ins x 20.64mm/52
No 2	190mm/7½ ins x 19.84mm/50
No 3	152mm/6 ins x 19.84mm/50
No 4	127mm/5 ins x 19.84mm/50

No 5 . . . . 168mm/6⅝ ins x 17.46mm/44
No 6 . . . . 152mm/6 ins x 16.67mm/42
No 7 . . . . 175mm/6⅞ ins x 15.08mm/38

SANTA DAMIANA

Hand-made. Quality, superior. Connecticut Shade wrapper. Mexican binder. Filler, blend of Dominican and Mexican tobacco. Mild. Launched in 1992 by Consolidated Cigars.

$$$$	**Seleccion No. 100**	. . 172mm/6¾ ins x 19.05mm/48
$$$	**Seleccion No. 300**	. . 140mm/5½ ins x 18.26mm/46
$$$	**Seleccion No. 500**	. . . 127mm/5 ins x 19.84mm/50
$$$	**Seleccion No. 700**	. . 165mm/6½ ins x 16.67mm/42
$$$	**Seleccion No. 800**	. . . 178mm/7 ins x 19.84mm/50
$$$	**Seleccion No. 200**	. . 140mm/5½ ins x 16.67mm/42
$$$	**Seleccion No. 400**	. . . 127mm/5 ins x 16.67mm/42
$$$	**Seleccion No. 600**	. . 113mm/4½ ins x 14.29mm/36
$$$	**Seleccion No. 700**	. . 165mm/6½ ins x 16.87mm/42
$$$	**Seleccion No. 800**	. . . 178mm/7 ins x 19.84mm/50

Brand relaunched in 1995 in four sizes with traditional names and blue and gold band, essentially for UK market. Has different blend from "Seleccion" range.

Churchill . . . . 178mm/7 ins x 19.05mm/48
Carona . . . . 140mm/5½ ins x 16.67mm/42
Petit Corona . . . . ★★★★★
127mm/5 ins x 16.67mm/42. Medium-bodied.
Good flavor and balance. Elegant. Well-made. For discerning smoker.
Panetela. . . . . . . 114mm/4 1/2 ins x 14.29mm/36

SANTIAGO

Hand-made. Connecticut wrapper. Dominican filler and binder.

$	**No 1** . . . . 171mm/6¾ ins x 19.1mm/48
$	**No 2** . . . . 178mm/7 ins x 14.3mm/36
$	**No 3** . . . . 165mm/6½ ins x 18.3mm/46
$	**No 4** . . . . 140mm/5½ ins x 18.3mm/46
$	**No 5** . . . . 127mm/5 ins x 15.9mm/40

★★★★★ Outstanding. A classic.   ★★★★ Excellent.
★★★ Good.   ★★ Fair, ordinary.   ★ Poor or faulty.
No Star Not evaluated.

SAVINELLI EXTREMELY LIMITED RESERVE

Hand-made. Connecticut wrapper. Dominican binder and filler. Small production. Owned by famous maker of pipes.

$$$$ **No 1 Churchill** . . . . . . 184mm/7¼ ins x 19.1mm/48

$$$$ **No 2 Corona Extra** . . 168mm/6⅝ ins x 18.3mm/46

$$$ **No 3 Lonsdale** . . . . **★★★★**
159mm/6¼ ins x 17.1mm/43. Beautiful, oily wrapper. medium-bodied, spicy. Good draw.

$$$ **No 4 Double Corona** . 152mm/6 ins x 19.84mm/50

$$$ **No 5 Extraordinaire** . . 140mm/5½ ins x 17.5mm/44

$$$ **No 6 Robusto** . . . . **★★★★★**
127mm/5 ins x 19.5mm/49. Fine Colorado wrapper. Extremely good, consistent construction. Draws well. Slow, even burning. Fairly mild, but has loads of spicy flavors. A cigar you would wish would go on forever. Difficult to get, so treasure the moment when you smoke it.

SERENDIPITY

Hand-made. Quality, superior. Connecticut Shade wrapper. Dominican filler and binder. Distributed by Mike's Cigars, Bay Harbour, Florida, USA.

$$$ Presidente . . . . 203mm/8 ins x 19.8mm/50

$$$ Churchill . . . . 165mm/6½ ins x 18.3mm/46

$$$ Torito . . . . 127mm/5 ins x 19.8mm/50

$$$ Coronita. . . . . 165mm/6½ ins x 17.5mm/44

SIGLO 21

Hand-made. Quality, superior. Ecuadorian wrapper. Dominican filler and binder. Created to celebrate the new millenium. Made by Puros de Villa Gonzalez SA. Distributed by Swisher Intl.

$$$ 21-1 . . . . 114mm/4½ ins x 19.8mm/50

$$$ 21-2 . . . . 165mm/6½ ins x 17.5mm/44

$$$ 21-3. . . . . 152mm/6 ins x 19.8mm/50

$$$ 21-4 . . . . **★★★★**
178mm/7 ins x 19.1mm/48. Uneven burn. Mild. Herby flavors. Daytime smoke.

$$$ 21-5. . . . . 203mm/8 ins x 19.8mm/50

¢ – Under $1.00 $ – $1–3.00 $$ – $3–4.00
$$$ – $5–8.00 $$$$ – $8–20.00 $$$$$ – $20+

SILLEM'S LAS TERENAS

Hand-made. Connecticut wrapper. Dominican binder and filler. Launched 1996. Exclusive to F&K Cigar Co.

Carabella	16.83mm/6⅝ ins x 16.67mm/42
Hidalgo	15.24mm/6 ins x 19.84mm/50
Baraja	11.43mm/4½ ins x 19.84mm/50
Levantado	19.05mm/7½ ins x 19.84mm/50
Talamquera	14.29mm/5⅝ ins x 16.67mm/42

SOSA

Hand-made. This brand was introduced 20 years ago by Juan Sosa. Wrapper from Ecuador and Connecticut. Binder from Honduras. Filler from Dominican Republic. Distributed by Antillian Cigar, Miami, Florida, USA.

$	**Magnum**	190mm/7½ ins x 20.64mm/52
$$$	**Piramides No 2**	178mm/7 ins x 25mm/64
$$	**Churchill**	176mm/6¹⁵⁄₁₆ ins x 19.05mm/48
$$	**Lonsdale**	165mm/6½ ins x 17.07mm/43
$$	**Governor**	152mm/6 ins x 19.84mm/50
$	**Brevas**	133mm/5½ ins x 17.07mm/43
$$	**Wavell**	120mm/4¾ ins x 19.84mm/50
$	**Santa Fe**	152mm/6 ins x 13.9mm/35

SOSA FAMILY SELECTION

Hand-made. Connecticut Shade wrapper. Dominican filler and binder. Owned by Antillian Cigar.

$$	**No 1**	171mm/6¾ ins x 17.1mm/43
$$$	**No 2**	159mm/6¼ ins x 21.4mm/54
$$	**No 3**	146mm/5¾ ins x 17.5mm/44
$$	**No 4**	127mm/5 ins x 15.9mm/40
$$	**No 5**	127mm/5 ins x 19.8mm/50
$$	**No 6**	159mm/6¼ ins x 15.1mm/38
$$	**No 7**	152mm/6 ins x 19.8mm/50
$$	**No 8**	171mm/6¾ ins x 19.1mm/48
$$$	**No 9**	197mm/7¾ ins x 20.6mm/52
$	**Intermezzo**	127mm/5 ins x 12.7mm/32

SPECIAL CARIBBEAN

Hand-made. Quality, superior. Connecticut wrapper. Very mild.

Corona	140mm/5½ ins x 17.07mm/43
Churchill	178mm/7 ins x 19.05mm/48
Fino	152mm/6 ins x 13.89mm/35
Nom Plus	140mm/5½ ins x 19.84mm/50

Port Au Prince . . . . 194mm/7⅝ ins x 20.64/52
No 1 . . . . 194mm/7⅝ ins x 17.07mm/43
No 2 . . . . 162mm/6⅜ ins x 16.67mm/42
No 898 . . . . 165mm/6½ ins x 17.86mm/42

SPECIAL CORONAS

Hand-made. Quality, superior. Ecuador wrappers. Made exclusively for Santa Clara, N.A. Mild to medium flavor. High-quality construction.

Pyramides . . . . 178mm/7 ins x 21.43mm/54
No 754 Light . . . . 178mm/7 ins x 21.43mm/54
No 2 Light . . . . 165mm/6½ ins x 17.76mm/45
No 54 Light . . . . 152mm/6 ins x 21.43mm/54
No 4 Light . . . . 140mm/5½ ins x 17.86mm/45
Victoria Obsequio . . 190mm/7½ ins x 20.64/52

SPECIAL JAMAICAN

Hand-made. Connecticut Shade wrapper. Mild. Sweet. Made in Jamaica until 1985. Exclusive to Santa Clara, N.A.

Rey del Rey . . . . 228mm/9 ins x 23.81mm/60
Mayfair . . . . 178mm/7 ins x 23.81mm/60
Pyramid . . . . 178mm/7 ins x 20.64mm/52
Churchill . . . . 178mm/7 ins x 20.64mm/52
Nobles (flared) . . . . . 178mm/7 ins x 19.84mm/50
Bonita Obsequio . . . . 152mm/6 ins x 19.84mm/50
A . . . . 165mm/6½ ins x 17.46mm/44
Fancytale Shape . . . . 165mm/6½ ins x 17.07mm/43
B . . . . 152mm/6 ins x 17.46mm/44
C . . . . 140mm/5½ ins x 17.46mm/44
B . . . . 152mm/6 ins x 19.84mm/50
Pica . . . . 127mm/5 ins x 12.7mm/32

TABANTILLAS

Hand-made. All Dominican tobacco. Distributed by Indian Head Sales.

Tabantillas A. . . . . 254mm/10 ins x 19.8mm/50
Gran Duque . . . . 203mm/8 ins x 19.8mm/50
Havana Club . . . . 184mm/7¼ ins x 15.1mm/38
1866 No 1 . . . . 171mm/6¾ ins x 15.1mm/38
Torerro . . . . 152mm/6 ins x 19.8mm/50

¢ – Under $1.00 $ – $1–3.00 $$ – $3–4.00
$$$ – $5–8.00 $$$$ – $8–20.00 $$$$$ – $20+

Condado Real	140mm/5½ ins x	18.3mm/46
No 4	133mm/5¼ ins x	16.67mm/42
Romero	114mm/4½ ins x	20.2mm/52

TABAQUERO

Hand-made. Quality, superior. Connecticut wrapper. Dominican filler and binder. Exclusive to Indian Head Sales.

No 850	203mm/8 ins x	20.84mm/50
No 746	178mm/7 ins x	18.3mm/46
No 650	152mm/6 ins x	20.84mm/50
No 644	152mm/6 ins x	17.5mm/44
No 638	152mm/6 ins x	15.1mm/38
No 542	127mm/5 ins x	16.67mm/42

TOPPER CENTENNIAL

Hand-made. Connecticut wrapper. Dominican filler. Mexican binder. Launched to mark founding of company in 1896. Owned by Topper Cigar Co.

Churchill	191mm/7½ ins x	20.6mm/52
Toro	152mm/6 ins x	20.84mm/50
Lonsdale	171mm/6¾ ins x	17.1mm/43

TRESADO

Hand-made. Quality, good. Medium flavor. Well-made. Mild. Indonesian wrapper. Dominican binder and filler.

$	**No 100**	216mm/8½ ins x	20.64mm/52
$	**No 200**	178mm/7 ins x	19.05mm/48
$	**No 300**	165mm/6 ins x	18.26mm/46
$	**No 400**	168mm/6⅝ ins x	17.46mm/44
$	**No 500**	140mm/5½ ins x	16.67mm/42

TROYA

Hand-made. Quality, superior. Connecticut Shade or maduro wrappers. Havana seed binder, long fillers. Made by Tabacos Dominicos. Brand owned in USA by Lignum-ll. Still made in Cuba with "Habana" on band.

$$$	**No 81 Torpedo**	★★★★

178mm/7 ins x 21.43mm/54. Easy draw, burns a little hot. Smooth. Medium- to full-bodied. Daytime smoke for beginners and experienced smokers alike.

$$	**No 72 Executive**	197mm/7¾ ins x	19.84mm/50
$$	**No 63 Churchill**	175mm/6⅞ ins x	18.26mm/46
$$	**No 54 Elegante**	178mm/7 ins x	16.67mm/43

$$ **No 45 Cetro** . . . . 160mm/6 1/4 ins x 17.46mm/44
$$ **No 36 Palma Fina**. . . . 178mm/7 ins x 14.29mm/36
$$ **No 27 Corona** . . . . ★★★★
      140mm/5½ ins x 16.67mm/42. Good, consistent
      construction. Easy draw. Mild to medium-bodied.
      Good finish. Complex flavors.
$$ **No 18 Rothschild**. . . 113mm/4½ ins x 19.84mm/50

TROYA CLASICO

Limited production. Long filler, double selection. Connecticut
Shade wrapper.

      Executive . . . . 197mm/7¾ ins x 19.84mm/50
      Corona. . . . . 133mm/5¼ ins x 20.64mm/52

VALDRYCH

Hand-made. Quality, superior. Produced with blends of Olor
Dominicano and Piloto Cubano tobacco. Sun-grown wrapper. A medium strength, full-bodied range with attractive, dark
wrappers. Close in flavor, texture and quality to that of genuine Havana. All tobacco is aged for at least three years. If
not properly humidified, wrappers become particularly frag-
ile. Good, consistent construction throughout range.

      Quisqueya Real . . . . . 254mm/10 ins x 19.8mm/50
      Monumento . . . . ★★★★★
      203mm/8 ins x 19.8mm/50. Good draw, even burn-
      ing. Smooth. Full-flavored. To follow good meal.
      This cigar is an occasion!
      Caballero . . . . 197mm/7¾ ins x 15.1mm/38
      Taino . . . . 152mm/6 ins x 19.8mm/50
      Conde . . . . 114mm/4½ ins x 20.6mm/52
      Carlos . . . . ★★★★★
      114mm/4½ ins x 19.8mm/50. Good draw. Medium
      strength with lots of flavor. Spicy. Good balance.
      For the connoisseur.
      1904 . . . . ★★★★
      171mm/6¾ ins x 18.3mm/46. Firm, but good draw.
      Slow, even burning. Smooth. Short finish.
      Francisco . . . . 140mm/5½ ins x 18.3mm/46
      Good draw. Burns a little unevenly. Makes long,
      white ash. Good balance and finish. Hint of coffee.
      To follow meal. For discerning smoker.
      Anacaona . . . . ★★★★
      140mm/5½ ins x 16.67mm/42. Burns and draws
      well. Smooth. A little more complexity would make
      this a stunning cigar. Daytime smoke.
      Sublime . . . . 102mm/4 ins x 16.67mm/42

VICTOR SINCLAIR

Hand-made. Quality, superior. Legend has it that this is the cigar that, in 1838, was appreciated by members of the Agricultural and Sporting Club of St. Simons Island. Connecticut Shade wrapper. Owned by Victor Sinclair Inc., St Simons Island, Georgia, USA.

	Churchill	19mm/7½ ins x 19.8mm/50
$$	**Robusto No 1**	140mm/5½ ins x 19.8mm/50
$$	**Robusto No 2**	114mm/4½ ins x 19.8mm/50
$$	**Lonsdale**	152mm/6 ins x 17.5mm/44
$$	**Pyramid**	179mm/7 ins x 21.4mm/54
$$	**Corona**	152mm/6 ins x 18.3mm/46

VICTOR SINCLAIR GRAND RESERVE

Hand-made. Quality, superior. All with maduro wrappers. Packed in boxes of 10 or 15. Owned by Victor Sinclair Inc., St. Simons Island, Georgia, USA.

$$	**Panetela**	179mm/7 ins x 15.1mm/38
$$	**Figurado**	127mm/5 ins x 18.3mm/44
$$$	**Belicoso**	146mm/5¾ ins x 20.6mm/52
$$$	**Pyramid**	152mm/6 ins x 21.4mm/54

VUELTABAJO

Hand-made. Connecticut Shade wrapper. Dominican binder and filler. Brand owned by Hollco Rohr.

$$	**Gigante**	203mm/8½ ins x 20.64mm/52
$$	**Churchill**	178mm/7 ins x 19.05mm/48
$	**Robusto**	113mm/4½ ins x 20.64mm/52
$$	**Lonsdale**	178mm/7 ins x 17.07mm/43
$	**Toros**	★★★★

152mm/6 ins x 19.84mm/50. Good flavor. Elegant. After-dinner cigar.

$	**Corona**	147mm/5¾ ins x 16.67mm/42

YUMURI

Hand-made. Quality, good. Dominican filler and binder. Connecticut Shade wrapper. Distributed by Brown Leaf Co., Miami, Florida, USA.

$$$	**Churchill**	178mm/7 ins x 19.1mm/48
$$$	**Lonsdale**	178mm/7 ins x 17.1mm/43

¢ – Under $1.00 $ – $1–3.00 $$ – $3–4.00
$$$ – $5–8.00 $$$$ – $8–20.00 $$$$$ – $20+

$$$	**Toro** . . . . ★★★	

152mm/6 ins x 19.8mm/50 Well-made. Slow, even burning. Mild. Daytime smoke. Ideal for beginners.

$$$ **Corona**. . . . . 140mm/5½ ins x 17.1mm/43

$$$ **Robusto** . . . . 121mm/4¾ ins x 20.6mm/52

Ecuador

PRIMERA BUNDLES

Hand-made. Distributed in USA by Phillips & King.

           No 1 . . . . 178mm/7 ins x 16.67mm/42

           No 2. . . . . 149mm/5⅞ ins x 17.46mm/44

           Toro . . . . 127mm/5 ins x 17.07mm/43

Germany

In 1950 there were more than 300 cigar factories in Germany. Today, although fewer than 10, cigar making (mainly cigarillos) is major industry. In 1995 exports to USA doubled to almost 5 million cigars over 1994. Cigar consumption in Germany has fallen in past 30 years from 5 billion to around 1 billion—about 5 percent of the total tobacco market.

AL CAPONE

Machine-made by Burger Söhne. Distributed in USA by Swisher Intl.

           Sweets (cognac dipped) . . . . 82mm/3¼ ins

           Pockets . . . . 70mm/2¾ ins

BRANIFF GOLDEN LABEL

Machine-made. Tobacco from Sumatra. Short filler. Dry cigar.

           Cigarillo. . . . . ★★

75mm/2¹⁵⁄₁₆ ins x 8.3mm/21. Good integrated flavors.

   ★★★★★ Outstanding. A classic.   ★★★★ Excellent.
  ★★★ Good.   ★★ Fair, ordinary.   ★ Poor or faulty.
               No Star Not evaluated.

CANDLELIGHT DRY CURED

Machine-made. Light green wrapper cured with heat to fix chlorophyll in leaf. Slightly sweet taste.

Mini
Senorita
Panetela
Corona Slim
Block Corona

CLUBMASTER

Machine-made. Quality, good. Produced by Arnold André-Zigarrenfabrik, largest cigar producer in Germany. Part of gaint Ebas Group which was established in 1989 as result of merger between Dutch companies, La Paz, Willem II and Arnold André. Key markets: Germany, Belgium and France. Known mainly for its Brazil cigar type. Mild and aromatic.

Export/Export Light . . . . 75mm/3 ins x 8.8mm/22
Superior Sumatra/Brazil . . . . ★
75mm/3 ins x 8.8mm/22. Slightly harsh.
Superior Mild Sumatra/Brazil
75mm/3 ins x 8.8mm/22
Finos Sumatra/Brazil
90mm/3⁹⁄₁₆ ins x 9mm/23
Selectos Sumatra/Brazil
92mm/3⅝ ins x 9mm/23
Elegantes Sumatra/Brazil
107mm/4³⁄₁₆ ins x 10.7mm/27
Long Sumatra/Brazil
145mm/5¹¹⁄₁₆ ins x 81.8mm/22
Panatelas Sumatra/Brazil
145mm/5¹¹⁄₁₆ ins x 11mm/28
Half Corona Sumatra/Brazil
125mm/4¹⁵⁄₁₆ ins x 13.8mm/35

DANNEMANN

Machine-made. Established 1873 by Geraldo Dannemann in Brazil. Made with Brazilian and Sumatran tobaccos. Homogenized (HTL) wrapper. In 1994, launched vigorous marketing campaign in USA where it is distributed by Swisher Intl. One of largest producers of cigarillos in world. Employs nearly 500 people in Germany and has about 33 percent share of local cigar market.

¢   **Lonja** (Brazil/Sumatra) . . . . ★★★★
    136mm/5⅜ ins x 9.92mm/25. Mild. Good balance.
    Spicy. Morning smoke. Ideal for beginners.
¢   **Speciale** (Brazil/Sumatra) . . . . ★★
    74mm/2⅞ ins x 9.92mm/25. Mild, pleasant aroma.
¢   **Imperial** (Sumatra/Brazil)
    108mm/4¼ ins x 9.92mm/25
¢   **Pierrot** (Sumatra leaf/Brazil)
    9.84mm/3⅞ ins x 11.11mm/28
¢   **Menor** (Sumatra) . . 9.84mm/3⅞ ins x 11.11mm/28
    Moods . . . . 73.2mm/2⅞ ins x 7.9mm/20

IRACEMA

Machine-made.

> **Iracema Autentico Fuma**
> 133mm/5¼ ins x 17.46/44
> **Iracema Macumba**
> 165mm/6½ ins x 16.67/42
> **Iracema Mata Fina**
> 210mm/8¼ ins x 17.46mm/44
> **Iracema Santo Amoro**
> 89mm/3½ ins x 9.95mm/25

JOHN AYLESBURY

Hand-made. Good quality. Tobacco from Brazil, Sumatra and Indonesia.

This group is based in Germany where it manufactures a range of cigars from Brazilian and Sumatran leaf. It also imports range of hand-made cigars from Dominican Republic and Honduras with "John Aylesbury" label.

Unique feature of this company is that distribution in Germany is guaranteed through a chain of 44 individually owned specialist cigar shops, with each shop owner having a share in the manufacturing business. This brand is exported to the United States. (See also "John Aylesbury" in Dominican Republic and Honduras sections.)

> **John Aylesbury**
> **Feinschmecker No 1 (Indonesian leaf)**
> **Feinschmecker No 2 (Indonesian leaf)**
> **Feinschmecker No 3 (Indonesian leaf)**

These sizes are repeated using Brazilian leaf.

> **John Aylesbury** (all from Sumatra leaf)
> **No 22**
> **No 23**
> **No 24**

Corona
Jubilee
Half Corona Number 1
Number 9
Pedito
Grandola
Tubo
Los Finos No 506
Los Finos No 509
Los Finos No 510
Half Corona

The above sizes are repeated using Brazilian leaf.

JOHN AYLESBURY CIGARILLOS

Machine-made.

No 1 (Brazilian and Sumatran leaf)
Mild and Small (Sumatran)
Black and Small (Brazilian)
Speciales (Brazilian)
Senoritas (Sumatran and Brazilian)
Longos (Sumatran and Brazilian)
Light Slenders (Sumatran)
Dark Slenders (Brazilian)
Twenty-One (Sumatran and Brazilian)
Japura (Brazilian)

JOHN AYLESBURY LOS FINOS

Machine-made.

Rondo (Sumatran)
No 501 (Sumatran and Brazilian)
No 502 (Sumatran and Brazilian)
Mini Cigarillo (Sumatran and Brazilian)

JOHN AYLESBURY SIR JOHN'S

Mini (Sumatran, Brazilian and Cuban)
Aromatic (Sumatran and Brazilian)
Selection 100 (Sumatran and Brazilian)
Selection 400 (Cuban)

SUERDIECK (SEE ALSO BRAZIL)

Machine-made.

Mandarim (Sumatran and Brazilian wrapper)

Holland

Holland is the largest global manufacturer of cigars, accounting for nearly half the world's production. It makes close to 3 billion (including cigarillos). About 95 percent is made by four companies: Agio, about 1 billion (of which 500 million are their own brands); Ebas, about 900 million; Henri Winterman, about 650 million and Ritmeester, about 130 million. Of the total production, about 50 percent is cigarillos. In 1995, exports to the USA increased from 3.26 million the previous year to 5.7 million. Local consumption is around 455 million pieces (decline of 3.3 percent from 1994) for a population of only 15 million. The country has a highly developed marketing infrastructure. There are still about 2,000 good tobacco shops, of which around 200 are top specialist shops. In 1995, for second year running, cigarillos accounted for more than 50 percent of the Dutch market. Senoritas and tuit sizes did well at the expense of larger cigars. The industry started in about 1830 on a small scale in Amsterdam. Until WWII most cigars were made by hand. Today, only about four brands are made that way. By 1860, there were 62 cigar makers in and around Amsterdam selling in grocery stores that specialized in colonial goods, such as coffee, tea, spices and tobacco. Now there are only two hand rollers left in Amsterdam: Harry Nak and his wife, situated opposite the famous and prestigeous Hajenius tobacco shop in what was the heart of the Amsterdam tobacco trade. By 1900, many cigar makers had settled around the towns of Eindhoven, near the Belgian border, and Veenendal in the center of Holland. The country was poor and there was plenty of cheap labor available. The industry built on what was, largely, a home industry. Cigar makers would call at the factories on Saturday to collect tobacco and then during the week the whole family—husband, wife, children and grandparents—

would make cigars, with the most skillful members adding the wrappers. Finished cigars were delivered to the factories the following Saturday when tobacco was collected for the next week. Cigars were entirely hand-rolled until the 1930s, when the first machines were introduced. These only made the "bunch" (the filler wrapped inside the binder leaf). The wrapper was still applied by hand. Today the entire process is mechanized. It was only after the end of WWII that the Dutch began to export cigars in earnest. At that time, there were hundreds of factories. As recently as 1963 there were still 22 cigar companies, but by 1982 the number had decreased to about 10. Holland has created a huge industry even though it produces no tobacco itself. It has always relied on its former colonies, particularly Indonesia, for raw material. Despite this, and extremely high labor costs, Holland has been able to create this vast industry because of the concentration of production in a few large, highly mechanized and automated factories. Amsterdam and Rotterdam used to be world centers for the trade in Indonesian and American tobacco. Today, all Indonesian tobacco is sold by auction in Bremen in Germany; Cameroon tobacco is sold in Paris. What has certainly contributed to the international popularity of the Dutch product is the variety of small cigars and cigarillos which have the taste of a true cigar and which can be smoked in a short time. Also, because of the link between disease and cigarettes, many cigarette smokers are switching to pure tobacco cigars which are less harmful, as many of the damaging elements, including nicotine, have been considerably reduced. In addition, Dutch cigars cost substantially less than a Havana and this was highlighted by Fons Maenen, export manager of the Ebas Group, who told me on a recent visit to Holland, "The Cubans make cigars for wealthy capitalists, while the Dutch make cigars for the mass market."

AGIO CIGARS

Machine-made. Dry cigars. Available in Sumatran and dark Brazilian wrappers. Big seller in Europe. Agio Sigaren-fabrieken is one of the largest cigar manufacturers in Europe. Head office is situated in Duizel, near the Belgium border. It produces about 1 billion cigars a year, of which about 500 million exported under own brand names to more than 100 countries outside Europe. Employs about 2,500 people world-wide. Family enterprise established in 1904 by Jacques Wintermans, grandfather of present chairman. Rapid growth of Agio, combined with shortage of manpower in the Dutch Kempen, led to the establishment, in 1961, of a subsidiary in Geel, Belgium, where all cigars are currently produced. Increased labor costs in Holland and Belgium sparked off sub-sidiaries in Malta in 1973, Sri Lanka in 1985 and the Dominican Republic in 1990. These companies process binders and wrappers on bobbins for Agio and, to an increas-ing extent, for other cigar manufacturers as well. The cigars are actually manufactured in the factory in Geel. Binder and filler tobacco are provided from the plant in Duizel. Final pro-cessing such as cutting, putting on the bands and wrapping in cellophane takes place in Duizel, where packing in wood or cardboard boxes is undertaken. Company has also devel-oped and manufactured bobbin machines for its own use as well as for other manufacturers.

AGIO

Machine-made, mass market. Quality, good. Short filler. Dry cigar.

Agio Lights (Connecticut Shade wrapper, light blue box) . . . . ★★★★
79mm/3⅛ ins x 8.3mm/21. Lemony aroma.
Smooth and mild.

Biddies (Brazilian wrapper, green box) . . . . . . ★★★
99mm/3⅞ ins x 9.1mm/23. Light-bodied, but good balance between strength and flavor.

Biddies (Sumatran wrapper, blue box) . . . . . . ★★★
99mm/3⅞ ins x 9.1mm/23. Medium-bodied.
Stronger and more flavor than Brazilian wrapper.

Biddies Light (Connecticut Shade wrapper, cream box) . . . . ★★★★
99mm/3⅞ ins x 9.1mm/23. Spicy flavor and aroma.
Smooth and mild.

Elegant Rich & Light (Cuban shade wrapper, blue box) . . . . ★★★
99mm/3⅞ ins x 9.6mm/24. Figurado shape (tuit cigar). Full flavor. Medium-bodied. Spicy. Also available with Sumatran wrapper.

Filter Tip (Cameroon wrapper, white box) . . . . ★★
79mm/3⅛ ins x 8.2mm/20. Plastic tip with charcoal filler. HTL binder. Touch of sweetness. Mild. Much like a cigarette.

Junior Tip (Cameroon wrapper, white box)
79mm/3 ⅛ ins x 8.2mm/20.

Mehari's Cigarillos (Cameroon wrapper, pale orange box) . . . . ★★
99mm/3⅞ ins x 9.1mm/23. Touch of sweetness. Medium-bodied. HTL binder.

Mehari's Cigarillos (Brazilian wrapper)
99mm/3⅞ ins x 9.1mm/23

Mehari's Mild & Light (Connecticut Shade wrapper, blue box) . . . . ★
99mm/3⅞ ins x 9.1mm/23. Sweet. Mild. HTL binder.

Agio Biddies (Brazilian) 85mm/3⅜ ins x 7.9mm/20

Agio Biddies (Sumatran) 85mm/3⅜ ins x 7.9mm/20

BALMORAL

Machine-made, premium. Quality, good. Short filler. Dry cigar. Owned by Agio. Heads are pre-cut.

Corona de Luxe (aluminum tubes)
122mm/4¾ ins x 16.6mm/42

Overland . . . . 132mm/5¼ ins x 13.4mm/34

Coronas No 4. . . . . ★★★★
132mm/5¼ ins x 13.4mm/34. Medium-bodied. Full creamy flavors.

Aristocrats . . . . 159mm/6¼ ins x 13.4mm/34

Valentine (figurado—tuit cigar)
85mm/3⅜ ins x 7.9mm/20

Cambridge (figurado—tuit cigar)
99mm/3⅞ ins x 9.6mm/24

Oxford (figurado—tuit cigar)
91mm/3⁹⁄₁₆ ins x 12.6mm/32

Cardinal (figurado—tuit cigar) . . . . ★★★
106mm/4³⁄₁₆ ins x 12.6mm/32. Sumatra wrapper. Good balance between flavor and strength. Surprisingly full-bodied for a small cigar.

Regentes (figurado—tuit cigar)
96mm/3¹⁄₁₆ ins x 14.5mm/37
Cumberland . . . . 112mm/4⅜ ins x 10mm/25
Senoritas No 5 . . . . 112mm/4⅜ ins x 10mm/25
Highlands . . . . 111mm/4⁵⁄₁₆ ins x 12.2mm/31
Midlands . . . . 103mm/4⅛ ins x 12.6mm/32
Panatella . . . . 124mm/4⅞ ins x 12.3mm/31
Diana . . . . 85mm/3⅜ ins x 7.9mm/20
Legende . . . . 97mm/3½ ins x 7.6mm/19
Shetlands . . . . 93mm/3¹¹⁄₁₆ ins x 9.4mm/24
Cigarillos No 3 . . . . 93mm/3¹¹⁄₁₆ ins x 9.4mm/24

HENRI WINTERMAN CAFE CREME

Machine-made, mass market. Short filler. Dry cigar. Quality, good. Entire production of about 650 million exported, mainly cigarillos. Company established in Eersel, near Belgium border, in 1934 to supply local market. Then, in 1950, because of severe competition from about 1,500 manufacturers, began exporting. Probably largest cigar exporter in world. Taken over by giant cigarette manufacturer, BAT. Operate separately because marketing of cigars different from that of cigarettes. However, uses parent company's expertise in emerging markets, such as the former Soviet Union countries and Eastern Europe. Presently exports to about 100 countries. Main markets are Australia, Ireland, Italy, Scandinavia and duty-free shops. Brand launched in 1963 to capture large sector of cigarillo market, that was growing as cigarette smokers switched to pure tobacco products. Packed in flat tins, bearing Café Crème logo, coffee cup symbol and cigar. These elements were added to the packaging to reinforce ideal partnership of the brand when enjoying a break, or a moment of relaxation. Annual sales exceed 100 million sticks.

Filter Tip (paper filter incorporated in plastic
mouthpiece) . . . . 98mm/3⅞ ins x 8.5mm/28
Mild . . . . 75mm/2⅞ ins x 8.5mm/28
Grand Café . . . . 92mm/3⅜ ins x 7.7mm/19
Mini/Mild . . . . x 8.5mm/28
Plus/Mild . . . . 74mm/2⅞ ins x 8.5mm/28
Specials . . . . 110mm/4⁵⁄₁₆ ins x 10mm/25

***

★★★★★ Outstanding. A classic.   ★★★★ Excellent.
★★★ Good.   ★★ Fair, ordinary.   ★ Poor or faulty.
No Star Not evaluated.

HENRY WINTERMAN CIGARS

Machine-made, mass market. Quality, superior. Sumatran wrapper. Java binder and filler blend of tobacco from Cuba and Brazil. Half-corona claimed to be top-selling cigar in UK.

- ¢ **Excellentes**. . . . . . . 160mm/6⅜ ins x 16.67mm/42
- ¢ **Royales**
- ¢ **Cello**
- ¢ **Golden Panetella**
- ¢ **Kentucky Kings**
- ¢ **Half Corona**. . . . . 95mm/3¾ ins x 13.5mm/34
- ¢ **Long Panatella**. . . . . . 131mm/5⅛ ins x 11.9mm/30
- ¢ **Slim Panatella** . . . . 143mm/5⅝ ins x 7.9mm/20
- ¢ **Corona de Luxe**. . . . 115mm/5⅛ ins x 16.67mm/42
- ¢ **Scooters**. . . . . 90mm/3½ ins x 7.9mm/20

JUSTUS VAN MAURIK

Machine-made. Quality, superior. Short filler. Dry cigar. Hand selected. Wrapper from Sumatra, binder from Java and filler blend of tobacco from Cuba, Brazil and Indonesia. Brand established in 1794. Now owned by Ebas Group. Packed in varnished cedar boxes.

Grand Corona . . . . . . 152mm/6 ins x 16.67mm/42
Corona No 1. . . . . 152mm/6 ins x 16.67mm/42
Coronation . . . . 135mm/5⁵⁄₁₆ ins x 16.67mm/42
After Dinner. . . . . . . 120mm/5¹¹⁄₁₆ ins x 14.5mm/37
Petit Corona . . . . 103mm/4¹⁄₁₆ ins x 14.9mm/38
Noblesse . . . . 130mm/5⅛ ins x 13.8mm/35
Sumatra Tuitnak (figurado) . . . . ★★★★★
112mm/4⁷⁄₁₆ ins x 12.15mm/32. Even, slow burn-
ing. Spicy, floral flavors and aroma. Medium- to
full-bodied, flavor gets going when full girth of
cigar is reached. Great daytime smoke.
Classique. . . . . 104mm/4¹⁄₁₆ ins x 12.6mm/32
Petit Panetela. . . . . 122mm/4¹³⁄₁₆ ins x 10.75mm/27
Zandblad Cigarillos . . . 94mm/3⁷⁄₁₆ ins x 8.2mm/21
Caresse . . . . ★★★
98mm/3⅞ ins x 8mm/20. Full flavor, but mild in
strength.

LA PAZ

Machine-made. Quality, good. 100 percent tobacco, undusted. Dry cigar. Uses tobacco from Sumatra, Java, Brazil and Cuba. Quality, superior. Brand established in 1814. Now owned by Ebas, which was established in 1989 as a result of merger between Dutch companies La Paz and Willem II and German company, Arnold André. Ebas produces more than 1 billion cigars annually, employs nearly 2,000 people in several countries. La Paz popularized concept of wilde cigars. Availability: Holland, France, Belgium, Germany, South Africa and duty-free shops. Foot of Wilde range is uncut, enabling smokers to see easily that the binder is pure tobacco leaf.

Mini Wilde . . . . ★★★
79mm/3⅛ ins x 7.6mm/19. Robust, full, integrated flavors.

Wilde Cigarillos Havana . . . . ★★★★
102mm/4 ins x 9.2mm/23. Good integrated flavors. Satisfying quick smoke.

Wilde Cigarillos Brazil . . 102mm/4 ins x 9.1mm/23
Wilde Panetela . . . . . 119mm/4¹¹⁄₁₆ ins x 10.5mm/27
Wilde Havana . . . . ★★★★
119mm/4¹¹⁄₁₆ ins x 12.7mm/32. Pleasant cool smoke. Good value.

Wilde Brazil . . . . ★★★★
119mm/4¹¹⁄₁₆ ins x 12.6mm/32. Dark maduro wrapper. Spicy. Vegetal aroma. Full-bodied and good flavor.

Wilde Corona . . . . . . 135mm/5⁵⁄₁₆ ins x 14.5mm/37
Cherie . . . . ★★★
102mm/4 ins x 12.7mm/32. Mild, pleasant, quick smoke.

Corona Superiores CK126 . . . . ★★★
114mm/4½ ins x 16mm/41. Good integated flavors with a creamy finish. Good morning smoke.

Especiales CK164 (tube)
162mm/6⅜ ins x 13.7mm/35

RITMEESTER

Machine-made, mass market. Short filler. Dry cigar. HTL binder. Quality, good. Designed for mass market. Good value range. Established in 1887. Reached high point in the 1930s, when torpedo shape developed. In 1937 employed 1,700 people; today, largely because of mechanization, figure down to about 200 employees. Produce about 130 million cigars annually. (5 million to South Africa, where it is the brand leader.) Popular in USA, Europe and South Africa. Mild cigar using tobacco mainly from Java and Brazil. Today Ritmeester is owned by Burger Söhne Company, manufacturers of Dannemann brand, in Switzerland.

Half Corona . . . . ★★
95mm/3¾ ins x 14.6mm/37. Dusted. Pleasant. Medium- to full-bodied.

PiKeur . . . . ★
101mm/4 ins x 12.5mm/32. Ordinary quick smoke. Dusted.

Riant (dusted). . . . . ★★
97mm/3⅞ ins x 18mm/46. Mild but slightly harsh finish.

PiKeur Mini Light . . . . . 83mm/3¼ ins x 7.8mm/20
Corona. . . . . 117mm/4⅝ ins x 16.3mm/41

Gracia (torpedo). . . . . ★★
108mm/4¼ ins x 19.8mm/50. HTL binder. Dusted.

Livarde . . . . ★★★
91mm/3⁹⁄₁₆ ins x 9.1mm/23. Dusted wrapper. Better burning and fuller body than Livarde Light.

Livarde Light . . . . 91mm/3⁹⁄₁₆ ins x 9.1mm/23
HTL binder. Good wrapper from Sumatra. Mild.

Livarde Mini Light. . . . . 83mm/3¼ ins x 7.8mm/20

Rozet. . . . . ★★
117mm/4⅝ ins x 10.7mm/27. Full-bodied. Bit harsh.

Royal Dutch Fresh and Mild
91mm/3⁹⁄₁₆ ins x 9.1mm/23

Royal Dutch Cigarillo
91mm/3⁹⁄₁₆ ins x 9.1mm/23

Royal Dutch Panatella
106mm/4³⁄₁₆ ins x 10.3mm/26

Royal Dutch Half Corona
95mm/3¾ ins x 11.6mm/29

Tip . . . . 75mm/3 ins x 8.7mm/22
Elites . . . . 136mm/5⅛ ins x 9.7mm/25

Wilde Havana . . . . ★★★★
120mm/4¾ ins x 12.7mm/32. Medium-bodied. Mild coffee aroma. Flavor little forward. Good cigar.

Corona Delecta . . . . ★★
132mm/5¼ ins x 17mm/43. Medium to full-bodied. Not particularly elegant cigar. Dusted.

Quick* . . . . 101mm/4 ins x 12.5mm/32

Whiff. . . . . 91mm/3⁹⁄₁₆ ins x 9.1mm/23
Senior* . . . . ★★★
100mm/3¹⁵⁄₁₆ ins x 10mm/25. HTL binder. Dusted.
Medium-bodied. Bit one dimensional.
Junior*. . . . . 90mm/3½ ins x 9.7mm/24
**Only available in South Africa.*

SCHIMMELPENNICK

Machine-made, mass market. Quality, superior. Made from
tobacco from Brazil, Cameroon and Indonesia. Dry cigar.
Started in 1924 and named after 19th-century Dutch governor. About 90 percent of total production exported to over
160 countries. Accounts for about 40 percent of dry cigars
sold in USA. Duet is world's best-selling thin panetela. Owned
by Rothmans.

¢   **Florina** . . . . 99mm/3⅞ ins
¢   **Half Corona** . . . . 95mm/3¾ ins
¢   **Nostra**. . . . . 74mm/2⅞ ins
¢   **Media** . . . . 76mm/3 ins
¢   **Montego Milds** . . . . 76mm/3 ins
¢   **Mono** . . . . 86mm/3⅜ ins
¢   **Vada** . . . . 99mm/3⅞ ins
     Mini Tips. . . . . 102mm/4 with tip
     Panatella 145 Miskleur
     Panatella 145 Miskleur Naturel
     Superior Milds
     Duet . . . . 143mm/5⅝ ins
     Media Brazil . . . . 79mm/3⅛ ins
     Duet Brazil . . . . 79mm/5⅛ ins
     Mini Cigar. . . . . 70mm/2¾ ins
     Mono Brazil . . . . 86mm/3⅜ ins
     Havana Milds . . . . 76mm/3 ins
     Swing
     VSOP Cigarillo de Luxe
     VSOP Senoritas de Luxe
     VSOP Duella de Luxe
     VSOP Corona de Luxe
     VSOP Grand Corona de Luxe
     VSOP Corona Royales (aluminum tube)

SWISHER SWEETS

Machine-made, mass market. Owned by Swisher Intl.

Mini Cigarillo (tins) . . 111mm/4⅜ ins x 11.1mm/28

WILLEM II

Machine-made, mass market. Short filler. Dry cigar. Quality, good. Sumatran wrapper. HTL binder. Willem was founded in 1916 by the tobacco merchant Hendrik Kersten. Factory still located in Valkenswaard, small rural village in south of Holland. Cigars exported to more than 100 countries and stocked in nearly all duty-free shops. Part of Dutch Ebas Group established in 1989 as result of merger between Dutch companies, La Paz, Willem II and German company, Arnold André.

Optimum . . . . ★
126mm/4¹⁵⁄₁₆ ins x 15.8mm/40 Draws too easily, tends to burn bit harsh. Mild. Uninspiring.
Corona de Luxe . . . . 126mm/4¹⁵⁄₁₆ ins x 15.8mm/40
Half Corona . . . . ★★★
94mm/3⅞₁₆ ins x 13.7mm/35 All tobacco. Spicy, vegetal aroma. Good balance. Smooth.
¢ **Extra Senoritas** . . . . 101mm/3¹⁵⁄₁₆ ins x 12.4mm/31
¢ **Long Panetella** . . . . ★★★
143mm/5⅝ ins x 9mm/23. Mild. Rich coffee and spice aroma. Touch of sweetness.
Whiff

WILLEM II WHIFF & MINIATURE

Mass market.
¢ **No 30** . . . . 89mm/3½ ins x 9.1mm/23
¢ **Java** . . . . 102mm/4 ins x 8.8mm/22
¢ **Indioz** . . . . 96mm/3¹³⁄₁₆ ins x 7.6mm/19
¢ **Primo** . . . . 96mm/3¹³⁄₁₆ ins x 7.6mm/19
¢ **Java Mini** . . . . 79mm/3⅛ ins x 7.6mm/19
¢ **Indioz Mini** . . . . 79mm/3⅛ ins x 7.6mm/19
¢ **Petitos** . . . . ★★★★
79mm/3⅛ ins x 7.6mm/19. Good flavor. Medium body. Good, quick smoke.
¢ **Sigretto** . . . . ★★★
70mm/2¾ ins x 9mm/23. Dark maduro wrapper. Surprisingly strong and full-bodied for such a small cigar.
Wee Willem Mild . . . . . . 70mm/2¾ ins x 8.1mm/21
Wee Willem Extra Mild . . 70mm/2¾ ins x 8.1mm/21

Wings No 75. . . . . 75mm/3 ins x 7.6mm/19
Wings No 105 . . . . 105mm/4⅛ ins x 7.6mm/19

ZINO

Machine-made. 100 percent tobacco. Dry cigar. Available in
Indonesian and dark Brazilian wrappers. Mild.

Zino Drie . . . . 147mm/5¾ ins x 15.87mm/40
Zino Jong Cigarillos . . . 108mm/4¼ ins x 12mm/30
Zino Panatellas (Sumatran leaf)
140mm/5½ ins x 7.14mm/18
Zino Panetellas (Brazilian leaf)
140mm/5½ ins x 7.14mm/18
Zino Cigarillos (Brazilian leaf) . . . . ★★★★
89mm/3½ ins. Mild with good flavor.
Zino Cigarillos (Sumatran leaf). . . . . ★★★★
89mm/3½ ins. More body than Brazilian leaf. Both
excellent cigarillos.

Honduras

Honduras is the second-largest exporter of premium
cigars to the United States, exporting in 1996 more
than 83.7 million. This accounted for 28 percent of
imports into USA of premium cigars. Main growing
areas are hot, coastal plains around San Pedro Sula and
cooler mountain regions of Santa Rosa de Copan
stretching to the hilly Nicaraguan border of Danli.
Tradition dominating the cigar industry in Honduras
is different from that of Cuba and the Dominican
Republic. Something between the rustic yet disciplined
air of Cuba's state-owned factories and the almost
industrial atmosphere of the Dominican Republic.
Honduras is clearly Third World, with factories dotting
the sparsely populated countryside or in small, fron-
tier-like towns with cobblestone streets and carts pulled
by bulls or horses. Many believe that Honduran
tobacco has the aroma and palate closest to that of true
Cuban tobacco, although supporters of cigars from
Nicaragua will deny this. Commercial tobacco opera-
tions in Honduras date back to mid-18th century. Most

tobacco in Honduras is grown from Cuban seed introduced as early as 1941. However, blue mold has devastated huge amounts of tobacco in Central America since the early 1980s. About 25 percent of the crop of some producers was lost to this disease in 1993. A field of several acres can be overcome by this scourge in a single night once the mold is present. To combat blue mold some growers in Honduras have altered their plant seasons from the milder, cooler months of November and December, which encourage the fungus, to the hotter, drier period in January and February. Mold is not able to prosper without the end-of-year cool nights and mornings wet with dew. Although Honduras is not as sophisticated as the Dominican Republic most factories employ strict quality control. However, it is not unusual to find producers who expect workers to produce 600 cigars a day working in teams of bunchers and rollers. This is, more or less, similar to the Dominican Republic.

AL CAPONE

Hand-made. Quality, superior. Brazilian wrapper. Nicaraguan binder and filler. Exclusive to Swisher Intl.

$$ Corona Grande . . . . . 171mm/6¾ ins x 17.1mm/43
$$ Robusto . . . . 121mm/4¾ ins x 19.8mm/50

ARANGO STATESMAN

Hand-made. All Honduran tobacco. Medium-bodied. Not to be confused with sister brand, Arango Sportsman, which is vanilla flavored, machine-made in Tampa, Florida, USA. Owned by Arango Cigar Co., Chicago, Illinois, USA.

$ **Barrister** . . . . ★★★
190mm/7½ ins x 18.26mm/46. Smooth claro wrapper. Burns evenly. Easy draw. Sweet vanilla finish.
$ **Executor**. . . . . 127mm/5 ins x 15.87mm/40
$ **Counselor** . . . . 140mm/5½ ins x 17.46mm/44

★★★★★ Outstanding. A classic.　★★★★ Excellent.
★★★ Good.　★★ Fair, ordinary.　★ Poor or faulty.
No Star Not evaluated.

ASTRAL

Hand-made. Quality, superior. Premium Connecticut Shade wrapper. Aged Honduran binder. Blend of Havana seed and Honduran long leaf filler. Super-premium with price range of $7 to $10, launched in June 1995. Distributed worldwide. Sales in 1996 nearly 6 million. Owned by U.S. Tobacco International. Distributed in USA by Miami Cigar.

$$$ **Maestro** . . . . ★★★★★
190mm/7½ ins x 20.64mm/52. Good balance between strength and flavor. Not as much body as one would expect from such big cigar. Discreet aroma and flavors. Elegant. Well-made. Appreciated by connoisseur and occasional smoker alike.

$$$ **Favorito** . . . . ★★★★
178mm/7 ins x 19.05mm/48. Spicy aroma before lit. Medium-bodied. Needs half an inch or so before it starts to show its pace.

$$$ **Perfeccion** . . . . ★★★★
178mm/7 ins x 19.05mm/48. Well-made. Medium-bodied. Smooth. Good balance.

$$$ **Lujos** . . . . ★★★★
165mm/6½ ins x 17.46mm/44. Firm draw. Medium-bodied. Short on flavor. Smooth. Even burning.

Besos . . . . ★★★★
127mm/5 ins x 20.64mm/52. Attractive wrapper. Full-bodied. Robust. Not for beginner.

BACCARAT HAVANA SELECTION

Hand-made. Quality, medium. Good value. Connecticut Shade wrapper. Mexican binder. Cuban seed filler. Launched in 1978. Made by Tabocos Rancho Jamastran. This company owns its own farms and in 1996 planted over 600 acres (300 hectares) of tobacco. Runs formal training school for rollers. Group owned by Eiroas Family. Imported exclusively into USA by Caribe in Miami, Florida, USA.

$ **Polo** . . . . ★★
178mm/7 ins x 20.64mm/52. Inconsistent construction. Mild. Lacks punch.

$ **Churchill*** . . . . ★★★★
178mm/7 ins x 19.84mm/50. Mild, with lots of flavor. Well-made.

$ **No 1** . . . . 178mm/7 ins x 17.46mm/44

$ **Panetela** . . . . 152mm/6 ins x 15.08mm/38

$ **Petit Corona** .... ★★★★
140mm/5½ ins x 16.67mm/42. Good draw.
Cinnamon and coffee undertones. Good balance.
Fine finish. Ideal daytime smoke for beginner and
experienced smoker alike. Value for money.

$ **Rothschild*** .... 178mm/7 ins x 19.84mm/50

$ **Bonita** .... 113mm/4½ ins x 12mm/30

$ **Luchadore** .... ★★★★
152mm/6 ins x 17.07mm/43. Firm draw. Robust
flavor with touch of sweetness.

$ **Platinum** .... 124mm/4⅞ ins x 12.7mm/32
Also available in maduro.

BALLENA SUPREMA DANLI COLLECTION

Hand-made. Quality, superior. Connecticut Shade wrapper.
Mexican binder. Filler is blend of Dominican Piloto from
Cuban seed and Mexican San Andres Morron. A range with
full flavor. Distributed by pipe tobacco specialist McClelland
Tobacco Co., Kansas City, Missouri, USA.

$$$ **Capitan** (pyramid) .... 178mm/7 ins x 21.4mm/54

$$$ **Encanto** .... 20.32mm/8 ins x 19.8mm/50

$$$ **Ventaja**. .... 178mm/7 ins x 17.5mm/44 8

$$$ **Alma**. .... 178mm/7 ins x 18.7mm/47

$$$ **Consuelo** .... 127mm/5 ins x 19.8mm/50

BANCES

Five hand-made, six machine-made. Good value. Made by
Villazon. Machine-made in their Tampa, Florida, USA plant
and hand-made in Honduras using Havana seed wrappers.
Good value.

¢   **Presidents*** .... ★★★★★
8½ ins x 52. Well-made. Good draw. Full flavor. Hint
of cinnamon and coffee. For experienced and
casual smoker alike. Value for money.

¢   **Corona Immensas*** .... ★★★★
172mm/6¾ ins x 19.05mm/48. Good draw, even
burning. Medium-bodied. Spicy. Daytime smoke.

¢   **Crowns Maduro** .... 147mm/5¾ ins x 19.84mm/50

¢   **Demi Tasse**. .... 102mm/4 ins x 13.89mm/35

¢   **Uniques*** .... 140mm/5½ ins x 15.08mm/38

¢   **Havana Holders** ...... 165mm/6½ ins x 12mm/30

¢   **Brevas*** .... ★★★★
140mm/5½ ins x 17.07mm/43. Good, consistent
construction. Medium-bodied. A pleasant smoke.
Value for money.

¢   **Palmas** .... 152mm/6 ins x 16.67mm/42

ȼ	**Palmas** (Boy or Girl). . 152mm/6 ins x 16.67mm/42
ȼ	**El Prados** . . . . 160mm/6¼ ins x 14.29mm/36
ȼ	**No 3** . . . . 147mm/5¾ ins x 18.26mm/46
ȼ	**Cazadores*** . . . . 160mm/6¼ ins x 17.46mm/44

**Hand-made.*

BELINDA

Hand-made. Quality, superior. Wrapper from Ecuador.
Binder from Honduras. Filler is blend of tobacco from
Honduras and Dominican Republic. Cigar of same name
made in Cuba with word "Habana" on band. Exclusive to
Santa Clara N.A. Good value.

$ **Belinda**. . . . . ★★★★
165mm/6½ ins x 14.29mm/36. Very mild. Ideal for
women.

$ **Breva Conserva** . . . . 140mm/5½ ins x 17.46/44
Good draw. Slow, even burning. Medium-bodied,
spicy with treacle undertones. Good finish. Value
for money.

$ **Cabinet**. . . . . 143mm/5⅝ ins x 17.86/45
Good, consistent construction and draw. Slow, even
burning. Smooth. Cinnamon and coffee undertones. Extremely good value for money.

$ **Ramon** . . . . 184mm/7¼ ins x 18.65/47

$ **Corona Grande** . . . . 160mm/6¼ ins x 17.46/44

$ **Medagla D'Oro** . . . . 113mm/4½ ins x 19.84/50

BERING

Machine-bunched and hand-finished. Quality, superior. First
made in 1905 in Tampa's famed Ybor City. End of last decade
entire operation moved to Honduras. Also produces range
with maduro and candela wrappers. Now with red and gold
bands only.

$ **Torpedo** . . . . 178mm/7 ins x 21.4mm/54

$ **Barons**. . . . . 184.9mm/7¼ ins x 16.67mm/42

$ **Casinos** Glass Tubes. . 181mm/7⅛ ins x 16.67mm/42

$ **Cazadores** . . . . 160mm/6¼ ins x 17.86mm/45

$ **Coronados** . . . . 132mm/5³⁄₁₆ ins x 17.86mm/45

$ **Grande** . . . . 215.9mm/8½ ins x 20.6mm/52

$ **Corona Royale** . . . . . . 152mm/6 ins x 16.27mm/41

$ **Gold No 1** . . . . 160mm/6¼ ins x 13.1mm/33

$ **Hispanos** . . . . ★★★★
152mm/6 ins x 19.84mm/50. Mild. Touch of cinna-
mon. Good daytime smoke.

$ **Robustos**. . . . . 120.6mm/4¾ ins x 19.8mm/50

$ **Imperials Boy/Girl** . . . .
133mm/5¼ ins x 16.67mm/42

$ **Imperials** . . . . ★★★★
133mm/5¼ ins x 16.67mm/42. Fairly hard draw.
Mild. Smooth. Lacks character. After-dinner cigar.

$ **Inmensas** . . . . 181mm/7⅛ ins x 17.86mm/45

$ **Plazas**. . . . . ★★★★
152mm/6 ins x 17.07mm/43. Well-made. Easy
draw. Spicy.

BERMEJO

Hand-made. Made by Villazon.

$ **Cazadores** . . . . 160mm/6¼ ins x 18.26mm/46

$ **Fumas**. . . . . 165mm/6½ ins x 17.86mm/45

BEVERLY HILLS—VIP

    No 535 . . . . 127mm/5 ins x 13.89mm/35
    No 550 . . . . 127mm/5 ins x 19.8mm/50
    No 644 . . . . 152mm/6 ins x 17.46mm/44
    No 736 . . . . 178mm/7 ins x 14.29mm/36
    No 749 . . . . 178mm/7 ins x 19.45mm/49

BLUE LABEL

Hand-made. Bundle. All Honduran tobacco. Distributed by
Mike's Cigars, Miami, Florida, USA.

$ **Bulvon** . . . . 168mm/6⅝ ins x 21.4mm/54
$ **Churchill** . . . . 175mm/6¼ ins x 19.1mm/48
$ **Finos** . . . . 179mm/7 ins x 11.9mm/3
$ **Imperial** . . . . 203mm/8 ins x 20.6mm/52
$ **No 1** . . . . 168mm/6⅝ ins x 17.5mm/45
$ **No 2** . . . . 152mm/6 ins x 16.67mm/42
$ **Palma**. . . . . 175mm/6⅝ ins x 13.9mm/35
$ **Presidente** . . . . 190mm/7½ ins x 19.84mm/50
$ **Rothschild** . . . . 121mm/4¾ ins x 19.84mm/50
$ **Toro** . . . . 159mm/6¼ ins x 19.84mm/50

C.A.O.

Hand-made. Quality, superior. Connecticut Shade wrapper.
Honduran binder. Filler blend of tobacco from Nicaragua and
Mexico. Made by Tabacos de Plasencia. Distributed by C.A.O.
Enterprises, Nashville.

$$ **Petit Corona**. . . . . 127mm/5 ins x 15.9mm/40

$$$ **Corona**. . . . . ★★★★
152mm/6 ins x 16.67mm/42. Good draw. Slow,
even burning. Medium-bodied. Touch of cinnamon. Good finish.

$$$ **Lonsdale**. . . . . 178mm/7 ins x 17.5mm/44
$$$ **Robusto** . . . . ★★★★
       114mm/4½ ins x 19.8mm/50. Good draw. Medium
       strength. Full flavor with nutty undertones.
       Smooth. To follow a meal for discerning smoker.
$$$ **Corona Gorda** . . . . ★★★
       152mm/6 ins x 19.8mm/50. Attractive, oily wrap-
       per. Slow, even burning. Full, nutty flavor. Good fin-
       ish. Ideal for beginner.
$$$ **Churchill** . . . . ★★★★★
       191mm/7½ ins x 21.4mm/54. Well-made. Even
       burning. Flavors improve all the time. Good bal-
       ance between strength and flavor. Medium
       strength. The size and quality make this cigar
       ideal for a special occasion.
$$$ **Triangulare** . . . . ★★★★
       178mm/7 ins x 21.4mm/54. Good draw. Slow, even
       burning. Smooth. Full-bodied with spicy flavors. For
       beginner and experienced smoker.

CAMACHO

Hand-made. Quality, good. Cuban seed wrapper, binder and
filler. Also with Connecticut Shade wrapper. Made by
Tabacos Rancho Jamastran (Eiroa Family). Imported exclu-
sively into USA by Caribe in Florida.

$$ **El Cesar** . . . . 216mm/8½ ins x 20.64mm/52
$$ **Executives** . . . . 197mm/7½ ins x 19.84mm/50
$$ **Churchill** . . . . ★★★
       178mm/7 ins x 19.05mm/48. Spicy and coffee
       aroma with cinnamon on palate. Starts with
       promise but soon loses its luster.
$$ **No 1** . . . . 178mm/7 ins x 17.46mm/44
$ **Monarca** . . . . 127mm/5 ins x 19.84mm/50
$ **Cetros** . . . . 165mm/6½ ins x 14.29mm/36
$ **Pan Especial**. . . . . 178mm/7 ins x 14.29mm/36
$ **Elegante** . . . . 155mm/6⅛ ins x 15.08mm/38
$ **Palmas** . . . . 152mm/6 ins x 17.07mm/43
$ **Nacionales** . . . . 140mm/5½ ins x 17.46mm/44
       Draws and burns well. Cinnamon and caramel
       flavors. Good everyday smoke. Value for money.

★★★★★ Outstanding. A classic.   ★★★★ Excellent.
★★★ Good.   ★★ Fair, ordinary.   ★ Poor or faulty.
No Star Not evaluated.

| $ | **Cazadores** . . . . | 165mm/6½ ins x 17.46mm/44 |
| $ | **Conchitas** . . . . | 140mm/5½ ins x 12.7mm/32 |

CAMORRA IMPORTED LIMITED RESERVE

Hand-made. Ecuadorian wrapper. Honduran filler and binder. Launched 1995. Distributed by G.A.T.E. Inc., Savannah.

$	**Capri** . . . . ★★
	140mm/5½ ins x 12.7mm/32. Inconsistent construction. Medium-bodied. Caramel undertones. Harsh.
$$$	**Napoli** . . . . 156mm/6⅛ ins x 15.1mm/38
$$$	**Roma** . . . . ★★★★
	127mm/5 ins x 19.84mm/50. Mild with creamy, nutty undertones. Daytime smoke. Ideal for casual smoker.
$$$	**Genova** . . . . ★★★★
	140mm/5½ ins x 17.5mm/44. Well-made cigar. Starts slightly harsh, but give it ½ inch (1cm) then becomes smooth and mellow. Creamy.
$$$	**Venzia** . . . . 165mm/6½ ins x 17.5mm/44
$$$	**San Remo** . . . . 178mm/7 ins x 19.1mm/48
$$	**Padova** . . . . 127mm/5 ins x 16.67mm/42

CARAMBA TWIN PACK

Hand-made. Made by Villazon.

$	**No 1** . . . . 203mm/8 ins x 17.46mm/44
$	**No 2** . . . . 190mm/7½ ins x 19.84mm/50
$	**No 3** . . . . 178mm/7 ins x 14.29mm/36
$	**No 4** . . . . 165mm/6½ ins x 17.46mm/44
$	**No 5** . . . . 152mm/6 ins x 19.84mm/50
$	**No 6** . . . . 140mm/5½ ins x 18.26mm/46
$	**No 7** . . . . 127mm/5 ins x 16.67mm/42
$	**No 8** . . . . 152mm/6 ins x 14.29mm/36

CASA MAYAN

Hand-made.

	Viajaute . . . . 216mm/8½ ins x 20.64mm/52
	Lonsdale . . . . 165mm/6½ ins x 17.46mm/44
	Robusto . . . . 140mm/5½ ins x 19.84mm/50
	Rothschild . . . . 113mm/4½ ins x 19.84mm/50
	No 4 . . . . 127mm/5 ins x 16.67mm/42
	President . . . . 190mm/7½ ins x 19.84mm/50

CAZ-BAR

Hand-made. Bundles. Short and long filler. Distributed by Miami Cigar.

$	**Cazadores** .... 175mm/6¾ ins x 17.46mm/44
$	**Fumas**............ 175mm/6¾ ins x 17.46mm/44
$	**Churchills**........ 190mm/7½ ins x 19.84mm/50
$	**Corona Lonsdale** ... 140mm/5½ ins x 19.84mm/50
$	**Petit Cazadore** ... 175mm/67/8 ins x 17.46mm/44

CCI GOLD SILK SELECTION

Hand-made. Connecticut wrapper. Honduran binder. Filler, blend of tobacco from Nicaragua and Honduras. Launched 1995. Small, select production. Owned by Cigar Club International.

> **No 1**............ 191mm/7½ ins x 19.84mm/50
> **No 2**............. 178mm/7 ins x 19.1mm/48
> **No 3**............ 152mm/6 ins x 19.84mm/50
> **No 4**............ 159mm/6¼ ins x 17.5mm/44
> **No 5**............ 127mm/5 ins x 19.84mm/50

CCI ROYAL SATIN SELECTION

Hand-made. Ecuador wrapper. Filler, blend of tobacco from Nicaragua and Honduras. Binder from Dominican Republic. Owned by Cigar Club International.

> **No 1**............ 191mm/7½ ins x 19.84mm/50
> **No 2**............. 178mm/7 ins x 19.1mm/48
> **No 3**............ 152mm/6 ins x 19.84mm/50
> **No 4**............ 159mm/6¼ ins x 17.5mm/44
> **No 5**............ 127mm/5 ins x 19.84mm/50

CERVANTES

Hand-made. Distributed by Phillips & King.

$	**Churchill** .... 184mm/7¼ ins x 17.86mm/45
$	**Corona**.......... 160mm/6¼ ins x 18.26mm/46
$	**Senadores**........................... ★★★

152mm/6 ins x 16.67mm/42. Medium strength. An everyday smoke. Good value.

CHARLES FAIRMORN

Hand-made. All Honduran tobacco. Distributed in USA by F&K Cigar.

> **Churchill** .... 175mm/6⅞ ins x 19.45mm/49
> **Coronas** .... 160mm/6¼ ins x 17.46mm/44

Elegante . . . . 172mm/6¾ ins x 15.08mm/38
Super Finos . . . . 113/4½ ins x 12.7mm/32

CIENFUEGO

Hand-made. Name means "100 fires" after famous fires in USA. Connecticut Shade wrapper. Mexican binder. Filler blend of tobacco from Mexico, Jamaica and Dominican Republic.

New York 1776 . . . . . . 203mm/8 ins x 21.43mm/54
Washington 1814 . . . . 178mm/7 ins x 20.64mm/52
Boston 1902 . . . . 178mm/7 ins x 21.43mm/54
Los Angeles 1965 . . . 216mm/8½ ins x 20.64mm/52
Chicago 1871 . . . . . . 197mm/7¾ ins x 19.84mm/50
Atlanta 1864 . . . . 152mm/6 ins x 19.84mm/50
Detroit 1805 . . . . . . 190mm/7½ ins x 18.26mm/46
Baltimore 1902. . . . . 165mm/5½ ins x 16.67mm/42
Richmond 1865 . . . . . 152mm/6 ins x 17.07mm/43
San Francisco 1906. . . 178mm/7 ins x 17.07mm/43

CLEMENTINE

Hand-made. Bundles. Ecuadorian wrapper. Brand owned by House of Oxford. Good value.

$	**Inmensas** . . . . 203mm/8 ins x 21.4mm/54
¢	**Churchills**. . . . . 178mm/7 ins x 19.1mm/48
¢	**Cetros** . . . . 159mm/6¼ ins x 17.5mm/44
¢	**No 1** . . . . 178mm/7 ins x 17.5mm/44
¢	**No 4** . . . . 140mm/5½ ins x 17.5mm/44
¢	**Panetelas** . . . . 178mm/7 ins x 14.3mm/36
¢	**Presidente** . . . . 197mm/7¾ ins x 19.8mm/50
¢	**Rothschild** . . . . 127mm/5 ins x 19.8mm/50
¢	**Toro** . . . . 152mm/6 ins x 19.8mm/50
$	**Viajante**. . . . . 216mm/8½ins x 20.6mm/52
$	**Torpedo** . . . . 191mm/7½ ins x 23.8mm/60

COLORADO BY DON LINO

Hand-made. Quality, superior. Attractive colorado Connecticut wrapper. Binder from Honduras. Filler blend of tobacco from Honduras and Nicaragua. Available in both cedar boxes and 25-cigar-capacity humidors. Distributed by Miami Cigar.

$$$ **Lonsdale** . . . . 165mm/6½ ins x 17.5mm/44
$$$ **Robusto** . . . . ★★★★
140mm/5½ ins x 19.84mm/50. Easy draw. Even, slow burning. Mild, but good flavor and balance. Well-made. Daytime smoke.
$$$ **Torpedo** . . . . 178mm/7 ins x 19.1mm/48
$$$ **Presidente** . . . . 190mm/7½ ins x 19.84mm/50

COLUMBUS

Hand-made. Quality, superior. All Honduran tobacco. Publicly launched in 1992. Previously only available for private consumption. Extremely well-made. Owned by El Tobacco Ltd, Athens, Greece. Available in Europe. Limited distribution in USA. Tubes remind one of Cuban made Montecristo and Romeo y Julieta tubes. Beautiful, consistent wrappers are feature.

Eleven Fifty . . . . 279mm/11 ins x 19.84mm/50
Double Corona . . . . ★★★★★
216mm/8½ ins x 19.84mm/50. Explodes with rich, creamy flavors. Burns perfectly. Extremely well-made. This cigar will make any occasion special.
Churchill . . . . ★★★★★
178mm/7 ins x 18.7mm/47. Good draw. Burns perfectly. Elegant. Lots of flavor with hint of choclate and leather. Cigar for connoisseur or special occasion.
No 2 Torpedo . . . . 155mm/6 ins x 20.6mm/52
Tubos . . . . ★★★★★
155mm/6 ins x 16.67mm/42. Smooth with rich flavors, hint of treacle. Good burning. For connoisseur and novice alike.
Short Churchill . . . . ★★★★★
127mm/5 ins x 19.84mm/50. Smooth. Creamy flavors. Did not burn quite as evenly as others in this range. To follow meal.
Columbus Columbus . 146mm/5¾ ins x 18.22mm/46
Perfectos . . . . 127mm/5 ins x 17.4mm/44
Especial . . . . 159mm/6¼ ins x 17.4mm/44
Brevas . . . . 137mm/5⅜ ins x 16.67mm/42
Tinas . . . . 114mm/4½ ins x 11.9mm/30

COMPETERE

Hand-made. Wrapper from Ecuador. Binder and filler from Honduras. Distributed in USA by Brick-Hanquer.

Havana Twist . . . . 178mm/7 ins x 17.46mm/44
Havana Breva . . . . 152mm/6 ins x 19.84mm/50
Churchill . . . . 178mm/7 ins x 17.46mm/44
No. 200 . . . . 152mm/6 ins x 17.07mm/43

CONNISSEUR GOLD LABEL

Hand-made. Bundles. Distributed in USA by Indian Head Sales.

No 1	190mm/7 ins x	17.07mm/43
No 3	190mm/7 ins x	14.29mm/36
No 4	140mm/5½ ins x	16.07mm/43
Goliath	203mm/8 ins x	25mm/64
Rothschild	113mm/4½ ins x	19.84mm/50
Viajante	216mm/8½ ins x	20.64mm/52
Imperial	178mm/7½ ins x	19.84mm/50
Gigante	203mm/8 ins x	21.43mm/54
Toro	152mm/6 ins x	19.84mm/50
Corona	152mm/6 ins x	17.46mm/44
Churchill	190mm/7 ins x	19.45mm/40

CUBA ALIADOS

Hand-made. Quality, superior. Wrapper and binder from Ecuador. Filler is blend of tobacco from Honduras, Brazil and Dominican Republic. Has three large beautifully made figurado shapes. General claimed to be world's largest commercially available cigar. Factory located in Danli, 15 miles (24 km) from Nicaraguan border, in abandoned motel. Rollers are in what used to be the lobby and sorting table was once registration desk. Word "Cuba" appears on band. Founder of Cuba Aliados Cigars Inc., Rolando Reyes Sr, launched Aliados brand in Cuba in 1955. Company has wholesale and retail operation in Union City, New Jersey, USA.

$$$$ **General**. . . . . 457mm/18 ins x 26.19mm/66

$$$$ **Figurin** (figurado) . . . . ★★★
254mm/10 ins x 23.8mm/60. Mild. Little oomph for what one would expect from such a big cigar. Becomes tedious.

$ **Valentino** (figurado). . 178mm/7 ins x 19.05mm/48

$$$ **Piramedes** (figurado) 190mm/7½ ins x 23.81mm/60

$$$ **Diamedes** (figurado) 190mm/7½ ins x 23.81mm/60

$ **Churchill** . . . . ★★★★★
181mm/7⅛ ins x 21.43mm/54. Dark oily wrapper. Medium- to full-bodied. Good balance. Strong finish. Top cigar for one who appreciates good things in life.

$ **Cazadore** . . . . 178mm/7 ins x 45

$ **Palma** . . . . 178mm/7 ins x 14.29mm/36

$ **Fuma** . . . . 165mm/6½ ins x 17.7mm/45

$ **Lonsdale** . . . . 165mm/6½ ins x 16.67mm/42

$ **Corona Deluxe** . . . . ★★★★
    165mm/6½ ins x 17.86mm/45. Lots of flavor. Mild.
    Smooth. Elegant. Good daytime smoke.
$ **Toro** . . . . 152mm/6 ins x 21.43mm/54
$ **Number 4** . . . . 140mm/5½ ins x 17.86mm/45
$ **Remedios** . . . . 140mm/5½ ins x 16.67mm/42
$ **Petite Cetro** . . . . 127mm/5 ins x 14.29mm/36
$ **Rothschild** . . . . ★★★
    127mm/5 ins x 20.24mm/51. Burns unevenly. Lacks
    punch. A boring smoke. An inexpensive cigar.

CUBAN TWIST

Hand-made. Mixed filler. Distributed in USA by Indian Head
Sales.

No 200 . . . . 127mm/5 ins x 14.29mm/36
No 400 . . . . 178mm/7 ins x 14.29mm/36
No 500 . . . . 152mm/6 ins x 19.84mm/50
No 600 . . . . 178mm/7 ins x 18.26mm/46

DA VINCI

Hand-made. Quality, superior. Ecuadorian wrapper. Dominican binder. Cuban seed Honduran, Nicaraguan and Dominican
filler. Distributed by Brimar Group, Dallas., Texas, USA

$$$ **Renaissance** (torpedo). 178mm/7 isn x 21.4mm/54
$$$ **Leonardo** . . . . 216mm/8½ ins x 20.6mm/52
$$$ **Ginerva de Benci** . . . . . 178mm/7 ins x 19.1mm/48
$$$ **Monalisa** . . . . ★★★★★
      152mm/6 ins x 19.8mm/50. Well-made. Good
      draw. Slow, even burning. Good complexity with
      medium-bodied. To follow meal. For discerning
      smoker.
$$$ **Cecilia Gallerani** . . . . . 152mm/6 ins x 17.1mm/43
$$$ **Madonna** . . . . 127mm/5 ins x 19.8mm/50

DANIEL MARSHALL HONDURAN RESERVE

Hand-made. Quality, superior. Connecticut Shade wrapper.
Honduran binder. Honduran and Nicaraguan filler. Top
humidor manufacturer, has now added a small but select
range of Honduran and Dominican cigars to complement
impressive range of humidors. Black, gold and white band
donates Honduran range. Natural pairing—a class cigar with
a class humidor. Distributed by D. Marshall Inc., Tustin,
California, USA.

$$$ **Churchill** . . . . 178mm/7 ins x 19.8mm/50
$$$ **Corona** . . . . 152mm/ 6 ins x 17.5mm/44

$$$ Robusto . . . . ★★★★★
127mm/5 ins x 19.8mm/50. Good draw. Slow, even burning. Cool. Medium strength with good balance of spicy, creamy flavors. Enjoy this when you can get it. For discerning smoker.

DANLYS

Hand-made bundles. All Honduran tobacco. Made by Tobacos de Plascencia. Distributed by House of Oxford.

- ¢   **Churchill** . . . . 178mm/7 ins x 19.8mm/50
- ¢   **Luchadore** . . . . ★★★★
  152mm/6 ins x 16.67mm/42. Medium to full-bodied. Well-made. Tends to fade.
- ¢   **Panetela** . . . . 152mm/6 ins x 15.1mm/38
- ¢   **Toro** . . . . 152mm/6 ins x 19.8mm/50
- ¢   **No 1** . . . . 178mm/7 ins x 16.67mm/42
- ¢   **No 4** . . . . 127mm/5 ins x 16.67mm/42

DON ASA

Hand-made. All Honduran tobacco. Made by US Tobacco for House of Oxford.

- $ **Blunts** . . . . 127mm/5 ins x 16.67mm/42
- $ **Cetros** . . . . 165mm/6½ ins x 17.5mm/44
- $ **Coronas** . . . . 140mm/5½ ins x 19.8mm/50
-     **Imperials** . . . . 203mm/8 ins x 17.5mm/44
-     **Presidents** . . . . 190mm/7½ ins x 19.8mm/50
- $ **Rothchilds** . . . . 114mm/4½ ins x 19.8mm/50

DON FIFE

Hand-made. Quality, superior. Connecticut and Ecuadorian wrappers. Cuban seed Honduran binder and filler. Owned by Don Fife Cigars Corp., Miami, Florida, USA.

-     **Churchill** . . . . 178mm/7 ins x 19.1mm/48
-     **Numero 1** . . . . 178mm/7 ins x 17.1mm/43
-     **Double Corona** . . . . . 165mm/6½ ins x 17.5mm/44
-     **Corona Gorda** . . . . 152mm/6 ins x 19.8mm/50
-     **Petit Cetro** . . . . 140mm/5½ ins x 17.1mm/43
-     **Petit** . . . . 114mm/4½ ins x 11.9mm

DON JOSE

Hand-made bundles of 20. All available in natural or maduro wrapper. Distributed by M&N.

- $ **Valrico** . . . . 114mm/4½ ins x 19.84mm/50
- $ **Granada** . . . . 152mm/6 ins x 17.1mm/43

$	**Turbo**	152mm/6 ins x 19.84mm/50
$	**San Marco**	178mm/7 ins x 19.84mm/50
$	**El Grandee**.	216mm/8½ ins x 20.6mm/52

DON LINO

Hand-made. Quality, superior. Connecticut wrapper. Binder and filler blend of tobacco from Honduras. Distributed by Miami Cigar.

$$	**Corona**	140mm/5½ ins x 19.84mm/50
$$	**Peticetro** . . . . ★★★★
	140mm/5½ ins x 16.67mm/42. Well-made. Mild with character. Good balance. Ideal for beginner.
$$	**Toros**	140mm/5½ ins x 18.3mm/46
$$	**No 1**	165mm/6½ins x 17.5mm/44
$$	**No 3**	152mm/6 ins x 14.3mm/36
$	**No 4**	127mm/5 ins x 16.67mm/42
$$	**No 5**	159mm/6¼ ins x 17.5mm/44
$$$	**Torpedo**	178mm/7 ins x 19.1mm/48
$$	**Churchill** . . . . ★★★★★
	190mm/7½ ins x 19.84mm/50. Dark oily wrapper. Spicy with woodsy undertones. Good balance and finish. After-dinner cigar for connoisseur.
$$	**Panetelas** . . . . ★★
	178mm/7 ins x 14.3mm/36. Hard draw. Harsh, slightly bitter.
$$	**Robustos** . . . . ★★★★
	140mm/5½ ins x 19.84mm/50. Smooth oily wrapper. Wet hay aroma. Creamy finish. Smooth. Well-made.
$$	**Rothchild** . . . . ★★★★
	114mm/4½ ins x 19.84mm/50. Dark, oily maduro wrapper. Well-made. Full flavors with hint of chocolate and caramel. After-dinner cigar for connoisseur.
$	**Epicures**	114mm/4½ ins x12.7mm/32
$$$$	**Supremos**	216mm/8½ ins x 20.6mm/52

DON LINO ORO

Hand-made. Quality, superior. Wrapper of Cameroon seed grown in Honduras. Binder and filler from Cuban seed grown in Honduras. Distributed by Miami Cigar. More robust than Don Lino range.

| $$ | **No 1** . . . . | 165mm/6½ ins x 17.5mm/44 |
| $$ | **Panetelas** . . . . | 178mm/7 ins x 14.3mm/36 |

$$ **Toro** .... ★★★
140mm/5½ ins x 18.3mm/46. Good draw. Slow,
even burning. Medium-bodied. Hint of caramel.
Daytime smoke.

$$$ **Churchill** .... 190mm/7½ ins x 19.84mm/50

DON MATEO

Hand-made bundles. All Honduran tobacco. Made by
Consolidated Cigar.

¢ **No 1** .... 178mm/7 ins x 12mm/30
¢ **No 2** .... 175mm/6⅞ ins x 13.89mm/35
¢ **No 3** .... 152mm/6 ins x 16.67mm/42
¢ **No 4** .... 140mm/5½ ins x 17.46mm/44
¢ **No 5** .... 143mm/5⅝ ins x 17.46mm/44
¢ **No 6** .... 175mm/6⅞ ins x 19.05mm/48
¢ **No 7** .... 120mm/4¾ ins x 19.84mm/50
¢ **No 8** .... 160mm/6¼ ins x 19.84mm/50
¢ **No 9** .... 190mm/7½ ins x 19.84mm/50
¢ **No 10** .... 203mm/8 ins x 20.64mm/52

DON MELO

Hand-made. All Honduran tobacco. Distributed by Cigars of
Honduras, Virginia, USA.

$$$ **Presidente** .... 216mm/8½ ins x 20.2mm/50
$$ **Churchill** .... 179mm/7 ins x 19.5mm/49
$$ **Corona Gorda** .... 152mm/6 ins x 17.5mm/44
$$ **Numero Dos** .... 152mm/6 ins x 16.67mm/42
$$ **Corona Extra** .... 140mm/5½ ins x 18.3mm/46
$ **Petit Corona** .... 140mm/5½ ins x 16.67mm/42
$ **Nom Plus** .... 121mm/4¾ ins x 20.2mm/50
$ **Cremos** .... 114mm/4½ ins x 16.67mm/42

DON REX

Hand-made. Connecticut Shade or Sumatra maduro wrap-
pers. Launched in 1987. Available in different wrappers grown
in Honduras: Connecticut seed shade, Sumatran seed and
maduro. Made by US Tobacco Co. Distributed by Miami Cigar.

$$ **Gigantes maduro** ... 216mm/8½ ins x 21.43mm/52
$$ **Presidentes** .... 190mm/7½ ins x 19.84mm/50

¢ – Under $1.00 $ – $1–3.00 $$ – $3–4.00
$$$ – $5–8.00 $$$$ – $8–20.00 $$$$$ – $20+

$ **Cetros No 2** .... ★★★
    165mm/6½ ins x 17.46mm/44. Fairly tight draw.
    Lacks flavor. Daytime smoke.
$ **Coronas** .... 140mm/5½ ins x 19.84mm/50
$ **Panetela Largas** ..... 178mm/7 ins x 14.29mm/36
$ **Blunts** .... 127mm/5 ins x 16.67mm/42

DON RUBIO

Hand-made. Bundles. Wrapper from Ecuador. Binder and filler from Honduras. Distributed by Brick-Hanauer.

No 1 .... 178mm/7 ins x 17.07mm/43
Cazadore (Sandwich)
160mm/6¼ ins x 17.46mm/44
Corona Extra ...... 140mm/5½ ins x 18.26mm/46
Corona Gorda ..... 160mm/6¼ ins x 17.46mm/44
Churchill .... 178mm/7 ins x 19.45mm/49
Grandios. .... 203mm/8 ins x 23.81mm/60
Lindas .... 140mm/5½ ins x 23.81mm/38
Monarchs .... 178mm/7 ins x 20.64mm/52
Nom Plus .... 127mm/5 ins x 19.84mm/50
Panatella .... 172mm/6¾ ins x 13.89mm/35
President .... 216mm/8½ ins x 19.84mm/50
Soberanos .... 197mm/7¾ ins x 19.84mm/50
Toro .... 152mm/6 ins x 19.84mm/50

DON TOMAS

Hand-made. Quality, superior. Cuban seed wrappers. All sizes available in four wrappers: natural/colorado, maduro and claro claro. Medium strength. Introduced in 1974. Owned by U.S. Tobacco International. Distributed in USA by Miami Cigar.

$$ **Gigantes**. .... 216mm/8½ ins x 20.64mm/52
$$ **Imperiales No 1** ..... 203mm/8 ins x 17.46mm/44
$$ **Presidentes** .... 190mm/7½ ins x 19.84mm/50
$ **Panetelas Largas**. .... 178mm/7 ins x 14.29mm/36
$ **Cetros No 2** .... 165mm/6½ ins x 17.46mm/44
$ **Corona Grandes** (tubed) .... ★★★★★
    165mm/6½ ins x 17.46mm/44. Dark smooth oily
    wrapper. Easy draw. Burns evenly. Ash falls off eas-
    ily. Spicy, earthy. Lots of flavor. Dignified cigar.
$ **Supremos**. .... ★★★★
    160mm/6¼ ins x 16.67mm/42. Easy draw. Even
    burn. Cool. Spicy. Mild to medium strength. Good
    cigar for beginner.
$ **Panetelas** .... 152mm/6 ins x 14.29mm/36
$ **Coronas** .... 140mm/5½ ins x 19.84mm/50

$	**Toros**	140mm/5½ ins x 18.26mm/46
$	**Matadors**	140mm/5½ ins x 16.67mm/42
$	**Rothschilds**	113mm/4½ ins x 19.84mm/50
$	**Epicures** . . . . ★★★★★

$ **Epicures** . . . . ★★★★★
113mm/4½ ins x 12.7mm/32. Good draw. Slow,
even burning. Smooth. Full, spicy flavors. Big
punch for a small cigar.

$ **It's a Boy/Girl** . . . . . 165mm/6½ ins x 17.46mm/44

DON TOMAS INTERNATIONAL SERIES

Hand-made. Quality, superior. Cuban seed tobacco.
Distributed by Miami Cigar.

$	**No 1**	165mm/6 1/2 ins x 17.46mm/44
$	**No 2**	140mm/5 1/2 ins x 19.84mm/50
$	**No 3**	140mm/5 1/2 ins x 16.67mm/42
$	**No 4**	178mm/7 ins x 14.29mm/36

DON TOMAS SPECIAL EDITION

Hand-made. Quality, superior. Connecticut, Cuban and
Dominican seed tobacco. Connecticut Shade wrapper.
Smooth and aromatic. Good quality. Owned by United States
Tobacco Company. Distributed by Miami Cigar.

$$ **No 100** . . . . 190mm/7½ ins x 19.84mm/50
$$ **No 200** . . . . ★★★★
165mm/6½ ins x 17.46mm/44. Touch of cinna-
mon. Fairly strong but balanced with flavor.
Suitable to follow meal.

$$ **No 300** . . . . 127mm/5 ins x 19.84mm/50
$$ **No 400** . . . . 178mm/7 ins x 14.29mm/36
$$ **No 500** . . . . ★★★★★
140mm/5½ ins x 18.26mm/46. Spicy. Touch of
coffee. Good balance. Smooth. Good burn.
After-dinner cigar. Smoke for connoisseur.

DON TONIOLI

Hand-made. Quality, superior. Ecuadorian wrapper.
Nicaraguan binder and filler. Tobacco aged for four years.
Cigars also aged for several months after rolling. Distributed
by Tony Borhani Cigars, La Jolla, California, who specializes
in setting up humidors in wine trade.

Super Torpedo. . . . . . 191mm/7½ ins x 25.4mm/64
Torpedo . . . . 152mm/6 ins x 20.6mm/52

Churchill . . . . 178mm/7 ins x 18.7mm/47
Robusto . . . . 127mm/5 ins x 19.8mm/50
Corona Extra . . . . 146mm/5¾ ins x 18.3mm/46

EL INCOMPARABLE

Hand-made. Quality, superior. Distinctive presentation. Inbued with 25-year-old Springbank Single Malt Whisky. Owned by Frenchman, Jean-Claude Marty. Made by Tobacos de Plasencia in Danli. Distributed in USA by Music City Marketing, Nashville, Tennessee, USA.

$$$$ **Churchill** . . . . ★★★★★
203mm/8 ins x 19.1mm/48. Well-made. Attractive, smooth, oily wrapper. Slow, even burning. Smooth. Wonderful complexity. A luxurious smoke for the connoisseur.
$$$$ **Torpedo** . . . . 179mm/7 ins x 22.2mm/56
$$$$ **Corona** . . . . 152mm/6 ins x 17.5mm/44
$$$$ **Robusto** . . . . 114mm/4½ ins x 19.8mm/50

EL PARAISO

Grande . . . . 203mm/8½ ins x 20.6mm/52
Presidente . . . . 190mm/7½ ins x 19.84mm/50
Double Corona . . . . . . 178mm/7 ins x 18.26mm/46
Panetelas . . . . 165mm/6½ ins x 14.29mm/36
Toro . . . . 152mm/6 ins x 19.84mm/50
Corona . . . . 147mm/5¾ ins x 17.07mm/43
Pequenos . . . . 127mm/5 ins x 12mm/30

EL REY DEL MUNDO

Hand-made. Quality, superior. 25 models. Heavy bodied Havana style cigar with Ecuador Sumatra wrapper grown in the Rio Jagna region of Spanish Honduras. Made by Villazon for Santa Clara, N.A. Same name as Cuban brand, which has "Habana" on band.

$ **Tino** . . . . 140mm/5½ ins x 15.08mm/38
$ **Rothschilde** . . . . ★★★★
127mm/5 ins x 19.84mm/50. Rich, medium strength, full flavors. Spicy aroma.
$ **Robusto Zavalia** . . . . . 127mm/5 ins x 21.43mm/54

$ **Robusto Suprema** . . . . ★★★★★
184mm/7¼ ins x 21.43mm/54. Dark oily wrapper.
Well-made. Range of flavors. Ideal to follow sweet
dessert.
Robusto Larga . . . . . . 152mm/6 ins x 21.43mm/54
Robusto. . . . . ★★★★★
127mm/5 ins x 21.43mm/54. Cool smoke with lots
of flavor. Top cigar for connoisseur. One of best in
this size.
Reynita . . . . 127mm/5 ins x 15.08mm/38
$ **Rectangulare** . . . . ★★★★
143mm/5⅝ ins x 17.86mm/45. Good draw. Slow,
even burning. Smooth. Full, spicy flavors. Big
punch for a small cigar.
Principale . . . . 203mm/8 ins x 18.65mm/47
Plantation . . . . 165mm/6½ ins x 12mm/30
$ **Petit Lonsdale** . . . . . 117mm/4⅝ ins x 17.07mm/43
Originale. . . . . ★★★★★
143mm/5⅝ ins x 17.86mm/45. Medium strength.
Rich, full flavor with touch of cinnamon. Smooth.
Well-made.
Montecarlo. . . . . 155mm/6⅛ ins x 19.05mm/48
Imperiale . . . . 184mm/7¼ ins x 21.43mm/54
Habana Club . . . . . . 140mm/5½ ins x 16.67mm/42
$$ **Flor del Mundo** . . . . ★★★★
184mm/7¼ ins x 21.43mm/54. Spicy. Medium-to
full-bodied. Lots of flavor. Smooth, but gets bitter
towards end.
$$ **Flor de Llaneza** (torpedo) . . . . ★★★★★
165mm/6½ ins x 21.43mm/54. Varnished cabinet
box of 35 cigars. Spicy aroma. Honeyed finish. Full-
bodied. If draw is too hard ensure that enough has
been cut off head. Great experience for connoisseur.
Elegante . . . . 136mm/5⅜ ins x 11.51mm/29
$ **Double Corona** . . . . ★★★★★
178mm/7 ins x 19.45mm/49. Strong, full flavored
cigar, beautifully presented in white tissue paper.
For connoisseur after rich meal.
$ **Coronation**. . . . . 216mm/8½ ins x 20.64mm/52
$ **Corona** . . . . ★★★★★
143mm/5⅝ ins x 17.86mm/45. Good, consistent
construction. Good draw. Rich flavors with long
finish. Good complexity.
Corona Inmensa . . . 184mm/7¼ ins x 18.65mm/47
Classic Corona. . . . . 143mm/5⅝ ins x 17.86mm/45

$ **Choix Supreme** . . . . ★★★★
     155mm/6⅛ ins x 19.45mm/49. Spicy, earthy. Slow
     to start but good flavor soon comes through.
     Elegant cigar. Good daytime smoke.
$ **Cedar** . . . . 178mm/7 ins x 17.07mm/43
$ **Cafe Au Lait**. . . . . . . 113mm/4½ ins x 13.89mm/35

EL SUBLIMADO

Hand-made. Quality, superior. Owned by Frenchman Jean-
Claude Marty. Made by Tobacos de Plasencias in Danli.
Distributed in USA by Music City Marketing, Nashville. Packed
in elegant and distinctive off-white aluminum tube with green
and gold band. Cognac-scented cigar launched in 1993. Some
people, including Churchill, follow practice of dipping end
of cigar into glass of cognac. This inelegant practice dissolves
some of the tar which has accumulated in the end of the cigar,
damaging cognac's flavor, while smoke's taste remains
unchanged. Many believe this is nothing more than sucking
cognac from a cigar. Some place a little cognac in their humidor, which does not appreciably alter the flavor when smoked.
Dipping leaves in cognac does affect tobacco flavors, while
simple spraying has only ephemeral effect and, some
believe, this does not develop desired synergy. Cognac used
is a 50-year-old "Noces d'Or" from Cognac A. Hardy & Co.

$$$$ **Torpedo** . . . . ★★★★★
       178mm/7 ins x 21.43mm/54. Launched in 1995.
       Breaks new barriers. A stupendous cigar for the
       self-confident, unconventional smoker.
$$$$ **Churchill** . . . . ★★★★★
       203mm/8 ins x 19.05mm/48. Mild. Smooth with
       distinctive character. Lots of flavor. Thicker girth
       of this size and Robusto does wonders. Most
       luxurious smoke.
$$$$ **Robusto**. . . . . ★★★★★
       113mm/4½ ins x 19.84mm/50. Mellow with lots of
       distinctive flavor, but not dominated by cognac. For
       discerning smoker who knows what he likes and has
       self-confidence not to be dictated to by convention.
$$$$ **Corona**. . . . . ★★★★
       152mm/6 ins x 17.46mm/44. If any tighter, would
       be hard to draw. Medium strength, smooth, good
       balance between strength and flavor. Cigar for dis-
       cerning smoker. suffers by comparison to larger
       girth of other three models.

ELEGANTE BLEND

Hand-made. Quality, good. Connecticut seed, Ecuadorian wrapper. Dominican and Honduran filler. Distributed by Tampa Rico Cigar Co., Tampa, Florida

$$	**Especial**	178mm/7 ins x 19.1mm/48
$	**Centimo**	178mm/7 ins x 17.5mm/44
$	**Petit Cetro**	152mm/6 ins x 16.67mm/42
$	**Queen**	127mm/5 ins x 19.8mm/50

ENCANTO

Hand-made.

Viajantes	216mm/8½ ins x 20.64mm/52
Churchill*	178mm/7 ins x 19.45mm/49
Grandotes 1	90mm/7½ ins x 18.65mm/47
Elegantes	178mm/7 ins x 17.07mm/43
Toro	152mm/6 ins x 19.84mm/50
Corona Larga	165mm/6½ ins x 17.46mm/44
Cetros*	152mm/6 ins x 16.67mm/42
Rothschild**	113mm/4½ ins x 19.84mm/50
Palma Fina	172mm/6½ ins x 14.29mm/36
Petit Corona*	140mm/5½ ins x 16.67mm/42
Luchadores	160mm/6½ ins x 17.46mm/44
Princesse	113mm/4½ ins x 12mm/30

* *Natural & claro claro.*
** *Natural & maduro.*

ESPADA

Hand-made. All Honduran tobacco.

Viajantes	216mm/8½ ins x 20.6mm/52
Presidente	216mm/8½ ins x 19.84mm/50
Torpedo	178mm/7 ins x 21.4mm/54
Monarch	178mm/7 ins x 20.6mm/52
Executive	197mm/7¾ ins x 19.84mm/50
Corona Gorda	159mm/6¼ ins x 17.5mm/44
Rothschild	127mm/5 ins x 19.84mm/50
Palma Fina	175mm/6⅞ ins x 14.3mm/36

EVELIO

Hand-made. Quality, superior. Ecuadorian wrapper. Binder and filler from Honduras. Launched 1996. Made by Tabacos de Plasencia. Exclusive to House of Oxford.

$$ **Corona**............................. ★★★★
146mm/5¾ ins x 16.67mm/42. Fairly strong. Loads of flavor. Smooth. Good finish.

$$$ **Double Corona**..................... ★★★★★
194mm/7⅞ ins x 18.7mm/47. Medium strength. Full-bodied, spicy with creamy finish. Well-made. To follow meal or with port or cognac.

$$ **No 1**............... 178mm/7 ins x 17.5mm/44

$$ **Robusto**........................... ★★★★★
121mm/4¾ ins x 21.4mm/54. Well-made. Good draw. Slow, even burning. Good balance. Medium-bodied. Spicy. For discerning smoker.

$$$ **Robusto Larga**..................... ★★★★★
152mm/6 ins x 21.4mm/54. Good, consistent construction. Slow, even burning. Good balance and finish. Medium- to full-bodied. Worth the time it takes.

$$$ **Torpedo**........................... ★★★★★
178mm/7 ins x 21.4mm/54. Good, consistent construction. Slow, even burning. Good balance and finish. Medium- to full-bodied. Worth the time it takes.

EXCALIBUR BY HOYO DE MONTERREY

Hand-made. Best quality. Connecticut Shade wrappers. Cuban seed binder and filler. Medium to full-bodied. Sold with Hoyo de Monterrey label in United States, but word "Excalibur" is on band. In Europe they are simply sold as Excalibur. Made by Villazon.

$ **Excalibur I** .... ★★★★★
184mm/7¼ ins x 21.43mm/54. Slow burning, cool, elegant cigars. Needs a cm or two (up to one inch) before it imparts its full, rich flavors. Ideal to enjoy with good cognac or port.

$ **Excalibur II** .... 172mm/6¾ ins x 18.65mm/47

$ **Excalibur III** .... ★★★★★
155mm/6⅛ ins x 19.05mm/48. Easy draw. Even, slow burning. Smooth. Top cigar for special occasion.

$ **Excalibur IV**....... 143mm/5⅝ ins x 18.26mm/46

$ **Excalibur V** .... ★★★★
160mm/6¼ ins x 17.86mm/45. Medium- to full-bodied. Good texture. Loses character after half-way, unlike No 1, that improves and enhances its personality. Daytime smoke or to follow meal.

$ **Excalibur VI**....... 136mm/5½ ins x 15.08mm/38

$ **Excalibur VII** . . . . ★★★★★
127mm/5 ins x 17.07mm/43. Good, earthy, spicy
flavors. Smooth. Long finish. Well-made. Ideal to
follow meal.

$$ **Banquets** (A/tube) . 172mm/6¾ ins x 19.05mm/48
¢   **Miniatures** . . . . ★★★★
76mm/3 ins x 8.7mm/22. Fairly strong, but
smooth. Ideal quick smoke. A top cigarillo.

EXECUTOR

Viajante	216mm/8½ ins x 20.6mm/52	
No 1	165mm/6½ ins x 17.5mm/44	
No 4	140mm/5½ ins x 17.1mm/43	
Cetros	152mm/6 ins x 17.5mm/44	
Churchill	178mm/7 ins x 19.1mm/48	
Rothschild	114mm/4½ ins x 19.8mm/50	
Panetela	178mm/7 ins x 13.9mm/35	
Toro	152mm/6 ins x 19.8mm/50	

F. D. GRAVE & SON

Hand-made. Connecticut wrapper. Honduran filler and
binder. Owned by F. D. Grave & Son in New Haven,
Connecticut. One of oldest companies in continuous pro-
duction.

$$ **Churchill** . . . . ★★★★
197mm/7¾ ins x 19.84mm/50. Good draw. Slow,
even burning. Full, earthy flavors.

$$ **Corona Grande** . . . . ★★★★
178mm/7 ins x 20.6mm/52. Dark, oily wrapper.
Good draw. Burns unevenly. Rich, full flavor. Robust.

$ **Lonsdale** . . . . ★★★★
159mm/6¼ ins x 17.5mm/44. Good draw. Slow,
even burning. Full, earthy flavors. The extra ring
gauge improves this cigar.

$ **Robusto** . . . . 127mm/5 ins x 19.8mm/50

FELIPE GREGORIO

Hand-made. All Honduran tobacco. Exclusive to Cigars of
Honduras, Virginia.

$$$$ **Glorioso*** . . . . 197mm/7¾ ins x 19.84mm/50
$$$$ **Suntouso** . . . . 178mm/7 ins x 19.1mm/48

¢ – Under $1.00 $ – $1–3.00 $$ – $3–4.00
$$$ – $5–8.00 $$$$ – $8–20.00 $$$$$ – $20+

$$$$ **Belicoso** (torpedo) . . . . ★★★★
      152mm/6 ins x 20.6mm/52. Dark, oily wrapper.
      Medium strength. Rich, full, complex flavors with
      coffee and caramel undertones.
$$ **Sereno** . . . . ★★★★
      146mm/5¾ ins x 16.67mm/42. Slow, even burning.
      Medium-bodied. If reasonably aged, a satisfying
      smoke.
$$ **Robusto** . . . . 127mm/5 ins x 19.84mm/50
$$ **Nino** . . . . 108mm/4¼ ins x 17.5mm/44
      Available with Maduro wrapper.

FIRST PRIMING

Hand-made. Bundles. All Honduran tobacco. Distributed by
Phillips & King.

$ **Grandees Natural** . . 216mm/8½ ins x 20.64mm/52
$ **Largos Natural** . . . . . 190mm/7½ ins x 19.84mm/50

FLOR DE ALLONES

Hand-made. Ecuadorian wrapper. Honduran binder. Filler,
a blend of tobacco from Honduras, Nicaragua and Dominican
Republic. Named after old Cuban brand, Ramon Allones.

      No 50 . . . . 159mm/6¼ ins x 19.84mm/50
      No 100 . . . . 114mm/4½ ins x 19.84mm/50
      No 110 . . . . 203mm/8 ins x 18.7mm/47
      No 150 . . . . 140mm/5½ ins x 15.1mm/38

FLOR DE CONSUEGRA

Hand-made. Quality, superior. Cuban seed wrapper. full-bod-
ied. Exclusive to Santa Clara, Inc.

      Corona . . . . 140mm/5½ ins x 16.67mm/42
      Corona Immensa . . . 184mm/7¼ ins x 18.65mm/47
      Cuban Corona . . . . . 143mm/5⅝ ins x 17.86mm/45
      Lonsdale . . . . 165mm/6½ ins x 16.67mm/42
      Panetela . . . . 136mm/5⅜ ins x 15.08mm/38
      President . . . . 216mm/8½ ins x 19.45mm/49
      Robusto . . . . 113mm/4½ ins x 19.84mm/50
      Corona Grande . . . . 160mm/6¼ ins x 17.86mm/45
      Corona Extra . . . . 152mm/6 ins x 16.67mm/42

FLOR DE PALICIO

Hand-made by Villazon for Phillips and King

$ **No 1** . . . . ★★★★
178mm/7 ins x 15.48mm/39. Medium strength
with complex flavors. Good finish. Value for money.

$ **No 2** . . . . 152mm/6 ins x 16.67mm/42

$ **Corona** . . . . ★★★★
172mm/6 3/4 ins x 19.45mm/48

FLOR DEL CARIBE

Hand-made. Quality, superior. Available in natural or
Maduro wrappers. All Honduran tobacco. Made by Villazon
for Arango Cigar.

$$$ **Sovereign** . . . . 178mm/7 ins x 20.6mm/52

$$ **Super Cetro** . . . . 178mm/7 ins x 18.3mm/46

$ **Duques** . . . . 140mm/5½ ins x 16.67mm/42
Medium- to full-bodied. Hint of cinamon. Well-
made. Ideal to follow meal. Underrated. Deserves
being discovered. Good value.

GILBERTO OLIVA

Hand-made. Quality, superior. Connecticut Shade wrapper.
Dominican and Nicaraguan Cuban seed filler. Named after
patriach of old Cuban tobacco family. Made by Gilberto Oliva
in Tobacos de Plascencia Factory. Distributed by Oliva Cigar
Co., Smyrna, Georgia.

$$$ **Churchill** . . . . ★★★★
178mm/7 ins x 19.8mm/50. Dark. oily wrapper.
Has good aging potential. Medium-bodied.
Smooth. Creamy finish.

$$$ **Viajante** . . . . ★★★★
152mm/6 ins x 19.8mm/52. Slow, even burning.
Smooth. Mild. Good finish.

$$$ **Torpedo** . . . . ★★★★★
152mm/6 ins x 19.8mm/52. Well-made. Smooth.
Good complexity with touch of sweetness. Buy if
you see it. For discerning smoker.

$$ **No 1** . . . . ★★★
165mm/6½ ins x 17.5mm/44. Some disturbing
flavors. Spicy.

$$ **Robusto** . . . . ★★★★★
140mm/5½ ins x 19.8mm/50. Slow, even burning.
Smooth. Well-made. Medium-bodied. Spicy. To
follow light meal. For discerning smoker.

H. A. LADRILLO

Hand-made. All Honduran tobacco.

Imperial	. . . .	191mm/7½ ins x 20.6mm/52
Triangulare	. . . .	178mm/7 ins x 19.84mm/50
Fabuloso	. . . .	178mm/7 ins x 19.1mm/48
Lancero	. . . .	165mm/6½ ins x 17.5mm/44
Robusto	. . . .	127mm/5 ins x 20.6mm/52

HABANA GOLD

Hand-made. Good value. Distributed by Gold Leaf Tobacco Co. Available in two ranges: Black label—Sumatran wrapper. Nicaraguan filler and binder. White label—all Nicaraguan tobacco. Dark wrapper.

$	**Petite Corona**	127mm/5 ins x 16.67mm/42
$	**Corona** . . . . ★★★★
	152mm/6 ins x 175mm/44. Good draw. Slow, even burning. Smooth. Mild. Good finish. Early morning smoke.	
$$	**Double Corona** . . . . ★★★
	190mm/7½ ins x 18.3mm/46. Medium-bodied with rich, spicy flavors. Smooth. Cool smoke.	
$	**Robusto**	127mm/5 ins x 19.8mm/50
$$	**Torpedo**	152mm/6 ins x 20.6mm/52
$$	**Churchill**	178mm/7 ins x 20.6mm/52
$$	**Presidente** . . . . ★★★★
	213mm/8½ ins x 20.6mm/52. Hard draw. Full, earthy flavors. Daytime smoke, but will take a lot of time. Ideal for beginners to this size.	
$$	**No 2**	157mm/6⅛ ins x 20.6mm/52

HAVANA RESERVE BY DON LINO

Hand-made. Quality, superior. All Honduran tobacco. Connecticut seed wrapper, aged for five years. Top of Don Lino range. Distributed by Miami Cigar.

$$	**No 1**	165mm/6¼ ins x 17.5mm/44
$$	**Toros**	140mm/5½ ins x 18.3mm/46
$$	**Panetelas**	178mm/7 ins x 14.3mm/36
$$	**Churchills**	190mm/7½ ins x 19.84mm/50
$$	**Torpedo**	178mm/7 ins x 19.1mm/48
$$	**Rothchild**	114mm/4½ ins x 19.84mm/50
$$	**Robusto**	140mm/5 1/2 ins x 19.84mm/50
$$	**Tubes**	165mm/6 1/2 ins x 17.5mm/44

HECHO-A-MANO-CAZ-BAR

Hand-made. (Short and long filler.) Bundles. Distributed in
USA by H. J. Bailey Co.

¢   **Cazadores** . . . . 172mm/6¾ ins x 17.46mm/44
¢   **Churchills**. . . . . 190mm/7½ ins x 19.84mm/50
¢   **Corona Lonsdale** . . . 140mm/5½ ins x 16.67mm/42
¢   **Fumas**. . . . . 175mm/6⅞ ins x 17.46mm/44

HOJA DEL REGAL

Hand-made bundles. Distributed by Brick-Hanauer Co.

Slim Panetela . . . . 152mm/6 ins x 14.29mm/36
Soberano . . . . 190mm/7½ ins x 19.84mm/50
Corona Gorda . . . . . 165mm/6½ ins x 17.46mm/44
Corona Extra . . . . 154mm/6 ins x 17.07mm/43
Rothschild . . . . 113mm/4½ ins x 19.84mm/50
No 4 . . . . 133mm/5½ ins x 17.46mm/44
El Toro . . . . 152mm/6 ins x 19.84mm/50
Viajante . . . . 216mm/8½ ins x 18.26mm/46
Corona Grande . . . . 190mm/7½ ins x 18.26mm/46

HONDURAN GOLD

Hand-made. Bundles. Wrappers from Ecuador. Filler and
binder from Honduras. Owned by Indian Head Sales.

$ **Mayor**. . . . . 140mm/5½ ins x 16.67mm/42
$ **Panetelas** . . . . 178mm/7 ins x 14.29mm/36
$ **Senator**. . . . . 178mm/7 ins x 17.07mm/43
$ **Governor** . . . . 152mm/6 ins x 19.84mm/50
$ **General** . . . . 178mm/7 ins x 19.45mm/49
$ **Presidente** . . . . 216mm/8½ ins x 20.6mm/52

HONDURAN IMPORT MADURO

Hand-made. Bundles. Sold in packs of two by 25. All with
maduro wrappers. All Honduran tobacco. Distributed by
Phillips & King.

Bandidos . . . . 143mm/5⅝ ins x 18.74mm/47
Delicosos . . . . 178mm/7 ins x 17.1mm/43
Granadas . . . . 152mm/6 ins x 19.84mm/50
Majestics. . . . . 203mm/8 ins x 18.74mm/47
Petzels . . . . 114mm/4½ ins x 19.84mm/50
Superbos . . . . 171mm/6¾ ins x 19.1mm/48

¢ – Under $1.00 $ – $1–3.00 $$ – $3–4.00
$$$ – $5–8.00 $$$$ – $8–20.00 $$$$$ – $20+

HONDURAS CUBAN TOBACCOS

Hand-made. Country of origin of tobacco used changes periodically. Made by Honduras Cuban Tobaccos Co., Danli, Honduras.

Viajantes	216mm/8½ ins x 21.4mm/54
Presidente	216mm/8½ ins x 20.6mm/52
Gigantes	203mm/8 ins x 21.4mm/54
Soberano	197mm/7¾ ins x 19.84mm/50
Corona Grande	191mm/7½ ins x 18.3mm/46
Palma de Mayorca	203mm/8 ins x 15.1mm/38
Torpedo	178mm/7 ins x 21.4mm/54
Monarch	178mm/7 ins x 20.6mm/52
Churchill	175mm/6⅞ ins x 19.5mm/49
Elegantes	178mm/7 ins x 16.67mm/42
Pincel	178mm/7 ins x 11.9mm/30
Palma Fina	175mm/6⅞ ins x 14.3mm/36
Corona Gorda	159mm/6¼ ins x 17.5mm/44
Matador	152mm/6 ins x 19.84mm/50
Cetros	152mm/6 ins x 17.1mm/43
Petit Coronas	140mm/5 ins x 16.67mm/42
Lindas	140mm/5½ ins x 15.1mm/38
Clasico	140mm/5½ ins x 13.5mm/34
Rothschild	127mm/5 ins x 19.84mm/50
Super Fino	114mm/4½ ins x 11.9mm/30
Moderno	114mm/4½ ins x 10.3mm/26

HOYO DE MONTERREY

Hand-made. Quality, superior. Most names in this range differ from those of Cuban range, which helps to avoid confusion. Bands maroon rather than red. Made from Cuban seed tobacco. Strong and full-bodied in flavor.

Loose cigars, without Hoyo band, are sold in Europe and are a bargain. Also sold in UK under Don Ramos label. Made by Villazon. Good value.

$ **President** .... ★★★★
216mm/8½ ins x 20.64mm/52. Medium-bodied. Spicy with touch of cinnamon. Good draw. Smooth. Big cigar. Needs 2 to 2½ hours to enjoy it.

$ **Sultan** .... 184mm/7¼ ins x 21.43mm/54

$ **Double Corona** .... ★★★★
172mm/6¾ ins x 19.05mm/48. Elegant cigar, smooth, medium-bodied with spicy aroma, to follow meal.

$ **Churchill** . . . . ★★★★
160mm/6¼ ins x 17.86mm/45. Good Colorado
Maduro wrapper. Rich flavors with spicy and floral
aroma. To follow robust meal.

$ **Ambassador** . . . . 160mm/6¼ ins x 17.46mm/44

$ **Cuban Largos** . . . . . . 184mm/7¼ ins x 18.65mm/47

Cetros . . . . 178mm/7 ins x 17.07mm/43

$ **Governor** . . . . ★★★★★
155mm/6⅛ ins x 19.84mm/50. Smooth, oily
Colorado Maduro wrapper provides good aging
potential. Wonderful, rich coffee and chocolate flavors with hint of spice. Full-bodied. Good balance
between flavor and strength. Great cigar to end
good meal.

$ **Largo Elegantes** . . . . 184mm/7¼ ins x 13.49mm/34

$ **Delights** . . . . 160mm/6¼ ins x 14.68mm/37

Dreams . . . . 147mm/5⅞ ins x 18.26mm/46

$ **Super Hoyos** . . . . . . 140mm/5½ ins x 17.46mm/44

$ **Cafe Royale** . . . . 143mm/5⅝ ins x 17.07mm/43

$ **No 1** . . . . 165mm/6½ ins x 17.07mm/43

$ **No 55** . . . . 133mm/5¼ ins x 17.07mm/43

$ **Culebras** . . . . 152mm/6 ins x 13.89mm/35

$ **Margaritas** . . . . 133mm/5¼ ins x 11.51mm/29

Petit . . . . 120mm/4¾ ins x 12.3mm/31

Rothschild . . . . 114mm/4½ ins x 19.84mm/50

$ **Corona** . . . . 143mm/5⅝ ins x 18.26mm/46

$ **Demitasse** . . . . 102mm/4 ins x 15.48mm/39

$ **Sabrosos** . . . . 127mm/5 ins x 15.87mm/40

HUGO CASSAR

Hand-made: Bundles. Connecticut Shade wrapper. Honduran
filler and binder. Owned by Hugo Cassar Cigars, California,
USA.

$ **No 1** . . . . 121mm/4¾ ins x 19.8mm/50

$ **No 2** . . . . 140mm/5½ ins x 18.3mm/46

$ **No 3** . . . . 171mm/6½ ins x 17.5mm/44

$ **No 4** . . . . 178mm/7 ins x 19.1mm/48

$ **No 5** . . . . 171mm/6¾ ins x 21.4mm/54

$ **No 6** . . . . 191mm/7½ ins x 19.8mm/50

$ **No 7** . . . . 203mm/8 ins x 20.6mm/52

HUGO CASSAR DIAMOND SELECTION

Hand-made. Quality, superior. Ecuadorian wrapper.
Dominican binder. Filler blend of tobacco from Mexico and
Nicaragua.

$$$	**Corona**............	140mm/5½ ins x 17.5mm/44
$$$	**Robusto**	127mm/5 ins x 19.84mm/50
$$$	**Lonsdale**	168mm/6⅝ ins x 18.3mm/46
$$$	**Torpedo**	152mm/6 ins x 21.0mm/53
$$$	**Double Corona**	159mm/6¼ ins x 20.6mm/52
$$$	**Presidente**	178mm/7 ins x 19.5mm/49
$$$	**Chairman**........	197mm/7¾ ins x 19.84mm/50

HUGO CASSAR PRIVATE COLLECTION

Hand-made. Ecuadorian wrapper. Honduran filler and binder.

$$	**Matador**.............	mm/6 ins x 16.67mm/42
$$	**Imperiale**.............	mm/7 ins x 17.5mm/44
$$	**Robusto**	mm/43/4 ins x 20.6mm/52
$$	**Elegantes**	mm/6 ins x 19.84mm/50
$$$	**Emperador**	mm/7¾ ins x 18.7mm/47

INDIAN

Hand-made. Ecuadorian Sumatra wrapper. Filler a blend of tobacco from Honduras and Nicaragua. An unusual feature in the construction is a second layer of binder called the "neutralizer." The logo is the same as that of the Indian Motorcycle Co. Exclusive to Indian Tobacco Co., Beverly Hills, California, USA.

$$$	**Chief**	191mm/7½ ins x 20.6mm/52
$$$	**TeePee** (pyramid) ...	140mm/5½ ins x 20.6mm/52
$$	**Warrior**...........	152mm/6 ins x 16.67mm/42
$$	**Boxer**...........	114mm/4½ ins x 19.84mm/50
$$	**Arrow**............	140mm/5½ ins x 13.5mm/34

INDIAN HEAD

Hand-made. Bundles. Quality, good. Connecticut Shade wrapper. Filler is blend of tobacco from Honduras and Dominican Republic. Made by Tobacos de Plascencia for Tropical Tobacco.

$	**Princesse**...........	113mm/4½ ins x 12mm/30
$	**Petit Coronas**......	140mm/5½ ins x 13.49mm/34
$	**Lindas**	140mm/5½ ins x 15.08mm/38
$	**Fumas***...........	178mm/7 ins x 17.46mm/44
$	**Cazadores***........	160mm/6¼ ins x 17.46mm/44
$	**Numero Cuatro**	140mm/5½ ins x 16.67mm/42
$	**Pinceles**............	178mm/7 ins x 12mm/30
$	**Numero Dos****......	160mm/6 ins x 17.07mm/43
$	**Panetelas**	175mm/6⅞ ins x 13.89mm/35
$	**Coronas Gorda**	160mm/6¼ ins x 17.46mm/44

$	**Rothschild****	127mm/5 ins x 19.84mm/50
$	**Numero Uno****	178mm/7 ins x 17.07mm/43
$	**Palma de Mayorca** . . .	203mm/8 ins x 15.08mm/38
$	**Emperador****	203mm/8 ins x 19.84mm/50
$	**Toros****	152mm/6 ins x 19.84mm/50
$	**Corona Grande**	190mm/7½ ins x 18.26mm/46
$	**Churchills****	175mm/6⅞ ins x 19.45mm/49
$	**Monarch**	178mm/7 ins x 20.64mm/52
	Soberanos**	197mm/7¾ ins x 19.84mm/50
$	**Viajante****	216mm/8½ ins x 20.64mm/52
$	**Gigantes****	203mm/8 ins x 21.43mm/54
$	**Torpedos**	190mm/7 ins x 21.43mm/54

*Mixed Filler

**Available with both Maduro and natural wrapper.

J. R. ULTIMATE

Hand-made. Quality, superior. Cuban seed tobacco from Honduras for binder and filler. Cuban seed from Nicaragua for wrapper. Aged for over one year. Wide selection of colors. Made exclusively for Lew Rothman of J.R. Tobacco Corporation, USA. Originally available only through this company, but now available nationwide. Full-bodied. Well-made.

Estelo Individual . . .	216mm/8½ ins x 20.64mm/52
Presidente	216mm/8½ ins x 20.64mm/52
No 1	184mm/7¼ ins x 21.43mm/54
Cetro	178mm/7 ins x 16.67mm/42
Super Cetro	210mm/8¼ ins x 17.07mm/43
Slims	175mm/6⅞ ins x 14.29mm/36
Palma Extra	175mm/6⅞ ins x 15.08mm/38
Double Corona	172mm/6¾ ins x 19.05mm/48
Padrons	152mm/6 ins x 21.43mm/54
Toro	152mm/6 ins x 19.84mm/50
No 5	155mm/6⅛ ins x 17.46mm/44
Corona	143mm/5⅝ ins x 17.86mm/45
Corona Tubus	127mm/5 ins x 17.86mm/45
Petit Cetro	140mm/5½ ins x 15.08mm/38
Rothschild . . . . ★★★★

113mm/4½ ins x 19.84mm/50. Rich, complex flavor. Well-made. Flavor fades slightly towards end.

Petit Corona	117mm/4⅝ ins x 17.07mm/43

JOHN AYLESBURY

Hand-made. Quality, superior. Full-bodied. Lacks subtlety. Well-made and a good substitute for Havana. Has elegant "JA" band. (See entry under Germany and Dominican Republic. Produced for John Aylesbury chain of cigar shops in Germany. Also exported to USA.) Distributed in USA by F & K Cigar Co.

> **Pinceles**
> **Puritos**
> **Panetela Larga**
> **Morning**
> **Panatela**
> **Pico**

JOHN AYLESBURY LA PINTURA

Hand-made. Quality, superior. Does not have elegant "JA" band. Distributed in USA by F & K Cigar Co.

> **Uno**
> **Dos**
> **Tres**

JOHN AYLESBURY PEDRO DE ALVARADO

Hand-made. Quality, superior. Full-bodied. Distributed in USA by F & K Cigar Co.

> **Grand De Luxe**
> **Cetros**
> **Supremos**
> **Crenas**

JOHN AYLESBURY SAN PEDRO SULA

Hand-made. Quality, superior. Brown and cream band with a crown and words "special seleccion."

> **Corona**
> **Panetela Corona**
> **Slim Panetela**

J.P.B.

Hand-made. All Honduran tobacco. Distributed by Lignum-2 Inc.

> **Imperiale** . . . . 191mm/7½ ins x19.8mm/50
> **Monarch** . . . . 178mm/7 ins x 18.3mm/46
> **Baron** . . . . 178mm/7 ins x 16.67mm/42
> **Royal Carona** . . . . 152mm/6 ins x 16.67mm/42

> **Regal** . . . . 159mm/6¼ ins x 13.9mm/35
> **Dugae** . . . . 140mm/5½ ins x 16.67mm/42

JOHN AYLESBURY SANTA ROSA DE COPAN

Hand-made. Quality, superior. Has "Santa De Copan," not "JA" band.

> **Uno**
> **Dos**
> **Tres**
> **La Douche**

JUAN LOPEZ

Hand-made. Bundles. All Honduran tobacco.

$ **No 300** . . . . 216mm/8½ ins x 19.84mm/50
$ **No 301** . . . . 191mm/7½ ins x 19.84mm/50
$ **No 302** . . . . 152mm/6 ins x 19.84mm/50
$ **No 303** . . . . 165mm/6½ ins x 16.67mm/42
$ **No 304** . . . . 140mm/5½ ins x 16.67mm/42

LA BALLA

Hand-made. Bundles. Maduro wrapper. All Honduran tobacco. Exclusive to Phillips & King.

> **La Balla** . . . . 171mm/6¾ ins x 18.3mm/46

LA DILIGENCIA

Hand-made. Quality, superior. Connecticut Shade wrapper. Dominican binder. Dominican, Honduran and Nicaraguan filler. Distributed by Swisher Intl.

$$ **Presidente** . . . . 216mm/8 1/2 ins x 20.6mm/52
$$ **Churchill** . . . . 178mm/7 ins x 19.1 mm/48
$$ **Toro** . . . . 152mm/6 ins x 19.8mm/50
$$ **Gran Corona** . . . . 152mm/6 ins x 17.5mm/44
$$ **Robusto** . . . . 121mm/4 3/4 ins x 19.8mm/50

LA FONTANA VINTAGE

Hand-made. Quality, superior. Connecticut Shade wrapper. Mexican binder and Cuban seed filler. Made by Tobacos Rancho Jamastran (Eiroa Family). Imported exclusively into USA by Caribe in Florida, USA.

$$ **Michelangelo** . . . . . . 190mm/7½ ins x 20.64mm/52
$$ **Da Vinci** . . . . ★★★
      175mm/6⅞ ins x 19.05mm/48. Good draw. Well-
      made. Mild cigar. Creamy. Touch of sweetness.

$$ **Puccini** . . . . 165mm/6½ ins x 17.46mm/44

$$ **Gallileo** . . . . ★★★★
127mm/5 ins x 19.84mm/50. A well-made cigar with spicy, floral aromas. Medium- to full-bodied with smooth, integrated flavors.

$ **Verdi** . . . . ★★★
140mm/5½ ins x 17.46mm/44. Medium- to full-bodied. Distinct cinnamon finish. Daytime smoke.

$ **Dante** . . . . ★★★★
140mm/5½ ins x 15.08mm/38. Rich spicy and coffee aroma. Full-flavored. Not such distinct cinnamon finish as on Verdi.

$ **Rossini** . . . . 140mm/5½ ins x 13.1 mm/33

$$ **Mona Lisa** (figurado) 121mm/4¾ ins x 18.3mm/46

$$ **Belicoso** (figurado) . . . 152mm/6 ins x 21.4 mm/54

LA GIANNA

Hand-made. Quality, superior. Ecuadorian wrapper. Nicaraguan binder and filler. Distributed by Gary Scott Intl., Massachusetts, USA.

Churchill . . . . 178mm/7 ins x 19.5mm/49
Rothchild . . . . 127mm/5 ins x 19.8mm/50
Torpedo . . . . 152mm/6 ins x 21.4mm/54
No 2 . . . . 159mm/6¼ ins x 17.5mm/44

LA INVICTA

Hand-made. Quality, good. Medium-bodied. Delicate, spicy flavor. Originally made in Jamaica. Made by Villazon for Hunters and Frankau, London, England.

Churchill . . . . 172mm/6¾ ins x 18.65mm/47
Corona . . . . ★★★★
140mm/5½ ins x 16.67mm/42. Pronounced cinnamon and cloves aroma and on finish. Burns well. Good after dinner cigar.
Magnum No 2 . . . . . 127mm/5½ ins x 19.84mm/50
Magnum No 3 . . . . . 113mm/4½ ins x 19.84mm/50
No 10 . . . . 127mm/5 ins x 19.84mm/50
Petit Corona . . . . 127mm/5 ins x 16.67mm/42

LA LLORONA

Hand-made. Bundles of 20. Connecticut wrapper. Nicaragua filler. Mexican binder. Made by Consolidated Cigar.

No 1 . . . . 165mm/6½ ins x 16.67mm/42
No 2 . . . . 140mm/5½ ins x 18.3mm/46

No 3	178mm/7 ins x 19.1mm/48
No 4	206mm/8½ ins x 19.84mm/50
No 5	127mm/5 ins x 20.6mm/52
No 6	171mm/6¾ ins x 21.4mm/54

LA MAXIMILIANA

Hand-made. All Honduran tobacco. Distributed by Cigars of Honduras, Virginia, USA.

$	**Luxus**	152mm/6 ins x 17.1mm/43
$	**Fumas**	179mm/7 ins x 17.5mm/44
$	**Dulcis**	140mm/5½ ins x 16.67mm/42
$$	**Optimus**	152mm/6 ins x 19.05mm/48

LA NATIVE

Hand-made. Connecticut wrapper. Honduran filler and binder.

Gigantes . . . . 203mm/8 ins x 20.6mm/52
Corona Grande . . . . . 191mm/7½ ins x 18.3mm/46
Churchill . . . . 175mm/6⅞ ins x 19.5mm/49
Cetros . . . . ★★★
152mm/6 ins x 17.1mm/43. Indifferent construction. Medium strength. Full flavor with chocolate and cinnamon undertones.
Rothchild . . . . 127mm/5 ins x 19.84mm/50
Super Fino . . . . 114mm/4½ ins x 11.9mm/30
Moderno . . . . ★★★
114mm/4½ ins x 10.3mm/26. Good, consistent construction. Uncomplicated, medium flavors. Because of price, ideal for everyday smoking.

LA PRIMODORA

Hand-made. Bundles. Natural or Maduro wrappers. Honduran wrapper. Dominican binder and filler. Brand owned by Swisher Intl. Good value.

$	**Emperor**	216mm/8½ ins x 19.84mm/50
$	**Solitaire**	152mm/6 ins x 19.84mm/50
$	**Starbite**	113mm/4½ ins x 19.84mm/50
$	**Falcon**	165mm/6½ ins x 13.49mm/34
$	**Excellentes**	165mm/6½ ins x 16.67mm/42
$	**Petite Cetros**	140mm/5½ ins x 16.67mm/42

LA REAL

Hand-made. All Honduran tobacco. Distributed by Cigars of Honduras, Virginia, USA.

Imperials . . . . 178mm/7 ins x 20.2mm/50
Baron . . . . 127mm/5 ins x 20.2mm/50

LA VENGA

Hand-made. Wrapper from Ecuador. Honduran binder. Filler blend of tobacco from Dominican Republic, Nicaragua and Honduras. Exclusive to Arango Cigar.

Fuma . . . . 140mm/5½ ins x 17.46mm/44
No 10 . . . . 140mm/5½ ins x 17.07mm/43
No 37 . . . . 113mm/4½ ins x 19.84mm/50
No 59 . . . . 184mm/7¼ ins x 21.43mm/54
No 61 . . . . 160mm/6¼ ins x 19.84mm/50
No 62 . . . . 140mm/5½ ins x 18.65mm/47
No 63 . . . . 184mm/7¼ ins x 18.26mm/46
No 70 . . . . 172mm/6¾ ins x 19.05mm/48
No 80 . . . . 216mm/8½ ins x 17.46mm/44

LAS CABRILLAS

Hand-made. Introduced in 1993. Connecticut Shade wrapper. Mexican binder. Nicaraguan filler. Made by Consolidated Cigar.

¢   **Columbus**. . . . . 209mm/8¼ ins x 20.64mm/52
$ **Balboa** . . . . 190mm/7½ ins x 21.43mm/54
$ **De Soto** . . . . 175mm/6⅞ ins x 19.84mm/50
$ **Ponce de Leon**. . . . . 172mm/6¾ ins x 17.46mm/44
$ **Magellan** . . . . ★★★★
152mm/6 ins x 16.67mm/42. Good draw and consistent construction. Even burning. Medium-bodied. Dry finish. Every day smoke.
¢   **Coronado**. . . . . 175mm/6⅞ ins x 13.89mm/35
¢   **Cortez**. . . . . ★★★
120mm/4¾ ins x 19.84mm/50. Good draw. Mild.
$$ **Maximilian** . . . . 178mm/7 ins x 22.2mm/56
¢   **Pizarro** . . . . 140mm/5 ins x 12.7mm/32

LEGACY

Hand-made. Bundles of 18. Wrapper from Ecuador. Binder and filler from Honduras. Brand owned by Lignum-2 Inc.

$ **Napoleon**. . . . . 216mm/8½ ins x 20.64mm/52
$ **Monarch**. . . . . 178mm/7 ins x 20.64mm/52
$ **Corona Grande** . . . . 190mm/7½ ins x 18.26mm/46
$ **Elegante** . . . . 178mm/7 ins x 17.07mm/43
$ **Rothchild** . . . . 127mm/5 ins x 19.84mm/50
$ **Super Cetro** . . . . 152mm/6 ins x 17.07mm/43

LEMPIRA

Hand-made. Bundles. Quality, good. Filler blend of tobacco from Nicaragua, Honduras and Dominican Republic. Made by Tobacos de Plasencia for Tropical Tobacco.

$$	**Toro**	152mm/6 ins x 17.07mm/50
$$	**Lanceros**	165mm/6½ ins x 15.08mm/38
$	**Lonsdale**	165mm/6½ ins x 17.46mm/44
$	**Robusto**	127mm/5 ins x 19.84mm/50
$$	**Churchills** . . . . ★★★★
	178mm/7 ins x 19.45mm/50. Good draw. Well-made. Slow, even burning. Spicy. Good balance.
$$	**Presidentes**	197mm/7¾ ins x 19.84mm/50

MARIA MANCINI

Hand-made. Quality, good. Medium to dark Havana seed wrappers. Exclusive to Santa Clara, N.A. Good value.

$$	**Palma Delgado**	178mm/7 ins x 15.48mm/39
$	**Grandes**	172mm/6¾ ins x 17.07mm/43
$	**Coronas Largas**	160mm/6¼ ins x 17.07mm/43
$	**Corona Classico**	127mm/5 ins x 16.67mm/43
$	**De Gaulle**	127mm/5 ins x 19.84mm/50

MAYA

Hand-made. Connecticut Shade wrapper. Filler blend of tobacco from Honduras and Dominican Republic. Made by Tobacos de Plasencia for Tropical Tobacco.

$$	**Executive***	197mm/7¾ ins x 19.84mm/50
$$	**Churchills***. . . . . ★★★★
	175mm/6⅞ ins x 19.45mm/49. Mild with good flavor. Ideal for beginner or casual smoker. Value for money.
$	**Coronas*** . . . . ★★★★
	160mm/6¼ ins x 17.46mm/44. Medium strength with tons of flavor. Cool. Good finish. Ideal to smoke with cognac or scotch.
$	**Matador***	152mm/6 ins x 19.84mm/50
$	**Robustos***.	127mm/5 ins x 19.84mm/50

*Available with Mexican Maduro wrapper.

★★★★★ Outstanding. A classic.   ★★★★ Excellent.
★★★ Good.   ★★ Fair, ordinary.   ★ Poor or faulty.
No Star Not evaluated.

MEDAL OF HONOR

Hand-made. Bundle. Connecticut Shade wrapper. Binder and filler from Honduras.

No 300	165mm/6½ ins x 16.67mm/42
No 500	190mm/7½ ins x 19.84mm/50
No 700	216mm/8½ ins x 20.64mm/52

MOCHA SUPREME

Hand-made. Quality, good. Havana seed wrappers. All Honduran tobacco. Made by Tobacos de Plasencia for Cigars by Santa Clara, N.A. Full-bodied.

$	**Rembrandt**	216mm/8 ins x 20.64mm/52
$	**Patron**	190mm/7½ ins x 19.84mm/50
$	**Lords**	165mm/6½ ins x 16.67mm/42
$	**Renaissance**	152mm/6 ins x 19.84mm/50
$	**Baron de Rothschild**	113mm/4½ ins x 20.64mm/52
$	**Sovereign**	140mm/5½ ins x 16.67mm/42
$	**Allegro**	165mm/6½ ins x 14.29mm/36
$	**Petites**	113mm/4½ ins x 16.67mm/42

MONTECASSINO

Hand-made. Bundles. All Honduran tobacco. Distributed by Mike's Cigars.

$	**Cazadores**	165mm/6½ ins x 17.5mm/44
$	**Imperial**	216mm/8½ ins x 20.6mm/52
¢	**Picador**	178mm/7 ins x 13.9mm/35
$	**Super Diamantes**	203mm/8 ins x 19.84mm/50

MONTELIMAR

Hand-made. Ecuadorian wrapper. Binder and filler from Nicaragua.

No 1	168mm/6⅝ ins x 17.46mm/44
Cetros	152mm/6 ins x 16.27mm/41
Churchill	175mm/6⅞ ins x 19.45mm/49
Elegante	175mm/6⅞ ins x 13.49mm/35
Joya Maduro	113mm/4½ ins x 20.64mm/52
Joya Natural	113mm/4½ ins x 20.64mm/52
Luchadore Mad	168mm/6⅝ ins x 17.46mm/44

★★★★★ Outstanding. A classic.   ★★★★ Excellent.
★★★ Good.   ★★ Fair, ordinary.   ★ Poor or faulty.
No Star: Not evaluated.

Luchadore Nat . . . . . 168mm/6⅝ ins x 17.46mm/44
Presidente . . . . 216mm/8 ½ ins x 20.64mm/52
Toro . . . . 152mm/6 ins x 19.84mm/50

MONTOYA PREMIUM

Hand-made. Bundles. Dominican wrapper. Binder and filler from Honduras. Made by Tabacos Rancho Jamastran (Eiroa Family) for Caribe in Florida, USA.

Presidente . . . . 52mm/8½ ins
Churchill . . . . 50mm/7½ ins
No 1 . . . . 43mm/6⅞ ins
Rothschild . . . . 50mm/5 ins
Petit Corona . . . . 43mm/5½ ins

NATIONAL BRAND

Hand-made. Bundles. All Honduran tobacco. Made by Tobacos Rancho Jamastran (Eiroa Family). Imported into USA by Caribe.

Imperial . . . . 216mm/8½ ins x 20.6mm/52
Churchill . . . . 191mm/7½ ins x 19.84mm/50
Lonsdale . . . . 165mm/6½ ins x 16.67mm/42
Corona . . . . 140mm/5½ ins x 16.67mm/42
Super Rothschild . . . . 152mm/6 ins x 19.84mm/50
Saberano . . . . 175mm/6⅞ ins x 18.7mm/46
Royal Palm . . . . 175mm/6⅞ ins x 14.7mm/37

NAT SHERMAN HOST SELECTION

Hand-made. Quality, superior. Ecuadorian seed wrapper. Honduran Cuban seed binder and filler. Full-bodied. Green, red and gold band. Named after New York State resorts.

$	Hudson . . . . 124mm/4⅞ ins x 12.7mm/32	
$$	Hamilton . . . . 140mm/5½ ins x 16.67mm/42	
$$	Hunter . . . . 152mm/6 ins x 17.07mm/43	
$$	Harrington . . . . 178mm/7 ins x 17.46mm/44	
$$	Hobart . . . . ★★★	

127mm/5 ins x 19.84mm/50. Tends to become dusty on finish and loses flavor and balance.

$$ Hampton . . . . 178mm/7 ins x 19.84mm/50

NESTOR VINTAGE

Hand-made. Quality, superior. Ecuadorian wrapper. Honduran binder and filler. Made by Tobacos de Plasencia. Named after famous owner, Nestor Plasencia. Distributed by House of Oxford.

$$ **No 1** . . . . 178mm/7 ins x 17.1mm/43

$$ **747** . . . . ★★★★
194mm/7⅝ ins x 18.7mm/47. Slow, even burning. Smooth. Creamy, with touch of cinnamon. Good finish.

$$ **654** . . . . ★★★★★
152mm/6 ins x 21.4mm/54. Oily wrapper. Medium strength with lots of flavor. Good balance. For discerning smoker. Ideal for aging.

$$ **454** . . . . ★★★★
121mm/4¾ ins x 21.4mm/54. Medium-bodied. Good draw. Slow, even burning. Doesn't have complexity one would expect from this ring gauge.

NORDING

Hand-made. Quality, superior. Connecticut Shade wrapper. Nicaraguan binder. Filler, a blend of tobacco from Dominican Republic and Nicaragua. Exclusive to Hollco Rohr.

Presidente . . . . 191mm/7½ ins x 20.6mm/52
Corona Grande . . . . . . 152mm/6 ins x 19.8mm/50
Robusto . . . . 121mm/4¾ ins x 20.6mm/52
Lonsdale . . . . 171mm/6¾ ins x 17.1mm/43
Corona . . . . ★★★
140mm/5½ ins x 17.1mm/43. Medium strength and flavor. Smooth. Good finish.

PADRON

Hand-made. Quality, superior. All Nicaraguan tobacco. Same range also made in Honduras where Connecticut Shade wrapper is used. Distributed by Piloto Cigars, Miami, Florida, USA.

$$ **Padron 3000** . . . . ★★★★
140mm/5½ ins x 20.6mm/52. Burns well with good draw. Spicy with touch of cinnamon.

$$ **Magnum** . . . . 229mm/9 ins x 19.84mm/50
$$ **Executive** . . . . 190mm/7½ ins x 19.84mm/50
$$ **Padron 2000** . . . . 127mm/5 ins x 19.84mm/50
$$ **Churchill** . . . . 175mm/6⅞ ins x 18.3mm/46
$$ **Delicias** . . . . 124mm/4⅞ ins x 18.3mm/46
$$ **Ambassador** . . . . 175mm/6⅞ ins x 16.67mm/42

$$	**Palmas**. . . . . 164mm/6⁵⁄₁₆ ins x 16.67mm/42
$$	**Londres** . . . . 137mm/5½ ins x 16.67mm/42
$$	**Grand Reserve** . . . . 203mm/8 ins x 16.3mm/41
$$	**Panetela** . . . . 175mm/6⅞ ins x 14.3mm/36
$$	**Chicos** . . . . 137mm/5½ ins x 14.3mm/38

PADRON SERRIE DE ANIVERSARIO

Hand-made. Quality, superior. Limited production. See notes on Padron.

$$$	**Pyramide** . . . . 175mm/6⅞ ins x 20.6mm/52
$$$	**Diplomatico** . . . . 179mm/7 ins x 19.84mm/50
$$$	**Exclusivo** . . . . ★★★★

137mm/5½ ins x 19.84mm/50. Medium-bodied. Touch of cinnamon. Elegant. Daytime smoke or after lunch.

| $$$ | **Monarca**. . . . . 165mm/6½ ins x 18.3mm/46 |
| $$$ | **Superior** . . . . ★★★ |

165mm/6½ ins x 16.67mm/42. Starts with good promise but flavor fades towards end. Looks so good, but disappoints.

| $$$ | **Corona** . . . . 152mm/6 ins x 16.67mm/42 |

PARTICULARES

Hand-made. Quality, superior. Filler blend of Cuban seed and 30 percent tobacco from Dominican Republic. Made by Tobacos de Plasencia for Tropical Tobacco. Connecticut Shade wrapper. Medium strength.

$	**Petit** . . . . 143mm/5⅝ ins x 13.49mm/34
$	**Numero Cuatro** . . . . 140mm/5½ ins x 16.67mm/42
$	**Panetelas** . . . . 175mm/6⅞ ins x 13.89mm/35
$	**Royal Coronas** . . . . ★★★

160mm/6¼ ins x 17.07mm/43. full-bodied and round-good cigar to follow lunch

$	**Rothschild*** . . . . 127mm/5 ins x 19.84mm/50
$	**Supremos** . . . . 178mm/7 ins x 17.07mm/43
$	**Matador*** . . . . 152mm/6 ins x 19.84mm/50
$	**Churchills**. . . . . 152mm/6⅛ ins x 19.45mm/49
$$	**Presidentes** . . . . 197mm/7¾ ins x 19.84mm/50
$$	**Viajantes***. . . . . 203mm/8½ ins x 20.64mm/52
$$	**Executive** . . . . 203mm/8½ ins x 20.64mm/52

*Also available in Maduro wrapper.

★★★★★ Outstanding. A classic.   ★★★★ Excellent.
★★★ Good.   ★★ Fair, ordinary.   ★ Poor or faulty.
No Star Not evaluated.

PEDRO IGLESIAS

Hand-made.

Crowns	127mm/5 ins x 17.86mm/45
Regents	152mm/6 ins x 17.46mm/44
Lonsdales	165mm/6½ ins x 17.46mm/44

PETRUS TABACAGE 89

Hand-made. Ecuadorian wrapper. Filler and binder from Honduras. Exclusive to Cigars of Honduras, Virginia, USA.

$$$ **Double Corona*** . . . . ★★★★★
197mm/7¾ ins x 20.2mm/50. Maduro. Black, oily wrapper. Well-made. Slow, even burn. Smooth. Rich, earthy flavors. Robust. A big smoke.

      Lord Byron . . . . 203mm/8 ins x 15.1mm/38

$$$ **Churchill*** . . . . 179mm/7 ins x 20.2mm/50

$$$ **No II*** . . . . 159mm/6¼ ins x 17.5mm/44

$$$ **No III** . . . . 152mm/6 ins x 20.2mm/50

$$ **No IV** . . . . 137mm/5⅜ ins x 15.1mm/38

$$ **Corona Subline*** . . . . . 140mm/5½ ins x18.3mm/46

$$ **Gregorius** . . . . 127mm/5 ins x 16.67mm/42

$$ **Rothschild*** . . . . 121mm/4¾ ins x 20.2mm/50

$$ **Chantaco** . . . . 121mm/4¾ ins x 13.9mm/35

$$ **Duchess** . . . . 114mm/4½ ins x 11.9mm/30

$$$ **Antonius*** (torpedo) . . 127mm/5 ins x 20.6mm/52

$$ **Palma Fina** . . . . ★★★★
165mm/6½ ins x 13.9mm/35. Firm draw, but acceptable. Slow, even burning. Robust, earthy flavor. Has "punch" for a thin cigar.
Available with Maduro wrappers.

PLASENCIA

Hand-made.

Viajante	216mm/8½ ins x 20.64mm/52
Gigante	203mm/8 ins x 21.43mm/54
Elegante	203mm/8 ins x 14.29mm/36
Imperial 1	90mm/7½ ins x 19.84mm/50
Churchill	178mm/7 ins x 19.45mm/49
No 1	178mm/7 ins x 17.07mm/43
No 3	178mm/7 ins x 14.29mm/36
No 4	140mm/5½ ins x 17.07mm/43
Toro	152mm/6 ins x 19.84mm/50
Corona Especial	152mm/6 ins x 17.46mm/44
No 5	140mm/5½ ins x 13.49mm/35
Rothchild	113mm/4½ ins x 19.84mm/50

PRIDE OF COPAN

Hand-made. Quality, superior. Connecticut wrapper. Honduran binder and filler. Distributed by Davidoff. Good value.

$	**No 1**	171mm/6¾ ins x 19.84mm/50
$	**No 2**	152mm/6 ins x 17.5mm/44
$	**No 3**	137mm/5⅜ ins x 15.1mm/38
$	**No 4** . . . .∴. . .	149mm/5⅞ ins x 13.9mm/35
$	**No 5**	159mm/6¼ ins x 11.9mm/30
$	**No 6**	121mm/4¾ ins x 11.9mm/30
$	**No 7**	105mm/4⅛ ins x 9.91mm/25

PRIMO DEL CRISTO

Hand-made. All Honduran tobacco.

Generals	216mm/8½ ins x 19.84mm/50
Inmensos	197mm/7¾ ins x 20.6mm/52
Churchills	165mm/6½ ins x 19.84mm/50
Toros	152mm/6 ins x 19.84mm/50
Rothschilds	127mm/5 ins x 19.84mm/50
No 1	165mm/6½ ins x 16.67mm/42
Coronas	140mm/5½ ins x 16.67mm/42
Palmas Reales	203mm/8 ins x 14.3mm/36
Palmas Extra	178mm/7 ins x 14.3mm/36
Reyes	127mm/5 ins x 16.67mm/42

PUNCH

Hand-made. Quality, superior. Havana seed wrappers. Names differ from those of Cuban range, with exception of Presidents, Double Corona, and Punch Punch. Bands are similar, but do not include "Habana." Made by Villazon. Sold in UK under La Invicta label. Made by Villazon.

$$	**Presidents**	★★★★★

216mm/8½ ins x 20.64mm/52. Well-made, good-looking cigar. Medium strength. Smooth, integrated flavors. Cigar to be seen smoking.

$	**Casa Grandes**	184mm/7¼ ins x 18.26mm/46
$	**After Dinner**	184mm/7¼ ins x 17.86mm/45
$	**Double Corona**	★★★★

172mm/6¾ ins x 19.05mm/48. Reminiscent of Havana Maduro wrapper, smooth and oily. Honeyed undertones. Loses its zest towards end.

$ **Pitas** . . . . ★★★★★
155mm/6⅛ ins x 19.84mm/50. Good balance
between strength and flavor. Coffee and spice aromas. Gets better. Cigar one doesn't want to put out.

$ **Cafe Royal** . . . . ★★★★★
143mm/5⅝ ins x 17.46mm/44. Well-made. Good
balance. Medium-bodied. Hint of cinnamon on finish. For discerning beginner and experienced
smoker alike.

$ **Punch Punch** . . . . . . 160mm/6¼ ins x 17.46mm/44
$ **Amatistas** . . . . 160mm/6¼ ins x 17.46mm/44
$ **No 1** . . . . 165mm/6½ ins x 16.67mm/43
$ **No 75** . . . . 140mm/5½ ins x 17.46mm/44
$ **Card Royal** . . . . 143mm/5⅝ ins x 17.46mm/44
$ **Elites** . . . . 133mm/5¼ ins x 17.46mm/44
$ **Largo Elegantes** . . . . . . 178mm/7 ins x 12.7mm/32
$ **Super Rothschild** . . . 133mm/5¼ ins x 19.84mm/50
$ **London Club** . . . . 127mm/5 ins x 15.87mm/40
$ **Rothschilds** . . . . ★★★
113mm/4½ ins x 19.84mm/50. Loose construction.
Burns hot, creating harshness. Not in same class as
others evaluated in this range.

$$ **Slim Panetela** . . . . 102mm/4 ins x 11.11mm/28
$ **Lonsdale** . . . . 165mm/6½ ins x 17.07mm43

PUNCH DE LUXE

Hand-made. Quality, superior. Havana seed wrappers. Full-
bodied. Only the Coronas have the same name as in the
Havana range. Not for the beginner.

$ **Chateau Lafitte** . . . . ★★★★★
184mm/7¼ ins x 21.43mm/54. Aristocratic, well-
made cigar. Elegant with integrated flavors. Maduro
wrapper. Good after-dinner cigar for connoisseur.

$ **Chateau Margaux** . . 147mm/5¾ ins x 18.26mm/46
$ **Coronas** . . . . 160mm/6¼ ins x 17.86mm/45
Good draw. Medium strength, full, rich flavors.
Touch of sweetness. Cinnamon undertones. For dis-
cerning smoker.

$ **Royal Coronations** (tube)
133mm/5¼ ins x 17.46mm/44

★★★★★ Outstanding. A classic.   ★★★★ Excellent.
★★★ Good.   ★★ Fair, ordinary.   ★ Poor or faulty.
No Star Not evaluated.

PUNCH GRAN CRU

Hand-made. Quality, superior. Havana seed wrappers. Particularly full-bodied. Appreciated by experienced smoker. Names not the same as Cuban range. Selected cigars. Made by Villazon.

$$ **Prince Consorts** . . . . 216mm/8½ ins x 20.64mm/52

$$ **Diademas** . . . . ★★★
184mm/7¼ ins x 21.43mm/54. Discreet, spicy aroma. Mild and smooth. Could do with more flavor. Lacks luster.

$$ **Monarcas** (tube) . . . . ★★★★
172mm/6¾ ins x 19.05mm/48. Good, consistent construction. Slow, even burning. Good complexity. Ideal for beginner and experienced smoker alike.

$ **Britania** . . . . ★★★★
160mm/6¼ ins x 19.84mm/50. Well-made cigar. Good texture and integrated flavors. Good after-dinner smoke.

$ **Robustos** . . . . ★★★★
133mm/5¼ ins x 19.84mm/50. Well-made. Good balance. Touch of cinnamon. Lacks complexity for this ring gauge.

$ **Superiors**. . . . . ★★★★★
140mm/5½ ins x 19.05mm/48. Lives up to its name. Full-bodied. Good balance between strength and flavor. Ideal to follow meal.

PUROS INDIOS

Hand-made. Quality, superior. Ecuadorian wrapper and binder. Filler blend of tobacco from Dominican Republic, Brazil, Jamaica and Nicaragua. Launched early 1996. Brand owned and made by Rolando Reyes Sr, founder of Cuba Aliados Cigars Inc., which as wholesale and retail operations in Union City, New Jersey, USA.

$$$ **Churchill Especial** . . . . ★★★★
184mm/7¼ ins x 21.0mm/53. Good draw. Slow, even burning. Smooth. Full-bodied. Good balance. To follow meal. Not for beginner.

$$$ **Presidente**. . . . . ★★★★★
184mm/7¼ ins x 18.7mm/47. Medium- to full-bodied. Rich, spicy. Good finish. Well made. Elegant. To follow special meal.

$$ **Nacionales**. . . . . ★★★★★
165mm/6½ ins x 18.3mm/46. Good, consistent
construction. Good balance between strength and
flavor. Creamy. For discerning smoker.

$$ **Piramide No 1** . . . . ★★★★
190mm/7½ ins x 23.8mm/60. Medium-bodied.
Smooth and elegant. I would prefer more "oomph"
for cigar of this size.

$$ **Piramide No 2** . . . . . . 165mm/6½ ins x 18.3mm/46
$$ **Toro Especial** . . . . 152mm/6 ins x 19.84mm/50
$$ **Rothschild**. . . . . ★★★★★
127mm/5 ins x 19.84mm/50. Attractive, oily wrap-
per. Good draw. Slow, even burning. Full-bodied.
Spicy. To follow meal.

$$ **Palmas Real** . . . . 178mm/7 ins x 15.1mm/38
$$ **No 4 Especial** . . . . 140mm/5½ ins x 17.5mm/44
$$ **Figurin** . . . . ★★★
254mm/10 ins x 23.8mm/60. Well-made. Burns
well. Don't expect much from this cigar. You could
be in for a long, boring smoke. Lacks punch for
cigar of this size. A cigar for showing, not smoking.

$$ **General** . . . . 457mm/18 ins x 26.2mm/66
$ **Petit Perla**. . . . . ★★★★★
127mm/5 ins x 15.1mm/38. Good draw. Slow, even
burning. Well-made. Surprising flavor for a small
cigar. Elegant. Good finish.

$$$ **No 1 Especial** . . . . 178mm/7 ins x 19.1mm/48
$$ **No 2 Especial**. . . . . . . 165mm/6½ ins x 18.3mm/46

RED LABEL

Hand-made. Bundles. Natural, Maduro and Claro wrappers.
Mexican wrapper and binder. Honduran filler.

Amatista	147mm/5¾ ins x 17.86mm/45
Casino	216mm/8½ ins x 16.67mm/42
Cetro	152mm/6 ins x 16.67mm/42
Chico	140mm/5½ ins x 17.07mm/43
Churchill Round.	152mm/6 ins x 19.45mm/49
El Dorado.	203mm/8 ins x 17.86mm/45
Elegante	178mm/7 ins x 15.08mm/38
Emperadore.	216mm/8½ ins x 20.64mm/52
Londre	178mm/7 ins x 15.87mm/40
Lonsdale	172mm/6¾ ins x 19.05mm/48
Magnifico.	184mm/7¼ ins x 21.43mm/54
Presidente	190mm/7½ ins x 17.86mm/45
Rothschild	113mm/4½ ins x 19.84mm/50
Super Cetro	160mm/6¼ ins x 17.46mm/44

REPEATER

Hand-made. Medium filler. Quality, good. Made by Tabacos Rancho Jamastram (Eiroa Family). Good value. Imported into United States by Caribe.

$	**Repeater 100**	140mm/5½ ins x 17.07mm/43
$	**Repeater 200**	152mm/6 ins x 17.07mm/43
$	**Repeater 300**	165mm/6½ ins x 17.07mm/43
$	**Havana Twist**	178mm/7 ins x 17.46mm/44
$	**Churchill**	★★★

178mm/7 ins x 19.45mm/49. A little underfilled. Good integrated flavor and aroma.

RIATA

Hand-made. Bundles. Mexican wrapper and binder. Honduran filler. Made by Consolidated Cigar.

$	**No. 100**	178mm/7 ins x 12mm/30
$	**No. 200**	175mm/6⅞ ins x 13.89mm/35
$	**No. 300**	152mm/6 ins x 16.67mm/42
$	**No. 400**	140mm/5½ ins x 17.46mm/44
$	**No. 500**	168mm/6⅝ ins x 17.46mm/44
$	**No. 600**	175mm/6⅞ ins x 19.05mm/48
$	**No. 700**	120mm/4¾ ins x 19.84mm/50
$	**No. 800**	160mm/6¼ ins x 19.84mm/50
$	**No. 900**	184mm/7¼ ins x 19.84mm/50
$	**No 1000**	203mm/8 ins x 20.6mm/52
$	**It's A Boy/Girl**	152mm/6 ins x 16.67mm/42

ROMEO Y JULIETA

Hand-made. Quality, superior. Havana seed wrapper. Good quality and well-made. Full-bodied. Reminiscent of a Havana. Also made in Dominican Republic and Cuba. The bands do not include the word "Habana." Brand owned in USA by Hollco Rohr.

Gigante	178mm/7 ins x 19.05mm/48
Celestiales	203mm/8 ins x 14.29mm/36
Especiales	160mm/6¼ ins x 17.07mm
Prado	140mm/5½ ins x 16.67mm
Princessa	133mm/5¼ ins x 15.48mm/39
Sublime	113mm/4½ ins x 19.84mm/50

ROYAL COURT

Hand-made. Bundles. Ecuadorian wrapper. Honduran filler and binder. Brand owned by Lignum-2 Inc.

Petit Corona.	140mm/5½ ins x 15.08mm/38
Panetela	175mm/6⅞ ins x 14.29mm/36
Cetro	152mm/6 ins x 17.86mm/43
Presidente	197mm/7¾ ins x 19.84mm/50
Viajante	216mm/8½ ins x 20.64mm/52

ROYAL HONDURAS

Hand-made. Quality, superior. Indonesian wrapper. Dominican binder. Honduran filler. Exclusive to Antillian Cigar Corp., Miami, Florida, USA.

$$	**Czar**	203mm/8 ins x 19.8mm/50
$$	**Sovereign**	178mm/7 ins x 19.1mm/48
$$	**Kings** (torpedo)	156mm/6⅛ ins x 21.4mm/54
$$	**Prince**.	178mm/7 ins x 17.5mm/44
$$	**Majesty**	127mm/5 ins x 19.8mm/50
$$	**Joker**	140mm/5½ ins x 16.67mm/42
$$	**Princess** (pyramid) . . .	127mm/5 ins x 15.1mm/38
$$	**Knight**.	152mm/6 ins x 19.8mm/50

ROYAL MANNA

Hand-made. Ecuadorian wrapper. Honduran filler and binder. Brand owned by Brick-Hanauer Co., Waltham, Massachusetts, USA.

$	**No 1**	7 ins x 17.07mm/43
$	**No 4**.	5½ ins x 16.67/42
$	**Manchego**.	152mm/6 ins x 14.29mm/36
$	**Churchill**.	190mm/17½ ins x 19.84 mm/50
$	**Largo Extra Fino Rothschild**	
	203mm/8 ins x 15.08mm/38	
$	**Toro**	152mm/6 ins x 19.84mm/50

SAN LUIS

Hand-made. Bundles. Mixed filler. Distributed by Indian Head Sales.

Soberanos	191mm/7½ ins x 19.84mm/50
Corona.	166mm/6½ ins x 17.5mm/44

★★★★★ Outstanding. A classic.   ★★★★ Excellent.
★★★ Good.   ★★ Fair, ordinary.   ★ Poor or faulty.
No Star Not evaluated.

Toro	. . . .	152mm/6 ins x 19.84mm/50
Panetelas	. . . .	166mm/6½ ins x 14.3mm/36
Cetros	. . . .	137mm/5⅜ ins x 16.67mm/42

SAN FERNANDO

Hand-made. All Honduran tobacco. Distributed by Cigars of Honduras, Virginia, USA.

Churchill	. . . .	179mm/7 ins x 19.1mm/48
Corona	. . . .	152mm/6 ins x 17.5mm/44
No 5	. . . .	127mm/5 ins x 20.6mm/52

SANTA ROSA

Hand-made. Ecuadorian wrapper. Honduran filler and binder. Distributed by Brick-Hanauer Co., Waltham, Massachusetts, USA.

$	**Numero Quatro**	127mm/5½ ins x 16.67mm/42
$	**Cetros**	152mm/6 ins x 16.67mm/42
$$	**Churchill**	178mm/7 ins x 19.45mm/49
$$	**Corona**	165mm/6½ ins x 17.46mm/44
$$	**Elegante**	178mm/7 ins x 17.07mm/43
$$	**Embajadore**	216mm/8½ ins x 20.64mm/52
$$	**Finas**	127mm/6½ ins x 11.9mm/30
$$	**President**	216mm/8½ ins x 19.8mm/50
$$	**Sancho Panza**	121mm/4¾ ins x 19.8mm/50
$$	**Torpedo**	127mm/5½ ins x 214mm/54
$	**Largos**	172mm/6¾ ins x 13.89mm/35
$	**Regulares** . . . . ★★★★
	140mm/5½ ins x 17.86mm/45. Don't judge this cigar too quickly. Flavor soon builds up with good complexity. For everyday smoking. Good value for money.
$$	**Toro**	152mm/6 ins x 19.84mm/50

SOLO AROMA

Hand-made. Bundles. Connecticut Shade wrapper. Filler blend of tobacco from Honduras and Dominican Republic. Made by Tabacos de Plasencia for Tropical Tobacco.

Fumas*	. . . .	178mm/7 ins x 17.46mm/44
Cazadores*	. . . .	160mm/6¼ ins x 17.46mm/44
Numero Cuatro	. . . .	140mm/5½ ins x 16.67mm/42
Numero Dos	. . . .	152mm/6 ins x 17.07mm/43
Corona Gorda	. . . . .	160mm/6¼ ins x 17.46mm/44
Rothchild	. . . .	127mm/5 ins x 19.84mm/50
Numero Uno	. . . .	178mm/7 ins x 17.07mm/43

Panetela	175mm/6⅞ ins x 14.29mm/36
Palma de Mayorca	203mm/8 ins x 15.08mm/38
Corona Grande	190mm/7½ ins x 18.26mm/46
Churchill	175mm/6⅞ ins x 19.45mm/49
Toro	152mm/6 ins x 19.84mm/50
Soberanos	197mm/7¾ ins x 19.84mm/50
Viajante	216mm/8½ ins x 20.64mm/52

Short filler.

SUPER SPECIAL

Hand-made. Bundles. Connecticut Shade wrapper. Brand owned by Brick-Hanauer Co, Waltham, Massachusetts, USA.

Toro	152mm/6 ins x 19.84mm/50
Churchill	178mm/7 ins x 19.45mm/49
Viajante	216mm/8½ ins x 20.64mm/52
No 1	172mm/6¾ ins x 16.67mm/42
Cetros	152mm/6 ins x 16.67mm/42
Rothschild	113mm/4½ ins x 20.64mm/52

SWISHER SWEEETS

Hand-made. Short filler. All tobacco. No binder. Rough cut and hand-rolled. Unique sweet taste. Packed in resealable pouch. Good value mass-market cigar. Owned by Swisher Intl.

Outlaws	★★★

108mm/4¼ ins x 11.1mm/28

TENA Y VEGA

Hand-made. Quality, superior. Cameroon wrapper. Honduran binder and filler. Mild. Exclusive to Santa Clara N.A.

Cetros	155mm/6⅛ ins x 16.67mm/42
Churchill	178mm/7 ins x 19.84mm/50
Double Corona	152mm/6 ins x 19.84mm/50
No 1	172mm/6¾ ins x 16.67mm/42

TESOROS DE COPAN

Hand-made. All Honduran tobacco. Wrapper is Honduran grown Connecticut seed. La Ruta Maya Foundation, dedicated to preservation of Central American rainforests and remains of Mayans, original users of tobacco, benefits from sale of these cigars. Distributed by Cigars of Honduras, Virginia, USA.

Churchill	179mm/7 ins x 20.2mm/50
Cetros	159mm/6¼ ins x 17.5mm/44
Toros	152mm/6 ins x 20.2mm/50

Corona . . . . ★★★
133mm/5¼ ins x 18.3mm/46. medium-bodied. Full
flavor. Good draw. Will benefit with aging.
Yumbo . . . . 121mm/4¾ ins x 20.2mm/50
Lindas . . . . mm/5⅜ ins x 15.1mm/38

THOMAS HINDS HONDURAN SELECTION

Hand-made. Ecquadorian wrapper. Honduran filler and
binder. Owned by Hinds Brothers Tobacco.

$$ **Presidente** . . . . ★★★★
216mm/8½ ins x 20.6mm/52. Medium-bodied.
Smooth. Spicy with creamy finish.

$$ **Torpedo** . . . . ★★★
152mm/6 ins x 20.6mm/52. Easy draw. Burns
unevenly. Medium-bodied. Earthy with cinnamon
undertones. Daytime smoke.

$$ **Churchill** . . . . ★★★★★
178mm/7 ins x 19.5mm/49. Slow, even burning.
Well-made. Rich, spicy flavor. Good finish. For dis-
cerning smoker.

$$ **Short Churchill**. . . . . . 152mm/6 ins x 20.84mm/50
$ **Supremo**. . . . . 178mm/7 ins x 20.1mm/43
$ **Robusto** . . . . 127mm/5 ins x 20.84mm/50
$ **Royal Corona** . . . . ★★★★★
152mm/6 ins x 20.1mm/43. Firm, but good draw.
Well-made. Medium strength. Full, complex flavors.
Ideal for beginner and experienced smoker.

$ **Corona** . . . . ★★★
140mm/5½ ins x 16.67mm/42. Earthy, wet hay
flavors. Attractive aroma. Ideal for beginner.

TIBURON

Hand-made. Bundles. Connecticut wrapper. Mexican binder.
Dominican filler. Distributed by Phillips & King and Swisher
Intl.

$ **Tiger Shark** . . . . 160mm/6¼ ins x 13.49mm/34
$ **Great White** . . . . 152mm/6 ins x 17.07mm/43
$ **Mako** . . . . 83mm/5¼ ins x 16.67mm/42

★★★★★ Outstanding. A classic.   ★★★★ Excellent.
★★★ Good.   ★★ Fair, ordinary.   ★ Poor or faulty.
No Star Not evaluated.

TOPPER

Hand-made. Honduran wrapper and binder. Filler, blend of tobacco from Mexico and Dominican Republic. Owned by Topper Cigar Co., established 1896.

Panetela	. . . .	178mm/7 ins x 13.5mm/34
Corona	. . . .	140mm/5½ ins x 17.1mm/43
No 1	. . . .	165mm/6½ ins x 17.1mm/43
Rothschild	. . . .	114mm/4½ ins x 20.84mm/50
Toro	. . . .	152mm/6 ins x 20.84mm/50
Churchill	. . . .	191mm/7½ ins x 20.84mm/50

TULAS

Hand-made. Bundles of 20. Connecticut wrapper. Nicaraguan filler. Mexican binder. Made by Consolidated Cigar.

¢	**No 1**	. . . .	165mm/6½ ins x 16.67mm/42
¢	**No 2**	. . . .	140mm/5½ ins x 18.3mm/46
¢	**No 3**	. . . .	178mm/7 ins x 19.1mm/48
¢	**No 4**	. . . .	216mm/8½ ins x 19.84mm/50
¢	**No 5**	. . . .	127mm/5 ins x 20.6mm/52
¢	**No 6**	. . . .	171mm/6¾ ins x 21.4mm/54

V CENTENNIAL

Hand-made. Quality, superior. Top of range from Tropical Tobacco. Made by Tabacos de Plasencia. Connecticut Shade wrapper. Mexican binder. Filler blend from five countries. Good value.

$$ **Torpedo** . . . . ★★★★
178mm/7 ins x 21.43mm/54. Spicy, hint of cinnamon. Flavor somewhat light for strength. Smooth. Well-made. Attractive presentation.

$$ **Presidente** . . . . 203mm/8 ins x 19.84mm/50

$$ **Churchills*** . . . . ★★★★
178mm/7 ins x 19.05mm/48. Attractive wrapper. Well-made. Spicy, hint of cinnamon. Smooth. Good finish.

$$ **Numero 1** . . . . ★★★★★
190mm/7½ ins x 15.08mm/38. Good draw. Slow, even burning. Good balance between strength and complex flavors.

$$ **Numero 2*** . . . . 152mm/6 ins x 19.84mm/50

$ **Cetros*** . . . . ★★★★★
160mm/6¼ ins x 17.46mm/44. Well-made. Good draw. Slow, even burning. Medium strength. Lots of spicy, creamy flavors. For discerning smoker.

$ **Robustos*** . . . . ★★★★
127mm/5 ins x 19.84mm/50. Lovely wrapper.
Perhaps not enough flavor for the strength. Robust.

$ **Coronas** . . . . 140mm/5½ ins x 16.67mm/42
*Also available in Maduro wrapper.

VSOP

Hand-made. Quality, superior. Connecticut Shade and Sumatra wrapper. Honduran binder and filler. Distributed by CEI Group, Northfield, Illinois, USA.

Churchill	178mm/7 ins x 19.8mm/50
Torpedo	152mm/6 ins x 21.4mm/54
Lonsdale	165mm/6½ ins x 16.67mm/42
Robusto	127mm/5 ins x 19.8mm/50
Corona	140mm/5½ ins x 16.67mm/42

VINTAGE HONDURAN

Hand-made. Medium- to full-bodied. All Honduran tobacco.

Cetro	165mm/6½ ins x 17.46mm/44
Governor	152mm/6 ins x 19.84mm/50
Imperial	203mm/8 ins x 17.46mm/44
Matador	140mm/5½ ins x 16.67mm/42
Panetela	152mm/6 ins x 14.29mm/36
Panetela Larga	178mm/7 ins x 14.29mm/36
President	190mm/7½ ins x 19.84mm/50
Rothchild	113mm/4½ ins x 19.84mm/50
Sultans	216mm/8½ ins x 20.64mm/52
Toro	140mm/5½ ins x 18.26mm/46

VIRTUOSO TORANO

Hand-made. Connecticut seed wrapper grown in Ecuador. Nicaraguan binder. Filler blend of tobacco from Nicaragua, Honduras and Mexico. Brand owned by Toraño Cigars, Miami, Florida, USA.

$$$ **Presidente** . . . . ★★★★
203mm/8 ins x 20.6mm/52. Good, consistent construction. Slow, even burning. Smooth. Good balance between strength and flavor. Touch of caramel and cinnamon. Fine ending to good meal.

$$ **Double Corona** . . . . ★★★★★
152mm/6 ins x 19.84mm/50 . Well-made. Good smoking qualities and balance between strength and flavor. Wonderful after-dinner cigar.

$$ **Robusto**. . . . . ★★★★★
121mm/4¾ ins x 20.6mm/52. Good consistent construction. Has complexity with nutty undertones. Long finish. Good introduction to this size for beginner.

$$ **Lonsdale**. . . . . 178mm/7 ins x 17.5mm/44

$$ **Cetros**. . . . . 152mm/6 ins x 17.1mm/43

VOYAGER

Hand-made. Connecticut Shade wrapper grown in Ecuador. Binder and filler from Honduras. Brand owned by Brick-Hanauer Co., Waltham, Massachusetts, USA.

$ **Atlantis**. . . . . 190mm/7½ ins x 18.26mm//46

$ **Columbia** . . . . 178mm/7 ins x 17.07mm/43

$ **Enterprise**. . . . . 152mm/6 ins x 16.67mm/42

W & D

Hand-made Bundles. Good value. Distributed in USA by Hollco Rohr.

Presidentes . . . . 190mm/7½ ins x 19.84mm/50

Cetros No 2 . . . . ★★★★
165mm/6½ ins x 17.46mm/44. Oily mid brown wrapper. Smooth. Good balance. Good daytime smoke or after light meal.

Coronas . . . . 140mm/5½ ins x 19.84mm/50

Panetela Largas . . . . . 178mm/7 ins x 14.29mm/36

Blunts . . . . ★★★
127mm/5 ins x 16.67mm/42. Fairly hard draw. Lacks luster.

Gigantes. . . . . 216mm/8½ ins x 20.64mm/52

YAGO

Hand-made. Bundles. All Honduran tobacco. Exclusive to Miami Cigar.

Fumas. . . . . 178mm/7 ins x 17.5mm/44

Cazadores. . . . . 178mm/7 ins x 17.5mm/44

Churchill . . . . 191mm/7½ ins x 19.84mm/50

Petit Cazadores . . . . . 140mm/5½ ins x 17.5mm/44

★★★★★ Outstanding. A classic.   ★★★★ Excellent.
★★★ Good.   ★★ Fair, ordinary.   ★ Poor or faulty.
No Star Not evaluated.

ZINO

Hand-made. Quality, superior. Named after Zino Davidoff.
Connoisseur series developed in 1987 for opening of
Davidoff shop in New York. Full, rich flavor. Mouton Cadet
range very mild and specially selected from Baronne
Philippe de Rothschild. Honduran series medium flavor. All
high-quality construction. Range of machine-made dry cigars also made in Holland.

\$\$ **Mouton Cadet No 1** . . . . ★★★★★
160mm/6½ ins x 17.46mm/44. Good, consistent
construction. Good complexity. Spicy. Good balance. Elegant.

\$\$ **Mouton Cadet No 2** . . 152mm/6 ins x 13.89mm/35
\$\$ **Mouton Cadet No 3** . 147mm/5¾ ins x 14.29mm/36
\$\$ **Mouton Cadet No 4** . . . 130mm/5⅛ ins x 12mm/30
\$\$ **Mouton Cadet No 5** . . . . ★★★★★
127mm/5 ins x 17.46mm/44. Spicy aroma with
touch of cinnamon and sweetness on palate.
Smooth. Well-balanced.

\$\$ **Mouton Cadet No 6** . . . . ★★★★★
127mm/5 ins x 19.84mm/50. A well-made cigar.
Good burning qualities. Smooth, creamy. Good finish. For discerning smoker.

        Connoisseur No 100 . . . . ★★★★
197mm/7¾ ins x 19.84mm/50. Firm draw. Slow,
even burning. Mild to medium-bodied. Complex
flavors develop. Good finish. For discerning
smoker.

        Connoisseur No 200 190mm/7½ ins x 18.26mm/46
        Connoisseur No 300 147mm/5¾ ins x 18.26mm/46

\$\$\$ **Veritas** . . . . ★★★★★
178mm/7 ins x 19.84mm/50. Silky, oily wrapper.
Well-made. Medium-bodied. Good flavor with chocolate undertones. Good finish. For discerning smoker.

\$\$ **Tradition** . . . . 160mm/6¼ ins x 17.46mm/44
\$\$ **Elegance** . . . . 172mm/6¾ ins x 13.49mm/34
\$\$ **Diamond** . . . . 140mm/5½ ins x 15.87mm/40
\$\$ **Junior** . . . . 172mm/6¾ ins x 12mm/30
\$\$ **Princesse** . . . . 113mm/4½ ins x 7.94mm/20
\$\$ **Zino Tubos No 1** . . . 172mm/6¾ ins x 13.49mm/34
\$\$ **Classic Sumatra** . . . . 120mm/4¾ ins x 18.65mm/47

$$	**Classic Brazil**	120mm/4¾ ins x 18.65mm/47
$$	**Relax Sumatra**	147mm/5¾ ins x 12mm/30
$$	**Relax Brazil**	147mm/5¾ ins x 12mm/30
$$$$	**Pantellas Sumatra**	
$$$$	**Panatellas Brazil**	
¢	**Cigarrillos Sumatra**	
¢	**Cigarrillos Brazil**	
$	**Demi Tasse**	

Indonesia

CELESTINO VEGA

Hand-made. Quality, superior. Indonesian wrapper and binder. Filler is blend of tobacco from Indonesia, Dominican Republic and Pennsylvania, USA. Available in conventional boxes or unique triangle boxes. Distributed by Caribbean Cigar Co., Miami, Florida, USA.

$$$	**Churchill**	178mm/7 ins x 19.8mm/50
$$$	**Cuban Perfecto**	152mm/6 ins x 19.1mm/48
$$	**Cuban Corona**	165mm/6½ ins x 16.67mm/42
$	**Cuban Panetella**	178mm/7 ins x 11.1mm/28
$$$	**Super Rothchild**	152mm/6 ins x 19.8mm/50
$$	**Rothchild**	127mm/5 ins x 19.8mm/50
$	**Senator**	89mm/3½ ins x 19.1mm/48
$	**Petit Corona**	121mm/4¾ ins x 15.9mm/40
$	**Senorita**	105mm/4⅛ ins x 12.7mm/32
$	**Tesorita**	92mm/3⅝ ins x 7.9mm/20

DJARUM

Machine-made by G.A. Andron.

   Cigarillos

Italy

   Antico Tuscano . . . . 152mm/6 ins x 10mm/25
   Machine-made. Specially aged for export. Dark
   maduro, uneven wrapper. Unusual shape. Tightly
   rolled, but fairly easy draw. Sweet floral aroma
   before lit. Strong, but good balance with flavor.
   Touch of sweetness. Rugged cigar. No finesse.

Jamaica

In 1996 Jamaica exported 15.5 million cigars to the USA, an increase of only 1.5 percent over 1995.

8-9-8 COLLECTION

Hand-made. Connecticut Shade wrapper. Dominican filler and binder. Distributed by Mike's Cigars, Miami, Florida, USA.

Churchill	. . . .	191mm/7½ ins x 19.5mm/49
Corona	. . . .	140mm/5½ ins x 16.67mm/42
Lonsdale	. . . .	165mm/6½ ins x 16.67mm/45
Monarch	. . . .	171mm/6¾ ins x 17.9mm/45
Robusto	. . . .	140mm/5½ ins x 19.5mm/49

CHEVERE

Hand-made. Bundle. All Jamaican leaf. Distributed by Mike's Cigars, Miami, Florida, USA.

Kingston	. . . .	178mm/7 ins x 19.5mm/49
Montego	. . . .	165mm/6½ ins x 17.9mm/45
Ocho Rios	. . . .	203mm/8 ins x 19.5mm/49
Antonio	. . . .	140mm/5½ ins x 17.1mm/43
Spanish Town	. . . . . .	165mm/6½ ins x 16.67mm/42

CIFUENTES BY PARTAGAS

Hand-made. Quality, superior. Limited edition of about 150,000, named after Ramon Cifuentes, the Partagas brand in Cuba before Castro's revolution. Went into Alfred Dunhill stores mid-1996. Aged for two years before boxing. Connecticut Shade wrapper. Cameroon binder and filler blend of tobacco from Dominican Republic and Mexico. Made by General Cigar.

$$$$	**Churchill**	. . . .	191mm/7½ ins x 19.5mm/49
$$$$	**Lonsdale**	. . . .	165mm/6½ ins x 16.67mm/42
$$$$	**Corona Gorda**	. . . . . .	140mm/5½ ins x 19.5mm/49
$$$	**Petit Corona**	. . . .	127mm/5 ins x 15.1mm/38

FUNDADORES

Hand-made. Connecticut Shade wrapper. Mexican binder. Filler blend of tobacco from Jamaica, Mexico and Dominican Republic. Made by Combined Tobacco Co. for House of Oxford.

King Ferdinand	. . . . . .	203mm/8 ins x 19.5mm/49

Rothschild . . . . ★★★★
165mm/6½ ins x 16.67mm/42. medium-bodied.
Spicy with hint of ginger. Daytime smoke for
experienced smoker. After dinner cigar for casual
smoker.
Ultra . . . . 152mm/6 ins x 19.84mm/50

GISPERT

Hand-made. US rights owned by Hollco Rohr. Old Cuban
brand, which has word "Habana" on band.

Kingston Town
Port Royal
Montego Bay
Port Antonio

GUARANTEED JAMAICA

Hand-made. Bundles. Ecuadorian wrapper. Mexican binder.
Filler, blend of tobacco from Jamaica, Mexico and Dominican
Republic. Made by Combined Tobacco Co., Kingston,
Jamaica.

No 1000 . . . . 191mm/7½ ins x 19.5mm/49
No 1002 . . . . 203mm/8 ins x 19.84mm/50
No 100 . . . . 165mm/6½ ins x 16.67mm/42
No 200 . . . . 140mm/5½ ins x 16.67mm/42
No 300 . . . . 171mm/6¾ ins x 15.1mm/38
No 600 . . . . 152mm/6 ins x 19.84mm/50
No 900 . . . . 152mm/6 ins x 17.9mm/45

JAMAICA BAY

Machine-bunched & hand-finished bundles. Connecticut
wrapper, Mexican binder and filler blend of tobacco from
Dominican Republic and Mexico. Good value. Distributed in
USA by Arango Cigar.

$ **No 100** . . . . 190mm/7½ ins x 19.45mm/49
$ **No 200** . . . . 152mm/6 ins x 19.85mm/50
$ **No 300** . . . . 172mm/6¾ ins x 17.86mm/45
$ **No 400** . . . . 165mm/6½ ins x 16.67mm/42
$ **No 500** . . . . 152mm/6¾ ins x 15.08mm/38
$ **No 600** . . . . 140mm/5½ ins x 16.67mm/42

¢ – Under $1.00 $ – $1–3.00 $$ – $3–4.00
$$$ – $5–8.00 $$$$ – $8–20.00 $$$$$ – $20+

JAMAICA GEM

Hand-made. Mexican grown Connecticut seed wrappers. Mexican binder and filler blend of tobacco from Mexico and Dominican Republic.

$	**Petit Corona**	127mm/5 ins x 15.87mm/40
$	**Palma**	172mm/6¾ ins x 13.49mm/34
$	**Corona**	140mm/5½ ins x 15.87mm/40
$	**Royal Corona**	152mm/6 ins x 16.27mm/41
$	**Corona Grande**	165mm/6½ ins x 17.07mm/43
$	**Churchill**	203mm/8 ins x 20.24mm/51
$	**Double Corona**	178mm/7 ins x 17.86mm/45
$	**Giant Corona**	190mm/7½ ins x 19.45mm/49
$	**Palmitas**	165mm/6½ ins x 12mm/30

JAMAICA GOLD

Hand-made. Connecticut Shade wrapper. Jamaican grown Connecticut seed wrapper. Mexican binder and filler from Dominican Republic

$	**Prince**	197mm/7¾ ins x 19.84mm/50
$	**Earl**	172mm/6¾ ins x 15.08mm/38
$	**Baron**	★★★

165mm/6½ ins x 17.46mm/44. Mild, little flavor. Easy draw. Daytime smoke. Good value. Ideal for novice.

$	**Queen**	160mm/6¼ ins x 17.07mm/43
$	**Count**	140mm/5½ ins x 15.08mm/38
$	**Duke**	140mm/5½ ins x 16.67mm/42
$	**Baron**	165mm/6½ ins x 17.76mm/44
¢	**Dutchess**	113mm/4½ ins x 12mm/30
	King	152mm/6 ins x 19.84mm/50
	Torpedo	178mm/7 x 36 ins x 20.64mm/52

JAMAICA HERITAGE

Hand-made. Bundle. Ecuadorian wrapper. Mexican binder. Filler is blend of tobacco from Jamaica, Mexico and Dominican Republic. Distributed by Lignum-2 Inc and House of Oxford.

¢	**No 100**	160mm/6½ ins x 16.67mm/42
¢	**No 200**	140mm/5½ ins x 16.67mm/42
¢	**No 600**	152mm/6 ins x 19.84mm/50
¢	**No 1000**	190mm/7⅛ ins x 19.5mm/49
¢	**No 1002**	203mm/8 ins x 19.84mm/50

JAMAICAN KINGS

Hand-made. Bundles. Connecticut Shade wrapper.

Petit Coronas	140mm/5½ ins x 16.67mm/42
Buccaneers	165mm/6½ ins x 16.67mm/42
Rapiers	178mm/7 ins x 14.29mm/36
Double Coronas	178mm/7 ins x 17.46mm/44
Imperials	190mm/7½ ins x 19.84mm/50

JAMAICAN PRIDE

Hand-made by General Cigar.

Churchill	203mm/8 ins x 19.5mm/49
Double Corona	178mm/7 ins x 19.5mm/49
Imperiales	165mm/6½ ins x 17.9mm/45
Lonsdales	152mm/6 ins x 17.9mm/45
Corona Deluxe	165mm/6½ ins x 16.67mm/42
Corona	140mm/5½ ins x 16.67mm/42
Petit Corona	127mm/5 ins x 15.5mm/39

MACANUDO

Hand-made. Connecticut Shade wrapper. Quality, superior. Originally founded in 1868. Now made by General Cigar. Blend is the same for both countries-Connecticut Shade wrapper, binder from Mexico and a blend of Jamaican, Mexican and Dominican tobacco for the filler. Largest-selling premium cigar brand in United Stated. In Spanish Macanudo means "the greatest." Excellent range of well-made cigars. Mild and smooth.

$$$$ Vintage No I . . . . ★★★★★
190mm/7½ ins x 19.45mm/49. Excellent claro wrapper. Spicy, floral aromas. Creamy finish. Balanced. Well-made.

$$$$ Vintage No II . . . . ★★★★★
165mm/6½ ins x 16.67mm/42. Spicy aroma. Medium-bodied. No harshness. A top cigar.

$$$$ Vintage No III . . . . . 140mm/5½ ins x 18.26mm/46

$$$$ Vintage No IV . . . . ★★★★★
113mm/4½ ins x 18.26mm/46. Medium-bodied. Elegant. Satisfying smoke with no harshness. Ideal to follow a meal.

$$$$ Vintage No V . . . . ★★★★
140mm/5½ ins x 19.45mm/49. Mild, smooth. Well-made, but could do with more flavor.

$$$$ Vintage No VII* . . . . 190mm/7½ ins x 15.08mm/38

$$$ Prince of Wales . . . . . 216mm/8½ ins x 20.6mm/52

$$$ Prince Philip . . . . . . 190mm/7½ ins x 19.45mm/49

Sovereign*...... 197mm/7 3/4 ins x 17.86mm/45

$$ **Baron de Rothschild** .... ★★★★
165mm/6½ ins x 16.67mm/42. Elegant, well-made
cigar. Excellent for average smoker.

Amatista* .... ★★★★
160mm/6¼ ins x 16.67mm/42. Good draw.
Elegant, mild and smooth.

Hampton Court .... 147mm/5¾ ins x 17.07mm/43

$$ **Duke of Devon** .... ★★★★
140mm/5½ ins x 16.67mm/42. Maduro wrapper.
Rich aroma. Honey on palate.

Lord Claridge* .... ★★★★
140mm/5½ ins x 15.08mm/38. Mild. Elegant. Hard
draw makes it difficult for beginners.

Somerset* .... 197mm/7¾ ins x 13.49mm/31

$$ **Portofino** .... 178mm/7 ins x 13.49mm/34

$$ **Claybourne**.......... 152mm/6 ins x 12.3mm/31

$$$ **Duke of Wellington*** 216mm/8½ ins x 15.08mm/38

$$ **Hyde Park**........................... ★★★
140mm/5½ ins x 19.45mm/49. Medium-bodied.
Lacks punch.

Earl of Lonsdale* .. 172mm/6¾ ins x 15.08mm/38
No. 800 .... 190mm/7½ ins x 19.45mm/49
No. 900 Portofino ... 178mm/7 ins x 14.29mm/36
No. 500 .... 172mm/6¾ ins x 15.08mm/38
No. 700 .... 165mm/6½ ins x 16.67mm/42
No. 1000 .... 140mm/5½ ins x 19.45mm/49
No. 600 .... 140mm/5½ ins x 16.67mm/42
No. 400 .... 140mm/5½ ins x 15.08mm/38

¢ **Ascots** (tin)........................... ★★★
108mm/4¼ ins x 12.7mm/32. Difficult burning.
Fairly strong for small cigar.

$$ **Trump***.......................... ★★★★★
165mm/6½ ins x 17.86mm/45. Good balance
between strength and flavor. Elegant and smooth.

$$ **Crystal** .... ★★★★
133mm/5½ ins x 19.45mm/49. Packed in glass
tube. Mild. Good flavor.

$$ **Duke of Windsor** .... 152mm/6 ins x 19.84mm/50
$ **Quill***........... 133mm/5¼ ins x 11.11mm/28

★★★★★ Outstanding. A classic.　★★★★ Excellent.
★★★ Good.　★★ Fair, ordinary.　★ Poor or faulty.
No Star Not evaluated.

$$ **Petit Corona** .... ★★★★
127mm/5 ins x 15.08mm/38. Mild, spicy and vegetal flavors. Smooth. A good daytime smoke.

$ **Caviar**............ 102mm/4 ins x 14.29mm/36
* *Manufacture of these cigars ceased early 1996 to make tobacco and production capacity available for more popular cigars. Most of these cigars have ring gauge of 40 or less, showing market preference for thicker cigars.*

MARIO PALOMINO

Hand-made by Palomino Brothers Tobacco Co. Connecticut Shade wrapper. Mexican binder and Jamaican filler. Distributed in USA by Topper Cigar.

Buccaneers.........	140mm/5½ ins x 12.7mm/32
Delicado...........	140mm/5½ ins x 12.7mm/32
Petit Corona.......	127mm/5½ ins x 16.27mm/41
Rapier	152mm/6 ins x 12.7mm/32
Festivale	152mm/6 ins x 16.27mm/41
Cetro	165mm/6½ ins x 16.67mm/42
Corona Immensa	152mm/6 ins x 18.65mm/47
Caballero	178mm/7 ins x 17.86mm/45
Presidente	190mm/7½ ins x 19.45mm/49

OCHO RIOS

Hand-made. Bundle. Ecuadorian wrapper. Mexican binder. Filler blend of tobacco from Jamaica, Mexico and Dominican Republic. Exclusive to House of Oxford.

¢	**President**	178mm/7 ins x 19.84mm/50
¢	**Toros**	152mm/6 ins x 19.84mm/50
$	**Vijantes**	210mm/8¼ ins x 20.6mm/52
¢	**No 4**	127mm/5 ins x 16.67mm/42
¢	**No 1**	178mm/7 ins x 17.1mm/43

OLD HARBOUR

Hand-made. Bundles.

No 100..........	140mm/5½ ins x 16.67mm/42
No 200..........	165mm/6½ ins x 16.67mm/42
No 300	178mm/7 ins x 17.86mm/45
No 400	190mm/7½ ins x 19.84mm/50

¢ – Under $1.00 $ – $1–3.00 $$ – $3–4.00
$$$ – $5–8.00 $$$$ – $8–20.00 $$$$$ – $20+

PRIDE OF JAMAICA

Hand-made. Connecticut wrapper. Mexican binder. Filler a blend of tobacco from Jamaica, Mexico and Dominican Republic.

Monarch . . . . 203mm/8 ins x 19.84mm/50
Churchill . . . . 191mm/7½ ins x 19.5mm/49
Magnum . . . . 152mm/6 ins x 19.84mm/50
Petit Churchill . . . . 152mm/6 ins x 17.9mm/45
Lonsdale . . . . 165mm/6½ ins x 16.67mm/42
President . . . . 171mm/6¾ ins x 15.1mm/38
Royal Corona . . . . . . 140mm/5½ ins x 16.67mm/42

SANTA CRUZ

Hand-made.

Monarch . . . . 190mm/7½ ins x 19.45mm/49
Churchill . . . . 152mm/6 ins x 19.84mm/50
Bristol . . . . 172mm/6¾ ins x 17.86mm/45
Corona Grande . . . . 152mm/6½ ins x 16.67mm/42
Majestic . . . . 172mm/6¾ ins x 15.08mm/38
Corona . . . . 140mm/5½ ins x 16.67mm/42
Palmette . . . . 152mm/6 ins x 12.3mm/31

TEMPLE HALL

Hand-made. Quality, good. Connecticut Shade wrapper. Mexican binder from San Andres area. Filler is blend of Jamaican, Dominican and Mexican tobacco. Subtle. Owned by General Cigar.

$$$ **No 700** . . . . 178mm/7 ins x 19.45mm/49
$$$ **No 675** . . . . 172mm/6¾ ins x 17.86mm/45
$$$ **No 550** . . . . ★★★★
      140mm/5½ ins x 19.84mm/50. Smooth, elegant, slow burning. Good introduction to this size. Excellent daytime smoke or after unspiced meal.
$$$ **No 625** . . . . 160mm/6¼ ins x 16.67mm/42
$$$ **No 450 Maduro** . . . . 113mm/4½ ins x 19.45mm/49
      Discreet, aromatic aroma. Slightly sweet, honeyed aftertaste.
$$$ **No 685** . . . . 175mm/6⅞ ins x 13.49mm/34
$$$ **No 500** . . . . ★★★
      127mm/5 ins x 12.3mm/31. Medium-bodied. Discreet, spicy aroma. Good daytime smoke.
$$$ **Belicoso** . . . . ★★★
      152mm/6 ins x 19.84mm/50. Medium- to full-bodied. Mild, spicy, floral aromas. Last third has bitter finish.

$$$	No 4 Trump	190mm/7½ ins x 19.45mm/49
$$$	No 1 Trump	165mm/6½ ins x 16.67mm/42
$$$	No 2 Trump	140mm/5½ ins x 19.84mm/50
$$$	No 3 Trump	140mm/5½ ins x 16.67mm/42

Mexico

San Andrés Valley produces finest tobacco and is center of cigar export business. In 1996, 14.5 million pieces exported to USA, up from 9.68 million in 1995. Mexican cigars are very popular in USA and offer good value for money.

AROMAS DE SAN ANDRES

Hand-made. Packed in amber tubes. Made by Tabacos Santa Claro.

Maximillian . . . . 190mm/7½ ins x 20.64mm/52
Gourmet . . . . ★★★★★
165mm/6½ ins x 16.67mm/42. Spicy, coffee flavors. Good balance between strength and flavor. Strong finish. Ideal for regular smoker.
Aficionado . . . . 152mm/6 ins x 19.84mm/50
Robusto . . . . 127mm/5 ins x 19.84mm/50

BALLENA SUPREMA SAN ANDRES COLLECTION

Hand-made. Quality, superior. Connecticut Shade wrapper. Mexican filler and binder. Distributed by pipe tobacco specialists, Mc Clelland Tobacco Co., Kansas City, Missouri, USA.

$$$	**Esperanza**	178mm/7 ins x 19.8mm/50
$$$	**Concordia**	178mm/7 ins x 19.1mm/48
$$$	**Patron** (torpedo)	165mm/6½ ins x 20.6mm/52
$$$	**Cordura**	127mm/5 ins x 20.6mm/52
$$$	**Cortes** . . . . ★★★★

178mm/7 ins x 16.67mm/42. Burns evenly. Nutty. Hint of harshness

BLACK LABEL

Hand-made. Bundles. All Mexican tobacco. Distributed by Mike's Cigars, Miami, Florida, USA.

Acapulco . . . . 152mm/6 ins x 16.67mm/42
Cancun . . . . 203mm/8 ins x 20.6mm/52
Guadalajara . . . . 168mm/6⅝ ins x 13.9mm/35
Jaliso . . . . 175mm/6⅞ ins x 21.4mm/54
Monterrey . . . . 190mm/7½ ins x 19.84mm/50

Robusto . . . . ★★★★
121mm/4 3/4 ins x 9.84mm/50. Full-flavored,
strong, but smooth. Ideal to follow spicy meal.
Toro . . . . 152mm/6 ins x 19.84mm/50
Veracruz . . . . 168mm/6⅝ ins x 18.3mm/46
Tijuana . . . . 127mm/5 ins x 12.7mm/32

CRUZ REAL

Hand-made. Quality, superior. All Mexican tobacco. Made by
Tabacos y Puro de San Andres SA. Distributed by Finck Cigar
Co., San Antonio, Texas, USA.

$$	**No 1** . . . . 168mm/6⅝ ins x 16.67mm/42	
$$	**No 2** . . . . ★★★★	
	152mm/6 ins x 16.67mm/42. Even burn. Spicy.	
	Medium-bodied. Daytime smoke.	
$	**No 3** . . . . 168mm/6⅝ ins x 13.9mm/35	
$$	**No 14** . . . . 191mm/7½ ins x 19.84mm/50	
$$	**No 19** . . . . 152mm/6 ins x 19.84mm/50	
$$	**No 24** . . . . 114mm/4½ ins x 19.84mm/50	
$$	**No 25** . . . . 140mm/5½ ins x 20.2mm/52	
$$	**No 28** . . . . 216mm/8½ ins x 21.4mm/54	
$$$	**Ministro Special Edition**	
	159mm/6¼ ins x 16.67mm/42	
	Emperador Special Edition	
	159mm/6¼ ins x 19.84mm/50	
	Canciller Special Edition	
	191mm/7½ ins x 19.84mm/50	

EL BESO

Hand-made. Available in Natural and Maduro.

Churchill . . . . 190mm/7½ ins x 19.84mm/50
Toro . . . . 168mm/6 ins x 19.84mm/50
No 1 . . . . 168mm/6⅝ ins x 16.67mm/42
Cetros . . . . 152mm/6 ins x 16.67mm/42

EL TRIUNFO

Hand-made. Distributed by Consolidated Cigars. Mexican
wrapper and binder. Filler is blend of tobacco from Mexico
and Nicaragua.

$	**No. 1 Mayans** . . . . . . 190mm/7½ ins x 19.84mm/50	
$	**No. 2 Aztecs** . . . . 168mm/6⅝ ins x 19.84mm/50	
$	**No. 3 Toltecs** . . . . 152mm/6 ins x 19.84mm/50	
$	**No. 4 Tulas** . . . . 168mm/6⅝ ins x 18.26mm/46	
¢	**No. 5 Palenques** . . . . . 152mm/6 ins x 18.26mm/46	

¢   **No. 6 Mitlas** . . . . 168mm/6⅝ ins x 16.67mm/42
¢   **No. 7 Pueblas** . . . . 152mm/6 ins x 16.67mm/42

EXCELSIOR

Hand-made. Quality, superior. All Mexican tobacco. Launched August 1996. Uncharacteristically full-bodied for Mexican cigar. Extremely well-made. Impressive packaging. Although premium price, still represents good value. Made by Nueve Matacapan Tabacos (manufacturers of Te-Amo). Distributed by Consolidated Cigars.

$$ **No 1** . . . . 159mm/6¼ ins x 16.67mm/42
$$$ **No 2** . . . . 171mm/6¾ ins x 17.5mm/44
$$$ **No 3** . . . . ★★★★★
    140mm/5½ ins x 20.6mm/52. Slow, even burning. Cool, rich, wonderful complexity of flavors. A cigar you don't want to put out. Smoking this cigar is an occasion!
$$$ **No 4** . . . . 178mm/7 ins x 19.05mm/50
$$$ **No 5** . . . . 203mm/8 ins x19.05mm/50
$$$$ **Individuale** . . . . 216mm/8½ ins x 20.6mm/52

FLOR DE MEXICO

Hand-made. Bundles. All Mexican tobacco. Brand owned by House of Oxford.

¢   **Churchill** . . . . 190mm/7½ ins x 19.84mm/50
¢   **Toro** . . . . 152mm/6 ins x 19.84mm/50
¢   **No 1** . . . . 168mm/6⅝ ins x 16.67mm/42
¢   **No 2** . . . . 152mm/6 ins x 16.67mm/42
¢   **No 3** . . . . 168mm/6⅝ ins x 19.9mm/35
¢   **No 4** . . . . 127mm/5 ins x 16.67mm/42

HOJA DE MEXICALI

Hand-made.

$ **Lonsdale Natural** . . . 168mm/6⅝ ins x 16.67mm/42
$ **Royal Corona Natural** 152mm/6 ins x 16.67mm/42
$ **Soberano Natural** . . . 190mm/7½ ins x 19.84mm/50
$ **Toro Natural/Maduro** 152mm/6 ins x 19.84mm/50
$ **Viajante Natural/Maduro**
    203mm/8½ ins x 20.64mm/52

¢ – Under $1.00 $ – $1–3.00 $$ – $3–4.00
$$$ – $5–8.00 $$$$ – $8–20.00 $$$$$ – $20+

HOJA DE ORO

Hand-made. Bundles. Wrapper is Mexican grown Sumataran seed. Mexican binder and filler.

$	**100**	178mm/7 ins x 19.84mm/50
$	**101**	178mm/7½ ins x 19.84mm/50
$	**103**	152mm/6 ins x 19.84mm/50
$	**104**	152mm/6¾ ins x 17.86mm/45
$	**105**	113mm/4½ ins x 19.84mm/50
$	**106**	152mm/6 ins x 17.86mm/45
$	**107**	127mm/5 ins x 17.86mm/45

HUGO CASSAR

Hand-made. Bundles. All Mexican tobacco. Owned by Hugo Cassar Cigars, California, USA.

$	**Tulum**	121mm/4¾ ins x 19.8mm/50
$	**Monterey**	152mm/6 ins x 16.67mm/42
$	**Durango**	171mm/6¾ ins x 18.3mm/46
$	**Veracruz**	178mm/7 ins x 21mm/54
$	**Yucatan**	191mm/7½ ins x 19.8mm/50
$	**Sierra Madre**	203mm/8 ins x 20.6mm/52

HUGO CASSAR PRIVATE COLLECTION

Hand-made. All Mexican tobacco.

$$	**Rothschild**	114mm/4½ ins x 19.84mm/50
$$	**Corona**	152mm/6 ins x 16.67mm/42
$$	**Toro**	165mm/6½ ins x 19.84mm/50
$$	**Robusto**	★★★★

140mm/5½ ins x 20.6mm/52. Good draw. Spicy. Uncharacteristically strong for a Mexican cigar. After-dinner smoke.

| $$ | **Churchill** | 191mm/7½ ins x 19.84mm/50 |

KINGSTON

Hand-made. All Mexican tobacco. Distributed by Brick-Hanauer Co. Waltham, Massachusetts, USA.

$	**Corona Grande**	165mm/6½ ins x 16.67mm/42
$	**Giant Corona**	191mm/7½ ins x 19.84mm/50
$	**Panetela Extra**	164mm/6⅜ ins x 13.9mm/35
$	**Royal Corona**	152mm/6 ins x 16.67mm/42
$	**Rothschild**	114mm/4½ ins x 19.84mm/50
$	**Toro**	152mm/6 ins x 19.84mm/50
$	**Viajante**	216mm/8½ ins x 20.6mm/52

LA DALMATA

Hand-made. Quality, superior. Sumatran wrapper. Mexican binder and filler. Distributed by Dalmation Cigar Co., New York, USA.

$$$	**Churchill**	178mm/7 ins x 19.8mm/50
$$$	**Toro**	152mm/6 ins x 19.8mm/50
$$$	**Corona Grande**	152mm/6 ins x 17.5mm/44
$$$	**Robusto**	127mm/5 ins x 19.8mm/50

MATACAN BUNDLES

Hand-made. Light brown and Maduro wrappers. Mexican wrapper and binder. Filler is blend of tobacco from Mexico and Nicaragua. Distributed by Consolidated Cigars.

$	**No 1**	190mm/7½ ins x 19.84mm/50
¢	**No 2**	152mm/6 ins x 19.84mm/50
¢	**No 3**	168mm/6⅝ ins x 18.26mm/46
¢	**No 4**	168mm/6⅝ ins x 16.67mm/42
¢	**No 5**	152mm/6 ins x 16.67mm/42
¢	**No 6**	168mm/6⅝ ins x 13.89mm/35
¢	**No 7**	108mm/4¼ ins x 19.84mm/50
$	**No 8**	203mm/8 ins x 20.64mm/52
¢	**No 9**	127mm/5 ins x 12.7mm/32
$	**No 10**	168mm/6⅝ ins x 21mm/54

MEXICAN EMPERADOR

Hand-made. Packed in single boxes. One of biggest cigars made in Mexico.

$$$	. . . .	349mm/13¾ ins x 19.45mm/49

MOCAMBO

Hand-made. All Mexican tobacco. Exclusive to Santa Clara N.A.

Churchill	178mm/7 ins x 19.84mm/50
Premier	168mm/6⅝ ins x 17.07mm/43
Empires	165mm/6½ ins x 15.48mm/39
Double Corona	152mm/6 ins x 20.24mm/51
Royal Corona	152mm/6 ins x 16.67mm/42

★★★★★ Outstanding. A classic.   ★★★★ Excellent.
★★★ Good.   ★★ Fair, ordinary.   ★ Poor or faulty.
No Star: Not evaluated.

NEW YORK, NEW YORK BY TE-AMO

Machine-made. Mexican grown Sumatran wrapper. Mexican binder and filler. Each size named after a famous New York street. Extremely mild. Made by Matacapan Tobacos. Distributed by Consolidated Cigars.

$	**Park Avenue**	168mm/6⅝ ins x 16.67mm/42
$	**Fifth Avenue**	140mm/5½ ins x 17.46mm/44
$	**7th Avenue**	165mm/6½ ins x 18.26mm/46
$	**Broadway**	184mm/7¼ ins x 19.05mm/48
$	**Wall Street**	152mm/6 ins x 20.64mm/52
$	**La Guardia**	127mm/5 ins x 21.43mm/54

NUDE MEXICAN

Hand-made. Bundles. Available in Claro and Maduro.

¢	**900**	113mm/4½ ins x 19.84mm/50
¢	**902**	140mm/5½ ins x 20.64mm/52
¢	**904**	152mm/6 ins x 16.67mm/42
¢	**906**	152mm/6 ins x 19.84mm/50
¢	**908**	165mm/6½ ins x 14.29mm/36
¢	**910**	168mm/6⅝ ins x 16.69mm/42
¢	**912**	190mm/7½ ins x 19.84mm/50
¢	**914**	216mm/8½ ins x 19.84mm/50

ORNELAS

Hand-made. All Mexican Tobacco. LTD shape cognac-treated wrappers. Five shapes treated with vanilla flavoring. Owned by Marcos Miguel Tobacco, Dallas, Texas.

$$$$	**LTD 40 Al Cognac** . .	159mm/6¼ ins x 16.67mm/42
$$	**No 1**	171mm/6¾ ins x 17.5mm/44
$$	**No 2**	152mm/6 ins x 17.5mm/44
$$	**No 3**	178mm/7 ins x 15.1mm/38
$$	**No 4**	127mm/5 ins x 17.5mm/44
$$	**No 5**	152mm/6 ins x 15.1mm/38
$$	**No 6**	127mm/5 ins x 15.1mm/38
$$$	**Churchill***	178mm/7 ins x 19.5mm/49
$$	**Robusto***	121mm/4¾ ins x 19.5mm/49
$$	**Cafetero Grande**	165mm/6½ ins x 18.3mm/46
$$	**Cafetero Chico**	140mm/5½ ins x 18.3mm/46
$$	**Matinee**	152mm/6 ins x 11.9mm/30
$$	**Matinee Lights**	121mm/4¾ ins x 11.9mm/30
$$$$$	**250**	232mm/9½ ins x 25mm/64
$$$	**No 1 Vanilla**	171mm/6¾ ins x 17.5mm/44
$$$	**No 5 Vanilla**	152mm/6 ins x 15.1mm/38
$$$	**No 6 Vanilla**	127mm/5 ins x 15.1mm/38

$$	**Matinee Vanilla**.	152mm/6 ins x 11.9mm/30
$$	**Matinee Lights Vanilla**.	121mm/4¾ ins x 11.9mm/30

Available with Maduro wrapper.

ORTIZ

Hand-made by Tabacos Santa Clara.

Churchill	190mm/7½ ins x 19.84mm/50
Club House	152mm/6 ins x 19.84mm/50
Double Corona	168mm/6⅝ ins x 17.07mm/43
Magnum	152mm/6 ins x 16.67mm/42
Mexican Emperadors	

349mm/13¾ ins x 19.45mm/49

SANTA CLARA "1830"

Hand-made. Quality, superior. Medium-flavored. Exclusive to Santa Clara, N.A., Inc. All Mexican tobacco. Made by Tabacos Santa Clara.

$$	**No I**	178mm/7 ins x 20.24mm/51
$	**No II**	165mm/6½ ins x 19.05mm/48
$	**No III**.	168mm/6⅝ ins x 16.67mm/43
$	**No IV**	127mm/5 ins x 17.46mm/44
$	**No V**.	152mm/6 ins x 17.46mm/44
$	**No VI**	152mm/6 ins x 20.24mm/51
$	**No VII**	140mm/5½ ins x 9.92mm/25
$	**No VIII**.	165mm/6½ ins x 12mm/30
¢	**Quino**	159mm/4¼ ins x 15.1 mm/38
$$	**Premier Tubes** (tubed)	
	171mm/6¾ ins x 15.1mm/38	
$	**Robusto**	113mm/4½ ins x 19.84mm/50

TE-AMO

Hand-made. Long filler. Quality, medium. Mild and medium strength. Medium available in choice of light brown and Maduro wrappers. Top selling Mexican brand in USA. Name means "I love you" in Spanish. Made by Matacapan Tabacos. Distributed by Consolidated Cigars.

$	**Torero**	165mm/6½ ins x 13.49mm/35
$	**No 4**	127mm/5 ins x 16.67mm/42
$	**Picador**.	178mm/7 ins x 10.72mm/27
$$	**C.E.O**	216mm/8½ ins x 20.64mm/52

¢ – Under $1.00 $ – $1–3.00 $$ – $3–4.00
$$$ – $5–8.00 $$$$ – $8–20.00 $$$$$ – $20+

$	**Epicure** . . . . 127mm/5 ins x 12mm/30	
$	**Contemplation** . . . . . 175mm/6⅞ ins x 17.46mm/44	
$$	**Churchill**. . . . . ★★★	

190mm/7½ ins x 19.84mm/50. Very mild. Burns a little hot.

$$	**Presidente** . . . . ★★★★	

178mm/7 ins x 19.84mm/50. Spicy. Smooth. Daytime smoke. Suitable for novice.

Robusto . . . . ★★★★
140mm/5½ ins x 21.43mm/54. Mild. Smooth. Flavor develops. Good balance.

Torito . . . . 113mm/4½ ins x 19.84mm/50
Toro . . . . 152mm/6 ins x 19.84mm/50
Figurado (torpedo) . . . . ★★★★
168mm/6⅝ ins x 19.84/50. Mild coffee flavors. Smooth.

Caballero . . . . 178mm/7 ins x 13.89mm/35
Impulse . . . . 127mm/5 ins x 12.7mm/32

$$	**Maximo** . . . . 178mm/7 ins x 21.43mm/54	
$$	**Celebration** . . . . . . 170mm/6¹¹⁄₁₆ ins x 17.46mm/44	

Satisfaction. . . . . 152mm/6 ins x 18.26mm/46

$$	**Grand Piramides** (pyramid)	

160mm/6¼ ins x 21.43mm/54

Relaxation . . . . 168mm/6⅝ ins x 16.67mm/42
Piramides . . . . 160mm/6¼ ins x 19.84mm/50

$$	**Meditation** . . . . 152mm/6 ins x 16.67mm/42	
¢	**Elegante** . . . . 140mm/5½ ins x 12mm/30	
¢	**Intermezzo** . . . . 178mm/7 ins x 21.43mm/54	
¢	**Pauser** . . . . 137mm/5⅜ ins x 13.89mm/35	

Following machine-made with short filler.

TE-AMO SEGUNDO

Good value.

$	**Churchill** . . . . 190mm/7½ ins x 19.84mm/50	
$	**Presidente** . . . . 178mm/7 ins x 19.84mm/50	
$	**Relaxation** . . . . 168mm/6⅝ ins x 17.46mm/44	
$	**Satisfaction**. . . . . 152mm/6 ins x 18.26mm/46	
$	**Toro** . . . . 152mm/6 ins x 19.84mm/50	
$	**Meditation** . . . . 152mm/6 ins x 16.67mm/42	
$	**Torero**. . . . . 166mm/6⁹⁄₁₆ ins x 13.89mm/35	

★★★★★ Outstanding. A classic.   ★★★★ Excellent.
★★★ Good.   ★★ Fair, ordinary.   ★ Poor or faulty.
No Star Not evaluated.

VERACRUZ

Hand-made.

Mina de Veracruz, Reserva Especial
160mm/6¼ ins x 16.67mm/42
Veracruz Magnum, Owner's Reserve
200mm/7⅞ ins x 19.1mm/48
Flor de Veracruz Carinas
118mm/4⅝ ins x 13.5mm/34
Poemas de Veracruz (tubed)
160mm/6¼ ins x 16.67mm/42
Veracruz L'Operetta
124mm/4⅞ ins x 13.5mm/34

Nicaragua

Many believe that Nicaragua produces tobacco closest to that of Cuba. Ten years of war and famine did much to damage cigar industry. Privatisation policy of present government is successful in restoring tobacco industry to meet increased demand and fulfill country's role as major exporter of cigars. In 1993, for first time in more than decade, good crop of oily Cuban seed wrapper was produced. In 1996 exported 18 million cigars to USA, up from 3.5 million in 1995.

BLUE RIBBON

Hand-made. Bundles.

$	**No 500**	190mm/7½ ins x 20.64mm/52
¢	**No 501**	152mm/6 ins x 19.84mm/50
¢	**No 502**	120mm/4¾ ins x 19.84mm/50
¢	**No 503**	160m/6½ ins x 17.46mm/44
¢	**No 504**	140mm/5½ ins x 16.67mm/42

CARLIN

Hand-made. Quality, superior. All Nicaraguan tobacco. Distributed by Arango Cigars and Swisher Intl.

$$	**Gigante**	203mm/8 ins x 20.6mm/52
$$	**Churchill**	178mm/7 ins x 19.1mm/48
$$	**Toro**	152mm/6 ins x 19.8mm/50
$$	**Corona**	140mm/5½ ins x 17.1mm/43
$$	**Robusto**	121mm/4¾ ins x 20.6mm/52

CASA DE NICARAGUA

Hand-made. All Cuban seed tobacco grown in Nicaragua. Distributed in USA by Indian Head Sales.

Rothschild . . . . 127mm/5 ins x 19.84mm/50
Petit Corona . . . . ★★★★
140mm/5½ ins x 19.84mm/50. Good draw. Spicy, full flavor. Medium strength. A good example of this size. Ideal for beginner and experienced smoker. Good value.
Corona . . . . 152mm/6 ins x 19.05mm/43
Toro . . . . 152mm/6 ins x 19.84mm/50
Panetela Extra . . . . . . 178mm/7 ins x 14.29mm/36
Double Corona . . . . . . 178mm/7 ins x 17.46mm/44
Churchill . . . . 178mm/7 ins x 19.49mm/49
Presidente . . . . 190mm/7½ ins x 20.64mm/52
Gigante . . . . ★★★★
203mm/8 ins x 21.43mm/54. Full, complex flavors, hint of caramel. Long finish. Medium strength.
Viajante . . . . 216mm/8½ ins x 19.84mm/50

DON JUAN

Hand-made. Packed 8-9-8 in wooden boxes. Quality, superior. Connecticut Shade wrapper. Nicaraguan binder. Filler blend of tobacco from Nicaragua and 30 per cent from Dominican Republic. Made by Tabacos de Plasencia. Distributed in USA by Tropical Tobacco. International distribution by Nica-Habano S|fwo Paulo, Brazil.

$ **Lindas** . . . . 140mm/5½ ins x 14.29mm/38
$ **Cetros** . . . . ★★★★
152mm/6 ins x 17.07mm/43. Easy draw. Even burn. Medium-bodied. Elegant. Good balance. Good daytime cigar or to follow lunch.
$ **Palma Fina** . . . . 175mm/6⅞ ins x 14.29mm/36
$ **Numero Uno** . . . . . . 168mm/6⅝ ins x 17.46mm/44
$ **Matador** . . . . 152mm/6 ins x 19.84mm/50
$$ **Churchills** . . . . 178mm/7 ins x 19.45mm/49
$$ **Presidents** . . . . 216mm/8½ ins x 19.84mm/50
$ **Robusto** . . . . 127mm/5 ins x 19.84mm/50

★★★★★ Outstanding. A classic.　★★★★ Excellent.
★★★ Good.　★★ Fair, ordinary.　★ Poor or faulty.
No Star Not evaluated.

FLOR DE JALAPA

Hand-made. Ecuadorian wrapper. Binder and filler from Nicaragua. Made by Tabacos de Plasencia. Brand owned by Swisher Intl. Introduced 1995.

Presidente	216mm/8½ ins x	20.6mm/52
Toro	152mm/6 ins x	19.84mm/50
Gran Corona	152mm/6 ins x	17.5mm/44
Churchill	178mm/7 ins x	19.1mm/48
Robusto	120mm/4¾ x	19.84mm/50

FLOR DE NICARAGUA

Hand-made. Ecuadorian wrapper. Nicaraguan filler and binder.

Viajante	216mm/8½ ins x	20.6mm/52
Presidente	203mm/8 ins x	21.4mm/54
Presidente Corto	184mm/7¼ ins x	21.4mm/54
Emperador	197mm/7¾ ins x	20.6mm/50
Emperador Corto	191mm/7½ ins x	20.6mm/50
No 1	168mm/6⅝ ins x	17.5mm/44
No 2	114mm/4½ ins x	16.67mm/42
No 3	152mm/6 ins x	17.5mm/44
No 5	175mm/6⅞ ins x	13.9mm/35
No 6	152mm/6 ins x	16.3mm/41
No 7	178mm/7 ins x	11.9mm/30
No 9	203mm/8 ins x	15.1mm/38
No 9 Corto	178mm/7 ins x	15.1mm/38
No 11	191mm/7½ ins x	18.3mm/46
Churchill	175mm/6⅞ ins x	19.1mm/48
Duke	152mm/6 ins x	20.6mm/50
Corona Extra	140mm/5½ ins x	18.3mm/46
Consul	114mm/4½ ins x	20.6mm/52
Nacional	140mm/5½ ins x	17.5mm/44
Seleccion B	140mm/5½ ins x	16.67mm/42
Elegante	165mm/6½ ins x	15.1mm/38
Corona	143mm/5⅝ ins x	19.1mm/48
Petits	140mm/5½ ins x	15.1mm/38
Senoritas	140mm/5½ ins x	13.5mm/34
Piccolino	105mm/4⅛ ins x	11.9mm/30

GRAND NICA

Hand-made. Quality, superior. All Nicaraguan tobacco. Distributed by Torano Cigars, Miami, Florida, USA.

Gigante	203mm/8 ins x	21.4mm/54
Churchill	178mm/7 ins x	20.6mm/52
Torpedo	165mm/6½ ins x	21.4mm/54

Lonsdale	. . . .	165mm/6½ ins x 19.8mm/50
Toro	. . . .	152mm/6 ins x 19.8mm/50
Robusto	. . . .	127mm/5 ins x 20.6mm/50

HABANICA

Hand-made. All Nicaragua tobacco. Full-bodied. Distributed by Cigars of Honduras, Virginia, USA.

$$$	**Serie 747**	179mm/7 ins x 18.7mm/47
$$$	**Serie 646**	152mm/6 ins x 18.3mm/46
$$$	**Serie 638**	152mm/6 ins x 15.1mm/38
$$$	**Serie 546**	140mm/5½ ins x 18.3mm/46
$$$	**Serie 550**	127mm/5 ins x 20.2mm/50

HOYO DE NICARAGUA MADURO DELUXE

$$	**Presidente**	203mm/8 ins x 21.43mm/54
$$	**Toro** . . . . ★★★★
	152mm/6 ins x 19.84mm/50. Full-bodied, rich flavors. Robust. Smooth. For experienced smoker.
$$	**Robusto**	121mm/4¾ ins x 20.64mm/52

HUGO CASSAR SIGNATURE SERIES

Hand-made. Quality, superior. Indonesian wrapper. Nicaraguan binder and filler. Owned by Hugor Cassar Cigars, Moorpark, California, USA.

$$	**Giant**	203mm/8 ins x 21.4mm/54
$$	**Churchill**	178mm/7 ins x 19.1mm/48
$$	**Toro**	152mm/6 ins x 19.8mm/50
$$	**Robusto**	121mm/4¾ ins x 20.6mm/52
$$	**Lonsdale**	171mm/6¾ ins x 17.5mm/44
$$	**Corona**	140mm/5½ ins x 16.67mm/42

JOYA DE NICARAGUA

13 models, all hand-made. Quality, superior. Started in 1965. Until Nicaraguan revolution in 1979 was considered one of best non-Havana brands. During revolution many tobacco fields and its factory damaged by fire. U.S. embargo in place between 1985 and 1990. Post-revolution cigars not as good as those made pre-revolution. Quality improving rapidly. Medium strength. Pleasant peppery flavor. Brand with same name made by two different factories.

$$$	**Viajante** . . . . ★★★★★
	216mm/8½ ins x 20.64mm/52. Easy draw. Good burning qualities. Well-balanced, smooth. A big cigar with lots of flavor. For experienced smoker.

$$	**Churchill**	. . . .	175mm/6⅞ ins x 19.05mm/48
$$	**Consul**	. . . .	★★★★

113mm/4½ ins x 20.64mm/52. Easy draw. Spicy, with touch of cinnamon. Medium- to full-bodied. Good balance between strength and flavor. Not particularly refined, but smooth. Daytime smoke for experienced smoker.

$	**Corona**	. . . .	143mm/5⅝ ins x 19.05mm/48
$	**No 1**	. . . .	168mm/6⅝ ins x 17.46mm/44
$	**No 2**	. . . .	113mm/4½ ins x 16.27mm/41
$$	**No 3**	. . . .	152mm/6 ins x 16.27mm/44
$	**No 5**	. . . .	175mm/6⅞ ins x 13.89mm/35
$	**No 6**	. . . .	152mm/6 ins x 16.67mm/42
$	**Petit**	. . . .	140mm/5½ ins x 15.08mm/38

LA CORDOBA

Hand-made. Bundles. Distributed in USA by Brick-Hanauer Co., Waltham, Massachusetts, USA.

Numero Uno	. . . . . .	165mm/6½ ins x 19.09mm/43
Numero Cuatro	. . . .	140mm/43 ins x 19.09mm/43
Gorda	. . . .	152mm/6 ins x 17.46mm/44
Churchill	. . . .	175mm/6⅞ ins x 19.45mm/49
Gigante	. . . .	203mm/8 ins x 21.43mm/54
Monarch	. . . .	184mm/7¼ ins x 21.43mm/54
President	. . . .	190mm/7½ ins x 20.64mm/52
Rothschild	. . . .	113mm/4½ ins x 20.64mm/52
Soberano	. . . .	197mm/7¾ ins x 19.84mm/50
Toro	. . . .	152mm/6 ins x 19.84mm/50
Viajante	. . . .	349mm/8½ ins x 20.64mm/52

LA FINCA

Hand-made. Quality, superior. All Nicaraguan tobacco. Full-bodied. Has good aging potential. Made by Tabacos de Plasencia, whose brands sell eight million cigars plus a year. Distributed in USA by Cigars by Santa Clara NA. International distribution by Nica-Habano, São Paulo, Brazil.

Robusto	. . . .	★★★★★

140mm/5½ ins x 19.5mm/49. Dark oily wrapper. Burns evenly with fairly tight draw. Rich, elegant, herbaceous with chocolate undertones. Well-made. To follow meal. For discerning smoker.

Romeos	. . . .	★★★★★

165mm/6½ ins x 16.67mm/42. Beautiful wrapper. Smooth, elegant with good balance. Well-made.

Corona . . . . 140mm/5½ ins x 16.67mm/42

Joyas . . . . ★★★★★
152mm/6 ins x 19.84mm/50. Dark oil wrapper.
Even, slow burning. Mildly spicy with hint of coffee.
Elegant with intergrated flavors. Classy cigar. Will
make any occasion special.
Bolivares . . . . 190mm/7½ ins x 19.84mm/50
Grand Finca . . . . 216mm/8½ ins x 206mm/52

MICUBANO

Hand-made. All Nicaraguan tobacco. Unusual feature is two
bands on each cigar-one near foot. Distributed by Lane Ltd.

No 450 . . . . ★★★★
121mm/4¾ ins x 19.84mm/50. Medium-bodied.
Smooth. Good balance. Well-made. Daytime smoke.
542 . . . . 140mm/5½ ins x 16.67mm/42
650 . . . . 152mm/6 ins x 19.84mm/50
644 . . . . 165mm/6½ ins x 17.5mm/44
748 . . . . 178mm/7 ins x 19.1mm/48
852 . . . . 216m/8½ ins x 20.6mm/52

NICARAGUA ESPECIAL

Hand-made bundles. Wrapper from Ecuador. Binder and
filler from Nicaragua. Distributed in USA by Lignum-2 Inc.

Linda . . . . 140mm/5½ ins x 14.29mm/38
Super Cetro . . . . 152mm/6 ins x 17.46mm/44
Matador . . . . 152mm/6 ins x 19.84mm/50
Presidente . . . . 188mm/7⅜ ins x 19.84mm/50
Viajante . . . . 216mm/8½ ins x 20.64mm/52

PURO NICARAGUA

Hand-made. Bundles. Connecticut Shade wrapper. Filler
blend of tobacco from Nicaragua and Dominican Republic.
Distributed in USA by Tropical Tobacco.

$ **Lindas** . . . . 140mm/5½ ins x 15.08mm/38
$ **Numero 4** . . . . 140mm/5½ ins x 16.67mm/42
$ **Rothschild** . . . . ★★★★
127mm/5 ins x 19.84mm/50. Full-bodied and aro-
matic. Wrapper slightly sweet. For experienced
smoker, after meal.
$ **Panetela Especial** . . . 175mm/6⅞ ins x 13.89mm/35

¢ – Under $1.00 $ – $1–3.00 $$ – $3–4.00
$$$ – $5–8.00 $$$$ – $8–20.00 $$$$$ – $20+

$ **Corona Gorda** ...... 152mm/6 ins x 17.46mm/44
$ **Numero 1** .... 168mm/6⅝ ins x 17.46mm/44
$ **Toro** .... 152mm/6 ins x 19.84mm/50
$ **Churchill** .... 178mm/7 ins x 19.45mm/49
$ **Soberano** .... 197mm/7¾ ins x 19.84mm/50
$ **Viajantes** .... 216mm/8½ ins x 20.64mm/52
$ **Gigantes** .... 203mm/8 ins x 21.43mm/54

ROYAL NICARAGUAN

Hand-made bundles. Distributed in USA by Indian Head Sales.

Numero 2 .... 216mm/8½ ins x 20.64mm/52
Numero 4 .... 203mm/8 ins x 21.43mm/54
Numero 6 .... 190mm/7½ ins x 20.64mm/52
Numero 8 .... 178mm/7 ins x 19.49mm/49
Numero 10 .... 178mm/7 ins x 17.46mm/44
Numero 12 .... 178mm/7 ins x 14.29mm/36
Numero 14 .... 152mm/6 ins x 19.84mm/50
Numero 16 .... 152mm/6 ins x 17.86mm/43
Numero 18 .... 140mm/5½ ins x 17.07mm/43
Numero 20 .... 127mm/5 ins x 19.84mm/50

SABROSO

Hand-made. Bundle. Ecuadorian wrapper. Binder and filler from Nicaragua. Introduced 1995. Made by Tabacos de Plasencia for Swisher Intl.

$ **Numero Uno** ...... 120mm/4¾ ins x 19.84mm/50
$ **Numero Dos** .... 152mm/6 ins x 17.5mm/44
$ **Numero Tres** .... 152mm/6 ins x 19.84mm/50
$ **Numero Quatro** ...... 178mm/7 ins x 19.1mm/48
$ **Numero Cinco** ...... 216mm/8½ ins x 20.6mm/52

SEBASTIAN RESERVA

Hand-made. Quality, superior. Connecticut, Sumatran and Cuban seed wrapper. Nicaraguan binder and filler. Distributed by Armenter Cigar Holding, New York, USA.

No 1 .... 216mm/8½ ins x 20.6mm/52
No 2 .... 203mm/8 ins x 21.4mm/54
No 3 .... 191mm/7½ ins x 19.8mm/50
No 4 .... 178mm/7 ins x 21.4mm/54
No 5 .... 175mm/6⅞ ins x 19.1mm/48
No 6 .... 165mm/6½ ins x 17.5mm/44
No 7 .... 152mm/6 ins x 16.1mm/41
No 8 .... 143mm/5⅝ ins x 19.1mm/48

No 9 . . . . 140mm/5½ ins x 20.6mm/52
No 10 . . . . 114mm/4½ ins 20.6mm/52

SEGOVIA

Hand-made. Ecuadorian wrapper. Filler and binder from Dominican Republic. Exclusive to Brick-Hanauer Co., Waltham, Massachusetts, USA. Good value.

$	**Crown Royal**	178mm/7 ins x 20.6mm/52
$	**Primo Gorda**	152mm/6 ins x 16.67mm/42
$	**Robusto**	127mm/5 ins x 20.6mm/52
$	**Toro**	152mm/6 ins x 19.84mm/50
$	**X-O**	165mm/6½ ins x 18.3mm/46

THOMAS HINDS NICARAGUAN SELECTION

Hand-made. All Nicaraguan tobacco. Made by Tabacos Puros de Nicaragua for Hinds Brothers Tobacco.

$$$	**Torpedo**	152mm/6 ins x 20.6mm/52
$$	**Churchill**	178mm/7 ins x 19.5mm/49
$$	**Short Churchill**	152mm/6 ins x 20.8mm/50
$$	**Lonsdale Extra**	178mm/7 ins x 17.1mm/43
$$	**Robusto**	127mm/5 ins x 20.84mm/50
$$	**Corona**	140mm/5½ ins x 16.67mm/42

TORCEDOR

Hand-made. Quality, superior. All Nicaraguan tobacco. Made by Tabacos de Plasencia. Exclusive to House of Oxford.

$	**No 1**	178mm/7 ins x 17.5mm/44
$$	**Churchill**	178mm/7 ins x 19.84mm/50
$	**Rothchild**	127mm/5 ins x 19.84mm/50
$	**Toro**	152mm/6 ins x 19.84mm/50
$$	**Vijante**	203mm/8 ins x 20.6mm/52

VEGAS GRAN RESERVA

Hand-made. Quality, superior. Colorado Sumatran wrapper. Nicaraguan binder and filler. Distributed by Andre Suarez Ltd., Miami Beach, Florida, USA.

Churchill	178mm/7 ins x 20.6mm/52
Piramide	165mm/6½ ins x 18.3mm/46
Double Corona	152mm/6 ins x 19.1mm/48
Panetela	152mm/6 ins x 15.1mm/38
Corona	140mm/5½ ins x 17.5mm/44
Robusto	127mm/5 ins x 20.6mm/50

Panama

In 1995 exported 308,000 cigars to USA.

BALBOA

Hand-made. Honduran wrapper. Mexican binder. Filler blend of tobacco from Honduras, Panama and Dominican Republic.

Viajante	216mm/8½ ins x 20.64mm/52
Churchill	178mm/7 ins x 19.1mm/48
No 1	178mm/7 ins x 17.09mm/43
No 2	165mm/6½ ins x 17.07mm/43
No 4	140mm/5½ ins x 16.67mm/42
Palma Extra	178mm/7 ins x 14.3mm/36

HIDALGO

Hand-made bundles. Wrapper from Ecuador. Mexican binder. Filler blend of tobacco from Panama, Honduras and Domincan Republic. Distributed in USA by Arango Cigar Co. Good value.

$	**Cazadore**	178mm/7 ins x 17.46mm/44
$	**Fuma**	178mm/7 ins x 17.46mm/44
$	**Corona**	140mm/5½ ins x 16.67mm/42
$	**Double Corona**	178mm/7 ins x 19.05mm/48
$	**Monarch**	216mm/8½ ins x 20.64mm/52

J. F. LLOPIS GOLD

Hand-made. Connecticut wrapper. Mexican binder. Filler blend of tobacco from Honduras, Panama and Dominican Republic.

$$	**Viajante**	213mm/8½ ins x 20.6mm/52
$$	**Churchill**	178mm/7 ins x 19.1mm/48
$$	**No 1**	191mm/7½ ins x 17.1mm/43
$$	**No 2**	165mm/6½ ins x 17.1mm/43
$	**No 4**	140mm/5½ ins x 16.67mm/42
$$	**Palma Extra**	175mm/7 ins x 14.3mm/36
$$	**Rothschild**	114mm/4½ ins x 19.84mm/50

★★★★★ Outstanding. A classic.   ★★★★ Excellent.
★★★ Good.   ★★ Fair, ordinary.   ★ Poor or faulty.
No Star Not evaluated.

Hand-made. Bundles. Wrapper from Ecuador. Binder from Mexico. Filler blend of tobacco from Panama, Dominican Republic and Honduras. Not to be confused with J. F. Llopis brand. Distributed in USA by Arango Cigar Co. Good value.

$$	**Viajante** . . . . 216mm/8½ ins x 20.64mm/52
$	**Churchill** . . . . 178mm/7 ins x 19.05mm/48
$	**No 1** . . . . ★★★★
	178mm/7 ins x 17.07mm/43. Good burning quali-
	ties. Mild, smooth. Elegant. Well-made.
$	**No 2** . . . . ★★★
	165mm/6½ ins x 17.07mm/43. Even burning.
	Light-bodied. Daytime smoke. Good value.
$	**No 4** . . . . ★★★★
	140mm/5½ ins x 17.07mm/43. Smooth, silky
	Connecticut wrapper. Good draw. Slow, even burn-
	ing. Smooth. Complex, creamy flavors. Well-made.
	Ideal for beginner and experienced smoker alike.
$	**Palma Extra** . . . . 178mm/7 ins x 14.29mm/36
$	**Rothschild** . . . . 121mm/4¾ ins x 19.84mm/50
$$	**Soberano** . . . . 184mm/7¼ ins x 20.64mm/52

Philippines

In 1995 exported 429,000 cigars to USA.

Hand-made. Bundles. Wrapper from Philippines. Binder from Java. Filler, a blend of tobacco from Indonesia and Java.

$	**Corona** . . . . 127mm/5 ins x 16.67mm/42
$	**Corona Grande** . . . . 209mm/8¼ ins x 18.65mm/47
$	**Double Grande** . . . . 216mm/8½ ins x 19.84mm/50
$	**Duque** . . . . 165mm/6½ ins x 16.67mm/42
$	**Especiale** . . . . 165mm/6½ ins x 19.84mm/50

Hand-made. Called Calixto Lopez in the USA and Carlos V in the United Kingdom. Havana seed wrappers. Binder and filler from Java and Indonesia.

$	**Czars** . . . . 203mm/8 ins x 17.86mm/45
$	**Corona Numero 1** . . 163mm/6⅜ ins x 17.86mm/45
$	**Corona Exquisito** . . . 137mm/5⅜ ins x 17.07mm/43

$ **Lonsdale Suprema**. . . . . ★★★★
172mm/6¾ ins x 16.67mm/42. Full-bodied. Rich,
full-flavored. Bold. Well-made. Good value.

$ **Palma Royale** . . . . ★★★★★
184mm/7¼ ins x 14.29mm/36. Good, consistent
construction. Good draw. Slow, even burning.
Medium- to full-bodied, robust, with range of spicy
flavors. Lots of complexity. An excellent cigar.
Exceedingly good value. Buy when you can.

$ **Gigantes**. . . . . 216mm/8½ ins x 19.84mm/50

$ **Nobles Extrafinos** . . 165mm/6½ ins x 19.84mm/50

DOUBLE HAPPINESS

Hand-made. Quality, superior. Connecticut Shade wrapper.
Binder and filler from Philippines. Owned by Splendid Seed
Tobacco Co., Manila, Philippines.

    Nirvana (pyramide) . . . 152mm/6 ins x 20.6mm/52
    Euphoria . . . . 165mm/6½ ins x 19.84mm/50
    Bliss . . . . ★★★
13mm/5⅛ ins x 19.1mm/48. Unique, twisted bun
on tuck end (foot). Uneven burn. Subtle, medium-
bodied. For the beginner. A good-looking cigar, but
construction not up to its looks.
    Rapture . . . . ★★★★
127mm/5 ins x 19.84mm/50. Good draw.
Consistent, good construction. Slow, even burning.
Rich, earthy flavors. Not for the beginner.
    Ecstasy . . . . 178mm/7 ins x 18.7mm/47

FIGHTING COCK

Hand-made. Quality, superior. Java wrapper. Binder and filler
from Philippines. Owned by Splendid Seed Tobacco Co.,
Manila, Philippines.

    Sidewinder (pyramide) 152mm/6 ins x 20.6mm/52
    Texas Red (square) . . . . ★★★
165mm/6½ ins x 19.84mm/50. Medium-bodied.
Peppery with touch of sweetness. Not for beginner.
    Smokin' Lulu (perfecto)
133mm/5¼ ins x 19.1mm/48
    Rooster Arturo . . . . 127mm/5 ins x 9.84mm/50
    C.O.D. . . . . 178mm/7 ins x 18.7mm/47

¢ – Under $1.00 $ – $1–3.00 $$ – $3–4.00
$$$ – $5–8.00 $$$$ – $8–20.00 $$$$$ – $20+

FLOR DE MANILA

Hand-made. All Philippine tobacco. Distributed by Hugo Cassar Cigars, California, USA.

Cetro Largo . . . . ★★★
191mm/7½ ins x 15.5mm/39. Medium-bodied. Spicy and peppery.
Cetro . . . . 152mm/6 ins x 15.5mm/39
Churchill . . . . 178mm/7 ins x 18.7mm/47
Corona Largo . . . . 178mm/7 ins x 18.7mm/44
Corona . . . . 140mm/5½ ins x 18.7mm/44
Cortado (torpedo)
Londres . . . . 146mm/5¾ ins x 18.7mm/44
Panetela . . . . 127mm/5 ins x 13.9mm/35

HARROWS

Hand-made. Quality, good. Sumatran wrappers.

Londonderry . . . . 203mm/8 ins x 19.05mm/48
Camelot . . . . 178mm/7 ins x 17.07mm/43
No 1 . . . . 160mm/6¼ ins x 19.07mm/43
Esquire . . . . 152mm/6 ins x 13.1mm/33
Regent . . . . 143mm/5⅝ ins x 17.46mm/44

LA FLOR DE LA ISABELA

Hand-made. Quality, superior. Made in Manila by company of same name. Distributed by Caribbean Cigar Co., Miami, Florida, USA.

$$ **Coronas Largas Especiales**
203mm/8 ins x 18.7mm/47
$$ **Coronas Largas** . . . . . 175mm/6½ ins x 17.5mm/44
$$ **Coronas** . . . . 140mm/5½ ins x 17.5mm/44
$$ **Coronas Sumatra** . . . . ★★★★
140mm/5½ ins x 17.5mm/44. Dark, almost Maduro wrapper. Mild to medium-bodied. Good balance between strength and flavor. Smooth. Burns evenly. Daytime smoke.
$$ **Brevas** . . . . ★★★
130mm/5 ins x 16.3mm/41. Attractive, dark wrapper. Fairly hard draw. Extremely mild and smooth. Not very exciting.

★★★★★ Outstanding. A classic.   ★★★★ Excellent.
★★★ Good.   ★★ Fair, ordinary.   ★ Poor or faulty.
No Star Not evaluated.

$$	**Half Coronas** . . . . 100mm/4 ins x 14.7mm/37
$$	**1881** . . . . ★★★★★

190mm/7½ ins x 16.67mm/42. Attractive wrapper. Good draw and balance. Medium-bodied with lots of flavor. Good finish. Well-made. For connoisseur. Also sold in impressive 30-cigar capacity humidor, complete with humidifier and hygrometer.

Following machine-made with short filler.

$	**Caprichos** . . . . 120mm/4¾ ins x 11.1mm/28
$	**Isabela** . . . . 150mm/5⅞ ins x 16.3mm/41
$	**Ideales** . . . . 130mm/5 ins x 16.3mm/41
$	**Brevas** . . . . 130mm/5 ins x 16.3mm/41
$	**Half Coronas** . . . . 100mm/4 ins x 14.7mm/37
$	**Conchas** . . . . 115mm/5⅛ ins x 16.3mm/41
$	**Panetelas Largas** . . . . 150mm/5⅞ ins x 13.9mm/35
$	**Damas** . . . . 100mm/4 ins x 13.9mm/35
$	**Panetelas** . . . . 120mm/4¾ ins x 13.9mm/35
$	**Cigarillos** . . . . 95mm/3¾ ins x 9.9mm/25
$	**Tips** (with pipes) . . . 135mm/5⁵⁄₁₆ ins x 11.1mm/28

TABACALERA

Hand-made. Filler from Philippines. Binder and filler from Java and Indonesia. Made by La Flor de la Isabela.

$	**Banderilla** . . . . 184mm/7¼ ins x 13.89mm/35
$	**Brevas** . . . . ★★★

133mm/5¼ ins x 17.46mm/44. Maduro wrapper. Good draw. Very mild, creamy flavor. Mellow. Not much character.

$	**Corona Larga Especiale**
	203mm/8 ins x 18.26mm/46
$	**Conde De Guell** . . . . . . 168mm/6⅝ ins x 12mm/38
$	**Corona** . . . . 133mm/5¼ ins x 16.67mm/42
$$	**Corona Larga** . . . . 178mm/7 ins x 17.07mm/43
$$	**Cortador** . . . . 127mm/5 ins x 17.86mm/45
$$	**Don Q** . . . . 184mm/7¼ ins x 16.27mm/41
$$	**Gigantes** . . . . 362mm/14¼ ins x 23.81mm/60
$$	**Panatella** . . . . 133mm/5¼ ins x 13.49mm/34
$$	**Panatella Larga** . . . . . . 152mm/6 ins x 13.49mm/34
$$	**El Conde De Guell Sr** 178mm/7 ins x 16.27mm/41
$$	**Brevas A La Conserva**
	133mm/5¼ ins x 17.07mm/43

¢ – Under $1.00 $ – $1–3.00 $$ – $3–4.00
$$$ – $5–8.00 $$$$ – $8–20.00 $$$$$ – $20+

Puerto Rico

DUTCH MASTERS

Machine-made by Consolidated Cigars. Short filler.
Homogenized binder. Available in regular or menthol. Part
of range machine-made in USA.

Cadet Regular . . . . . 120mm/4¾ ins x 11.11mm/28
Perfecto . . . . 120mm/4¾ ins x 17.46mm/44
Panetela . . . . ★★★
140mm/5½ ins x 14.29mm/36. Floral spicy aroma.
Medium- to full-bodied. Smooth. Daytime cigar.
Belvedere . . . . 124mm/4⅞ ins x 18.65mm/40
President . . . . 143mm/5⅝ ins x 17.46mm/41
Corona Deluxe . . . . ★★★
147mm/5⅞ ins x 17.07mm/43. Natural
Connecticut wrapper. HTL binder. Pierced hole in
head. Spicy, cardamom and peppery aroma. Full-
bodied.
Elites . . . . 156mm/6⅛ ins x 11.5mm/29

DUTCH MASTERS COLLECTION

Machine-made. Short filler. Natural Connecticut wrapper.
Homogenized binder. Made by Consolidated Cigars.

Cigarillos . . . . 120mm/4¾ ins x 10.75mm/27
Panetelas De Luxe . . . . . 137mm/5⅜ ins x 14.00/36
Palmas Maduro . . . . ★★
Good Maduro wrapper. Pierced hole in head.
Sweet, cherry, coffee aroma and flavor. Dusty finish.

MURIEL

Machine-made.

Magnum . . . . 117mm/4⅝ ins x 18.65mm/47
Sweet Coronas . . . . . 143mm/5⅝ ins x 16.27mm/41
Air Tips Regular . . . . . . 127mm/5 ins x 12.3mm/31
Sweet Little Cigars
Air Tips Pipe Aroma . . 127mm/5 ins x 12.3mm/31
Air Tips Menthol . . . . . 127mm/5 ins x 12.3mm/31
Air Tips Sweet . . . . 127mm/5 ins x 12.3mm/31
Coronella . . . . 117mm/4 5/8 ins x 12.3mm/31
Coronella Pipe Aroma . 117mm/4⅝ ins x 12.3mm/31
Coronella Sweet . . . . . . 17mm/4⅝ ins x 12.3mm/31
Sweet Minis . . . . 102mm/4 ins x 12.7mm/32

ROI-TAN

Machine-made. HTL wrapper and binder. Made by Consolidated Cigars.

Bankers . . . . 127mm/5 ins x 16.27mm/41
Blunts . . . . 143mm/5⅝ ins x 16.27mm/41
Falcons* . . . . 160mm/6¼ ins x 12.3mm/34
Panetelas . . . . 140mm/5½ ins x 14.29mm/36
Perfecto Extras . . . . . 127mm/5 ins x 16.27mm/41
Tips . . . . 130mm/5⅛ ins x 10.72mm/27
*Available in "Its A Girl" and "Its A Boy" packings.

South Africa

Produces tobacco virtually sufficient for large local cigarette industry. In the past, unsuccessful attempts made to produce low-priced, mass-market cigars. Late 1995 saw launch of first serious attempt by Gauteng Cigar Factory to produce top-quality, hand-made cigars from tobacco imported from Sumatra, Java and Brazil. Consumption of imported cigars in 1980 was 15 million, but fell to around 10 million in 1994. However, sales in 1997 are expected to be around 12 million. Market leader is Ritmeester (three models) with about 50 percent of sales. Small but discerning market for premium hand-made cigars from Cuba, Dominican Republic and Honduras. Two most important importers are L. Suzman & Co. and Brasant Enterprises.

SERENGETI

Hand-made. Quality, Superior. Dry cigar. Leaf from Indonesia. Established in 1995 in Roodepoort, in Province of Gauteng, near Johannesburg, by Tom and wife, Jon, van der Marck, Hollanders, now resident in South Africa. He has 32 years experience as tobacco buyer and blender with Dutch, Swiss, German and American companies. Company previously called Gauteng Cigar Co. Rolled in tradition that made Holland

---

★★★★★ Outstanding. A classic.   ★★★★ Excellent.
★★★ Good.   ★★ Fair, ordinary.   ★ Poor or faulty.
No Star Not evaluated.

famous in 1940s and 1950s, now all but disappeared. This is a range for connoisseurs of dry cigars.

$$ **Corona Kudu** . . . . ★★★★★
140mm/5½ ins x 15.8mm/40Mild to medium-bodied. Good balance, flavor and finish. Elegant. Well-made.

$$$ **Churchill Rhino** . . . . ★★★★★
165mm/6½ ins x 19.5mm/49. Mild to medium-bodied. Good balance, flavor and finish. Elegant. Well-made. Good daytime smoke.

$$ **Corona Bushbuck** . . . . ★★★★★
140mm/5½ ins x 15.8mm/40. Medium-bodied. Good flavors with coffee undertones. Long creamy finish. Well-made.

$$$ **Churchill Buffalo** . . . . ★★★★★
104mm/4⅛ ins x 15.8mm/40. Medium-bodied. Good flavors with coffee undertones. Long creamy finish. Well-made. Good daytime smoke.

Spain

First cigars to be made in similar fashion to those of today were produced by the tobacco monopoly, Tabacalera, in Seville, Spain in the early 18th century. It was then that the idea of constructing a cigar with filler, binder and wrapper was invented. The process was exported to Cuba, and in 1740, a Spanish Royal Decree created a tobacco monopoly in Cuba, called Royal Trading Company (Real Compania de Comerrio de la Habana). As a result, Cuba has maintained its cigar links with Spain, even when it had strong ties with the former Soviet Union-such ties endured even with a Communist Castro in power in Cuba and a fascist Franco dictatorship in Spain. The monopoly makes about 350 million machine-made cigars a year in Spain and hand-made ones through CITA, its subsidiary in the Canary Islands. It also imported around 28 million cigars in 1996-about half of Cuba's exports of hand-made cigars and around 10 percent of its machine-made cigars. The value of these imported was in excess of $35 million. Spain also imports about 75 percent of Cuba's export leaf production for use in its local industry. The value of leaf imports exceeds $70 million (46 million). Production of cigars in Spain is controlled by huge monopoly, Tabacalera, which is partnership of Government and private sector. In 1997, entered U.S. market with acquisition of California-based Max Rohr for $53 million. Because of small tax on tobacco products and the narrow profit margins, both for wholesalers and retailers, Spain has significantly low prices for Havanas. Spain may be considered cigar-friendly country, as smoking allowed in vast majority of restaurants, all good ones having cigars for sale. Tobaccos most commonly used for cigar production are those from Cuba, Brazil, Dominican Republic, Java and Sumatra.

CARIBES

Machine-made.

No 1	. . . .	152mm/6 ins x 16.67mm/42
No 2	. . . .	134mm/5¼ ins x 16.67mm/42

DUCADOS

Machine-made.

Cigarritos (tins)	. . . .	74mm/2⅞ ins x 8.7mm/23
Panetelas	. . . .	146mm/5¾ ins x 8.4mm/21
Extra	. . . .	90mm/3½ ins x 8.9mm/23
Suaves	. . . .	74mm/2⅞ ins x 8.7mm/22

ENTREFINOS

Machine-made.

Cortados	. . . .	90mm/3½ ins x 11mm/28
Java	. . . .	90mm/3½ ins x 11mm/28
Java Largos	. . . .	150mm/5⅞ ins x 11mm/28
Java Superiors	. . . .	100mm/4 ins x 12.4mm/31

FARIOS

Machine made. Leading machine-made brand with about 250 million cigars, accounting for over 60 percent of Tabacelera's production.

Centenario . . . . 121mm/4¾ ins x 16.2mm/41
Superiores . . . . 116mm/6⅜ ins x 16mm/40
No 1 . . . . 120mm/4¹¹⁄₁₆ ins x18.3mm/46
Superiores Especinles
115mm/6¹¹⁄₁₆ ins x 15.5mm/39
Chico . . . . 100mm/4 ins x 12.5mm/31
Purito. . . . . 88mm/3⅞₁₆ ins x 11mm/28
Club. . . . . 90mm/3½ ins x 8.7mm/22

FINOS CORTADOS

Machine-made. . . . . 90mm/3½ ins x 9.5mm/24

MONTECRISTO MINI

Machine-made. All Cuban tobacco.

. . . . 82mm/3¼ ins x 7.6mm/19

TARANTOS

Machine-made. . . . . 100mm/4 ins x 12.4mm/30

VEGAFINA

Machine-made.

Delicias . . . . 90mm/3½ ins x 8.7mm/22
Mini . . . . 77mm/3 ins x 8.7mm/22

Switzerland

In 1995 exported 1.436 million cigars to the USA.

DANNEMANN

Machine-made.
$$	**Lights-Sumatra**	152mm/6 ins x 13.49mm/34
$$	**Lights-Brazil**	152mm/6 ins x 13.49mm/34
$$	**Lights-Brazil Boy/Girl**	152mm/6 ins x 13.49mm/34
$$	**Espada-Sumatra**	127mm/5 ins x 17.86mm/45
$$	**Espada-Brazil**	127mm/5 ins x 17.86mm/45
¢	**Originale**	
¢	**Sweet Brazil**	

INDIANA SLIMS

Machine-made.

> **Indiana Slims** . . . . 82mm/3¼ ins

PEDRONI

Machine-made.

¢   **Classico** . . . . 92mm/3⅝ ins x 13.5mm/34

VILLIGER

Machine-made. Made from leaf from Mexico, Dominican Republic, Java, Columbia and Brazil. Cuban tobacco also used in cigars not exported to USA. Some all tobacco while others use homogenized binder. Today made in Switzerland, Germany and Ireland. Produce over 450 million cigars and cigarillos of which nearly 100 million exported to 70 countries. Also makes pipe tobacco and bicycles. Top mass-market cigar.

¢   **Villiger-Kiel Mild** . . . . 165mm/6½ ins
¢   **Villiger-Kiel Brasil**. . . . . 165mm/6½ ins
¢   **Villiger-Kiel Junior Mild** . . . . 113mm/4½ ins
¢   **Villiger-Kiel Junior Brasil** . . . . 113mm/4½ ins
¢   **Villiger Menorca** (wood chest)
¢   **Villiger Jewels Wood chest of 28**
¢   **Villiger Export** . . . . 102mm/4 ins
¢   **Villiger Export Kings** . . . . 130mm/5⅛ ins
¢   **Villiger Premium No 4** . . . . 102mm/4 ins
¢   **Villiger Premium No 7** . . . . ★★
       102mm/4 ins. Full-bodied. Dusty. Slightly harsh.
¢   **Villiger Premium No 10** . . . . 70mm/2¾ ins
       Braniff No 1 . . . . 89mm/3½ ins
       Braniff No 2 . . . . 113mm/4½ ins
       Braniff No 3 . . . . 95mm/3¾ ins
       Braniff No 8 . . . . 102mm/4 ins
       Braniff Cortos Filter Light . . . . 76mm/3 ins

---

United Kingdom

Imports around six million Cuban cigars, some 500,000 hand-made cigars from Central America and about 28 million mass market machine-made cigars from various countries.

ALTON

Only hand-made cigar company in England. Situated in Nottingham. Use Havana wrappers and binders and Jamaican filler.

HAMLET

Machine-made. Mild. Mass-market cigar.

> **Slim Panetelas**
> **Special Panetelas**
> **Panetelas**
> **Short Panetelas**

United States

Cigar industry established early 1800s. Tobacco production from Cuban seed started around 1825. Connecticut tobacco today providing some of best wrapper leaf to be found outside Cuba. In 1900 there were more than 25,000 active TP numbers (government registered tobacco product or producer numbers). Today fewer than 100 in active use. Between two World Wars there was huge influx of trained cigar makers from Cuba. Consumer market is estimated at 2.33 billion in 1994, of which about two billion, mainly machine-made, manufactured locally. Consumption peaked in 1993 at nine billion and from 1964, due to Surgeon-General's health warning on smoking, consumption, fell to around two billion in 1992. Then in 1993 and 1995 consumption increased by over 28 percent to present levels. In 1996 imports of premium cigars rose 66 percent on 1995 figure. It is estimated that past two years have seen the arrival of over five million new cigar smokers. Whereas, previously the average cigar smoker was more than 50 years old, these new smokers are aged 25 to 35, of which an important percentage are women. Year 1996 characterised by out-of-stock positions in retail shops and manufacturers holding back-orders of two to six months, particularly for bigger sizes. For the best part of 100 years the corona-size cigar has been the most popular in the world. Today, in the USA, there is a shift to larger cigars with the robusto, churchill and torpedo shapes becoming increasingly in demand. With the exception of a small number of manufacturers with Cuban origins, mainly in Little Havana in Miami and Union City, New Jersey, who make hand-made cigars, most of the local output is machine-made. The main producers are: Consolidated, 900 million (Antonio y Cleopatra, Dutch Masters, Muriel Roitan, Backwoods, Masters Collection, El Producto, La Corona, Harvester, Roi-Tan, Super Value, Rustlers, Supre Sweets, Super Value Little Cigars, Dutch Treats and Ben Franklin); Swisher International, 600 million (King Edward, Directors, Dexter, Landres, Keep Moving, El Trelles, Santa Fe, Swisher Sweets, Optimo, Outlaws, Dixie Made, As You Like It and Pom Pom Operas); General Cigar, 350 million (White Owl, Garcia y Vega, Tijuana Smalls, Robert Burns and Wm. Penn); Villazon/Danby-Palicio Group, 55 million (Lord Beaconsfield, Pedro Iglesias, Villa de Cuba, Villazon Deluxe and Topstone). These manufacturers also produce hand-made cigars in other countries, principally, Dominican Republic, Honduras, Mexico and Jamaica. Main imports into the United States are: Dominican Republic (138.6 million); Honduras (83.7 million), Jamaica (15.5 million); Mexico (14.5 million); Nicaragua (18 million) and the rest (23.45 million). Figures quoted are for 1996.

★★★★★ Outstanding. A classic.   ★★★★ Excellent.
★★★ Good.   ★★ Fair, ordinary.   ★ Poor or faulty.
No Star Not evaluated.

AMERICAN EAGLE

Hand-made. Cameroon wrapper. Filler blend of tobacco from Dominican Republic and Brazil. Made by Tampa Rico Cigar, Tampa, Florida, USA.

Statesman. . . . . 191mm/7½ ins x 19.1mm/48
Citation . . . . 178mm/7 ins x 17.5mm/44
Centennial . . . . 165mm/6½ ins x 14.3mm/36
Independence . . . . . . 152mm/6 ins x 16.67mm/42

ANTELO

Machine-made.

No 1 . . . . 172mm/6¾ ins x 16.27 mm/42
No 5 . . . . 130mm/5⅛ ins x 16.67 mm/42
Panatela . . . . 17.46mm/6⅞ ins x 14.29 mm/36
Presidente . . . . 193mm/7⅝ ins x 19.84mm/50
Super Cazadore . . . . 190mm/7½ ins x 18.26mm/46
Churchill . . . . 175mm/6⅞ ins x 18.26mm/46
Cetros. . . . . 147mm/5¾ x 16.67 mm/42
Wavell . . . . 130mm/5⅛ ins x 18.26 mm/46

ANTONIO Y CLEOPATRA

Machine-made. Short filler. Distinctive light green color called claro claro or candela. Also known as AMS (American Market Selection) because this was color most cigar smokers in USA used to favor. Made by Consolidated.

¢   **Grenadiers Whiffs** . . . . 92mm/3⅝ ins x 9.52mm/24
¢   **Grenadiers Mini** . . . . ★★★
     113mm/4½ ins x 11.11mm/28. Spicy vegetable aroma. Sweet finish. Pleasant quick smoke.
¢   **Grenadiers Mini Dark**
¢   **Grenadiers Mini Light**
¢   **Tribunes**
¢   **Panetelas Deluxe**. . . . . ★★
     13.65mm/5⅜ ins x 14.29mm/36. Natural Connecticut wrapper. Medium-bodied spicy. Dusty finish.
¢   **Grenadiers**. . . . . 160mm/6¼ ins x 13.49mm/34
¢   **Grenadiers Boy/Girl**
¢   **Classics Coronas** . . . . ★★
     168mm/5⅝ ins x 17.07mm/43. Natural Connecticut wrapper. Full-bodied. Pleasant smoke.
¢   **Grenadiers Tubos** . . 168mm/5⅝ ins x 17.07mm/43

¢   **Grenadiers/Presidentes** . . . . ★★★★
     Natural Connecticut wrapper. HTL binder. Good
     value cigar.

ARANGO SPORTSMAN ★★★

Machine-made in Tampa, Florida, USA. Vanilla flavored. Made
with tobacco from Honduras, Dominican Republic and
Ecuador. Be careful not to store these in same humidor as
non-flavored cigars. Mild. Owned by Arango Cigar.

¢	**No 100**	147mm/5¾ ins x 13.49mm/34
¢	**No 200** (Boy & Girl)	160mm/6¼ ins x 16.67mm/42
$	**No 300**	178mm/7 ins x 18.26mm/46
$	**No 350**	147mm/5¾ ins x 19.05mm/48
$	**No 400**	190mm/7½ ins x 19.05mm/48
	Little Cigars	

AS YOU LIKE IT

Machine-made by Swisher Intl.

¢	**No 18**	152mm/6 ins x 16.27mm/41
¢	**No 22**	113mm/4½ ins x 16.27mm/41
¢	**No 32**	152mm/6 ins x 17.07mm/43
¢	**No 35**	133mm/5¼ ins x 13.1mm/33

B-H

Machine-made.

	B-H Blunt	152mm/6 ins x 17.46mm/44
	B-H Blunt Boy & Girl	152mm/6 ins x 17.46mm/44
	B-H Corona	165mm/6½ ins x 16.67mm/42
	B-H Golden Corona Boy & Girl	
	165mm/6½ ins x 16.67mm/42	
	B-H Kings	165mm/6½ ins x 16.67mm/42
	B-H Special No 76 . .	165mm/6½ ins x 16.67mm/42

BACKWOODS ★★★

Machine-made. Connecticut Broadleaf wrapper, aged for one
year. Filler blend of tobacco from Phillipines, Malawi and
Mexico. Has wilde (uncut) foot. Is sealed in unique, eight
pack, pouch-lined with aluminum foil to keep humidity. Looks
like old-fashioned home-rolled cigar. Good value. Made by
Consolidated Cigars.

¢	**Original**	104mm/4⅛ins x 10.72mm/27
¢	**Sweet Aromatic**	104mm/4⅛ ins x 10.72mm/27
¢	**Black 'n Sweet**	104mm/4⅛ ins x 10.72/27

BANCES

Machine-made. Brand established 1840. Made in Tampa, Florida, USA by Villazon. Larger sizes hand-made in Honduras.

¢   **Crown** . . . . 147mm/5¾ ins x 19.84mm/50
¢   **Dermitasse** . . . . 102mm/4 ins x 13.89mm/35
¢   **Havana Holders** . . . . . . 165mm/6½ ins x 12mm/30
¢   **Palmas** . . . . ₂152mm/6 in x 16.67mm/42
¢   **Palmas** (Girl or Boy) . . 152mm/6 in x 16.67mm/42
¢   **No 3** . . . . 147mm/5¾ ins x 18.26mm/46

BEN BEY

Machine-made.

    Crystals . . . . 143mm/5⅝ ins x 17.46mm/44

BEN FRANKLIN★★

Machine-made by Consolidated Cigars.

    Perfectos
    Blunts

BLACK & MILD

Machine-made. Brand owned by John Middleton Inc.

    Pipe Tobacco Cigars . . 127mm/5 ins x 11.9mm/30

BLACK HAWK

Machine-made.

    Chief . . . . 130mm/5⅛ ins x 17.86mm/45

BOUQUET SPECIAL

Hand-made. Quality, superior. Owned by F.D Grave & Son in New Haven, Connecticut. One of oldest factories in continuous production. Founded 1884. Occupies same building since beginning of century.

    (in glass tubes) . . . . . 130mm/5⅛ ins x 18.26mm/46

BUDD SWEET

Machine-made

    Perfecto . . . . 127mm/5 ins x 17.07mm/43
    Panatela . . . . 133mm/5¼ ins x 13.49mm/34

¢ – Under $1.00 $ – $1–3.00 $$ – $3–4.00
$$$ – $5–8.00 $$$$ – $8–20.00 $$$$$ – $20+

CABANAS

Machine-made.

Coronas	. . . .	140mm/5½ ins x 16.67mm/42
Exquisitos	. . . .	165mm/6½ ins x 19.05mm/48
Premiers	. . . .	143mm/6⅜ ins x 16.67mm/42
Royales	. . . .	143mm/5⅝ ins x 18.26mm/46
Estupendos	. . . . . .	190mm/7½ ins x 19.84mm/50
Grandes	. . . .	152mm/6 ins x 19.84mm/50

CALLE OCHO

Hand-made. Quality, superior. Ecuadorian wrapper. Mexican binder. Filler blend of tobacco from Mexico, Nicaragua and Dominican Republic. Launched in 1996 by Carribean Cigar Factory. See details of company under "Santiago Cabana" brand in USA section. Distributed by Miami Cigar.

$$$	**Ninas**	127mm/5 ins x 15.1mm/38
$$$	**Festivale**	140mm/5½ ins x 17.5mm/44
$$$	**Gordito**	127mm/5 ins x 19.84mm/50
$$$	**Gordito Largo**	★★★★★

152mm/6 ins x 19.84mm/50. Attractive, oily wrapper. Good draw. Slow, even burning. Consistent construction. Light to medium strength with loads of flavor. Good complexity. For discerning smoker.

$$$	**Perfect Corona**	165mm/6½ ins x 16.67/42
$$$	**Laquito**	190mm/7½ ins x 15.1mm/38
$$$	**Churchill**	★★★★★

184mm/7¼ ins x 19.84mm/50. Medium-bodied. Good balance. Hint of pepper and spice. Smooth. Well-made. Daytime smoke for experienced smoker.

$$$$	**Immenso**	190mm/7½ ins x 21.4mm/54
$$$$	**Torpedo**	165mm/6½ ins x 21.4mm/54
$$$$	**Pyramide**	184mm/7¼ ins x 21.4mm/54
$$$$	**Embajador**	229mm/9 ins x 23.8mm/60

CARIBBEAN FAMILY

Machine-made. Mass-market.

¢	**Rounds**	184mm/7¼ ins x 18.26mm/46
¢	**Casinos**	160mm/6¼ ins x 18.26mm46
¢	**Royales**	160mm/6¼ ins x 13.49mm/34
¢	**Petite**	120mm/4¾ ins x 13.49mm/34

★★★★★ Outstanding. A classic.   ★★★★ Excellent.
★★★ Good.   ★★ Fair, ordinary.   ★ Poor or faulty.
No Star Not evaluated.

CHARLES DENBY

Machine-made. Mass-market.

Invincible . . . . 140mm/5½ ins x 17.07mm/43

CHAVELO

Hand-made.

No 1 . . . . 175mm/6⅞ ins x 17.46mm/44
No 2 . . . . 175mm/6⅞ ins x 17.46mm/44
Churchill . . . . 175mm/6⅞ ins x 19.05mm/48
Presidente . . . . 162mm/7⅜ ins x 19.84mm/50
Panatela . . . . 168mm/6⅝ ins x 14.29mm/36

CHERRY BLEND

Machine-made. Owned by John Middleton Inc.

Pipe-tobacco cigars . . . 127mm/5 ins x 12.3mm/30

CIBAO

Machine-made.

Brevas . . . . 133mm/5¼ ins x 19.84mm/50
Corona Deluxe . . . . . 140mm/5½ ins x 17.07mm/43
Diamantes . . . . 172mm/6¾ ins x 14.29mm/36
Churchills . . . . 172mm/6¾ ins x 18.26mm/46
Elegantes . . . . 178mm/7 ins x 17.46mm/44
Especiales . . . . 203mm/8 ins x 19.84mm/50

COJIMAR BY DON RENE DE CUBA

Hand-made. Quality, superior. Connecticut Shade wrapper. Dominican Piloto Cuban seed filler and binder. Named after the small Cuban fishing village that inspired Hemingway's classic novel, "The Old Man and the Sea." Brand established March 1996. Owned and distributed by The Cigar Connection, Miami Beach, Florida, USA.

Presidente . . . . 203mm/8 ins x 19.8mm/50
Torpedo . . . . 152mm/6 ins x 21.4mm/54
Laguito . . . . 171mm/6¾ ins x 15.1mm/38
Cortaditos . . . . ★★★★
171mm/6¾ ins x 15.1mm/38. Wrapper features two attractive shades of both Maduro and Colorado Claro in barber pole construction that adds additional dimension of flavor. Mild. Well-made. For discerning smoker.
Senoritas . . . . 127mm/5 ins x 11.9mm/30
Coronita . . . . 171mm/6¾ ins x 17.5mm/44
Toro . . . . 140mm/5½ ins x 19.84mm/50

CONNISSEUR GOLD LABEL

Machine-made. Natural and maduro wrappers.

Viajante	216mm/8½ ins x 20.64mm/52
Gigante	203mm/8 ins x 21.43mm/54
Elegante	203mm/8 ins x 14.29mm/36
Imperial 1	90mm/7½ ins x 19.84mm/50
Churchill	178mm/7 ins x 19.45mm/49
No 1 Nat	178mm/7 ins x 17.07mm/43
No 3 Nat	178mm/7 ins x 14.29mm/36
Toro Nat	152mm/6 ins x 19.84mm/50
Corona	152mm/6 ins x 17.46mm/44
No 4	140mm/5½ ins x 17.07mm/43
Rothschild	113mm/4½ ins x 19.84mm/50
Goliath	203mm/8 ins x 25.04mm/64

CONNISSEUR SILVER LABEL

Especiales	216mm/8½ ins x 19.84mm/50
Elegantes	178mm/7 ins x 17.46mm/44
Churchills	175mm/6⅞ ins x 18.26mm/46
Diamantes	172mm/6¾ ins x 14.29mm/36
Corona	140mm/5½ ins x 16.67mm/43
Brevas	133mm/5¼ ins x 19.84mm/50

CONQUISTADOR

No 100	165mm/6½ ins x 13.89mm/35
No 300	152mm/6 ins x 17.46mm/44
No 500	168mm/6⅝ ins x 17.46mm/44
No 700	175mm/6⅞ ins x 19.05mm/48
No 900	120mm/4¾ ins x 19.84mm/50
No 1100	160mm/6¼ ins x 19.84mm/50
No 1300	190mm/7½ ins x 19.84mm/50

CUESTA-REY

Machine-made in Tampa, Florida, USA. Established in 1884 by Angel LaMadrid Cuesta, a Spanish cigar maker, apprenticed in Cuba. In 1985 bought by Newman family's M & N Company in USA. First company to wrap cigars in cellophane. Some styles made by hand in Dominican Republic.

$ **Corona** (Cameroon wrapper)
$ **No 240**
$ **No 120**
$ **Palma Supreme**
$ **Caravelle**

CUETO

Machine-made. . . . . 124mm/4⅞ ins x 17.86mm/45

CYRILLA

Machine-made bundles in Tampa, Florida, USA by Villazon for Arango Cigar.

$ **Nationals** . . . . 152mm/6 ins x 16.67mm/42
$ **Kings** . . . . 178mm/7 ins x 18.26mm/46
$ **Senators** . . . . 190mm/7½ ins x 19.05mm/48
$ **Slims** . . . . 165mm/6½ ins x 14.29mm/36

DENOBILI

Machine-made. Mass-market.

Toscani
Toscani Longs
Twin Pack
Popular Amm
¢ **Kings** . . . . 10.8mm/4¼ ins

DEXTER LONDRES

Machine-made. Mass-market.
. . . . 133mm/5¼ ins x 16.67mm/42

DIRECTORS★★★

Machine-made. Mass-market. HTL binder. Mild, smooth with lots of flavor. Good value. Touch of sweetness. Owned by Swisher Intl.

Panetela . . . . 137mm/5⅜ ins x 14.3mm
Corona . . . . 152mm/6 ins x 16.67mm/42

DOMINO PARK

Hand-made. Quality, superior. Ecuadorian wrapper and binder. Nicaraguan and Dominican filler. Made by Caribbean Cigar Co., Miami, Florida, USA.

$$$ **Presidente** . . . . 203mm/8 ins x 20.6mm/52
$$ **Churchill** . . . . 178mm/7 ins x 19.8mm/50
$$ **Corona** . . . . 165mm/6½ ins x 16.67mm/42
$$ **Robusto Larga** . . . . 152mm/6 ins x 19.8mm/50
$$ **Robusto** . . . . 127mm/5 ins x 19.8mm/50

¢ – Under $1.00 $ – $1–3.00 $$ – $3–4.00
$$$ – $5–8.00 $$$$ – $8–20.00 $$$$$ – $20+

DON CESAR

Machine-made. Long filler.

> **Palma**. . . . . 143mm/5⅝ ins x 16.67mm/42

DON RENE

Hand-made. Quality, good. Dominican and Nicaraguan filler. Honduran binder. Ecuadorian wrapper. Made by Cigar Connection, Miami Beach, Florida, USA.

$	**Presidente**	216mm/8½ ins x 19.8mm/50
$	**Churchill**	184mm/7¼ ins x 19.8mm/50
$	**Torpedo**.	165mm/6½ ins x 21.4mm/54
$	**Lancero**	178mm/7 ins x 15.1mm/38
$	**Corona**.	165mm/6½ ins x 17.5mm/44
$	**Toro**.	140mm/5½ ins x 18.3mm/46
$	**Coronita**.	140mm/5½ ins x 16.67mm/42
$	**Robusto** . . . . ★★★

140mm/5½ ins x 19.8mm/50. Good draw. Slow, even burning. Mild to medium strength with good flavor. Every-day smoke. Ideal for beginners.

$	**Senoritas**	127mm/5 ins x 11.9mm/30

DRY SLITZ

Machine-made.

DUTCH MASTERS★★★

Machine-made. Mass-market. Short filler. HTL binder and natural wrapper. Big seller. Made by Consolidated Cigars.

¢	**Cadet Tip**.	140mm/5⅛ ins x 10.72mm/27
¢	**Cadet**	
¢	**Carona Deluxe***	
¢	**President**	143mm/5⅝ ins x 16.3mm/41
¢	**Belvedere**.	134mm/4⅞ ins x 18.7mm/47
¢	**Elites***	156mm/6⅛ ins x 11.9mm/30
¢	**Panetela Deluxe**	
¢	**Palma**	

*HTL binder and natural wrapper. Mild. Good value.

DUTCH TREATS★★★

Machine-made. HTL binder. Made by Consolidated Cigars.

¢	**Regular**	99mm/3⅞ ins x 7.94mm/20
¢	**Menthol**.	99mm/3⅞ ins x 7.94mm/20
¢	**Pipe Aroma**	99mm/3⅞ ins x 7.94mm/20
¢	**Sweet**.	99mm/3⅞ ins x 7.94mm/20
¢	**Ultra Lite**.	99mm/3⅞ ins x 7.94mm/20

EL CANELO

Hand-made. Long filler. Some good cigars in an inconsistent range. This range is also available under "Infiesta" and "Beck" brands. Made in St. Augustine and Miami, Florida, USA by El Canelo.

Soberanos. . . . . 203mm/8 ins x 19.84mm/50

Churchill. . . . . ★★★
178mm/7 ins x 19.1mm/48. Hard draw. Somewhat dusty flavor. Good-looking cigar. Daytime smoke or to follow light meal.

Fumas . . . . ★★★★
178mm/7 ins x 17.5mm/44. Smooth. Colorado Maduro wrapper. Medium strength. Hint of coffee and caramel. Good introduction to this size.

Cazadores. . . . . 178mm/7 ins x 18.3mm/46

Governos . . . . ★★★★
152mm/6 ins x 19.84mm/50. Medium-bodied. Good draw. Burns evenly. To follow lunch.

San Marcos . . . . ★★★
152mm/6 ins x 18.3mm/44. Fairly coarse Colorado Maduro wrapper. Medium-bodied. Flavors not fully integrated. Robust cigar.

No 1 . . . . ★★★★★
178mm/7 ins x 17.1mm/43. Medium-bodied. Good balance. Burns evenly. Well-made, elegant cigar to follow dinner.

Cetros No 2 . . . . 165mm/6½ ins x 16.67mm/42

Panetela No 3 . . . . ★★
178mm/7 ins x 14.3mm/36. Has curly head. Very mild with little character. Difficult burning.

No 4 . . . . 140mm/5½ ins x 16.67mm/42

St George . . . . ★★★
178mm/7 ins x 11.9mm/30. Very mild, but has some flavor. Not easy to smoke due to its size.

Miniatures . . . . ★★★
114mm/4½ ins x 11.9mm/30. Even burning. Has punch for small cigar. Tends to become harsh. Quick smoke to follow a light meal.

EL IMPERIO CUBANO

Hand-made. Quality, good. Ecuadorian wrapper. Made by Antillian Cigar Corp., Miami, Florida, USA.

$$$$	**Torpedo** . . . . ★★★★	

159mm/6¼ ins x 21.4mm/54. Well-made. Slow, even burning. Medium-bodied.

$$$	**Churchill**	171mm/6¾ ins x 19.1mm/48
$$$	**Toro**	152mm/6 ins x 19.8mm/50
$$$	**Robusto**	127mm/5 ins x 19.8mm/50
$$$	**Lonsdale**	171mm/6¾ ins x 17.1mm/43
$$$	**Corona**	140mm/5½ ins x 17.1mm/43

EL MACCO

Machine-made.

Puritano . . . . 120mm/4¾ ins x 17.86mm/45

El Producto . . . . ★★★
Machine-made. HTL binder and wrapper. Promoted by comedian George Burns who, until his death at the age of 100 in 1996, smoked an average of 10 of these cigars a day. Made by Consolidated Cigars.

Little Coronas . . . . . . 118mm/4⅝ ins x 12.3mm/31

Blunts . . . . 143mm/5⅝ ins x 16.27mm/41

Bouquets . . . . 120mm/4¾ ins x 17.46mm/44

Panetelas . . . . 130mm/5⅛ ins x 15.87mm/40

Finos . . . . 124mm/4⅞ ins x 18.2mm/46

Coronas . . . . 147mm/15¾ ins x 17.07mm/43

Favoritas . . . . 127mm/5 ins x 19.05mm/48

¢　**Escepcionales** . . . . . . 130mm/5⅛ ins x 20.64mm/52
Natural wrapper. HTL binder.

¢　**Queens** . . . . 143mm/5⅝ ins x 16.67mm/42
Natural wrapper. HTL binder.

EL RICO HABANO

Hand-made by El Credito in Miami, Florida, USA. See details of company under "La Gloria Cubana" brand in USA section. Wrapper from Ecuador. Binder from Nicaragua. Filler blend of tobacco from Dominican Republic and Nicaragua. Fuller-bodied than Hoya Selecta.

$$	**Gran Habanero Deluxe**	

194mm/7⅝ ins x 19.84mm/50. Earthy. Smooth. Good balance. Well-made. Finishes strongly.

$	**Double Coronas**	178mm/7 ins x 18.65mm/47
$	**Gran Coronas** . . . . ★★★★	

143mm/5⅝ ins x 18.26mm/46. Rich, spicy. Well-made. Fades on finish.

$	**Lonsdale Extra**	158mm/6³⁄₁₆ ins x 17.46mm/44
$	**Coronas**	142mm/5⅝ ins x 16.67mm/42
$	**Petit Habanos**	126mm/5 ins x 15.87mm/40

¢   **Habano Club** . . . . . . 124mm/4⅞ ins x 19.05mm/48
¢   **No 1** . . . . 190mm/7½ ins x 15.08mm/38

EL TRELLES

Machine-made. Mass-market.

¢   **Bankers** . . . . 152mm/6 ins x 17.07mm/43
¢   **Blunt Extra** . . . . 133mm/5¼ ins x 17.86 mm/45
¢   **Club House** . . . . 152mm/6 ins x 16.27mm/41
¢   **Kings** . . . . 152mm/6 ins x 16.27mm/41
¢   **Tryangles Deluxe** . . . 133mm/5¼ ins x 17.86mm/45

EL VERSO

Machine-made. Mass-market.

Corona Extra . . . . . . 147mm/5⅞ ins x 18.65mm/47
Bouquet . . . . 107mm/4⅜ ins x 17.86mm/45
Commodore . . . . 152 mm/6 ins x 14.29mm/36
Bouquet Light Leaf. . 120mm/4⅜ins x 17.86mm/45
Mellow . . . . 133mm/4¼ ins x 11.51mm/29

ELEGANTE

Hand-made. Connecticut Shade wrapper. Dominican filler and Honduran binder. Made by Tampa Rico Cigar Co., Tampa, Florida, USA.

$$ **Grande** . . . . 203mm/8 ins x 19.1mm/48
$$ **Especial** . . . . 178mm/7 ins x 19.1mm/48
$ **Centimo** . . . . 178mm/7 ins x 17.5mm/44
$ **Petit Cetro** . . . . 152mm/6 ins x 16.67mm/42
$ **Queen** . . . . 121mm/4¾ ins x 19.8mm/50

EMERSON

Machine-made. Mass-market.

Diplomat. . . . . 120mm/4¾ins x 17.07mm/43

ERIK

Machine-made. Mass-market.

¢   Natural (Filter Tipped). . . . . 99mm/3⅞ ins
¢   Menthol (Filter Tipped) . . . . 99 mm/3⅞ ins
¢   Cherry Flavor (Filter Tipped) . . . . 99m/3⅞ ins

EVERMORE

Machine-made. Mass-market.

¢   **Original** . . . . 117mm/4⅜ ins x 17.86mm/45
¢   **Palma**. . . . . 152mm/6 ins x 16.67mm/42
¢   **Corona Grande** . . . . 147mm/5⅞ ins x 18.65mm/47

FARNAM DRIVE

Machine-made. Mass-market.

     Original. . . . . 130mm/5⅛ ins x 179mm/45

FIGARO

Machine-made. Mass-market. Available in Natural and Maduro.

     . . . . 165mm/6½ ins x 15.87mm/40

FLAMENCO

Machine-made. Mass-market.

     Brevas SMS . . . . 141mm/5⁹⁄₁₆ ins x 16.67mm/42

FLOR DE FLOREZ

Hand-made. Quality, superior. Honduran Cuban seed filler and binder. Connecticut Shade wrapper. Good value. Named after family patriach, Carlos Florez, who operated a tobacco plantation in pre-Castro Cuba. Made by Flor de Florez Dist., Inc., Hoboken, New Jersey, USA.

$$	**Presidente**	178mm/7 ins x 19.5mm/49
$	**Cetros**.	165mm/6½ ins x 17.5mm/44
$	**Corona**	152mm/6 ins x 19.5mm/49
$	**Rothschild**	124mm/4⅞ ins x 18.7mm/47
$	**Blunt**.	127mm/5 ins x 16.67mm/42

FLOR DE FLOREZ CABINET SELECTION

Hand-made. Quality, superior. Nicaraguan Cuban filler and binder. Ecuadorian wrapper. Made by Flor de Florez Dist., Inc., Hoboken, New Jersey, USA.

$$$ **Gigante** . . . . ★★★★★
       191mm/7½ ins x 19.5mm/49. Well-made. Slow, even burning. Dark, oily wrapper. Full-bodied with complex, spicy flavors. To follow meal for connoisseur.

$$ **Sir Winston**. . . . . 178mm/7 ins x 18.7mm/47

$$ **Gran Panatela** . . . . ★★★★★
       178mm/7 ins x 15.1mm/38. Dark, oily wrapper. Well-made. Good draw. Surprisingly good burning for this size. Medium-bodied. Earthy, spicy flavor. Good balance and long finish. Pleasant aroma. Is worth the time. For the connoisseur.

$$ **Belicoso** . . . . 165mm/6½ ins x 20.6mm/52

$$ **Florez-Florez** . . . . 140mm/5½ ins x 18.3mm/46

$$ **Coronitas** . . . . 127mm/5 ins x 16.67mm/42
$$ **Robusto** . . . . 127mm/5 ins x 19.8mm/50

FREE CUBA

Hand-made. Quality, superior. Java wrapper. Nicaraguan binder. Cuban seed. Dominican filler. Made by Caribbean Cigar Co., Miami, Florida, USA.

$$$ **Perfecto** . . . . 165mm/6½ ins x 19.1mm/48
$$$ **Torpedo** . . . . 165mm/6½ ins x 21.4mm/54
$$$ **Churchill** . . . . 184mm/7¼ ins x 19.8mm/50
$$$ **Double Corona** . . . . . 191mm/7 ½ ins x 18.3mm/46
$$ **Corona** . . . . 165mm/6½ ins x 16.67mm/42
$$$ **Robusto Largo** . . . . 152mm/6 ins x 19.8mm/50
$$$ **Robusto** . . . . 127mm/5 ins x 19.8mm/50
$$ **Miniature** . . . . 127mm/5 ins x 14.3mm/36

GARCIA Y VEGA★★★

Machine-made. Mass-market. HTL binder. Natural wrapper. Mild. Good value mass-market cigar. Made by General Cigar.

¢ **Cigarillos*** . . . . 108mm/4¼ ins x 10.72mm/27
¢ **Chico*** . . . . ★★
108mm/4¼ ins x 10.72mm/27
¢ **Tips**** . . . . 133mm/5¼ ins x 12mm/30
¢ **Miniatures** . . . . 117mm/4⅝ ins x 11.51mm/29
¢ **Whiffs**** . . . . 95mm/3¾ ins x 9.13mm/23
¢ **Bravura**** . . . . 136mm/5⅜ ins x 13.94mm/34
Good looking cigar. Mild.
¢ **Panatella Deluxe*** . . 136mm/5⅜ ins x 13.49mm/34
¢ **Senators*** . . . . 113mm/4½ ins x 16.27mm/41
¢ **Blunts**** . . . . 120mm/4¾ ins x 16.27mm/41
¢ **Bouquets****. . . . . 117mm/4⅝ ins x 17.86mm/45
¢ **Delgado Panetela**** . 136mm/5⅜ ins x 13.49mm/34
¢ **Elegantes*** . . . . 162mm/6⅜ ins x 13.49mm/34
¢ **Gallantes****. . . . . 162mm/6⅜ ins x 13.49mm/34
¢ **Presidente****. . . . . . . 147mm/5¾ ins x 16.27mm/41
¢ **Napoleon*** . . . . 147mm/5¾ ins x 16.27mm/41
¢ **English Coronas**** (Tubed) . . . .
133mm/5¼ ins x 16.27mm/41
¢ **English Coronas Boy/Girl****
133mm/5¼ ins x 16.27mm/41
¢ **Granadas*** (tubed). . 162mm/6⅜ ins x 13.49mm/34
Difficult to smoke due to thinness. Mild. Little flavor.
¢ **Romeros**** . . . . 162mm/6⅜ ins x 13.49mm/34

¢   **Gran Coronas** (Tubed) .... 155mm/6¼ ins x 16.27mm/41
¢   **Gran Premios**** (Tubed)........ 155mm/6¼ ins x 16.27mm/41
¢   **Crystals No 100**** ... 155mm/6⅜ ins x 13.5mm/34
A good, simple cigar.
¢   **Crystals No 200** .... 155mm/6¼ ins x 16.27mm/41
Mild, one dimensional cigar.
*Available Only In Claro wrapper.
**Available Only In Natural wrapper.

GOLD & MILD

Machine-made. Mass-market. Owned by John Middleton Inc.
    Pipe Tobacco Cigars .... 127mm/5 ins 11.9mm/30

HARVESTER

Machine-made. Mass-market. Owned by Consolidated Cigar.

¢   **Perfecto**
¢   **Record Breaker**

HAUPTMANN'S

Machine-made. Mass-market.
    Perfecto Light/Dark 130mm/5⅛ ins x 17.86mm/45
    Broadleaf .... 133mm/5¼ ins x 17.07mm/43
    Corona .... 133mm/5¼ ins x 17.07mm/43
    Panetela .... 147mm/5¾ ins x 15.08mm/38

HAV-A TAMPA

Machine-made. Mass-market. Distinctive, self-contained, wooden mouthpiece introduced in late 1940s. Has huge following. Owned by Havatampa Inc.

¢   **Jewel**, Wood Tip
¢   **Jewel Sweet**, Wood Tip
¢   **Jewel Classic**, Wood Tip

HAVANA BLEND

Machine-made. Short filler. All tobacco, 20 percent of filler from 1959 Cuban crop. Made in San Antonio, Texas, USA. Distributed by Hollco Rohr.

$	**Petit Corona**	121mm/4¾ ins x 15.1mm/38
$	**Palma Fina**	165mm/6½ ins x 11.5mm/29
$	**Coronado** . . . . ★★★

127mm/5 ins x 17.1mm/43Easy draw. Burns evenly.
Full-bodied. Robust smoke.

$	**Delicado** . . . . ★★★★

146mm/5¾ ins x 17.1mm/43. Rich, full flavors.
Touch of coffee and sweetness. Smooth.

$	**Rothschild** . . . . ★★★★

127mm/5 ins x 19.8mm/50. Dark, almost black
wrapper. Full-bodied. Rich. Not subtle.

$	**Doubloon**	165mm/6½ ins x 16.67mm/42
$	**Churchill**	178mm/7 ins x 18.7mm/47

HAVANA CLASSICO

Hand-made. Quality, superior. Ecuadorian wrapper. Binder
from Dominican Republic. Filler blend of tobacco from
Mexico, Honduras and Dominican Republic. Launched in
1996 by Carribean Cigar Factory. See details of company
under "Santiago Cabana" brand in USA section. Distributed
by Miami Cigar.

$$$	**Puntas**	127mm/5 ins x 15.1mm/38
$$$	**Varadero**	140mm/5½ ins x 17.5mm/44
$$$	**Robusto**	127mm/5 ins x 19.84mm/50
$$$	**Robusto Largo**	152mm/6 ins x 19.84mm/50
$$$	**Corona Classic**	165mm/6½ ins x 16.67mm/42
$$$	**Double Corona**	190mm/7½ ins x 18.3mm/46
$$$	**Churchill** . . . . ★★★★★

184mm/7¼ ins x 19.84mm/50. Full-bodied. Good
balance. Complex, spicy flavors. Cool. Well-made,
elegant. Ideal for regular smoker. To follow heavy
meal.

$$$$	**Presidente**	190mm/7½ ins x 21.4mm/54
$$$$	**Torpedo**	165mm/6½ ins x 21.4mm/54
$$$$	**Pyramide**	184mm/7¼ ins x 21.4mm/54
$$$$	**Malelcon** . . . . ★★★★★

229mm/9 ins x 23.8mm/60. Appealing, oily wrapper. Good, consistent construction. Easy draw. Slow,
even burning. Smooth. Medium strength with lots
of complex flavors. Good balance. It will take time,
but will be worth it. For discerning smoker.

★★★★★ Outstanding. A classic. ★★★★ Excellent.
★★★ Good. ★★ Fair, ordinary. ★ Poor or faulty.
No Star Not evaluated.

HAVANA SUNRISE

Hand-made. Quality, superior. Medium- to full-bodied. Good,
consistent construction throughout range. Made by Havana
Sunrise Cigar Co. Miami.

Presidente . . . . 203mm/8 ins x 20.6mm/52
Churchill. . . . . 190mm/7½ ins x 19.84mm/50
Lancero . . . . 190mm/7½ ins x 15.08mm/38
Pyramid . . . . 178mm/7 ins x 23.8mm/60
Havana . . . . ★★★★★
171mm/6¾ ins x 18.3mm/46
Well-made. Good draw. Slow, even burning. Good
balance between strength and flavor. Complex fla-
vors. Appreciate this cigar if you can get it. For the
connoisseur.
Emperador. . . . . 159mm/6¼ ins x 21.4mm/54
Double Corona. . . . . . 152mm/6 ins x 19.1mm/48
Corona . . . . 152mm/6 ins x 17.5mm/44
Torpedo . . . . ★★★★★
152mm/6 ins x 21.4mm/54. Dark, oily wrapper.
Good draw. Slow, even burning. Cool. Well-made.
Rich flavor with good complexity. Good finish.
Ideal after-dinner cigar for the connoisseur.
Robusto . . . . 127mm/5 ins x 19.84mm/50
Panetela-Cache. . . . . . . 127mm/5 ins x 11.1mm/28

HOUSE OF WINDSOR

Machine-made.

Palmas . . . . 165mm/6½ ins x 13.49mm/34
Imperiales . . . . 203mm/8 ins x 17.07mm/43
Panetela . . . . 165mm/6½ ins x 13.49mm/34
Sportsman . . . . 127mm/5 ins x 17.07mm/43
Crook . . . . 127mm/5 ins x 15.9mm/45
Magnate . . . . 165mm/6½ ins x 17.07mm/43

IBOLD

Machine-made.

Blunt . . . . 124mm/4 7/8 ins x 17.46mm/44
Black Pete. . 124mm/5⅞ ins x 4⅞ ins x 17.46mm/44
Breva . . . . 130mm/5⅛ ins x 20.24mm/51
Cigarillo . . . . 108mm/4¼ ins x 11.51mm/29

¢ – Under $1.00 $ – $1–3.00 $$ – $3–4.00
$$$ – $5–8.00 $$$$ – $8–20.00 $$$$$ – $20+

INDIAN TABAC

Hand-made. Quality, good. Ecuadorian Sumatra wrapper. Mexican binder. Honduran and Nicaraguan filler. Made by Indian Tabac.

$$	**Chief**	191mm/7½ ins x 20.6mm/52
$$	**Buffalo** . . . . ★★★★★

152mm/6 ins x 20.6mm/52. Even burning. Cool. Medium strength. Well-balanced. Good finish. A cigar that will bring happiness even in the darkest circumstance. Appreciate it if you can get it. Scarce.

$$	**Warrior**.	152mm/6 ins x 16.67mm/42
$$	**Teepee** (pyramid) . . .	152mm/6 ins x 16.67mm/52
$$	**Boxer**	114mm/4½ ins x 19.8mm/50
$$	**Arrow**	140mm/5½ ins x 13.5mm/34

ISLAND AMARETTO

Hand-made. Quality, good. Amarello flavored. Medium filler. Made by Caribbean Cigar Co., Miami, Florida, USA.

$	**Gran Bella**	178mm/7 ins x 18.3mm/46
$	**Bellissima**.	127mm/5 ins x 15.1mm/38

JON PIEDRO

Jon Piedro Acapulco Breva*
152mm/6 ins x 16.67mm/42
Jon Piedro Acapulco Slims*
165mm/6½ ins x 14.29mm/36
Jon Piedro Acapulco Cazadores
165mm/6½ ins x 17.86mm/45
Connecticut Broadleaf Rounds
165mm/6½ ins x 18.26mm/46
**Natural & Claro Claro*

JOSE MELENDI

Machine-made. Vega series available in Cameroon wrappers. Named after a former master cigar blender from Cuba who established a factory in New York.

$	**Vega I**	5⅜ ins x 14.7mm/37
$	**Vega II**	5½ ins x 17.1mm/43
$	**Vega III**.	6 ins x 16.67mm/42
$	**Vega IV**.	6½ ins x 13.5mm/34
$	**Vega V**.	6½ ins x 17.7mm/45
$	**Vega VII**	7 ins x 17.7mm/45
$	**Wild Maduro**	6⅜ ins x 13.5mm/34
$	**Rothschild Maduro**	5 ins x 19.8mm/50

JOYA DEL REY

Numero 35 . . . . 178mm/7 ins x 13.49mm/35
Numero 42 . . . . 140mm/5½ ins x 16.67mm/42
Numero 43 . . . . 178mm/7 ins x 17.07mm/43
Numero 49 . . . . 178mm/7 ins x 19.45mm/49
Numero 50 . . . . 152mm/6 ins x 19.84mm/50
Numero 52 . . . . 216mm/8½ ins x 20.64mm/52

JUDGE'S CAVE

Hand-made and machine-made. Quality, superior. All Connecticut leaf. Brand established in 1884. Owned by Historic F.D. Grave & Son in New Haven, Connecticut. One of oldest companies in continuous production. Occupied same building since beginning of century.

KING EDWARD★★★

Machine-made in Georgia, USA. Mass-market. This is probably the biggest selling brand in the world. HTL binder and wrapper. Sold in over 60 countries. Unique blend of tobacco and flavoring. A mild, sweet cigar. Good value mass-market cigar. Made by Swisher Intl.

¢　**Invincible Deluxe** . . . . . . 140mm/5½ ins x 16.67/42
¢　**Panetela Deluxe** . . . . 133mm/5¼ ins x 14.29mm/36
¢　**Cigarillo Deluxe** . . . . 108mm/4¼ ins x 11.51mm/29
¢　**Imperial** . . . . 127mm/5 ins x 16.27mm/41
¢　**Specials**. . . . . 111mm/4⅜ ins x 11.51mm/29
¢　**Tip Cigarillo** . . . . 124mm/4⅞ ins x 11.11mm/28
¢　**Wood Tip Cigarillo**. . 140mm/5½ ins x 11.51mm/29

LA CORONA

Machine-made. Mass-market. Owned by Consolidated Cigar.

¢　**Whiffs** . . . . ★★
　　92mm/3⅝ ins x 9.52mm/24. Touch of sweetness on palate. Smooth.

LA CORONA VINTAGE

Machine-made. Owned by Consolidated Cigar.

¢　**Corona Chicas** . . . . . 140mm/5½ ins x 16.67mm/42
¢　**Coronas**. 152mm/6 in/17.07mm/43
¢　**Aristocrats** . . . . 155mm/6⅛ ins x 14.29mm/36
¢　**Directors**. . . . . 165mm/6½ ins x 18.26mm/46

LA FENDRICH

Machine-made.

Favorita . . . . 130mm/5⅛ ins x 17.9mm/45
Buds . . . . 108mm/4¼ ins x 12.7mm/32

LA FONTANA

Hand-made.

Dante . . . . 140mm/5½ ins x 17.46mm/38
Verdi . . . . 140mm/5½ ins x 17.46mm/44
Galileo . . . . 127mm/5 ins x 19.84mm/50
Puccini . . . . 165mm/6½ ins x 17.46mm/44
Da Vinci . . . . 175mm/6⅞ ins x 19.05mm/48
Michelangelo . . . . . . 190mm/7½ ins x 20.64mm/52

LA GLORIA CUBANA

Hand-made. Quality, superior. Wrappers from Ecuador. Binders from Dominican Republic. Fillers are blend of Dominican, Brazilian and American leaf. All sizes available in Maduro, which is Connecticut broad leaf. Full-bodied. El Credito, like many small producers, is unable, due to space and finance, to buy and store large quantities of tobacco. However, due to genius of owner, Cuban born Ernesto Carillo, who has great understanding of characteristics of different tobacco and how they work together, is able to alter blends to achieve a consistent result. Of all the cigars I have smoked, made outside Cuba, those from La Gloria Cubana are closest in flavor, texture and quality to that of genuine Havana. To achieve this Carillo sometimes uses tobacco from Nicaragua, Dominican Republic, Brazil, Sumatra, Mexico and USA. Production in 1995 was 1.4 million cigars across range of three brands of which La Gloria Cubana was almost 1 million. To overcome critical shortage of skilled workers in Miami, Carillo expanded operation to Dominican Republic in 1996 by leasing two-floor, 32,000 sq. ft. factory, built to his specification. Annual production in Dominican Republic is expected to reach 1.5 million cigars by end of 1997.

$$ **Crown Imperial** . . . . . 228mm/9 ins x 19.45mm/49
$$ **Soberano** . . . . ★★★★★
   203mm/8 ins x 20.64mm/52. Medium-bodied.
   Good balance between strength and flavor. Cool.
   Cigar for memorable occasion.
   Charlemagne . . . . . . 184mm/7¼ ins x 21.43mm/54
   Double Corona . . . . . 197mm/7¾ ins x 19.45mm/49
   Churchill . . . . 178mm/7 ins x 19.84mm/50

Glorias Inmensas . . . . ★★★
190mm/7½ ins x 19.05mm/48. Full-bodied. A little
harsh.
Corona . . . . 152mm/6 ins x 20.64mm/52
Wavell . . . . ★★★★★
127mm/5 ins x 19.84mm/50. Dark, oily wrapper.
Spicy, floral aroma. Rich honeyed undertones on
finish. Smooth. For the connoisseur.
Glorias Extra . . . . . . 160mm/6¼ ins x 18.26mm/46
Coronas Extra Large . . . . ★★★★
197mm/7¾ ins x 17.46mm/44. Medium-strength.
Lots of flavor. Long finish. Connoisseur's cigar for
all occasions.
Medaille D'Or No 1 . 172mm/6¾ ins x 17.07mm/43
Medaille D'Or No 2 . 160mm/6¼ ins x 17.07mm/43
Glorias. . . . . 130mm/5 1/2 ins x 17.07mm/43
Minutos . . . . 113mm/4 1/2 ins x 15.87mm/40
Panetela De' Luxe . . . . 178mm/7 ins x 14.8mm/37
Medaille D'Or No 3 . . 178mm/7 ins x 11.11mm/28
Medaille D'Or No 4 . . 152mm/6 ins x 12.07mm/32
Torpedo No 1 . . . . 165mm/6½ ins x Tapered
Piramides . . . . ★★★★★
184mm/7¼ ins x Tapered. Spicy, leathery aroma.
Full-bodied. Good balance between strength and
flavor. Wonderful cigar to follow wonderful meal.
This cigar is an occasion!

LA HOJA SELECTA

Hand-made. Connecticut Shade wrapper. Dominican,
Brazillian and Mexican filler. Dominican binder. Has loyal fol-
lowing. Originally made in Cuba. Now made in USA by El
Credito in Miami. See details of company under "La Gloria
Cubana" brand in USA section.

        Chateau Sovereign . . 190mm/7½ ins x 20.64mm/52
        Cosiac. . . . . 178mm/7 ins x 19.05mm/48
        Choix Supreme . . . . . 152mm/6 ins x 19.84mm/50
        Palais Royals . . . . . 120mmm/4¾ ins x 19.84mm/50
        Selectos No 1 . . . . . . 165mm/6½ ins x 16.67mm/42
        Cetros de Oro . . . . . 147mm/5¾ ins x 17.07mm/43
        Bel Aires. . . . . 172mm/6¾ ins x 15.08mm/38
        Geneves . . . . 165mm/6½ ins x 12.7mm/32

LA PLATA

Hand-made. Connecticut wrapper. Ecuadorian binder. Filler blend of tobacco from Ecuador and Dominican Republic. Made by La Plata Cigar Co. Founded in 1947, is last large-scale cigar manufacturer in Los Angeles, California, USA.

Hercules . . . . 140mm/5½ ins x 21.4mm/54
Enterprise Classic . . . . 178mm/7 ins x 20.6mm/52
Grand Classic . . . . 152mm/6 ins x 17.5mm/44

LA PLATA MADUROS

Hand-made. Tobacco as in standard La Plata range, but with Maduro wrapper. Made by La Plata Cigar Co.

Royal Wilshire . . . . 178mm/7 ins x 20.6mm/52
Robusto Uno . . . . 114mm/4½ ins x 20.6mm/52
Magnificos . . . . ★★★★
152mm/6 ins x 17.5mm/44. Rich, full flavor with touch of sweetness. For the bold, experienced smoker.

LANCER

Machine-made.

Havana Slims . . . . 127mm/5 ins x 12.7mm/32

LORD BEACONSFIELD

Machine-made. Mass-market. Short filler. Homogenized binder. Honduran filler. Full flavor. Originally made for British market. Made by Villazon in Tampa, Florida, USA.

¢ **Directors** . . . . 197mm/7¾ ins x 18.26mm/46
¢ **Rounds** . . . . 184mm/7¼ ins x 18.26mm/46
¢ **Lords** . . . . 178mm/7 ins x 13.49mm/34
¢ **Corona Superbas** . . . 160mm/6¼ ins x 16.67mm/42
¢ **Lindas** (girl or boy) . 165mm/6½ ins x 14.29mm/36
¢ **Cubanolas** . . . . 140mm/5½ ins x 17.46mm/44
Available with EMS, Claro Claro or Maduro wrappers.

LORD CLINTON

Machine-made. Mass-market.

Perfecto
Corona Gorda . . . . . 160mm/6¼ ins x 17.46mm/44
Churchill . . . . 178mm/7 ins x 19.45mm/49
Nom Plus . . . . 113mm/4½ ins x 19.84mm/50
President . . . . 216mm/8½ ins x 19.84mm/50
Toro . . . . 152mm/6 ins x 19.84mm/50

MACABI

Hand-made by Antillian Cigar, Miami, Florida, USA. Long filler. Good quality.

$$	**Super Corona**.......	197mm/7¾ ins x 20.6mm/52
$$	**Double Corona**......	175mm/6⅞ ins x 19.5mm/49
$$	**Corona Extra**........	152mm/6 ins x 19.8mm/50
$$	**Royal Corona**........	127mm/5 ins x 19.8mm/50
$$	**No 1**..............	171mm/6¾ ins x 17.5mm/44
$	**Media Corona**	140mm/5½ ins x 17.1mm/43
$$$	**Belicoso Fino** (triangular)	
	159mm/6¼ ins x 20.6mm/52	

MAESTRO

Hand-made. Quality, good. All have Maduro wrappers. Mexican and Honduran filler. Factory established 1994. Made by Cuban Cigar Factory, San Diego, California, USA.

$$$$	**No 1**..............	152mm/6 ins x 21.4mm/54
$$$$	**No 2**..............	165mm/6½ ins x 20.2mm/50
$$$	**No 3**..............	121mm/4¾ ins x 20.6mm

MARK IV

Machine-made. Mass-market.

Magnates
Maduro Supremes

MARSH

Machine-made. Mass-market.

¢	**Mountaineer**.......	140mm/5½ ins x 13.49mm/34
¢	**Virginian**..........	140mm/5½ ins x 14.68mm/37
¢	**Pioneer**...........	140mm/5½ ins x 14.68mm/37
¢	**Old Reliable**.......	140mm/5½ mm x 13.1mm/33
¢	**Deluxe**	178mm/7 ins x 13.49mm/34

MIFLIN'S CHOICE

Machine-made.

Deluxe II	178mm/7 ins x 13.49mm/34
Corona............	127mm/5 ins x 17.07mm/43
Panatela	162mm/6⅜ ins x 12.7mm/32

★★★★★ Outstanding. A classic. ★★★★ Excellent.
★★★ Good. ★★ Fair, ordinary. ★ Poor or faulty.
No Star Not evaluated.

MORRO CASTLE

Hand-made. Quality, superior. Ecuadorian wrapper. Nicaraguan binder and filler. Made by Caribbean Cigar Co., Miami, Florida, USA.

$$$	**Perfecto**	165mm/6½ ins x 19.1mm/48
$$$	**Torpedo**	165mm/6½ ins x 21.4mm/54
$$$	**Churchill**	184mm/7¼ ins x 19.8mm/50
$$$	**Double Corona**.	191mm/7½ ins x 18.3mm/46
$$	**Corona**	165mm/6½ ins x 16.67mm/42
$$$	**Robusto Largo**	152mm/6 ins x 19.8mm/50
$$$	**Robusto**	127mm/5 ins x 19.8mm/50
$$	**Miniature**	127mm/5 ins x 14.3mm/36

MUNIEMAKER

Machine-made. All American tobacco. Brand launched in 1916 by F.D. Grave & Son in New Haven, Connecticut, USA. One of oldest companies in continuous production. Occupied same building since beginning of century.

¢	**Regular**.	113mm/4½ ins x 18.65mm/47
¢	**Straights**	130mm/5¼ ins x 19.05mm/48
¢	**Longs**	152mm/6 ins x 18.26mm/46
¢	**Breva 100's Oscura**. .	130mm/5¼ ins x 19.05mm/48
¢	**Panetela 100's Oscura** .	152mm/6 ins x 13.1mm/33
¢	**Palma 100's**	152mm/6 ins x 18.26mm/46
¢	**Perfecto 100's**	133mm/5¼ ins x 18.65mm/47
¢	**Boy/Girl**.	113mm/4½ ins x 18.65mm/47

ODIN

Machine-made. Mass-market.

Viking.	120mm/4¾ ins x 16.67mm/42

OLD HERMITAGE

Machine-made. Mass-market.

Golden Perfecto . . .	140 mm/5½ ins x 17.86mm/45

OPTIMO★★

Machine-made. Mass-market. Natural leaf wrapper. HTL binder. Spicy, coffee aroma. Dry finish. Mild. Made by Swisher Intl.

¢	**Diplomat**	155mm/6¼ ins x 13.1mm/33
¢	**Admiral**	152mm/6 ins x 16.27mm/41
¢	**Admiral Boy/Girl**. . . .	152mm/6 ins x 16.27mm/41
¢	**Admiral Just Married** .	152mm/6 ins x 16.27mm/41

¢	**Coronas** .... 133mm/5¼ ins x 16.67mm/42
¢	**Palmas** .... 152mm/6 ins x 16.67mm/41
¢	**Panetela** .... 132mm/5¼ ins x 13.1mm/33
¢	**Sports** .... 113mm/4½ ins x 16.67mm/4

ORO BLEND

Hand-made. All Honduran tobacco. Made by Tampa Rico Cigar, Tampa, Florida, USA.

| **24** .... 191mm/7½ ins x 19.84mm/50 |
| **22** .... 165mm/6½ ins x 17.5mm/44 |
| **18** .... 140mm/5½ ins x 16.67mm/42 |
| **14** .... 152mm/6 ins x 14.3mm/36 |
| **10** .... 114mm/4½ ins x 11.4mm/50 |

PALMA LITES

Machine-made.

Palmas

PARODI

Machine-made. Dry cigar. All tobacco.

| **Ammezzati**..................... 89mm/3½ ins |
| **Economy**...................... 102mm/4 ins |
| **Kings** .... 104mm/4⅛ ins |
| **Avanti** .... 113mm/4½ ins |
| **Avanti Cont'l**.................. 113mm/4½ ins |
| **Ramrod Deputy**................. 113mm/4½ ins |
| **Ramrod Original**............... 113mm/4½ ins |
| **Kentucky Cheroots** .... 136mm/5⅜ ins |

PEDRO IGLESIAS

Machine-made. Short filler. Made by Villazon in Tampa, Florida, USA.

| **Lonsdales** .... 165mm/6½ ins x 17.46mm/44 |
| **Regents**............ 152mm/6 ins x 17.46mm/44 |
| **Crowns**............ 127mm/5 ins x 17.86mm/45 |

PETRI

Toscani
AA Cello
Sigaretto King
Sigaretto Reg.
Squillo
Toscanelli

¢ – Under $1.00 $ – $1–3.00 $$ – $3–4.00
$$$ – $5–8.00 $$$$ – $8–20.00 $$$$$ – $20+

PHILLIES

Machine-made in Selma, Alabama, USA, by Phillies Cigar.

Perfecto . . . . 147mm/5¾ ins x 17.07mm/43
Titan . . . . 160mm/6¼ ins x 17.46mm/44
Coronas . . . . 136mm/5⅜ ins x 16.27mm/41
Blunts . . . . 120mm/4¾ ins x 16.67mm/42
Panatella . . . . 140mm/5½ ins x 13.49mm/34
Sport . . . . 147mm/5¾ ins x 17.07mm/43
Cheroot . . . . 127mm/5 ins x 12.7mm/32
King Cheroot . . . . . . 140mm/5½ ins x 12.7mm/32
Mexicali Slim . . . . . . 117mm/4⅝ ins x 12.7mm/32
Juniors . . . . 127mm/5 ins x 16/27mm/41
Sweets . . . . 147mm/5¾ ins x 16/67mm/43
Tips (tipped) . . . . . . 113mm/4½ ins x 11.11mm/28
Tip Sweet (tipped) . . 113mm/4½ ins x 11.11mm/28

POLLACK

Machine-made.

Crown Drum . . . . 140mm/5½ ins x 13.1mm/33

PRINCE ALBERT

Machine-made. Owned by John Middleton Inc.

Soft & Sweet Vanilla . . . 127mm/5 ins x 11.9mm/30
Traditional . . . . 127mm/5 ins x 11.9mm/30
Cool Mint . . . . 127mm/5 ins x 11.9mm/30

R.G. DUN

Machine-made.

Admiral
Babies
Bouquet
Cigarillo

RED DOT

Machine-made.

Perfecto . . . . 127mm/5 ins x 16.67mm/42
Panetela . . . . 133mm/5¼ ins x 13.5mm/34

★★★★★ Outstanding. A classic.   ★★★★ Excellent.
★★★ Good.   ★★ Fair, ordinary.   ★ Poor or faulty.
No Star Not evaluated.

REY DEL MAR

Hand-made. Quality, superior. Connecticut Shade and Maduro wrapper. Dominican filler. Owned by Caribbean Cigar Factory, Miami, Florida, USA.

Churchill	. . . .	178mm/7 ins x 19.1mm/48
Piramides	. . . .	165mm/6 1/2 ins x 17.5mm/44
Petit Corona	. . . .	152mm/6 ins x 15.1mm/38
Corona	. . . .	140mm/5 1/2 ins x 17.1mm/43
Robusto	. . . .	114mm/4 1/2 ins x 20.6mm/52

RICO HAVANA BLEND

Hand-made. Long filler. Ecuadorian wrapper. Dominican binder and filler. Made by Tampa Rico Cigar Co., Tampa, Florida, USA.

$$$	**Rough Rider**	229mm/9 ins x 19.84mm/50
$$$	**Churchill**	203mm/8 ins x 19.1mm/48
$$$	**Double Corona**	178mm/7 ins x 19.1mm/48
$	**Plaza**	178mm/7 ins x 17.5mm/44
$	**Corona**	152mm/6 ins x 16.67mm/42
$	**Panetela**	178mm/7 ins x 13.5mm/34
$	**Duke**	121mm/4¾ ins x 19.84mm/50
$	**Habanero**	114mm/4½ ins x 16.67mm/42

RIGOLETTO CIGARS

Machine-made in Tampa. Two models hand-made in Dominican Republic. Made by M & N, Tampa, Florida, USA.

$	**Londonaire**	159mm/6¼ ins x 17.1mm/43
$	**Black Jack**	137mm/5⅜ ins x 18.3mm/46
$	**Natural Coronas**	152mm/6 ins x 16.67mm/42
$	**Palma Grande**	152mm/6 ins x 16.3mm/41

ROBERT BURNS

Machine-made in Dotham, Alabama, USA. Mass-market. Short filler. Homogenized binder. Made by General Cigar.

¢	**Cigarillos** . . . . ★★	
	113mm/4½ ins x 10.72mm/27. Quick burning. Hint of sweetness.	
¢	**Black Watch**	140mm/5 1/2 ins x 16.27mm/41

ROSEDALE

Machine-made. Mass-market.

Perfecto
Londres

RUM RIVER

Machine-made. Mass-market.

> **Crooks Rum**
> **Crookettes Rum**

RUM RUNNER

Hand-made. Quality, good. Rum flavored. Medium filler. Made by Caribbean Cigar Co., Miami, Florida, USA.

$$	**Pirate**	178mm/7 ins x 18.3mm/46
$	**Buccaneer**	140mm/5½ ins x 17.5mm/44
$	**Wench**	127mm/5 ins x 15.1mm/38

RUSTLERS★★

Machine-made. Mass-market. Filter tipped. HTL wrapper and binder. Very mild, sweet. Made by Consolidated Cigars.

Black 'n Cherry	99mm/3¾ ins x 9.13mm/23
Sweets	99mm/3¾ ins x 9.13mm/23
Menthol	99mm/3¾ ins x 9.13mm/23

SFS SPECIAL SELECTION

Machine-made. Mass-market.

> **Almond Liqueur**
> **Cafe Cubano** (Coffee)

SAN FELICE

Machine-made. Mass-market.

> **Original**

SAN LUIS

Machine-made.

Soberanos	190mm/7½ ins x 19.84mm/50
Corona	165mm/6½ ins x 17.46mm/44
Toro	152mm/6 ins x 19.84mm/50
Panetelas	165mm/6½ ins x 14.29mm/36
Panetelas Boy	165mm/6½ ins x 14.29mm/36
Panetelas Girl	165mm/6½ ins x 14.29mm/36
Cetros	136mm/5⅜ ins x 16.67mm/42

SAN VICENTE BLEND

Hand-made. All Honduran tobacco. Made by Tampa Rico Cigar Co., Tampa, Florida, USA.

| **Supremo** | 165mm/6½ ins x 17.5mm/44 |
| **Panetela** | 152mm/6 ins x 14.3mm/36 |

Matador . . . . 140mm/5½ ins x 16.67mm/42
Presidente . . . . 203mm/8 ins x 19.8mm/50
Rothchild . . . . 127mm/5 ins x 19.8mm/50

SANTA FE

Machine-made. Mass-market.

¢   **Biltmore** . . . . 152mm/6 ins x 16.27mm/41
¢   **Fairmont** . . . . 152mm/6 ins x 16.67mm/43
¢   **Panetela** . . . . 133mm/5¼ ins x 13.1mm/33
¢   **Patties** . . . . 140mm/5½ ins x16.67mm/42

SELLO DE ORO

Mixed filler. Mass-market.

Fumas
Cazador
Super Cazador

SIGNATURE COLLECTION BY SANTIAGO CABANA

Hand-made. Quality, superior. Ecuadorian wrapper. Mexican binder. Filler blend of tobacco from Honduras, Nicaragua and Dominican Republic. Launched late 1995. Made by Caribbean Cigar Factory. First major manufacturer of hand-made cigars to open in USA in past 30 years. Main factory in Miami, Florida, USA. Has shops with manufacturing facilities in Key Largo, Key West and Miami South Beach. Company founded by former air traffic controller, Kevin Doyle, and financial adviser and venture capitalist, Mike Risley, to seek listing on New York Stock Exchange. Company presently employs about 40 cigar rollers. Has plans, during 1996, to open another factory in trade free zone in Dominican Republic. This brand named after Santiago Cabana, Cuban cigar roller who created range. Distributed by Miami Cigar.

$$$ **Chicas** (torpedo) . . . . . 127mm/5 ins x 15.1mm/38
$$$ **Caribe** . . . . 130mm/5½ ins x 17.5mm/44
$$$ **Robusto** . . . . 127mm/5 ins x 19.8mm/50
$$$ **Lancero** . . . . 190mm/7½ ins x 15.1mm/38
$$$ **Double Corona** . . . . . . 190mm/7½ ins x 18.3mm/46
$$$ **Churchill** . . . . ★★★★★
     184mm/7¼ ins x 19.8mm/50. Well-made. Medium-bodied. Spicy, full flavors with undertone of wet hay. Good balance and finish.
$$$ **Presidente** . . . . 190mm/7½ ins x 21.4mm/54

$$$$ **Torpedo** . . . . ★★★★★
165mm/6 ½ ins x 21.4mm/54. Medium to full-bod-
ied. Good balance. Spicy, nutty flavors. Good finish.
Well-made cigar for special occasion.

$$$ **Corona** . . . . ★★★★★
165mm/6½ ins x 16.67mm/42. Spicy with touch of
nutmeg. Medium-bodied. Good balance. Smooth. A
well-made, elegant cigar for connoisseur.

SUPER VALUE PIPE TOBACCO CIGARS★★

Machine-made by Consolidated Cigars. Mass-market.

Black 'n Cherry
Black 'n Sweet

SUPRE SWEETS★★

Machine-made by Consolidated Cigar. Short filler. Mild and
slightly sweet. Good value, mass-market cigar.

Tip Cigarillo . . . . . . 130mm/5⅛ ins x 10.72mm/27
Cigarillo . . . . 120mm/4¾ ins x 11.11mm/28
Perfectos . . . . 120mm/4¾ ins x 17.46mm/44
Little Cigars . . . . 99mm/3⅞ ins x 7.94mm/20

SUPRE VALUE LITTLE CIGARS★★

Machine-made by Consolidated Cigars. Good value, mass-mar-
ket cigar.

Menthol . . . . 99mm/3⅞ ins x 7.94mm/20
Cherry . . . . 99mm/3⅞ ins x 7.94mm/20
Sweet . . . . 99mm/3⅞ ins x 7.94mm/20
Ultra Mild . . . . 99mm/3⅞ ins x 7.94mm/20

SWISHER SWEETS★★

Machine-made. Mass-market. Short filler. HTL wrapper and
binder. One of America's top-selling brands. Unique blend
of tobacco and flavoring, creating a mild, sweet cigar. Made
by Swisher Intl.

¢   **Kings**. . . . . 140mm/5½ ins x 16.67mm/42
¢   **Perfecto Slims** . . . . . . 127mm/5 ins x 16.27mm/41
¢   **Coronella** . . . . 127mm/5 ins x 11.11mm/28
¢   **Cigarillo** . . . . 111mm/4⅜ ins x 11.51mm/29
¢   **Tip Cigarillo** . . . . . . 124mm/4⅞ ins x 11.11mm/28
¢   **Wood Tip Cigarillo** . . 124mm/4⅞ ins x11.51mm/29

¢ – Under $1.00 $ – $1–3.00 $$ – $3–4.00
$$$ – $5–8.00 $$$$ – $8–20.00 $$$$$ – $20+

TAMPA NUGGET

Machine-made. Mass-market cigar.

Sublime Perfecto . . . 120mm/4¾ ins x 17.07mm/43
Blunt Blunt . . . . 127mm/5 ins x 17.07mm/43
Panetela Panatela . . . 140mm/5½ ins x 14.29mm/36
Tip Regular Cigarillo . 127mm/5 ins x 11.11mm/28
Tip Sweet Cigarillo . . . 127mm/5 ins x 11.11mm/28
Juniors Miniature . . . . 113mm/4½ ins x 12.3mm/31
Juniors Panetela . . . . . 113mm/4½ ins x 12.3mm/31

TAMPA SWEET

Machine-made. Mass-market cigar. HTL wrapper and binder.

¢ **Perfecto** . . . . 4¾ ins x 17.07mm/43
¢ **Cheroot** . . . . 4¾ins x 12.3mm/31
¢ **Tip Cigarillo** . . . . 5 ins x 11.11mm/28

TIJUANA SMALLS

Machine-made. Mass-market. HTL wrapper and binder. Made
by General Cigar.

¢ **Aromatic** . . . . 89mm/3½ ins x 8.33mm/21
¢ **Cherry** . . . . ★★
     89mm/3½ ins x 8.33mm/21. Aromatic and sweet.
¢ **Regular** . . . . ★
     89mm/3½ ins x 8.33mm/21. One dimensional.
     Much like mild cigarette.

TIPARILLO

Machine-made. Mass-market.

¢ **Mild Blend** . . . . 108mm/4¼ ins x 10.32mm/26
¢ **Sweet Blend** . . . . 108mm/4¼ ins x 10.32mm/26
¢ **Aromatic** . . . . 108mm/4¼ ins x 10.32mm/26
¢ **Menthol** . . . . 108mm/4¼ ins x 10.32mm/26

TOPPER

Machine-made by Topper Cigar Co.

Old Fashioned Perfecto . . . . ★★★★
124mm/4⅞ ins x 17.46mm/44. Oily Maduro wrap-
per. Milder than it looks. Medium-bodied. Good,
creamy flavors. Slightly sweet aroma. Probably best
value for money.

¢ – Under $1.00 $ – $1–3.00 $$ – $3–4.00
$$$ – $5–8.00 $$$$ – $8–20.00 $$$$$ – $20+

Old Fashioned Extra Oscuro
Breva . . . . 140mm/5½ ins x 17.86mm/45
Ebony . . . . 140mm/5½ ins x 17.46mm/44
Grande Corona . . . . . 152mm/6 ins x 17.46mm/44

TOPSTONE

Machine-made. Connecticut broadleaf. Long filler. Made by Villazon.

$ **Supreme** . . . . 152mm/6 ins x 16.67mm/42
$ **Extra Oscuro** . . . . . . 140mm/5½ ins x 18.26mm/46
$ **Grande** . . . . 147mm/5¾ ins x 18.26mm/46
$ **Panetela** . . . . 152mm/6 ins x 15.48mm/39
$ **Bouquet** . . . . 140mm/5½ ins x 18.26mm/46
$ **Oscuro** . . . . 140mm/5½ ins x 18.26mm/46
$ **Directors** . . . . 197mm/7½ ins x 18.65mm/47

TOPSTONE—NATURAL DARKS

Machine-made. Connecticut broad leaf. Maduro. Long filler. Made by Villazon in Tampa, Florida, USA.

$ **Executives** . . . . 184mm/7¼ ins x 18.65mm/47
$ **Coronas** . . . . 160mm/6¼ ins x 17.46mm/44
$ **Panetela** . . . . 152mm/6 ins x 15.48mm/39
$ **Breva** . . . . 140mm/5½ ins x 18.26mm/46

TORQUINO

Hand-made. Long filler. Triangular bundles. Ecuadorian wrapper. Mexican filler and binder. Made for Brick-Hanauer Co., Waltham, Massachusetts, USA.

Breva Corona . . . . 146mm/5¾ ins x 17.1mm/43
Classic Corona . . . . 178mm/7 ins x 17.1mm/43
Delicioso . . . . 178mm/7 ins x 20.6mm/52
Torquino . . . . 178mm/7 ins x 19.84mm/50
Privada No 1 . . . . 152mm/6 ins x 18.3mm/46
Pyramide . . . . 165mm/6½ ins x 23.8mm/60
Rothschild . . . . 114mm/4½ ins x 19.84mm/50
Toro . . . . 152mm/6 ins x 19.84mm/50
Torpedo . . . . 178mm/7 ins x 21.4mm/54

★★★★★ Outstanding. A classic.   ★★★★ Excellent.
★★★ Good.   ★★ Fair, ordinary.   ★ Poor or faulty.
No Star Not evaluated.

TRADITIONALES

Hand-made. Quality, good. Connecticut Shade wrapper. Mexican and Honduran filler. Factory established 1994. Made by Cuban Cigar Factory, San Diego, California, USA.

$$$	**Presidente**	197mm/7¾ ins x 20.6mm/52
$$$	**Cuban Round Larga**. .	184mm/7¼ ins x 20.2mm/50
$$$$	**Torpedo**	178mm/7 ins x 20.2mm/50
$$	**El Cubano**	171mm/6¾ ins x 17.5mm/44
$$	**Havana**.............	152mm/6 ins x 18.3mm/46
$$	**Corona**	146mm/5¾ ins x 16.67mm/42
$$$	**Montecristo**	140mm/5½ ins x 20.6mm/52
$$$	**Robusto**	127mm/5 ins x 20.2mm/50

VILLA DE CUBA

Machine-bunched with homogenized binder. Mass-market. Made by Villazon in Tampa, Florida, USA. Available since early 1930s.

¢	**Corona Grande**	184mm/7¼ ins x 17.86mm/45
¢	**Majestics**..........	162mm/6¾ ins x 17.07mm/43
¢	**Brevas**............	147mm/5¾ ins x 17.46mm/44

VILLAZON DELUXE

Machine-made. Medium filler. Made by Villazon.

$	**Chairman**	197mm/7¾ ins x 17.07mm/43
¢	**Cetros**	182mm/7⁹⁄₁₆ ins x 17.46mm/44
¢	**Senators**	172mm/6¾ ins x 17.46mm/44

VILLAZON DELUXE AROMATICS

Machine-made. Mass-market. Short filler. Made by Villazon in Tampa, Florida, USA.

	Commodores	152mm/6 ins x 16.67mm/42
	Panetela	147mm/5¾ ins x 13.49mm/34

WEST INDIES VANILLA

Hand-made. Quality, good. Vanilla flavored. Medium filler. Made by Caribbean Cigar Co., Miami, Florida, USA.

$$	**Carmella**...........	178mm/7 ins x 18.3mm/46
$	**Carmelita**	127mm/5 ins x 15.1mm/38

¢ – Under $1.00 $ – $1–3.00 $$ – $3–4.00
$$$ – $5–8.00 $$$$ – $8–20.00 $$$$$ – $20+

WHITE OWL

Machine-made. Mass-market. Short filler. Homogenized binder. A top seller in USA. Launched in 1902. Made by General Cigar.

¢   **Coronetta** . . . . 117mm/4⅝ ins x 11.51mm/29
¢   **Demi-Tip** . . . . 108mm/4¼ ins x 12.7mm/32
¢   **Miniatures** . . . . ★★★
     117mm/4⅝ ins x 11.49mm/34. Medium-bodied. Good flavor for cigarillo. Good quick smoke.
¢   **Panetela Deluxe** . . . . ★★
     133mm/5¼ ins x 13.49mm/34. Uninspiring. Smooth.
¢   **Invincible** (Boy/Girl). 136mm/5⅜ ins x 16.67mm/41
¢   **New Yorker**. . . . . 143mm/5⅝ ins x 16.67mm/41
¢   **Ranger** . . . . 162mm/6⅜ ins x 13.49mm/34
¢   **Blunts** . . . . ★★
     120mm/4¾ ins x 16.67mm/41. Mild. Good finish. Touch of sweetness.

WILLIAM ASCOT

Machine-made in Tampa, Florida, USA. Mass-market. Distributed by Arango. All available with Natural, Maduro and Claro Claro wrappers.

$ **Palma** . . . . 159mm/6¼ ins x 16.67mm/42
¢   **Panetela**. . . . . 133mm/5¼ ins x 13.5 mm/34

WILLIAM PENN

Machine-made. Mass-market. HTL wrapper and binder. Made by General Cigar.

¢   **Willow Tips** . . . . 108mm/4¼ ins x 10.32mm/26
¢   **Braves** . . . . ★
     117mm/4⅝ ins x 11.51mm/29. Medium-bodied. Sweet. One-dimensional.
¢   **Perfecto** . . . . 116mm/5⅜ ins x 16.27mm/41
¢   **Panetela** . . . . 133mm/5¼ ins x 13.49mm/34

WINCHESTER

Machine-made. Mass-market.

¢   **Winchester Little Cigars**
¢   **Winchester Menthol Little Cigars**
¢   **Winchester Sweets 100's Little Cigars**
¢   **Winchester 100's Little Cigars**

WOLF BROTHERS

Machine-made. Mass-market.

- € **Rum Crooks** . . . . 140mm/5½ ins x 12mm/30
- € **Crooks Sweet Vanilla Nippers**. . . . . . 83mm/3¼ ins

Venezuela

SABANA

Hand-made. Quality, good. Ecuadorian wrapper. Venezuelan filler and binder. Distributed in USA by Inversione Housto de America, Houston, Texas, USA.

- $$ **No 3** . . . . 146mm/5¾ ins x 18.3mm/46
- $$ **No 2** . . . . 140mm/5½ ins x 16.67mm/42
- $$ **No 1** . . . . 40mm/5½ ins x 15.1mm/38
- $$ **Especial** . . . . 114mm/4½ ins x 15.9mm/40

Identifying brands with countries

Gloria Palmera CI
Gold & Mild . . . . USA
Goya CI
Grand Nica . . . . Nic
Griffin's . . . . Dom
Gross Glockner . . . . . . Aus
Guaranteed Jamaica . . . Jam

H. A. Ladrillo . . . . Hon
H. Upmann . . . . Dom
Habana . . . . Hon
Habanica . . . . Nic
Habanos Hatuey . . . . . Dom
Hamlet . . . . UK
Harrows . . . . Phi
Harvester . . . . USA
Hauptmann's . . . . USA
Hav-a-Tampa . . . . USA
Havana Blend . . . . USA
Havana Classico . . . . . USA
Havana Reserve . . . . . Hon
Havana Sunrise . . . . . . USA
Hecho-A-Mana
　　Caz-Bar . . . . Hon
Henri Winterman . . . . . Hol
Henry Clay . . . . Dom
Hildalgo . . . . Pan
Hoja de Mexicali . . . . . Mex
Hoja de Oro . . . . Mex
Hon Duras Cuban Tob Hon
Honduran Gold . . . . . Hon
Honduran Import . . . . Hon
Honduras Cuban . . . . Hon
House of Windsor . . . . USA
Hoyo de Monterrey . . Hon
Hoya de Nicaragua . . . . Nic
Hoya del Regal . . . . . . Hon
Hugo Cassar . . . Dom, Hon,
　　　　　　　　　Mex, Nic

Ibold . . . . USA
Indian Tabac . . . . USA
Indiana Slims . . . . Swi

Indian Head . . . . Hon
Iracema . . . . Bra, Ger
Island Amaretto . . . . . USA

J. Cortes . . . . Bel
J. F. Llopis Gold . . . . . Pan
J. R. Ultimate . . . . Hon
Jamaica Bay . . . . Jam
Jamaica Crown . . . . . . Jam
Jamaica Gem . . . . Jam
Jamaica Gold . . . . Jam
Jamaica Heritage . . . . Jam
Jamaican Kings . . . . . . Jam
Jamaican Pride . . . . . . Jam
Jamaican Supreme . . . Jam
John Aylesbury . . . . . Dom,
　　　　　　　　Ger, Hon
John T's . . . . Dom
Jon Piedro . . . . USA
Jose Benito . . . . Dom
Jose Llopis . . . . Pan
Jose Marti . . . . . Dom, Hon
Jose Melendi . . . . USA
Joya del Rey . . . . USA
Joya de Nicaragua . . . . Nic
Juan Clemente . . . . . . Dom
Juan Lopez . . . . Hon
Judge's Cave . . . . USA
Justus Van Maurik . . . Hol

King . . . . Dom
King Edward . . . . USA
Kingston . . . . Mex
Kiskeya . . . . Dom
Knockando . . . . Dom

La Aurora . . . . Dom
La Balla . . . . Hon
La Cordoba . . . . Nic
La Corona . . . . . Dom, USA
La Dalmata . . . . Mex
La Diligencia . . . . Hon
La Diva . . . . Dom

Comments, suggestions and possible additions are welcome for the next edition.

Feel free to contact Theo Rudman at:

    P.O. Box 5223, Helderberg, 7135, South Africa.

    Telephone: (27)(21) 905-3600

    Fax: (27)(21) 905-2188

    E-mail: 101663.3231@compuserve.com